D1497875

A MORALIST IN AND OUT OF PARLIAMENT

To John Stewart,
a wonderful colleague
from whom I have learned
so much, and who I
will miss.
[illegible]
July 22, 1992.

The Father of Political Economy, illustrated initial,
Punch, 21 March 1868, p.122

A Moralist In and Out of Parliament

John Stuart Mill at Westminster 1865–1868

BRUCE L. KINZER
ANN P. ROBSON and
JOHN M. ROBSON

UNIVERSITY OF TORONTO PRESS
Toronto Buffalo London

Toronto Buffalo London
Printed in Canada

ISBN 0-8020-5949-X

Printed on acid-free paper

Canadian Cataloguing in Publication data

Kinzer, Bruce L., 1948–
A moralist in and out of Parliament

Includes index.
ISBN 0-8020-5949-X

1. Mill, John Stuart, 1806–1873. 2. Great Britain – Politics and government – 1837–1901. I. Robson, Ann P., 1931– II. Robson, John M., 1927– III. Title.

B1606.K55 1992 192 C91-095663-4

This book has been published with the help of a grant from the Social Science Federation of Canada, using funds provided by the Social Sciences and Humanities Research Council of Canada.

Contents

Illustrations

Preface

This book on John Stuart Mill's parliamentary years was first conceived more than a decade ago, when the editorial team of the Mill project, headed by John M. Robson, began preliminary work on the material that would ultimately make up the two volumes of Mill's *Public and Parliamentary Speeches* (vols. XXVIII–XXIX of the *Collected Works*). After a protracted period of proceeding by fits and starts (there seemed to be more of the former than the latter), we decided there were no further excuses for putting off the concentrated effort required to complete the task. We regret none of it, especially now that it is done.

The collaboration that produced this book sprang from a long-standing partnership, personal and professional, of two of the parties (the ones with the same surname), to which was added, for the purpose of this project, a third person who had come to share their interests, sympathies, and friendship. Although the organization and execution of the whole have been a collective endeavour throughout, an assortment of stylistic attributes may be detected among the parts. These arise from the distribution of responsibility for the drafting of specific chapters. The introduction came out of committee and bears the marks of each of the authors. The chapters on the 1865 and 1868 Westminster elections were drafted by John M. Robson; that on women's suffrage, by Ann P. Robson; those on parliamentary reform, Ireland, and Jamaica, by Bruce L. Kinzer. The formulation of the overall strategy that governed the selection of topics to be covered and the analytical approach to be adopted for each was the product of a consensual understanding arrived at after careful deliberation. Once a complete manuscript had been assembled, the process of revision entailed each of the authors tackling all of the chapters, from which there somehow emerged a final press copy. Limited liability does not apply.

Acknowledgments: We are greatly indebted to librarians, archivists, and collections at the British Library Reference and Newspaper divisions, British Library of Political and Economic Science (London School of Economics), Yale University Library, Somerville College Library, Fawcett Library at the Central London Polytechnic, the Library of University College London, Institute of Historical Research (University of London), Hambleden Archive (W.H. Smith and Co.), Fisher and Robarts libraries of the University of Toronto, the Pierpont Morgan Library, the Russell Archives of McMaster University, Victoria University Library, and Randall Library of the University of North Carolina at Wilmington. Among the individuals who over too many years have contributed information and offered advice are Marion Filipiuk and Jean O'Grady of the Mill project, Stefan Collini of Cambridge University, J.B. Conacher, Michael Laine, and Trevor Lloyd of the University of Toronto, Brian Harrison of Oxford University, and Barbara McCrimmon. Rosemary Shipton, once more to our delight our copy-editor, has made the straight way almost easy for us by professional tact and personal charm. Much helpful detailed criticism and the index originated with Ann Christine Robson Bacque, most dear to us.

Material from publications by each of us has been used in various ways, but not without considerable revision. These include Bruce Kinzer's "J.S. Mill and Irish Land: A Reassessment," *Historical Journal*, 27 (1984), 111–27, "John Stuart Mill and the Irish University Question," *Victorian Studies*, 31 (1987), 59–77, and "Introduction," *Public and Parliamentary Speeches*, ed. John M. Robson and Bruce L. Kinzer, *Collected Works of John Stuart Mill*, vols. XXVIII–XXIX (Toronto: University of Toronto Press, 1988); Ann P. Robson's "The Founding of the National Society for Women's Suffrage 1866–67," *Canadian Journal of History*, 8 (Mar. 1973), 1–22, and "No Laughing Matter: John Stuart Mill's Establishment of Women's Suffrage as a Parliamentary Question," *Utilitas*, 2 (May 1990), 88–101; and John M. Robson's "Mill in Parliament: The View from the Comic Papers," *Utilitas*, 2 (May 1990), 102–42.

Editorial practice: In nineteenth-century newspapers small capitals were used for personal names and to indicate emphasis: we have substituted the normal forms in the former case, and in the latter used italic type.

A MORALIST IN AND OUT OF PARLIAMENT

ONE

Contexts

At the end of the general election in July 1865, the poll in the city of Westminster read:

Capt. R.W. Grosvenor (L)	4534
Mr. John Stuart Mill (L)	4525
Mr. W.H. Smith (C)	3824

So in this constituency, where each elector had two votes to elect two members, Mill was within ten votes of the top of the poll, well and truly elected.

In November 1868, at the end of the next election, the poll read:

Smith	7648
Grosvenor	6584
Mill	6284

So Mill, at the bottom of the poll, was well and truly defeated, in a constituency that had at every election since the First Reform Act returned two Liberals, with the single exception of 1841, when a Conservative gained one of the seats.

In the concluding part of his *Autobiography*, written in the winter of 1869–70, just a year after his defeat, Mill says: "That I should not have been elected at all would not have required any explanation; what excites curiosity is that I should have been elected the first time, or, having been elected then, should have been defeated afterwards."[1] The implications

1 *Autobiography* [A], in *Autobiography and Literary Essays*, ed. John M. Robson and Jack Stillinger, *Collected Works of John Stuart Mill* [CW], vol. I (Toronto: University of Toronto Press, 1981), p. 288.

of that comment drive the argument of this examination of Mill's brief parliamentary career. The comment suggests that although initially he did not see himself as a politician, once elected he did so; it appears that he did not appreciate in what ways his view did not match the Westminster electors' notions of a politician.

Joseph Hamburger has well identified the young Mill and his energetic Philosophic Radical allies in the 1830s as "intellectuals in politics";[2] that label is not inapt for Mill in the 1860s, especially in view of the initial response to his candidature. But by that time the force propelling his intense desire for reform was more clearly moral: he believed that his part in the utilitarian scheme was to demonstrate, by incorporating principle in example, that subordinating selfish goals to community good was essential to the greatest happiness. To that end, he saw it as his duty not to disguise his allegiances to what he saw as moral causes, even though prudence would have led to qualification when they were generally perceived as radical and dangerous. Although Mill was not one to indulge publicly in high-minded harangue, there can be no doubt that the surprising enthusiasms revealed during his parliamentary life led the public to question his practical wisdom.

What follows is a selective account of John Stuart Mill's years as a member of parliament. The discussion of the two election campaigns focuses on both Mill's and the electorate's view of a moralist as member for Westminster and the effects of those views on the course and the success of the campaigns. The middle chapters give an outline of the general pattern of his activities, going into detail only on those matters that affected his political reputation and hence his attempt at re-election. In the retrospective account of his parliamentary career in his *Autobiography*,[3] Mill mentions a number of matters in passing, but only electoral reform, Ireland, Jamaica, and women's suffrage were regarded by him as of sufficient importance to warrant an entire paragraph or more. Our emphasis has turned out, hardly surprisingly, to be not unlike his. This is not to say that Mill's involvement with these issues is necessarily seen with hindsight as having the same significance he gave them. It is to say that Mill had excellent cause for identifying these issues as the most critical ones he faced during his Westminster years.

They were for him matters of principle and matters that as a public

2 Joseph Hamburger, *Intellectuals in Politics: John Stuart Mill and the Philosophic Radicals* (New Haven: Yale University Press), 1965. For a differing interpretation, see William Thomas, *The Philosophic Radicals: Nine Studies in Theory and Practice, 1817–1841* (Oxford: Oxford University Press, 1979).

3 See *A*, *CW*, vol. I, pp. 272–86.

figure he could not dissociate himself from while remaining faithful to himself. Mill did not run for parliament because he wanted a parliamentary career; he ran for parliament because he was in his own estimation one of the country's leading political moralists, if not the leading political moralist, and his influence would be increased by the publicity his views would obtain in an election campaign. If he accepted the nomination on his own highly principled terms, he could perhaps raise the tone of public life. At least he might set an example. Disraeli's reference to Mill as the "finishing governess" had much truth in it (as one would expect from Disraeli). The issues he stresses in the *Autobiography* are the ones he saw as the most important moral issues during his parliamentary years.

To Mill's surprise he was elected, and his obligation to make known his views took on an unsought urgency that the private Mill had rarely known. Many of his crusades were largely conducted outside the halls of Westminster, including his campaign against Governor Eyre, much of his work for Ireland (especially on the question of the secular university), and indeed a great deal of his labour for women's suffrage; however, these questions were all for him issues that, now that he had actively involved himself in the public arena, he was morally bound to act upon. Unlike many others, he made no distinction between Mill in parliament and Mill out of parliament, except that his being in parliament made even more essential that he stand up, and be seen to stand up, for right and truth. And, being more newsworthy than he had ever been, making his opinions known was almost too easy for his reputation as a rational philosopher. The fulfilment of this obligation led him to appear at times little short of quixotic to many of the electors.

The other parliamentary matters mentioned briefly in the *Autobiography* include his very interesting speech on capital punishment;[4] his notable contribution to the debate on the right of search and seizure at sea with respect to neutral vessels transporting the goods of England's enemies;[5] his parliamentary initiatives on metropolitan government (which took much of his—not the House's—time, and get little space in his account, probably because "on that subject the indifference of the House of Commons was such that I found hardly any help or support

4 For an interesting comment on Mill and capital punishment, see L.W. Sumner, "Mill and the Death Penalty," *Mill News Letter*, 11 (winter 1976), 2–7.

5 For a useful study of this and other issues pertinent to liberal ideology and British maritime power in the nineteenth century, see Bernard Semmel, *Liberalism and Naval Strategy: Ideology, Interest, and Sea Power during the Pax Britannica* (Boston: Allen & Unwin, 1986).

within its walls");[6] his distinctive speech on the malt duty and the national debt (those well-disposed towards Mill would rather recall his impassioned plea on behalf of posterity than his too pessimistic forecast, based on W.S. Jevons's *The Coal Question*, that Great Britain's workable coal seams would be exhausted within three generations); and his participation in the discussions on amendment of the extradition law.[7] Since in Mill's eyes and those of his contemporaries these issues were less significant, they are also for our purposes and are not dwelt upon.

Mill gives more space in the *Autobiography* to his Westminster years, in actual as well as proportional length, than he does to any other period of his life, the "mental crisis" not excepted. It may well be that he wished to have the first and the last word on his parliamentary career. Written not long after his defeat at the 1868 general election, what he says in the *Autobiography* reveals more about his state of mind following that defeat than it does about his political disposition in early 1866. Forcibly detached from Westminster by his former constituents, Mill may have been inclined in retrospect and by way of explanation to dwell on the independent character of his conduct in parliament. The reader is told that in the House of Commons he reserved himself "for work which no others were likely to do"; most of his interventions, he adds, "were on points on which the bulk of the Liberal party, even the advanced portion of it, either were of a different opinion from mine, or were comparatively indifferent." The task he set for himself was "to do work which others were not able or not willing to do"; his duty had been "to come to the front in defence of advanced Liberalism on occasions when the obloquy to be encountered was such as most of the advanced Liberals in the House, preferred not to incur."[8] On a number of occasions Mill indeed acted in a manner

6 A, CW, vol. I, p. 276. A good examination of the issues involved in the reform of metropolitan government can be found in David Owen, *The Government of Victorian London, 1855–1889: The Metropolitan Board of Works, the Vestries and the City Corporation* (Cambridge, Mass.: Harvard University Press, 1982).

7 For a valuable study of the context within which the extradition question ought to be placed, see Bernard Porter, *The Refugee Question in Mid-Victorian Politics* (Cambridge: Cambridge University Press, 1979). These efforts, along with everything else Mill did in the House of Commons, are now easily accessible in *Public and Parliamentary Speeches* [PPS], ed. John M. Robson and Bruce L. Kinzer, CW, vols. XXVIII–XXIX (Toronto: University of Toronto Press, 1988). See, for capital punishment, vol. XXVIII, pp. 266–72; for England's maritime rights, vol. XXVIII, pp. 220–7; for metropolitan government, vol. XXVIII, pp. 162–5, 230–1, 273–6, 290–5, 300–1, and vol. XXIX, pp. 437–542 (see also vol. XXXI, pp. 389–406); for malt duty and the national debt, vol. XXVIII, pp. 69–73; and for extradition, vol. XXVIII, pp. 115–18, 119, 120–3, 227–30, and vol. XXIX, pp. 542–71.

8 A, CW, vol. I, pp. 275–6.

justifying this conception of his role. But such actions formed only a part of the story of his enterprise in the House, although undoubtedly they formed most of the public's perception of the member for Westminster. The chief purpose, thinly disguised at best, of the account in the *Autobiography* is to defend this aspect of a controversial political record that had come in for intense public scrutiny following his defeat.[9]

Mill, of course, did not have the last word. It was Gladstone, not Mill, who put the deepest mark upon Mill's posthumous reputation as a member of the House of Commons. In view of the powerful impression Gladstone would make on Mill's imagination during the Westminster period, there is a striking fitness, metaphorical and otherwise, in this fact, but Mill would not have been altogether pleased. Gladstone's judgment became public when he responded to a request from W.L. Courtney, one of Mill's first biographers. Gladstone wrote:

> We well knew . . . Mr. Mill's intellectual eminence before he entered Parliament. What his conduct there principally disclosed, at least to me, was his singular moral elevation. I remember now that at the time . . . I used familiarly to call him the Saint of Rationalism, a phrase roughly and partially expressing what I now mean. Of all the motives, stings, and stimulants that reach men through their egoism in Parliament, no part could move or even touch him. His conduct and his language were, in this respect, a sermon. Again, though he was a philosopher, he was not, I think, a man of crotchets. He had, I think, the good sense and practical tact of politics, together with the high independent thought of a recluse. I need not tell you . . . that for the sake of the House of Commons at large, I rejoiced in his advent, and deplored his disappearance. He did us all good. In whatever party, whatever form of opinion, I sorrowfully confess that such men are rare.[10]

Gladstone surely intended this as high praise; he added that the House of Commons was a better place for Mill's presence.

Gladstone's words usually call up Mill as an almost disembodied political spirit that had by chance descended into an alien region barely

9 In this section of the *Autobiography*, Mill's capacity for self-criticism, so evident in other parts of the story, is conspicuously absent. The predominant message conveyed to the reader is that the mid-Victorian political system had not yet evolved to the point where it could do appropriate honour to the independence, integrity, and virtue exemplified by the late member for Westminster.

10 W.L. Courtney, *Life of John Stuart Mill* (London: Scott, 1889), pp. 141–2.

capable of supporting such a life-form. Courtney's relevant chapter in his *Life of John Stuart Mill* (1889) carries as a subtitle "A Saint of Rationalism," and Michael St. J. Packe borrows the term for his chapter on Mill's parliamentary years in his biography of Mill (1954).[11] Mill, however, saw himself as a substantial force, not in the least bereft of "the good sense and practical tact of politics"—to use other of Gladstone's words. He was by training hard-working and dutiful; his attendance at the House was exemplary, and, within the limits he himself recognized as inevitable for an advanced radical, effective. In his view he was not a saint of rationalism but a committed partisan—perhaps both if that is possible. Certainly the paucity of analytical work done on his parliamentary career since the publication of the *Autobiography* seems to have left available both interpretations. The account given there has not been superseded. The curious combination has then continued: from Courtney in 1889 to Packe in 1954, the narrative of the Westminster years has followed closely the summary presented in the *Autobiography* under the Gladstonian captions.

Mill's summary, however, implies possibly fewer errors of judgment than anyone then or now would care to claim; to an outsider it does not appear an unqualified success. But an understanding of Mill's own expectations qualifies the unqualified. As is well known, he got off to a rocky start with a somewhat intemperate speech on the condition of Ireland—a subject on which the governing classes were especially sensitive at the time of the Fenian threat—thus temporarily losing "the ear of the House."[12] The quality of his speech on parliamentary reform in April 1866, however, earned him very high marks and put him on a firm footing within the House. Although he occasionally stumbled thereafter, he did not fall. Measured against the standing and performance of the average backbencher, Mill could be said to have acquired and sustained a position of considerable weight and consequence in parliament.

The exalted public stature he took with him into the House was potentially a mixed blessing. At the outset his reputation assured him of an attentive audience, but there was risk in satisfying its curiosity. More than a few members would not have been displeased had the eminent philosopher cut but a poor figure in the house of the politicians. The reputation that preceded his arrival could easily have become a rapidly wasting asset. Mill had to prove his mettle, and by and large he did precisely that, his idiosyncrasies as a speaker notwithstanding. Although

11 See ibid., pp. 140–59; Michael St. John Packe, *The Life of John Stuart Mill* (London: Secker and Warburg, 1954), pp. 446–75.

12 *A*, *CW*, vol. I, pp. 276–7.

on the hustings he had shown readiness and wit, in the House he was more hesitant; his prestige afforded him opportunities to accustom the House to his style. Perhaps the House expected, and after his Irish speech he seems to have realized it expected, not intemperate volubility but temperate rationalism from the author of the *Logic* and the *Principles*.

The House's reaction is engagingly portrayed by one who knew it well and did not much like it. In his journal for 24 February, William White, the Door-Keeper of the Commons, reported the judgment that Mill's first appearances marked him as "a failure," and explained at length:

> This big giant, whom we were all so much afraid of, is, after all, no giant at all, but a mere pigmy. This is the decision; but then, please to remember, readers, that it was the pigmies of the House that delivered the verdict, and pigmies—at least intellectual pigmies—are no fit judges of a giant. . . . And so one may imagine Squirt saying to Squidlibet, as they sipped their wine at Lucas's, or smoked their havannah below: "Did you hear this great Mill, about whom there has been so much talk?" "Yes." "What did you think of him?" "Well, I should say he was a failure. I could see nothing in him." "Nor I. By the way, what has he done that so much noise was made about him?" "Oh! written some books." "Ah! these writing fellows never show well in the House." Then Mr. Mill is not a failure? . . . No; Mr. John Stuart Mill has not failed, nor can he fail. To ascertain whether a man is a failure we must ascertain what he aims at. Mr. Mill never thought to startle and dazzle the House by his oratory, as Disraeli did when he first rose to speak. Mr. Mill has no oratorical gifts, and he knows it. Nor can he be called a rhetorician. He is a close reasoner, and addresses himself directly to our reasoning powers; and though he has great command of language, as all his hearers know, he never condescends to deck out his arguments in rhetorical finery to catch applause. His object is to convey his thoughts directly to the hearer's mind, and to do this he uses the clearest medium. . . . Mr. Mill, we should say, cares very little for applause. . . . He would, perhaps, ask, with the old Roman orator, "What foolish thing have I said that these people applaud?"

As to delivery, White is candid but ever supportive (of Mill, but not of the view that the House was irritated by what it heard):

> True, his first speech was scarcely in any way a success, for few could hear it. Mr. Mill was in an entirely new position, and what wonder

> if he was nervous? Moreover, not having tested the acoustic properties of the House, he could not tell what exertion was necessary to make himself heard; and here we may remark that, so close is Mr. Mill's reasoning and so concise his sentences, that if you cannot hear all that he says you might as well hear nothing. There are speakers in the House out of whose speeches every third word might be taken, and the speeches would be all the better for the operation; but Mr. Mill uses no superfluous words—every word is necessary to make his meaning clear. . . .[13] Mr. Mill's subsequent speeches were heard in all parts of the House and commanded silent attention. He has not a powerful voice, but then it is highly pitched and very clear. . . . The giant, then, is not a failure; no, except in the eyes of the pigmies.[14]

Whatever the judgment of his initial appearances, Mill's speech on the Liberal Reform Bill made a considerable impression. J.A. Roebuck—not a disinterested witness—described it as "the outpouring of a great, honest, yet modest mind; the vigorous expression of well-considered & accurate thought."[15] William White was even more encomiastic, calling it "something entirely new in the debates of the House. Search *Hansard* from the time that record first began, and you will find nothing like it for purity of style and closeness of reasoning; and, secondly, as we venture to think, nothing like it for the effect which it produced upon the House."[16]

As to his overall performance, the general impression seems to have been favourable. Sir John R. Robinson, who had been a parliamentary reporter, and so closely aware of matter and manner in the House, gives a sympathetic but qualified account: "As an orator, it is well known Mill was a success, though his liability to pause as if he had lost the thread of his discourse, made his friends painfully apprehensive of a breakdown. This is all the more strange as all his speeches were carefully prepared and

13 As White well knew, apart from the immediate audience, who might or might not hear what was said, the public, informed through newspapers or *Parliamentary Debates* [PD], was unlikely to be aware of what anyone's words in the House actually had been. See John M. Robson, *What Did He Say? Editing Speeches from Hansard and the Newspapers* (Lethbridge: Lethbridge University Press, 1988).

14 William White, *The Inner Life of the House of Commons*, 2 vols. (1897) (Freeport, NY: Books for Libraries Press, 1970), vol. II, pp. 31–3.

15 Letter to Edwin Chadwick, 14 April 1866, J.S. Mill Papers, Yale University Library.

16 White, *Inner Life*, vol. II, p. 42. For confirmation of White's opinion, see the enthusiastic audience reactions reported in the press: PPS, CW, vol. XXVIII, pp. 59–68.

were communicated to the Press."[17] Sir William Fraser, much less sympathetic, had a far lower opinion of Mill's abilities:

> Not only was a man entering the House with a reputation out of doors looked at with the keenest severity; but he soon learnt, if he were capable of learning . . . that your reputation must be made within its walls: there you must be born again: and that it was by your own fault or your own incapacity if you failed to make a just reputation. I have seen striking instances of men, with deserved renown, who never were able to comprehend the "Genius Loci"; and whose failure was undeniable. Perhaps the most conspicuous of these was John Stuart Mill. I heard most of the speeches which he made. He entirely failed to affect the House; it was not in him: powerful as he was as a writer, he had not those peculiar gifts which the House of Commons requires: as regards that place, "His name is writ in water."[18]

Curiously, Fraser's hero, Disraeli, seems at least sometimes to have held another view—or rather, and not curiously, views: when Mill first spoke, Disraeli is reported to have said, "Ah, I see, the finishing governess"; but in October 1867 his comment was quite other: "Mill has recovered himself politically now & is listened to as every first-rate man must be listened to in the House."[19]

Leslie Stephen's account, which similarly describes both the strengths and weaknesses of Mill's parliamentary performances, best evokes the member for Westminster in parliament:

> Mill took up his duties with his usual assiduity; he watched business as closely as the most diligent of partisans, and was as regular in the House as he had been in his office. The scenes in which he appeared as an orator were remarkable. His figure was spare and slight, his voice weak; a constant twitching of the eyebrow betrayed his nervous irritability; he spoke with excessive rapidity, and at times lost the thread of his remarks, and paused deliberately to regain self-

17 Frederick Moy Thomas, ed., *Fifty Years of Fleet Street, Being the Life and Recollections of Sir John R. Robinson* (London: Macmillan, 1904), p. 81.

18 William Fraser, *Disraeli and His Day*, 2nd ed. (London: Kegan Paul *et al.*, 1891), pp. 286–7. That Fraser and Mill might differ on oratorical effect is shown by Fraser's judgment that Connop Thirlwall, whom Mill thought the best speaker he had ever heard (*A*, *CW*, vol. I, p. 129), though "famous as an historian, was a clear, but common-place, speaker" (*Disraeli and his Day*, p. 387).

19 W.F. Monypenny and G.E. Buckle, *Life of Benjamin Disraeli*, 6 vols. (London: 1916), vol. V, p. 501; and J.I. Brash, "Disraeli's Visit to Arniston House, October 1867," *Disraeli Newsletter*, 5 (spring 1980), p. 10.

> possession. But he poured out continuous and thoroughly well-arranged essays—lucid, full of thought, and frequently touching the point epigrammatically. . . . The tone of the debates, as was said by competent witnesses, was perceptibly raised by his speeches.[20]

Stephen also refers in his account to another important aspect of the impression Mill made. In the political context, Mill, he says, "appeared to be a thorough party man. He fully adopted, that is to say, the platform of the Radical wing, and voted systematically with them on all points."[21] How does this dogmatic judgment tally with Mill's comments in the *Autobiography*? Mill, well aware of the uncompromising and peculiar nature of his political principles and the public's knowledge of them, knew such was not the case. He singled out a number of issues on which his views were idiosyncratic: "Several of my speeches, especially one against the motion for the abolition of capital punishment, and another in favour of resuming the right of seizing enemies' goods in neutral vessels, were opposed to what then was, and probably still is, regarded as the advanced liberal opinion."[22]

Mill's role in the 1867 Reform Bill debates and divisions adds complexity to his position. On more than one crucial division a sizeable group of Radicals, anxious to keep the bill alive, voted with the Tory government and against Gladstone. Yet whenever Gladstone put his authority and prestige on the line in these debates, Mill, unlike other Radicals, supported him, judging that the pursuit of some of his own most cherished political goals could not prudently be separated from Gladstone's ambitions.[23] Mill's support of Gladstone was given not as a party man in the usual sense of that characterization; he wanted not to further his career but his ideals; he saw himself, in his own words, as "the defender of advanced liberalism." This view complicated his outward allegiances in the political groupings of the 1860s, but the inner motivation was consistent.

20 Leslie Stephen, *The English Utilitarians*, 3 vols. (London: Duckworth, 1900), vol. III, p. 64.

21 Ibid., p. 66.

22 *A*, *CW*, vol. I, p. 275.

23 John Vincent accepts Stephen's designation of Mill as "a good party man in Parliament." Vincent's valuable contribution to the literature on Mill's parliamentary career, however, lies in his recognition that the party to which Mill belonged was Gladstone's. With so many fish to fry in *The Formation of the Liberal Party*, Vincent is obliged to toss Mill into the pan in a fashion that precludes the possibility of revealing why this was so. John Vincent, *The Formation of the Liberal Party, 1857–1868* (London: Constable, 1966), pp. 158–60.

Since the 1830s Mill had defined the age in which he lived as one of transition; in an age of transition it was essential for social stability that the forces of progress, not the forces of stagnation, should predominate. France after 1830 had proved his hypothesis,[24] and England would too, he feared, especially if the years of stagnation under Palmerston were followed by a conservative ministry. Years earlier Mill had realized there was danger in a period of transition that the leadership of the country would fall into the hands of a man "whose object has been to resist innovation, to keep things as they are, to uphold institutions, and when abuses are inextricably interwoven with the texture of the institutions, to uphold abuses; . . . who has been consistently conservative, who has opposed a bold and unyielding front to the spirit of the age."[25]

Mill could understand the sincerity and the attraction of such a man and, therefore, the danger. In contrast was the minister

> whom we could allow to take to himself, to whom we could cheerfully give, a large share of credit for his administration, . . . a man who, taking the reins of office in a period of transition, a period which is called, according to the opinions of the speaker, an age of reform, of destruction, or of renovation, should deem it his chief duty and his chief wisdom to moderate the shock: to mediate between adverse interests; to make no compromise of *opinions*, except by avoiding any ill-timed declaration of them, but to negociate the most advantageous compromises possible in actual *measures*: to reform bit-by-bit, when more rapid progress is impracticable, but always with a comprehensive and well-digested plan of thorough reform placed before him as a guide.[26]

In 1866 Gladstone appeared to Mill as the great hope to lead a party of movement and to complete England's transition into the brighter future that history promised. Gladstone as the Grand Old Man is history's image, not Mill's. Three years younger than Mill, Gladstone was in his mid-fifties and at the height of his powers. In a reform debate the year before the 1865 election, he had appalled Palmerston and startled the House by declaring in full voice: "I venture to say that every man who is not presumably incapacitated by some consideration of personal unfitness or of political danger, is morally entitled to come within the pale of the

24 For a fuller discussion see Ann P. Robson, "Introduction," *Newspaper Writings* [*NW*], *CW*, vol. XXII, pp. lxiv ff.

25 Ibid., vol. XXIII, p. 598.

26 Ibid., pp. 598–9.

Constitution."[27] Oxford, disbelieving Gladstone's protest that his words did not imply support for universal suffrage and suspecting his views on Church Establishment not totally sound, rejected him after eighteen years. Gladstone turned to South Lancashire with words that echoed throughout the country, "At last, my friends, I am come among you, and I come among you 'unmuzzled.' "[28] After Palmerston's death, this was the new leader of the House of Commons.

Actual measures, although obviously important, were not as important as the understanding Gladstone showed of the spirit of the age. It was Gladstone's belief in movement, in progress, his conviction that history showed this to be a time in transition that gave him Mill's allegiance. Mill could not have wished for a better chastisement of the opponents of reform than Gladstone's famous peroration in April 1866:

> You cannot fight against the future. Time is on our side. The great social forces which move onward in their might and majesty . . . are against you. And the banner which we now carry in this fight, though perhaps at some moment it may droop over our sinking heads, yet it soon again will float in the eye of Heaven, and it will be borne by the firm hands of the united people of the three kingdoms, perhaps not to an easy, but to a certain and to a not far distant victory.[29]

Mill would not count on, but he would not reject, the help of Heaven in his task of uniting the advanced Liberals and the working classes in the reforming movement. He believed that Gladstone, whether or not with supernatural aid, had the principled, well-digested plan; if some of the reforms were not thorough enough, it was part of Mill's assumed role to bring the party and the country along the radical road. Through his own candidacy and its successful outcome he could work to form the advanced opinion both in and out of parliament that would allow the "rapid progress" of "thorough reform" that was not immediately possible. His goal was a true party of movement, led by Gladstone, and radicalized by the moralist from Blackheath.

Mill was not rejected by his Westminster constituents in 1868 because

27 *PD*, vol. 175, col. 324 (11 May 1864).

28 John Morley, *The Life of William Ewart Gladstone*, 3 vols. (London: Macmillan, 1903), vol. II, p. 146. An excellent evocation of the Gladstonian public personality and rhetoric at this time is given by Philip Magnus, *Gladstone* (London: Murray, 1954), although Richard Shannon, *Gladstone 1809–1865* (London: Hamish Hamilton, 1982), is most authoritative in its coverage.

29 *PD*, vol. 183, col. 152 (27 April 1866).

he had been a "thorough party man." Quite the opposite. His electoral demise had more to do with his being seen as one who had carried moral and theoretical principle to practical excess. This truth Mill saw more clearly in his *Autobiography* than Stephen in his appraisal. As a national political figure intent on using his influence to make the Liberal party an effective instrument of thoroughgoing reform, as champion of the right of the working classes to meet in Hyde Park, as eloquent advocate of fixity of tenure for Irish tenants, and as resolute adversary of Governor Eyre, J.S. Mill flashed a well-honed, familiar, radical lance. Mid-Victorian readers of Mill the logician, the political economist, and the political philosopher knew full well his substantial targets. With the windmills they had less cause to be familiar before 1865, though the windmills had always been part of Mill's vision. His was a difficult plan to follow and to understand, involving as it did both support and radicalization. To many of the public the connection between the main road and the byways was hard if not impossible to see, and they much preferred the orthodox Liberal path. In any case it was better to read Don Quixote than to meet him on the hustings. To some in 1868—but, it should be stressed, not to 6284 voters—Mill the moralist in parliament appeared a more menacing figure than had Mill the moralist in Blackheath.

The question as to why the moralist left Blackheath for Westminster also takes one back through his life. The thought of a political, if not a parliamentary career, had been in Mill's mind sporadically since, at sixteen, he dreamt of being an English Girondist.[30] His experience of politics was considerable, not all of it vicarious. He came to the hustings in 1865 not as an innocent, but as one who had written at length on the theory of politics as an engaged but distant sage, and also, and more importantly, as one who had written for the newspapers accounts of immediate events at exciting moments of political upheaval.

After his enthusiastic propagandizing for radical reform in the 1820s, Mill took little part in the Reform Bill agitation of the early 1830s. The explanation would seem to be—and this matter is very little commented on in the literature—that he, like many of his contemporaries, especially the Cambridge group of Coleridgeans with whom he became intimate after 1828, and under the influence of Carlyle as well as that of the Saint-Simonians, was imaginatively seized by the possibilities of a social revolution pointed by a political one. Certainly the French Revolution of 1830, of which he wrote weekly accounts in the *Examiner* promoting

30 *A*, *CW*, vol. I, p. 67.

English understanding and, thus, English radicalism, had provided for him an inspiriting if finally inadequate example. Following initially with elation and then growing dismay the course of political reforms under Louis-Philippe, Mill struggled to understand how the young men, especially those around Armand Carrel, whom he admired greatly, could have failed to achieve great things. He watched as the high principles espoused by those heroes degenerated into courtroom posturing and the real life of the country was directed by the party of stagnation under Guizot.

The example of Carrel continued to inspire Mill, however, as he looked for a leadership role through journalism.[31] He expended enormous effort to create a climate of opinion supportive of an effective radical party in the reformed British House of Commons after 1832.[32] Mill, himself, because of his position as an employee of the East India Company, was not free to seek election, though there is no doubt he regretted his inability during the middle years of the 1830s. He hoped much from those in the House, especially from George Grote, ably supported by William Molesworth, John Arthur Roebuck, and Joseph Hume.[33] The mere listing of these names shows how limited and heterogeneous were the ingredients for Mill's radical pudding; it was unlikely to rise, or even to turn out. For four years he struggled hopefully, and for two more years valiantly—with his eye turning more realistically if still far from usefully to Lord Durham as leader. He lost both time and money and, temporarily at least, some of his mental peace and some of his friends, in

31 For a fuller account of these matters, see Ann P. Robson and John M. Robson, "'Impetuous Eagerness': The Young Mill's Radical Journalism," in Joanne Shattock and Michael Wolff, eds., *The Victorian Periodical Press: Samplings and Soundings* (Leicester: Leicester University Press, 1982), pp. 59–77, and "Private and Public Goals: John Stuart Mill and the *London and Westminster Review*," in Joel H. Wiener, ed., *Innovators and Preachers: The Role of the Editor in Victorian England* (Westport, Conn.: Greenwood Press, 1985), pp. 231–57.

32 Mill described the attempt in his *Autobiography*: "In the meanwhile had taken place the election of the first Reformed Parliament, which included several of the most notable of my Radical friends and acquaintances; Grote, Roebuck, Buller, Sir William Molesworth, John and Edward Romilly, and several more; besides Warburton, Strutt, and others, who were in parliament already. Those who thought themselves, and were called by their friends, the philosophic radicals, had now, it seemed, a fair opportunity, in a more advantageous position than they had ever before occupied, for shewing what was in them; and I, as well as my father, founded great hopes on them. These hopes were destined to be disappointed." (*A*, *CW*, vol. I, p. 203.)

33 Especially in the early draft of the *Autobiography*, Mill emphasizes the role of Grote (pp. 202–4).

an attempt through the editorship of the *London and Westminster Review* to concentrate radical opinion with enough force to give the small group in the House the power to impose reforms on the government, or at least to prevent political stagnation. Not only did Mill solicit articles from writers of advanced views but he tried to direct from behind the scenes the tactics of the small radical force of members of parliament. He talked to, corresponded with, walked miles beside, wrote speeches for, and publicized the doings of the group he saw as a pale reflection (but the only one he had) of the *moustachioed* heroes surrounding Armand Carrel and *Le National*, and also those within the Chamber of Deputies spurring on the party of movement during the glorious early days of the French Revolution of 1830. What is abundantly evident throughout this period is the high tone, moralizing as much as moral, he adopted, not realizing that Hector is not the model for political success.

There is no doubt that the decade of the 1830s was one of reassessment for Mill, and he emerged from it a chastened visionary. Commenting on his movement in the 1830s away from his roots, he says in the *Autobiography*:

> I had, at the height of that reaction, certainly become much more indulgent to the common opinions of society and the world, and more willing to be content with seconding the superficial improvement which had begun to take place in those common opinions, than became one whose convictions, on so many points, differed fundamentally from them. I was much more inclined, than I can now approve, to put in abeyance the more decidedly heretical part of my opinions, which I now look upon as almost the only ones, the assertion of which tends in any way to re-generate society.[34]

This afterthought is not directed primarily towards his political allegiances in the 1830s, but throws incidental light on his reaction to what he had seen as practical politicking. Putting in abeyance his heretical opinions had given him no practical victories. Yet disheartening though those years were, he gained considerable insight into the workings of governing bodies and into the heads making up those governing bodies.[35] Wishful thinking certainly would not remould the world, but apparently neither

34 *A*, *CW*, vol. I, pp. 237–9.

35 Part of his trouble came through his inexperience in running a periodical and in selecting and supervising an assistant editor. Certainly his attitude to effective political commentary changed after he gave away the *London and Westminster* in 1840.

would careful explanations to potential governors of the abstract moral principles determining the rational steps to be taken for the improvement of mankind. In specifically political areas, he had learnt, attention had to be directed to the immediate, not the ultimate goals, with repeated illustrations and explanations. In 1849 he wrote in the *Westminster Review*:

> The English are fond of boasting that they do not regard the theory, but only the practice of institutions; but their boast stops short of the truth; they actually prefer that their theory should be at variance with their practice. If any one proposed to them to convert their practice into a theory, he would be scouted. It appears to them unnatural and unsafe, either to do the thing which they profess, or to profess the thing which they do. A theory which purports to be the very thing intended to be acted upon, fills them with alarm; it seems to carry with it a boundless extent of unforeseeable consequences. This disagreeable feeling they are only free from, when the principles laid down are obviously matters of convention, which, it is agreed on all parts, are not to be pressed home.[36]

After 1840, however, Mill turned to theory and, much to his surprise (and contrary to his judgments about the English), he made a great success in 1843 with his *System of Logic* and, later in the decade, with his *Principles of Political Economy*. As is perfectly evident, especially in the successive editions of these works, his polemical bent was still well exercised and his political views veiled but not forgone. Even more significantly, the ground for what he later so much valued, his more "heretical opinions," was therein laid.

He cannot have been much attracted to a political career in the 1840s and 1850s, when Radical fortunes were in woeful decline, his own eminence as an author constantly growing, and his duties in the India Office increasing; further, he had withdrawn from what little of society he had begun to mingle with before his liaison with Harriet Taylor began, and they both could not tolerate the kind of relations normal to political figures. Still, his eminence and known sympathies towards Ireland, on whose plight he had written sympathetically if dispassionately in the 1840s, led in the early 1850s to a proposal that he stand for an Irish seat; this he declined, apparently without serious consideration, instancing his position in the East India Company.[37] But his retirement from the company in

36 "Vindication of the French Revolution of February 1848," *Essays on French History and Historians*, CW, vol. XX (Toronto: University of Toronto Press, 1985), pp. 331–2.

37 *A*, CW, vol. I, p. 272.

1858, followed that same year by Harriet's death, altered his circumstances so much that he agreed, somewhat oddly and reluctantly, to stand for Westminster in 1865. It was, in many respects, but promise deferred; in other respects the road not earlier taken was only too well paved with good intentions. In going on the public stage he knew he was giving up his now more accustomed part, that of the careful observer and analyst, the "Logician" or "Scientist" in his own terminology.

He had long been accustomed to view reform as a three-stage process, which was instigated by the "Artist" who dreamt the dreams that powered the enterprise, to be developed by the "Scientist" with an eye to means tested for utility and practicability, and to be put into practice by the "Artist" who had persuasive powers and force.[38] Seeing his wife as the ideal embodiment of the Artist in both roles, he viewed himself as the mere middle person, essential but unexciting. But she was gone, leaving her dreams with him, and perhaps he saw at least a chance to be her "vice" in parliament, moving the ideal closer to reality. Here, as will be shown, the split between the two artistic roles caused difficulties. In some matters the kind of enthusiasm more appropriate to the Artist's first role emerged, and his behaviour was seen as inapt and inept. But in his major parliamentary campaigns, for women's suffrage, proportional representation, purity in elections, and municipal reform, he showed marked ability to estimate chances, seek support, and work through regular persuasive channels; even though these campaigns, especially the first two, were difficult and immediately losing efforts, one cannot fault his performance on normal parliamentary grounds. It is interesting that it was in this kind of activity that he most obviously exaggerated Harriet Taylor's skills.

He had a strong desire to be effective, and a shrewd idea, based on years of experience with the East India Company, of how to be so:

> I am disposed to agree with what has been surmised by others, that the opportunity which my official position gave me of learning by personal observation the necessary conditions of the practical conduct of public affairs, has been of considerable value to me as a theoretical reformer of the opinions and institutions of my time. Not, indeed, that public business transacted on paper, to take effect on the other side of the globe, was of itself calculated to give much practical knowledge of life. But the occupation accustomed me to see and hear the difficulties of every course, and the means of obviating them,

38 For an account of this scheme in relation to Mill's self-perception, see John M. Robson, "Harriet Taylor and John Stuart Mill: Artist and Scientist," *Queen's Quarterly*, 73 (1966), 167–86.

> stated and discussed deliberately . . . ; above all it was valuable to me by making me, in this portion of my activity, merely one wheel in a machine, the whole of which had to work together. As a speculative writer, I should have had no one to consult but myself. . . . But as a Secretary conducting political correspondence, I could not issue an order or express an opinion, without satisfying various persons very unlike myself, that the thing was fit to be done. I was thus in a good position for finding out by practice the mode of putting a thought which gives it easiest admittance into minds not prepared for it by habit; while I became practically conversant with the difficulties of moving bodies of men, the necessities of compromise, the art of sacrifing the non-essential to preserve the essential. I learnt how to obtain the best I could, when I could not obtain everything; instead of being indignant or dispirited because I could not have entirely my own way, to be pleased and encouraged when I could have the smallest part of it. . . . I have found, through life, these acquisitions to be . . . a very necessary condition for enabling any one, either as a theorist or as practical man, to effect the greatest amount of good compatible with his opportunities.[39]

Mill's experience in the company, combined with his experience in the 1830s and his maturity—he was now in his fifty-ninth year—had shaped a shrewd man, an idealist but a shrewd idealist. He had a better understanding of his fellow citizens. He had succeeded not only in divining the type of prophet they wanted but also in portraying himself in that mould—a man of expediency, eschewing general truths, a man whose proposals John Bull, especially blue-collar John Bull, could understand and approve. Publicly, as reactions to his parliamentary career demonstrated vividly, he was seen before his election not as a political activist, not as an enthusiast, but as a calm reasoner.

Yet despite his long political engagement, his political journalism, his administrative and executive experience, and his lifelong struggle with the relations between theory and practice, Mill was not by temper or habit a close observer of the inner workings of the House; if one compares him with Walter Bagehot, for instance, Mill's naivety—the word is not too strong—stands out. All during his endeavours of the 1830s he had been an outsider, a polemicist looking in. He himself had not been able to chance his arm in the House but had had to be content with the vicarious role of coach. What makes his behaviour even more explicable is the

39 *A*, *CW*, vol. I, p. 87.

realization that his most useful political role, as he saw it, was in putting forward "heretical" views—radicalizing Liberal opinion. (It is not obvious, as his earlier experience had led him to question, that the Commons was the best vehicle, especially now when Palmerston had given way to Gladstone, the leader from whom Mill hoped much.) The practical mode he had adopted was not pragmatic but moral, the MP as preceptor not producer, the latter being the role of the first Artist. Here his success was undoubted; the prominence he gained for his views both as candidate and as elected member was startling.

Yet Mill the Scientist did not forget that his overall goal, in less abstract and ideal terms, was still, as it had been in the 1830s, to help forge a political party that would serve as a constant force for the improvement of humankind. While he knew the chance was dicey, the stakes were irresistible. As he said when his active role was just beginning: "Time will show whether it was worth while to make this sacrifice for the sake of anything I am capable of doing towards forming a really advanced liberal party which, I have long been convinced, cannot be done except in the House of Commons."[40] But first he had to get there.

40 To Theodor Gomperz (22 Aug. 1866), *Later Letters* [*LL*], *CW*, vol. XVI (Toronto: University of Toronto Press, 1972), p. 1197. See also *A*, *CW*, vol. I, p. 276.

TWO

The Election of 1865

At the beginning of 1865 John Stuart Mill was fifty-eight years old, well-off, retired by his own choice after a quiet but distinguished career as a civil servant, and living with a companion, his step-daughter Helen Taylor, who shared passionately his beliefs and was capable and willing to give him all her support in principle and in practice. He was well known as an author with a keen theoretical knowledge of politics based on careful examination of issues. In March of that year he received a request from James Beal, representing a committee organized to serve the Radical interest in the borough of Westminster, to allow his name to be put forward as a possible candidate for the general election expected before the year was out. The background to that offer affords a perspective on Mill's acceptance of it and on the subsequent history of his relations with the constituency.

In the 1860s Westminster was recognized by everyone as having been a Liberal and Radical stronghold at least from the time of Charles James Fox. In the previous parliament it had been represented by two rather undistinguished Liberals, General De Lacy Evans, who had been a member from 1833 till 1841, and then again since 1846, and Sir John Villiers Shelley, first elected in 1852.[1] In 1865 there had not been a single Conservative member for many years either in a metropolitan constituency or in Middlesex, and the county of Surrey could boast of only two. As

1 General George De Lacy Evans (1787–1870), a hero of the Spanish campaigns though not a prominent MP, was seen as a loyal radical. Sir John Shelley (1808–1867), seventh baronet, who served as chairman of the Bank of London, was lieutenant-colonel of the 46th Middlesex Rifle Volunteers, 1861–7. "During his parliamentary career, the late baronet was always strongly in favour of vote by ballot, the extension of the suffrage to all rate-payers, and a strenuous opponent of religious endowments." *Gentleman's Magazine*, ns 3 (March 1867), 383.

for Westminster, there had been four candidates in only two of the previous nine general elections; in those two, three Liberals and one Conservative had run, and two Liberals had been elected. In the two previous general elections, of 1857 and 1859, Evans and Shelley had been returned unopposed, so there had not been even a candidate in the Conservative interest since 1852.

But the liberal forces, though triumphant, had not been firmly united. The Westminster Reform Society, responsible for the election of De Lacy Evans, had taken over in the early 1830s from a less radical group dating back to the election of 1780 and had maintained its coherence until 1852. At that time it was joined by still "more advanced and more practical Liberals,"[2] who immediately objected to the choice of Shelley as candidate. Evidently his supporters had brought him forward on no better grounds than that "he was the son of a baronet, that he lived in a park, that he was good looking, and could pay the expenses." The younger group, led by Charles Westerton and James Beal, seceded and found their own candidate in William Coningham (who will reappear late in this account playing a very different role). However, they failed badly in the election, when Shelley headed the poll, followed by Evans, with the Conservative candidate, Lord Maidstone, in third place and Coningham a sad last. Subsequently, in the general elections of 1857 and 1859, the splinter group (like the Conservatives) could not find a candidate willing to take on the expenses in an unpromising contest. In retrospect, the "advanced" group persuaded themselves that this period of evident inactivity had actually strengthened them by maturing their views and had weakened their opposition, now identified as "the Rump," who had in their "presumed security" been left "without a constituency, without organisation and incompetent to resist a vigorous effort to elevate the representation, and once more give to it the prominence its ancient and noble antecedents justified."[3]

Evans became ill during the session of 1864—he was in the seventy-eighth year of his life and the thirty-second since the beginning of his parliamentary service—and was forced to retire. His announced intention to withdraw in February 1865 signalled the need for one Liberal replacement, since Shelley was still in the field. A meeting of "the leading Liberal electors and Liberal members of the vestries" was held on 13 February with Dr. William Brewer in the chair, to give the electors an opportunity

2 This is the estimate of one of them, taken from a pamphlet, *Mr. J.S. Mill and Westminster: The Story of the Westminster Election, 1865*, p. 2, issued by the group after Mill's election, which provides details not to be found elsewhere.

3 Ibid., p. 3.

to air their views without advancing any special political creed and "to facilitate the progress of the popular Liberal candidate who might offer himself." Without "in the least degree undervaluing any organisation which existed, past or present," Brewer said, the intention was to form a new body with "branches in every parish, district, and ward."[4]

In fact, the organizers of the meeting believed that the Whiggish "Rump" had already betrayed their pretended wish for Liberal unity by bringing forward a candidate as soon as Evans had intimated his intention to retire. On 11 February, two days before this meeting, an advertisement had appeared in the press announcing the candidature of Robert Wellesley Grosvenor, thirty years old, an untried scion of the Grosvenor family, the major aristocratic landowners in Westminster. At the meeting on 13 February the Westerton-Beal group, believing Grosvenor not a fit and proper person to represent the "blue riband" constituency of liberalism, welcomed a motion to transfer the consideration of candidates from the public session to the proposed new organization, which would act as an executive committee. Before the meeting ended, the names of three possible candidates were mentioned: Viscount Amberley,[5] the Hon. Lyulph Stanley—and John Stuart Mill. To theirs were added, once the committee had convened, those of James Hudson, William Coningham (again), Samuel Laing, Edwin Chadwick, and John Thwaites. The committee's choice fell on Mill and Laing, with Stanley as replacement if either refused. Only Mill's name remained after both Laing and Stanley declined.[6]

These approaches were actually part of an elaborate strategy reflecting the liberal group's desire to broaden if not completely democratize the process of selection, as well as its determined opposition to the candidate of "the Rump," there being no Conservative candidate in sight as yet. The plan adopted, unusual though not unique, was outlined fully in a letter from Chadwick, early in the field,[7] to Beal, who boasted that he hap-

4 "Election Intelligence," *The Times*, 14 Feb. 1865, p. 6.

5 Lord Amberley, son of Lord John Russell and brother-in-law of Lyulph Stanley, was at this time a member of Grosvenor's election committee, but later withdrew to join Mill's. He and his wife became close friends of Mill and Helen Taylor, who were to be god-parents to the Amberley's second son, Bertrand Russell.

6 *Mr. J.S. Mill and Westminster*, p. 4. Stanley, without knowing that Mill's name was in consideration, recommended him or Goldwin Smith (ibid.).

7 In April 1859 Chadwick had written to Beal asking for his support in running for parliament, especially for Westminster, and proposing a circular letter to electors asking for pledges. Beal in reply warned that Chadwick's attacks on vestries and his reputation as a centralizer would prevent his winning in Westminster (and in Middlesex for slightly different reasons), but he offered his support, thinking

pened "to have more or less of a party in every Metropolitan vestry."[8] In saying that he wished his name to stand if "other candidates can be induced to consent to adopt the method" proposed, Chadwick gave the details:

> That method, I understand is the one you used to some extent to ascertain the sense of the electors, on the occasion of the election of a Coroner. It is to appoint, by agreement of the candidates, if practicable, a committee or an umpire, to send by post to each elector, each candidates [sic] statement, or his friends [sic] statement of his pretensions, with a blank form, which the elector will be requested to fill up with the name or names of the candidates he prefers and will promise to vote for. Or if it were thought fit to do away with the notion of sectional dictation or selection, the elector might be invited to name any other whom he would prefer to those on the list submitted to him. The returns would be examined by the committee or the umpire, and only the candidates who had the greatest number of promises would be put in nomination.[9]

The method would, in Chadwick's opinion, provide an important precedent for the Metropolis and other places with large constituencies. Among its many advantages, it would bring into the process electors who were hard to canvass and who never attended meetings:

> The usual electoral meetings, you will be aware are commonly composed for the greater part of non electors, and are illusory as tests of opinion. By the method proposed, you get at electors alone, and all of them, direct and at an inconsiderable expense. By it candidates will be induced to come forward who have strength of head for the position, without having great power of lungs, for very large and frequent electoral meetings.

Finally, Chadwick turned to the Westminster contest: "If in this instance

---

Chadwick might win in a metropolitan district if he modified his tactics. University College London [UCL], Chadwick MSS, No. 264, f. 5, 25 April 1859.

8 Ibid.

9 Chadwick goes on to say that the method had been tried successfully at the last election for the University of Cambridge to avoid the annoyance and expense of a contest, and that it had the approval of Lord Brougham and of a committee of the National Association for the Promotion of Social Science considering ways to prevent electoral bribery.

it should turn out that the majority of the electors are content with their remaining representative, or with the position, family connexion and promise of the new candidate already presented to them, the fact would be early determined with the least amount of trouble or expence to those gentlemen and their friends."[10]

As Chadwick well knew, Beal and his friends were far from content with Grosvenor, "the new candidate." Grosvenor's position, outlined in the advertisement of 11 February, was only *pro forma* Liberal, and not reassuring to their more extensive reforming desires:

> Determined to work in the paths of that constitution which has carried this country through so many storms in safety, whilst other nations have been shaken to their foundation, I cannot yet understand why we are not to proceed to enlarge the basis of our representative system by the extension of the suffrage; why we are not to protect the voter in the discharge of his duty from an undue influence, let it come from what quarter it may; why, in short, we are to halt in any of those measures of progress by which alone, in my opinion, the benefits arising from the conquests won for the cause of civil, religious, and commercial freedom can be maintained.

After expressing fulsome regrets at Evans's need to withdraw, Grosvenor's address continues: "I venture to think that it will not detract from my claims that I belong to a family deeply interested in the prosperity of the city of Westminster, one member of which [his father] was politically connected with it whilst member for the county of Middlesex, and all of whom are Reformers."[11]

Immediately following in *The Times* on that same day was another advertisement inviting "communications" about Grosvenor's candidacy, and, drawing on the family's extensive local influence, his supporters quickly put together a committee, that essential element of electoral activity in the period. On 17 February, long before the reforming group had settled on a candidate, Grosvenor's supporters held a meeting in St. Martin's Hall. Since his address was typical of his performances, a summary is called for.

Grosvenor began in his normal jokey manner with a reference to his

10 Chadwick concludes the long letter by asserting that his qualifications are revealed by his past labours, demonstrated in published works, and approved by many, including Bentham, Hume, James Stephen, the Earl of Carlisle, Lord Brougham, and Earl Russell. UCL, Chadwick MSS, No. 264, ff. 12–16, 20 Feb. 1865.

11 *The Times*, 11 Feb. 1865, p. 4.

election address having appeared, "it seemed, to the prejudice of 'peculiar trousers' and the adorable Menken . . . on the sacred pillars of the Marble Arch,"[12] and then went on to his most important claim on the electors, that he had lived in Westminster all his life and bore a name that was "a 'household word.' (*Cheers.*)" Dwelling on the Whig arguments of his connection with the electors by "the social tie of property" and the family's "championship of civil and religious liberty," he went on more liberally to assert that the present time of comparative political quiet provided an opportunity to consider the great social questions, such as the Poor Laws, extension of education, the treatment of criminals, and (a local issue) the displacement of working people by the construction of railways and public works. He then turned to issues before parliament: though a supporter of the Established Church, he would vote for the abolition of church rates (again he won cheers), support the ballot and revision of the Poor Law, and, though aware of the dangers of drink, oppose the attempts to legislate temperance. Touching on a tender religious nerve, he expressed the hope that Catholics would voluntarily accept the need for inspection of convents. His view of moderate reform of the franchise encompassed household suffrage in the boroughs. His most impassioned remarks, it seems, were reserved for his description of the U.S. Civil War as revealing "the collapse of democracy" and his approval of the present state of British neutrality, which, however, did not reach to countenancing insults from the North: "if the patience of John Bull should be at last exhausted, and he should have to knock Brother Jonathan into the middle of next week—(*hisses*)—he thought a jury of disinterested Europeans would say, 'Sarve him right.' " (The audience responded with mixed approval and dissent to these views.) In closing he announced that he had been told "there was a man of surpassing eloquence and superlative talent coming forward for the honour of representing them. He might be Garibaldi, the Pope, Count Bismarck, Jeff Davis, or General Tom Thumb—(*oh*)—," but he himself came "forward independent of all parties or sections, and, if elected, would not be the delegate of any, but the representative of all."[13]

12 The *Morning Star* has "Sydenham trousers" for *The Times*'s equally attractive "peculiar trousers." (The reference is partly elucidated below, though the trousers remain peculiar.) Grosvenor's tone contrasts sharply with those of the other candidates once they were in the field and greatly offended the radical group while amusing the readers of the satirical papers, but may not actually have done him much damage with the group most likely to support him.

13 Accounts of 18 Feb. 1865, in the *Daily Telegraph*, p. 3, *The Times*, p. 12, and the *Morning Star*, p. 5.

The reforming group, in whose opinion Grosvenor had been supported "by an array of most disreputable men in the body of the meeting, who acted under the leadership of a well-known *claqueur*,"[14] kept a keen eye on his activities and were not behind in making their opposition known. When on 4 March an advertisement appeared in *The Times* announcing a second Grosvenor meeting for the 9th in St. James's Hall, immediately below it was another advertisement, over the names of the chairman and secretary of the Liberal committee, Charles Westerton and E.D. Berry, that signalled not only their opposition but also some anxiety about the progress of their plan: "Representation of Westminster—The Westminster Liberal Electoral Committee earnestly invites their fellow-electors to withhold promises of their votes for the next election until steps have been taken to ensure to them the choice of able and proper representatives."

At the meeting on 9 March Grosvenor did not do well: he referred ineffectually to the advertisement asking Liberal electors to withhold promises, dealt equally weakly with his own qualifications and, after mentioning again his views on religion and political reform, alluded to his remarks of 17 February on the United States. The third-person account in the *Morning Star* captures his style and the mood of the audience:

> He said then what he still said, that the unfortunate state of affairs in America conveyed to his mind an impression of the failure of purely democratic institutions. (A perfect storm of disapprobation was raised by this remark.) He was not again going to use the words he did on the occasion referred to, because maturer thought induced him to think that they were calculated to give unnecessary offence, but he would first give their effect—and he put the case now as then on purely hypothetical grounds—that if England, goaded to resistance by insult and attacks from America, were to engage in a struggle with that country, and were to come out of that struggle successful, the unprejudiced opinion of Europe would be that America had brought the chastisement on herself. Could this be construed into a rash love of war? Did it not, on the contrary, rather tend to another doctrine which, if it had been observed, would have eradicated nine-tenths of the blood-stained pages of history? He rather leaned towards the weak than the strong. He leaned towards independence.

This comment was fatal to the success of the meeting: it was met by the cry

14 *J.S. Mill and Westminster*, p. 10.

of "'Slavery, slavery,' and uproar." The account in *Mr. J.S. Mill and Westminster* records Grosvenor's response thus: "he had the bad taste, in disgust at the opposition expressed to his Southern and slave-owning sympathies, to turn his back upon his audience, and was recalled to a sense of decorum only by the most vehement sibilation."[15] The report in the *Morning Star* confirms that account (in the square brackets commonly used in newspapers of the time to indicate "colour" commentary):

> [The hon. gentleman turned his back on the audience, and addressed himself to the gentlemen who occupied the platform. His remarks, in the midst of the hubbub excited thereby, were inaudible until he resumed his original position.]

He concluded quickly and, after one question concerning Catholic convents, the standard motion for approval of Grosvenor's candidature was made by H. Grenfell, MP, who felt compelled, however, to say that his general approval of Grosvenor's opinions did not extend to those on the U.S. Civil War; he was himself "entirely in favour of the North," but added that "as a soldier, it was not surprising that Captain Grosvenor should look favourably on the gallant defence which had been made by the South."

At this point the opposition took over the floor, with Brewer making some pungent comments on the failure of parliament to proceed with reform. Beal followed with a long speech in which he put finely detailed questions to Grosvenor, allowing him to escape "an open display of his utter incompetency by the misplaced kindness of that gentleman [Beal], in permitting him to defer his replies to the next meeting." And when the question about his candidature was put, "the number of hands contra so evenly balanced those pro that the chair's declaration that the motion was carried was loudly and clamorously questioned."[16]

What Mill thought of the moves against Grosvenor is not known, but he was by this time aware that he had been considered as a possible alternative to the representative of the "powerful local interest." He also knew that Chadwick, his lifelong friend, anxiously wished to be considered, and supported his effort wholeheartedly. For the moment he proposed to do nothing, he told Chadwick on 22 February, saying he would emulate him and wait to see if anything further came of the

15 Ibid.
16 *Morning Star*, 9 March 1865, p. 5.

proposal. He heard officially from the committee on 6 March, when Beal wrote asking that he allow his name to go forward during the first stage of the scheme, which included the committee's promise to assume "all the trouble of the election."[17]

Mill's reply of 7 March set forth his agreement that his name should be "submitted to the electors in the proposed manner," which he praised highly, if the committee held to its intention after reading his "explanations." First, private considerations being against his candidacy, his only personal object would be to serve the Liberal cause as usefully as possible, and he was uncertain whether he could not be of more use as a writer. Second, his usefulness could only be as an advocate of opinions such as those known through his works; he would be perfectly open to questions about these opinions, which were already before the world, and would, if elected, explain his votes in the House. Third, he would attend to no local constituency business. Fourth, he would undertake no expenses towards his election, on principle and because he could not afford them. Fifth, though he would be proud of their suffrages, he would not present himself to the electors to win their votes. Furthermore, he hoped that more than two names would be recommended by the committee to the electors in the winnowing-down process: he himself would suggest Sir John Romilly and Chadwick.[18]

This reply satisfied the committee that Mill was willing to stand and, very likely with an eye to the next Grosvenor public meeting on the 27th, they published it in the daily papers of 23 and 24 March. The response, especially in the *Daily Telegraph*, could not have been more cheering to the committee, its lauding of Mill being matched by its praise for their method of choosing candidates and by its denigration of Grosvenor (though not by name):

> A magnificent opportunity has presented itself to the electors of Westminster. The name of John Stuart Mill is suddenly placed at their disposal for representation in Parliament. It was of such a name as this that we were thinking lately in commenting on the titled nobodies and prosperous nonentities who get into Parliament by marches stolen on public opinion; and it was such a constituency as Westminster to which we looked to redeem great communities from the shame of becoming the prey of local landholders and bustling agents.

17 *Later Letters* [*LL*], ed. Francis E. Mineka and Dwight N. Lindley, *Collected Works* [*CW*], vols. XIV–XVII (Toronto: University of Toronto Press, 1972), vol. XVI, pp. 999–1000.

18 Ibid., pp. 1005–7.

Nothing could more justify the candidature of "one whom in the very largest sense Plato would have called *sophos*" than his "admirable letter" to Beal. "No political thinker of the present day has exercised an influence like this man, . . . [whose] published works on Representative Institutions, Governments, and Liberty have long stamped [him as] . . . the profoundest and yet most practical debater of the problems which engage modern society." As to the "new and most promising electoral method" proposed by Beal and "the leading men of Westminster," if adopted it will soon put an end to

> the evil days of room-hiring, placard-buffoonery, and parliamentary agency; we shall have done with the dirty hands which vainly acclaim election to the noisiest candidate. We shall begin to get rid of personal solicitation, canvassers, and clique elections. . . . It will be death to the swarm of titled and untitled gnats that buzz, nowadays, about a vacant metropolitan seat. . . . Singular and felicitous indeed will be the combination, and full of new hope for the cause of Liberalism, if the historical centre of that high political creed, in returning its foremost intellectual professor, accomplishes its choice by a new method, itself the precursor of purer elections and juster representation.[19]

An editorial in the *Morning Star* was, though typically less florid and more thoughtful than that in the *Daily Telegraph*, equally unstinting in its praise of Mill, of whom "it seems superfluous to say" that he "is one of the greatest of living Englishmen," though even at this early date the *Morning Star* raised the question of the comparative worth of his labours in and out of parliament. It also, specifically though more briefly, made allusion to Grosvenor as "a young scion of the aristocracy, personally unknown to even the smallest section of the political world, and apparently not quite clear in his own mind as to the political opinions which it would be his duty to express. Fortune could hardly devise a greater practical antithesis than by offering to Captain Grosvenor an opponent in the person of Mr. John Stuart Mill."[20]

Grosvenor's meeting on 27 March in the Temperance Hall, Broadway, was an even worse fiasco than its predecessor. He began his remarks by complaining about an attack on him in the *Saturday Review*, and then dwelt at length on Beal's behaviour at the previous meeting before going

19 *Daily Telegraph*, 24 March 1865, p. 6.

20 *Morning Star*, 25 March 1865, p. 5. This issue also contained an advertisement for Grosvenor's next two meetings, on 27 March and 4 April.

on to specific topics. He struck a new note by expressing opposition to capital and corporal punishment, though he was not a complete abolitionist with reference to the latter. He tried again to explain his views on the United States, and made what at least some of his auditors found unsatisfactory comments on the virtues of the Liberal leaders in parliament. Then he made another untactful move: "Coming next to the question of Reform, he said there were revolutionary Reformers, who were, in fact, no Reformers at all, but revolutionists—(*uproar*)—who would take away, for objects best known to themselves, the whole political power of the governing classes and hand it over to the class most numerous, and which, being uneducated, was most unfit for the monopoly. (*Hisses.*)"

At this Beal must have felt the same surge of triumph that Huxley had when he said, during the famed Oxford debate with Bishop Wilberforce, "The Lord hath delivered him into my hand!" In the question period a Mr. Monsey asked "what the hon. candidate meant by calling them revolutionists?" Grosvenor could do no better than to say that "his remark was those 'reckless' men, &c., were revolutionary Reformers, and he should not for a moment imagine that any gentlemen who sought an explanation of the kind, or indeed any person in the assembly, was either reckless or revolutionary." This drew laughter, though the account does not say of what kind and, after a few other interchanges, the customary motion was made. However, it was followed by an amendment: "'That the Hon. Mr. Grosvenor is not a fit and proper person to represent the city of Westminster in Parliament.' (*Applause and laughter.*)" Beal then intervened with another long attack on Grosvenor, in which the only affirmative note was the questionable assertion that at least he was getting a bit better on each occasion; his approval of the amendment was followed by a vote, during which the "greatest confusion prevailed," and the chair ultimately decided, "with much regret," that the opinion was against Grosvenor.[21]

There was clearly ground to be made up at his next meeting on 4 April in the Pimlico Rooms, with E.P. Bouverie, MP, in the chair,[22] and it would appear that Grosvenor's committee succeeded in gathering a majority of supporters. It seems unwise to suggest any more success than that, for though the final vote was in his favour, Grosvenor seemed fated or determined to alienate the "advanced" Liberals. In the course of a

21 Ibid., 29 March 1865, p. 4.

22 Bouverie, who in the new parliament was close to joining Grosvenor's better-known uncle in the Adullamite cave, played a significant part, as will be seen, in Mill's campaign for re-election in 1868.

review of his earlier speeches, he referred to his having carried the vote at two of the three meetings, and said that at the third he "believed that the majority against him was made up of non-electors. (*Cries of 'No, no.'*) The dirty hands were held up against him, but the clean hands in favour—(*oh and interruption*)—and he believed that the vast majority of the electors of Westminster had clean hands. (*Applause and interruption.*)" Grosvenor was able to continue with an account of his opinions after this little sally, and ventured an allusion to the proposed candidacy of Mill: "It would not be wise for Westminster to elect a man, however vast his intellect and mighty his power, who would not take an interest in their local matters."[23] The reference to "dirty hands" certainly rankled in the minds of the radical group, however, and was used by them in their campaign; in the summary from their point of view following the election, when presumably all Liberal differences had been accommodated, the repugnant sentence is cited, with comment:

> When this insult to labour was uttered, great surprise was expressed that Sir F. Crossley, who moved the resolution [in favour of Grosvenor's candidacy], and who knew the value and worth of honest hands blackened by toil, did not resent it, and enforce an apology. This insult was the more apparent, as the seconder of Capt. Grosvenor was the same Mr. Dundas, M.P., who had proposed in the House, as "a remedy for Reform demands, the trailing of 6-pounders amongst the mob."
>
> This excited meeting closed for a time the public appearance of the candidate. Captain Grosvenor was in no sense accepted by the constituency.[24]

The bias of that account is evident, but it serves to illustrate the strength of feeling surrounding these early stages of the campaign and to suggest the temper of the canvassing in the constituency. The Westminster Liberal Electoral Committee moved quickly following Grosvenor's meeting to convene a relatively small gathering in St. James's Hall on 6 April for the purpose of "ascertaining specifically the political sentiments" of Mill and Coningham. Mill was not present, being represented by Chadwick; Coningham also was absent, and indeed signalled that his name should not be in consideration, having notified Westerton that it was "evident to him there was no chance of his obtaining a majority of votes."

23 *Daily Telegraph*, 5 April 1865, p. 3.
24 *J.S. Mill and Westminster*, p. 10.

Chadwick's remarks were not reported at length in the press, but the summary indicates that he stayed close to Mill's own comments in his letter of 7 March, using them as an explanation for Mill's absence. W.D. Christie, Mason Jones, and Henry Fawcett also spoke for Mill, but the centrepiece of the reports, and undoubtedly of the meeting, was an impromptu speech by John Arthur Roebuck, MP. The strength of Roebuck's feeling when he turned to reminiscence evidently prompted the reporter for the *Morning Star* to switch into the first person:

> He and I (said Mr. Roebuck) were young men together, and he, in fact, though the younger of the two was the leader on the occasion. He taught me pretty much all I know upon politics and philosophy. He was my guide. I followed him, and I owe him a greater debt of gratitude than I owe to any man, living or dead. I cannot help thinking of those days and those hours we spent together in the investigation of great subjects—
>
> "For we spent them, not in toys, or lust, or wine,
> But in search of deep philosophy,
> Wit, eloquence, and poetry—
> Arts which I loved; for they, my friend, wert thine."

In asking whether Mill was "a fit and proper person to represent the city of Westminster," Roebuck considered the question first in relation to Westminster and then to the House of Commons. Knowing well the proud disposition of the Liberal electors, he played on the ancient and exemplary status of the constituency and imbedded the happy assumption that the Liberals could elect whomever they chose. Turning to the House, Roebuck fell back on the kind of eulogy that made him in these years a target of Matthew Arnold's satire: "any man who knows the House must know that every word said in it re-echoes throughout the world. There is no such assembly on the earth's surface." And in that assembly, he averred, it was well that there should be "railway contractors," "gallant men, who have won battles," and "persons in trade who had made a fortune," because the "House of Commons ought to be an epitome of England, and . . . ought to represent not only the interests but the feelings of the English people. (*Applause.*)" However, there also ought to be "some man whose mind is of that order that he shall represent the thought, the philosophy, the great powers of the thinking people of England." Again winning applause by that comment, Roebuck went on to identify Mill as that man: "His mind has been trained, and he has studied legislation as a science and not as a mere matter of talk over the evening dinner-table or the morning breakfast." Not "a mere talker," but "a man . . . who should hold the thought of that House, whose every word should be weighed, whose every sentence should be recollected," Mill would go there, Roebuck continued, getting to the necessary theme in these circumstances,

> not for the purpose of winning renown, for that he has gained. Then what does he go for? Because he believes he can do his country good. (*Applause.*) If I were to consult Mr. Mill's private comfort I would tell him, "Don't go to that House—you don't know that House as well as I do; my life has been passed in it, the turmoil and trouble of that House will be to you something very disagreeable." . . . [B]ut if I consult the interests of my country, if I consult the interests of those who are represented in the House of Commons, I would go down on my knees for Mill to stand.

That unfortunately worded image did not inhibit the audience's applause. The meeting closed with approval of a motion that Mill be adopted as a candidate on the terms of his letter of 7 March, and "that, to mark the spontaneity of the act on the part of the electors, subscriptions should be invited to defray the expenses of his election," and of a further motion that "the electors of Westminster and the friends of Mr. Mill be invited to form a committee to further his return."[25]

From that time the Westminster Liberal Committee seems not to have considered looking seriously for anyone else in order to have an advance poll. Mill was annoyed by this development and continued to encourage Chadwick through May. He had, however, by that time carried his resolve not to interfere in the electoral process to the length of removing himself to his French home in Avignon, where he had spent about half of each year since his wife's death there. In doing so, he was not being more awkward than he had said he would be: before the question of his standing had arisen he had planned to go to Avignon and, by 2 April, had arranged to leave by the 11th, as he did. His plans also included a trip through the Auvergne in June, with his return to England governed not

25 *Morning Star*, 7 April 1865, p. 2. The second motion, made by Beal, led to advertisements over his name as honorary secretary: "Westminster Election.—Mr. J. Stuart Mill for Westminster.—Gentlemen, being electors of Westminster and others anxious to promote the Election of Mr. Stuart Mill, and to subscribe to return him free of expense, are invited to communicate with the undersigned." See, for example, *Daily Telegraph*, 13, 15, and 17 April 1865.

by the date of the election, which as late as 23 May he still proposed to take no part in, but by his promise to be at a meeting of the Political Economy Club on 7 July.[26]

The election, however, was beginning to take a different shape. To this point, it will be recalled, one Liberal candidate, Shelley, was in the field, and two Liberal candidates, Grosvenor and Mill (or possibly another candidate chosen by the Westminster Liberal Committee), were being proposed. There being no Conservative candidates, it could be assumed that at least one of the new Liberal candidates would be elected. However, after Evans's retirement was announced, the Conservatives initiated some quiet activity, though they made no open move. By the end of March, William Henry Smith, the "Son" but now the moving spirit of the well-known bookselling firm, in his fortieth year, had been invited to stand by an informal group[27] and was preparing an address to the electors that he circulated to his close advisers for comment.[28] The political allegiance of Smith was less than dogmatic. In fact, his first solicitation as a potential candidate came in 1856 from the Liberal party in Boston. And in 1857 he was approached by Liberals in Exeter. In both cases, although he saw himself as holding "politically and religiously liberal" principles, he refused to stand on the practical grounds that the local parties were not

26 Mill had proposed the topic for the meeting: "Does the high rate of Interest in America and in new Colonies indicate a corresponding high rate of profits? and if so, What are the causes of that high rate." *Miscellaneous Writings*, ed. John M. Robson, *CW*, vol. XXXI (Toronto: University of Toronto Press, 1989), p. 410.

27 The group included tradesmen and aristocrats, as he informed his sister Augusta (Gussie), on 31 March 1865, saying he was considering the proposal on the understanding that he would not stand "at all unless I am absolutely assured of success in a contest, if any takes place." Quoted in Herbert Maxwell, *Life and Times of the Rt. Hon. W.H. Smith, M.P.*, 2 vols. (Edinburgh and London: Blackwood, 1893), vol. I, pp. 117–18, and in E.A. Akers-Douglas (Viscount Chilston), *W.H. Smith* (London: Routledge and Kegan Paul, 1965), p. 49.

28 A letter to Smith of 30 March 1865, from Robert Grimston, commenting on the address, is in the W.H. Smith Papers, Hambleden Archive, PS 1/1. Grimston, who was Smith's main agent in 1868, is considered by his own and Smith's biographers not to have taken an active role in the campaign of 1865; however, though he certainly was less prominent, he seems to have been as energetic as anyone else on Smith's behalf in the first of these elections. See, for example, a letter of 22 May 1865, from him to Smith on paper headed "*Westminster Election.* / Mr. Wm. Hy. Smith's Central Committee Rooms, / Trafalgar Hotel, / 34, Spring Gardens. S.W." Ibid., PS 1/34. See pp. 238 ff. below for Grimston's role in the second election.

Smith's feelings about his prospects are seen in a series of letters to his sister, printed in Maxwell, *Smith*, vol. I, pp. 118, 125–6, and in Akers-Douglas, *Smith*, pp. 49–52.

strong enough to elect a second Liberal to join the sitting member.[29] Smith's biographer asserts that his move to Conservatism resulted from his being blackballed at the Reform Club in 1862 because he was a "tradesman."[30] But certainly doubt remained. The proprietor of the *Daily Telegraph*, Edward Levy-Lawson, then a staunch Liberal though later, after his own conversion in the mid-1870s, a vigorous Conservative, met Smith in the Strand and promised him support, assuming he was a Liberal; when informed that he had Conservative support, he vowed opposition.[31] Similarly, George Cubitt, the influential London builder and Conservative MP for Surrey (later Baron Ashcombe), who became Smith's intimate friend and supporter, felt compelled in 1865 after seeing Smith's election address to consult the Conservative "whipper-in," Colonel T.E. Taylor, as to the prudence of support. Taylor's reply settled the question, and ultimately the issue: "Take him. . . . I don't fancy his politics much myself, but you'll get nobody better."[32]

In his address, Smith said he came forward to give the

> more moderate or Conservative portion of the constituency an opportunity of marking their disapproval of the extreme political

29 Maxwell, *Smith*, vol. I, pp. 113–14. Summarizing Smith's Liberalism in the early 1850s, Maxwell says it would "scarcely satisfy thorough-going Radicals of the present day [1904], for although he was in favour of abolishing Church Rates he was opposed to Disestablishment; though advocating the promotion of popular education by fresh legislation, he would not have made it compulsory; though holding the opinion that naval and military expenditure should be reduced (the Crimean war had then just been brought to a close), it must not be brought below the point of complete efficiency; and he could not look with favour on the introduction of vote by ballot."

30 See ibid., pp. 116–17, and compare Akers-Douglas, *Smith*, p. 49. John F. Isaacson, who organized Smith's committee and seems to have been the initiator of the campaign, recommended that his address give both town addresses, Hyde Park Street and Strand, to emphasize his local attachment to Westminster, but if either were omitted it should be the latter, his business address, presumably because of the trade stigma. Hambleden Archive, PS 1/2; for his initiative, see ibid., PS 1/3. During the campaign "An elector" wrote to Smith in abusive terms, referring to his being "Son of an Advertising Agent and Billsticker, which in itself is somewhat disparaging," and worse, lacking "merit and qualification." Ibid., PS 1/33.

31 Maxwell, *Smith*, vol. I, pp. 114–15; Akers-Douglas, *Smith*, p. 48. Maxwell dates the anecdote to 1864, though presumably it occurred after Smith had decided to run for Westminster in March-April 1865.

32 Maxwell, *Smith*, vol. I, pp. 121–2; Akers-Douglas, *Smith*, pp. 50–1. That Cubitt took the advice and put his weight behind Smith is shown in the Hambleden Archive, for example, in a letter of 1 May, 1865 (PS 1/14).

> doctrines which have been avowed by the Candidates already in the field. . . . Unconnected with either of the great political parties, I should desire to enter Parliament as an independent Member, at liberty to vote for measures rather than for men. I should not be a party to any factious attempt to drive Lord Palmerston from power, as I feel that the country owes a debt of gratitude to him for having preserved peace, and for the resistance he has offered to reckless innovation in our domestic institutions.

In addition to his advocacy of "an amicable adjustment of the question of Church rates," Smith went on to endorse a carefully considered extension of the suffrage, to lay emphasis on the need for educational legislation and "popular thrift," and to indicate his opposition to the ballot on the grounds that the voter who was afraid to act openly was "scarcely worthy of the trust which he is supposed to discharge for the benefit of the commonwealth."[33]

This platform can hardly be seen as founded on bedrock Conservatism, and Smith's ambivalence shows even more clearly in his response to what he interpreted (though no one else would be likely to do so) as hearty and handsome Conservative support:

> You are fully aware of the independence of party which I felt it necessary to stipulate for when it was proposed by the Committee that I should stand for Westminster, but I am not sure that your friends would gather as much from my address. It will be well, therefore, to repeat that I am not a member of the Conservative party as such—nor am I a member of the Liberal party, but I believe in Lord Palmerston,[34] and look forward ultimately to a fusion of the moderate men following Lord Derby and Lord Palmerston into a strong Liberal Conservative party, to which I should be glad to attach myself. Such an expectation may be chimerical but I cannot help indulging it—and I wish to stand by it.

33 See Maxwell, p. 123. We have found no comment on his close resemblance to Mill on the last issue.

34 Grimston had been disturbed by the exact terms of Smith's support for Palmerston, commenting that in his address it was wrong to say he would "*give him an independent support*"; rather he should say that he "would support him certainly if he brought forward a measure that you approved, but not otherwise," because, without this qualification, the comment was inconsistent with Smith's "previous declaration for measures and not men: and besides would appear so very antagonistic to the party that proposes to support you." Letter of 30 March 1865, Hambleden Archive, PS 1/1.

He adds that he is opposed to Baines's bill (extending suffrage in boroughs), the ballot, and "the unconditional abolition of Church rates and all similar radical measures," and asks that Taylor make clear to his friends where Smith stands, "as I would rather retire now than fairly lay myself open to the reproach of obtaining party support under false pretences." To this Taylor replied: "I consider your letter an extremely fair one, and I shall advise the Westminster Conservatives to give you their unreserved support."[35]

Still, many supporters remained aloof, and Smith's campaign was slow in starting, partly because of his professing a Liberal-Conservative faith, but also because though "known to the few as a practical philanthropist and steady churchman," he was known "to the many as the owner of the bookstalls."[36] His friends found it difficult to enlist a good committee until Earl Percy (two years later to become the sixth Duke of Northumberland) agreed to be chairman. Then the prospects brightened somewhat, as Smith "appeared to make an excellent impression and offers of support rolled in in gratifying numbers."[37] Overall, however, the expectations are probably best expressed by Smith's friend Robert Cheese, who was of opinion that his only chance would come "from a split in the Camp of the Radicals," and that, although sufficient money would come in for the campaign, ". . . I fear tho' you will make a real good fight you will not get in."[38]

35 Letter to Taylor, 26 April 1865, and from Taylor, 28 April 1865, Hambleden Archive PS 1/9, quoted in Maxwell, *Smith*, vol. I, p. 122n. In the letter to his sister cited above, Smith says: "If I go to Parliament it will be as an independent man and the printed paper I send you contains a general sketch of my opinions. . . . I can afford the expense and my business will be well managed."

36 Maxwell, *Smith*, vol. I, p. 119. As Maxwell admits (pp. 123–4), Smith's election address was not a very exciting document. He was not attractive to the aristocratic householders of Belgravia and Mayfair, many of whom were of course close to the Marquis of Westminster and other Grosvenors, and his fellow West End tradesmen held aloof (quite a few of whom, though Maxwell does not say so, were attracted to Mill).

37 Akers-Douglas, *Smith*, p. 51. That confusion about his actual political position remained is seen in a letter to Smith from "One of Westminster" (6 April 1865), in which he is implored not to stand on the side of "the *privileged classes*" against "the *popular side*" (Hambleden Archive, PS 1/4). The *Morning Advertiser*, which violently opposed Mill, promised to cover Smith's meetings, even though his political views did not harmonize with its position (ibid., PS 1/18, letter of 3 May 1865).

38 Cheese concludes that while he wants Smith to try for "the cause sake," as a "private friend" he would attempt to dissuade him from standing (Hambleden Archive, PS 1/5, 7 April 1865). The Hambleden Archive PS 1 series gives a good picture of the kind of support Smith attracted and of the advice he received:

Gentlemen.

I cannot be of the least use in any electioneering work. but you may use my name, as that of one who would very heartily rejoice in Mr Mill's success – provided you throw no responsibility on me –

I am. Gentlemen

Your faithful Servt.

J Ruskin.

Letter from John Ruskin to Mill's committee in 1865, Pierpont Morgan Library

The campaign for Mill's election, meanwhile, was continuing in his absence. He had accepted the nomination of the Liberal electors' meeting of 6 April only on 17 April in a letter to James Beal, though he must have known before he left for Avignon that he had been nominated and had almost certainly decided to accept (and perhaps had done so informally), for he had asked John Plummer to clip and send him newspaper notices bearing on the Westminster election and himself.[39] The committee started to advertise his candidacy by seeking subscriptions towards his election fund, frequently publishing lists of

noteworthy is the recommendation that he emphasize local issues, such as municipal institutions and defending local property owners against compulsory alienation of sites for railway and other improvements. For example, one canvasser reported that Samuel Hughes, a friend of Mill's main supporter, James Beal, was disinclined to Mill because "he declares he can pay no atttention to local matters," has no liking for Grosvenor, and feels that Evans "has for years done nothing for Local matters & Sir J. Shelley is indolent, & is moved to action with difficulty"; consequently Hughes would work and vote for Smith if he can be "assured that you [Smith] would look after Local Interests" (PS 1/16). Such issues were central in Smith's cultivation of the constituency during the interval between the elections of 1865 and 1868.

39 *LL*, *CW*, vol. XVI, p. 1029. Plummer did.

subscribers and amounts. On 21 April they also published his letter of acceptance. In the fashion of the times, this letter served as an "election address," though it was much more detailed and incomparably more principled than most. Both the style and *a fortiori* the contents were most unusual.

After acknowledging the request and agreeing to it, Mill indicated how honourable it was for the committee to have chosen someone with no personal claim on them, who would neither solicit nor pay; their example should be followed by other constituencies, who should also note the excellent plan to solicit other names and to poll through a circular letter. He then went on to give his opinions on particular matters, as Beal had requested in a letter of 12 April.[40] As to parliamentary reform, he would go beyond the proposals of Baines and Locke King[41] (though he would vote for them) and open the suffrage to all men and women who could read, write, and do a sum in the rule of three,[42] and who had not had parish relief for a small number of years; also, abominating all class ascendancy, he would not support any proposals that would swamp all but the most numerous, but would advocate minority representation and other palliating devices; nonetheless, he would support proposals to give the working class immediately one-half of the representation. As to taxation, he favoured a mixture of direct and indirect levies. He was opposed to intervention in other nations' affairs, except when third parties had already intervened directly or indirectly; even then, while intervention might be right, he thought it would not always be expedient. He would support the abolition of all religious disabilities. The secret ballot, he averred, was not wanted. While control over military expenditures was needed, he did not favour blind retrenchment. Probate duty should apply to landed property; payment should be on the full value, and not just on a life interest. He was opposed to purchase of commissions, so long as the alternative was not jobbing. Flogging, in or out of the army, should be abolished, except for crimes of brutality, when in some cases it remained very appropriate. Finally, concerning trade-union disputes, he stated his opposition to legal intervention in strikes, except to protect equal rights of all to combine or refrain from combination, and men-

40 See ibid., p. 1031n.

41 Sir Edward Baines brought forward a bill to reduce the borough property qualification in parliamentary elections from £10 to £6; Peter John Locke King proposed to extend the franchise to all £10 occupiers, borough and county alike.

42 This now obscure term was then a commonplace for elementary mathematical knowledge: it denotes the "rule of proportion" for finding a number x in the equation "a is to b as c is to x" when a, b, and c are known.

tioned his objection to enforceable arbitration: a better rule than compromise might eventually arise.[43]

With the publication of this letter on 21 April in the *Daily News* and other papers, Mill's candidacy was recognized and the contest began to take its conclusive form. Highly laudatory leading articles appeared in the *Morning Star* on 21 April and in the *Daily Telegraph* on 22 April; the latter was strongly critical of Grosvenor. On the 22nd also the *Daily News* published an important letter from Arthur Stanley, dean of Westminster, giving his support to Mill; and *The Times* gave a favourable signal in an editorial of the 24th.[44]

Among those of liberal leanings, Mill's positions generally elicited admiration, though usually tempered with surprise. The enthusiasm was sincere enough, however, to make *Punch*'s response seem apt. Eulogizing Mill's attempt to promote purity of election, *Punch* called special attention to his refusal to spend any money on his election or to canvass the constituents; also to his recommendation of other worthy candidates: "Mr. Mill has answered the solicitation to represent Westminster just as *Mr. Punch* would have answered an entreaty to represent London. Only *Mr. Punch* could not have named anybody so fit to do that as himself."[45] To demonstrate his support, Mr. Punch contributed a strong letter "to the Electors of Westminster," in which Mill is contrasted with the contemptible Whig candidate, the young Captain Grosvenor, who had been reckless enough to reveal himself as a devotee of homeopathy.[46] Grosvenor's

43 *LL*, *CW*, vol. XVI, pp. 1031–5.

44 Of lesser weight but still significant were other public responses: F.H.F. Berkeley, for example, published a long and strong assault on Mill's repudiation of the ballot—a cause dear to Berkeley's heart—Thomas Hare responded on Mill's behalf, and Berkeley again attacked. *Daily News*, 24 April, p. 2; 2 May, p. 6; and 13 May, p. 3. Berkeley, it may be noted, referred in his first letter to Mill's describing himself as "an isolated thinker" in a letter of 16 March to Thomas Potter (*LL*, *CW*, vol. XVI, pp. 1012–14) that may have been written without reference to the campaign, but became moot when published with the response Potter had elicited from Cobden just before the latter's death; the exchange was published under the title, "Cobden's Last Letter," *Daily News*, 19 April, p. 6.

A confusion of names led to a Grosvenor supporter's insisting in the *Daily News* that he was not the Miles listed in one of Beal's lists as a subscriber to Mill's expenses. Francis Newman responded to a request for support by outlining his agreement with Mill on various points—one sentence of Mill's, he says, should be immortal: "common despotism is tyranny militant, but a slaveowner's despotism is tyranny triumphant"—but he disagreed on several points, particularly on governing India, where he finds Mill too repressive, and on the liquor trade, where he finds him too permissive. See p. 40 above for a typical response from John Ruskin.

45 *Punch*, 1 April 1865, p. 134. For the letter to Beal, see *LL*, *CW*, vol. XVI, pp. 1005–7.

46 *Punch*, 15 April 1865, p. 156. Since Mill's election committee featured medical

pretension is illustrated in "The Height of Impudence": "This celebrated summit has just been reached by a juvenile member of the Aristocracy. Mr. Grosvenor continues to offer himself for Westminster, although Mr. John Stuart Mill is ready to become a candidate. The Alpine Club has shut up in despair."[47]

On 4 May, the day after the public statement of Smith's candidacy, Sir John Villiers Shelley, who had been silent, advertised his intention to seek re-election, even though more than one Liberal candidate, as he acknowledged, was now active. Shelley based his claim on having served for thirteen years and having been elected three times—no assertion of principles was given.[48] That move seems to have excited no public attention, and no committee or meetings were announced.[49] Smith's committee published lengthy lists of his adherents, however, and Grosvenor responded with a substantial list.[50]

Meanwhile Mill, who was being informed by Chadwick and Plummer of developments, continued to believe that Chadwick was still in the field, though he was disturbed to see that the advertisements for subscriptions gave his name only, and he pledged £50 to Chadwick if he had to stand as an independent. Finally, in a letter to Chadwick of 28 April, he more or less conceded, with considerable annoyance, that the original plan of the Liberal Committee to circulate the names of potential candidates had

men, it is not surprising to find a "War-Song of the Westminster Doctor" in *Punch*: "Ye Medical Electors, vote for Mill, / And efficacious draught, and active pill. / Grosvenor and inert globules both eschew, / And let him represent the Quacks, not you" (24 June 1865, p. 260). Compare "Medicine and Member for Westminster," ibid., 8 July 1865, p. 2.

47 Ibid., 15 April 1865, p. 147. For other abuse of Grosvenor at this time, see ibid., p. 155; 8 April, p. 137; 29 April, p. 178. After the election, a fanciful garland of the elected shows "intellectual Mill" in contrast to Grosvenor, "smoking a cheroot" (10 Feb. 1866). Indeed one searches in vain for any eulogies of Grosvenor, the universal tone being that adopted by *Tomahawk* in 1867, when it employed heavy irony in describing the "real service" he had done the country in calling, with "gravity," the home secretary's attention "to 'certain noctural depredations recently committed in Belgravia upon the flowers and plants with which some people delight to decorate their dining-room windows.' . . . We denounce with him the atrocity of these midnight marauders, and we call upon Sir Richard Mayne to do his duty and place a policeman in front of every flower-pot" (29 July 1867, p. 93).

48 See, for example, *Daily News*, 4 and 6 May 1865, p.2.

49 Shelley was not completely forgotten, however; a pro-Smith letter in the *Standard* on 8 May 1865, p. 5, called for his defeat on the somewhat surprising grounds that he was anti-cabdrivers and proprietors.

50 For Smith, see, for example, *Daily Telegraph*, 3 and 11 May 1865, p. 9; for Grosvenor, *Daily News*, 8 May 1865, p. 4.

been given up because, as Lankester and others had argued, a second candidate of the same stamp would imperil their chances of electing one.[51]

Chadwick was of opinion that the publication of Mill's second letter to Beal, that of 17 April, had been harmful, but Mill was sanguine and unrepentant, saying, "the only purpose for which I care to be elected is to get my opinions listened to."[52] It is easier to understand Mill's attitudes if one realizes that he was thinking at this time primarily of his candidacy rather than of his election, for he saw a distinction between the two—a distinction that affected his behaviour. However much Mill may have thought of a parliamentary career over the years, at this point the chances of his being elected seemed to him to be slight, and he did not worry about the revelation of his attitudes increasing the unlikelihood.

Education of the public was a large part of Mill's goal in accepting the offer. As a candidate, he should and could put before the world his views; they were, moreover, there for all to see in his books. At this stage a happy turn of events had given him the means with minimal exertion to spread his general principles more widely than ever before. He told Chadwick: "I have gained this by it, that what are thought the most out of the way of all my opinions, have been, and are, discussed and canvassed from one end of the country to the other, and some of them (especially women's voting) are obtaining many unexpected adherents. I reckon this is a good stroke of practicality, whether I am elected for Westminster or not."[53] Practicality was important for Mill, and he was not above enjoying a very utilitarian materialistic by-product: "Certainly this election affair is a better *propaganda* for all my political opinions than I might have obtained for many years; and it is selling my cheap editions, and indeed the dear ones too, in a most splendid manner."[54]

Again, the candidacy itself being of primary importance, and his views being made available through the press as well as his books, there was no need for him to behave like those whose main goal was election. Further, even admitting that some of his views, especially those revealing his judgments on the limitations of the English mind, including the working-class mind,[55] were unpopular, he could afford to be cavalier about the public revelation of his "crotchets." Some of these notions, such as his views on women's suffrage, were long-held, including his

51 *LL*, *CW*, vol. XVI, pp. 1038–9.
52 Ibid., pp. 1049–51 (15 May).
53 Ibid., p. 1050.
54 Ibid., pp. 1060–1, to Thomas Hare (29 May 1865).
55 See ibid., p. 1506 (4 Dec. 1868).

opposition to canvassing the electors. In 1832 he had written:

> When all other things are equal, give your votes to him who refuses to degrade himself and you by personal solicitation. To entrust a man with a burthensome duty (unless he means to betray it) is a compliment indeed, but no favour. The man who manifests the highest opinion of the electors, is not he who tries to gain them over individually by civil speeches, but he who assumes that their only object is to choose the fittest man, and abstains from all canvassing, except by laying his pretensions before them collectively, on the hustings, at public meetings, or through the press.[56]

And now, thirty-three years later, he had a chance to put his theory to the practical test. He wrote to his close friend John Elliot Cairnes: "The greatest pleasure which public life could give me would be if it enabled me to shew that more can be accomplished by supposing that there is reason and good feeling in the mass of mankind than by proceeding in the ordinary assumption that they are fools and rogues."[57] In brief, as Roebuck had said, Mill would go into parliament not "for the purpose of winning renown, for that he [had already] gained"; as he could have added were it politic, Mill had nothing to lose by standing, as well as nothing personally to gain by being elected. It was an enviable position.

Olympian though he might be, he was not above some allusions to the battle on the plains, referring ironically to Smith as "the illustrious man," adding "I do not think the Tories expect their man to come in, otherwise some more considerable person would have started in that interest. But," he continued, striking a note that was to resound through his comments on elections for the next three years, the Tories "are glad when anybody with money to spend, is willing to venture it on the chance."[58]

By 15 May he was pleased to see a copy of the list of his committee that Chadwick had sent him.[59] He was still not in the least inclined to qualify

56 *Newspaper Writings* [*NW*], ed. Ann P. and John M. Robson, *CW*, vols. XXII–XXV (Toronto: University of Toronto Press, 1986), vol. XXIII, p. 492.

57 *LL*, *CW*, vol. XVI, p. 1027 (6 April).

58 Ibid., pp. 1049–51. From the beginning Smith had admitted that expenses would be high, writing to his sister: "A contest would be expensive, but when a man once becomes a Member for Westminster, he may retain his seat pretty nearly for life if his personal or moral character is good and he attends reasonably to his duties." (Maxwell, *Smith*, p. 118; Akers-Douglas, *Smith*, p. 49.)

59 *LL*, *CW*, vol. XVI, p. 1051; in the same letter Mill reluctantly agreed to supply a photograph for publication, but only on his return to London. The list of his committee was not published until 27 May. See, for example, *The Times*, 27 May 1865, p. 5; the list fills nearly two columns.

his declaration, which he pointed out had been praised, or to take any part in the election beyond answering questions from the members of the committee and reprinting any articles they might wish to put before the public (including "The Enfranchisement of Women," which he insisted must be acknowledged as his wife's).[60]

During the latter half of May the Westminster Liberals continued their busy efforts to keep Mill's name foremost. Advertisements appeared announcing public meetings, two of which were held on 19 May in the Temperance Hall, Broadway, for electors of St. Margaret's and St. John's parishes, and in St. Martin's Hall, for those of St. Paul's, Covent Garden, and "other electors of Westminster," and listing the names of the speakers at each.[61] Another meeting to be held on 26 May in the Whittington Club, Strand, was advertised; it was aimed at the electors of St. Clement Danes and St. Mary-le-Strand.[62] At this meeting the chair was taken by Sir John Bowring who, as representative of the old Westminster reformers, seems to have forgotten or decided to ignore the estrangement between him and Mill that dated back to the late 1820s. The enthusiastic speakers—all on Mill's committee list—included Grant Duff, MP, who described the candidates as an "entirely unknown" Tory, another known "only from family and territorial 'influence,' " and a third of "transcendent personal merit" who was known throughout the world.[63] From Grant Duff's remarks, it would seem that Shelley had withdrawn.

But not so. A meeting was called for subscribers to the Westminster Liberal Registration Society at Caldwell's Assembly Rooms, Soho, on 29 May, which fully revealed the splits in the ranks. The aim, Mr. Diprose, secretary of the society, said, was to establish support for two of the three Liberal candidates, with the decision to be binding on all. Apparently this plan was seen by Shelley's supporters as designed to cut him out, and anti-Mill comments were made. Mr. Bidgood, for example, indicated that a decision in favour of an untried, if undoubtedly clever man would not be accepted by him; he noted that Grosvenor had been in the field for three months before Mill's name had been introduced to sow dissent. He also produced that most telling spectre, the likelihood that Smith would be elected if the Liberal vote were split and their tried and experienced member, Shelley, would lose (presumably to Grosvenor). Another speaker, George, had no fear of Mill's succeeding; he would poll no more

60 *LL*, *CW*, vol. XVI, pp. 1058–60 (28 May)—a point that some critics ignore.

61 *Daily News*, 18 and 19 May 1865, p. 4. The meeting in St. Martin's Hall is reported ibid., 20 May, p. 5.

62 See *Daily News*, 23, 25, and 26 May 1865, p. 4.

63 *The Times*, 27 May 1865, p. 5.

than 1200. His support for Shelley was echoed by Jeffreys, a member of both Shelley's and Grosvenor's committees, who lamented what seemed to be common knowledge but escaped report—the opposition to Shelley engendered by accusations against him by "some female members of Mr. Train's family."[64]

Mill, though clearly not the society's favourite, was not entirely without supporters, however, and Mr. Sainsbury expressed the view that all three Liberal candidates should meet with the electors who should then decide which two to support. Mr. Dunkley indicated (without citing any evidence) that Mill had promised to withdraw if he had insufficient support, and questioned the ability of Grosvenor and Shelley to run hand in hand. He was assured that Grosvenor had indicated his willingness so to do. And so the discussion went on, with agreement to a final resolution that committees should be formed in the parishes to support Shelley after the chairman said that Liberals' first votes should go to Shelley and their second to Grosvenor, and that if Mill's supporters objected, they should alter the Society.[65]

In the event they had no need to. On 1 June, Shelley announced his withdrawal from the contest on the grounds that he feared the Liberal vote would be split. As a leader in *The Times* commented: ". . . Westminster has exhibited an unseemly division in the Liberal camp. Sir John Shelley has honourably retired to prevent disunion, and it is to be presumed that Mr. Mill's and Mr. Grosvenor's Committees will now unite their forces against the redoubtable Mr. Smith."[66] Shelley's retirement may well have been honourable, and quite unconnected to females of the Train family or events in St. James's Street; however, the Westminster radical group had a readier explanation—unease in the formidable Grosvenor camp. Grosvenor, they later averred, "enforced the retirement of Sir J.V. Shelley; and 'the Rump,' in bringing forward the Guardsman, lost their favourite. Lord Ebury [the captain's father] and the Marquis of Westminster were severely blamed for the course they pursued in forcing upon the constituency a man utterly unqualified."[67] The issue was now plain: Would the two Liberal groups continue to battle one another, with the potential result of carrying only one seat, or combine to defeat the Tory?

Mill, who was apparently able to convince himself there was still room

64 The mystery is not lessened by a later, parallel reference by Mr. Dunkley to "the St. James's-street affair."

65 *Daily News*, 30 May 1865, p. 3.

66 *The Times*, 2 June 1865, p. 9.

67 *Mr. J.S. Mill and Westminster*, p. 11.

for yet another Liberal candidate in addition to Grosvenor and himself, took virtually no notice of the changed and newly charged electoral situation. As planned, he took a botanizing trip through the Auvergne in June, though information by letter and telegram continued to reach him quickly, indicating he had notified London of his movements. Having said in a letter to Chadwick of 8 June that he continued to favour the original plan for seeking a Liberal candidate, that the talk of splitting the vote was inappropriate given that plan, and that he still wanted Chadwick's name to go forward, he commented to Chadwick on 22 June, after hearing of Shelley's withdrawal: "I do not think either of us will be elected. I would at present lay considerable odds on Grosvenor and Smith."[68] However, not wishing evidently to lengthen the odds, Mill—who was not in any case a betting man, unlike his distinguished predecessor as representative for Westminster, Charles James Fox—felt it necessary to tell Chadwick that this letter was private.[69]

Absent in body, and congratulating himself on that absence, Mill was nevertheless speaking loudly not just to Westminster but to a wide constituency in the country and indeed in much of the world through his writings. He comments in his *Autobiography* as he had to his friends, and quite correctly as Longmans' records confirm, that his election campaign greatly increased the sale of his books.[70] What is evident also, though he does not dwell on it, is just how much his books contributed to his election, not only because his *System of Logic, Principles of Political Economy, On Liberty,* and *Representative Government* had given him an unrivalled eminence, but also because his most recent work, *An Examination of Sir William Hamilton's Philosophy,* which appeared in mid-April 1865, had an unexpectedly powerful impact. This work, not now much admired, sold more quickly than any other of his writings and prompted far more immediate responses than the now more famous ones. By the time the campaign for Mill was well underway, the first edition of the *Examination* had nearly sold out (its second edition appeared in July) and was providing exciting copy for the papers, which, in a way that is understood but not always fully appreciated, reflected the intensity of religious controversy in the nineteenth century.

68 *LL, CW,* vol. XVI, pp. 1067, 1072.

69 Ibid., pp. 1071–2.

70 In that one year there appeared, in addition to the periodical and book versions of *Auguste Comte and Positivism* and the first two editions of *An Examination of Sir William Hamilton's Philosophy,* the sixth Library Editions of both the *Logic* and the *Principles,* and the third Library Edition of *Representative Government,* as well as the first People's Editions of *On Liberty* (six printings totalling 10,000 copies), of the *Principles* (two printings), and of *Representative Government* (four printings).

The scene is perhaps best established by the opening sentence of the *Spectator*'s review of the *Examination* in late May: "We hold this to be Mr. Mill's greatest book, requiring far greater powers both of imagination and exposition than are required by his *Political Economy*, and showing those powers in a higher degree than his *System of Logic*."[71] Although this favourable judgment was far from unanimous—Sir William Hamilton, who had been greatly revered by his students, had powerful defenders against Mill's onslaught—on balance it must be said that Mill's attack specifically against Hamilton's intuitionist positions was generally accepted to have won the field. A sympathetic—but clerical—reviewer said (again in late May):

> The effect of Mr. Mill's review is the absolute annihilation of all Sir W. Hamilton's doctrines, opinions, of all he has written or taught. Not himself only, but all his followers, pupils, copyists, are involved in the common ruin. The whole fabric of the Hamiltonian philosophy is not only demolished, but its very stones are ground to powder.[72]

Hamilton's followers and many of the public were less convinced of their ruin, however, on one specific issue. A vigorous battle in which no quarter was asked or given had as its focal point the moral status of the theology of the Rev. H.L. Mansel, one of Hamilton's best-known disciples, who had pushed his "Philosophy of the Conditioned" to an extreme that Mill found repugnant. A few sentences of Mill's, much quoted but worth repeating, were at the centre of the fierce controversy:

> If, instead of the "glad tidings" that there exists a Being in whom all the excellences which the highest human mind can conceive, exist in a degree inconceivable to us, I am informed that the world is ruled by a being whose attributes are infinite, but what they are we cannot learn, nor what are the principles of his government, except that "the highest human morality which we are capable of conceiving" does not sanction them; convince me of it, and I will bear my fate as I may. But when I am told that I must believe this, and at the same time call this being by the names which express and affirm the highest human morality, I say in plain terms that I will not. Whatever power such a being may have over me, there is one thing which he shall not do: he shall not compel me to worship him. I will call no being good, who is

71 *Spectator*, 27 May 1865, p. 584.

72 Mark Pattison, "J.S. Mill on Hamilton," *The Reader*, 20 May 1865, p. 562.

> not what I mean when I apply that epithet to my fellow-creatures; and if such a being can sentence me to hell for not so calling him, to hell I will go.[73]

The *Spectator*, while expressing ignorance about how far Mill himself accepted the glad tidings of which he so eloquently speaks, says that the passage "is the true language of prophets and apostles about God, who never yet asked any one to worship Him without declaring His goodness in the language in which it had been manifested in our Lord and comes straight home to the heart of man."[74] But the *Record* was appalled: under the heading "Mr. J.S. Mill and his Supporters," it mentioned that thirty years earlier *Blackwood's Magazine* had called Shelley and his fellows "the Satanic School," and went on to introduce its quotation of the passage from Mill by commenting that *Blackwood's* epithet "might be more fitly applied to certain prose writers of the present day," for example, Mill. The sting is in the tail: after the quotation, and a brief explanation of its danger, the account concludes:

> Language equally bold may be found in Voltaire, or, more recently, in Holyoake. But the strange thing is, to find, immediately after this, a list of Mr. Mill's supporters in the Westminster election, containing the names of the Rev. F.D. Maurice, the Rev. J.L. Davies, the Rev. Leslie Stephen, the Attorney-General, *Sir R. Palmer*, with the appended sanction of the Dean of Westminster, and the *Right Hon. W.E. Gladstone*![75]

In fact, if at all well informed, the writer in the *Record* could hardly have been surprised to find the name of Maurice, Mansel's most bitter opponent, in the list, nor those of Davies, Stephen, or Dean Stanley, all of whom had had friendly relations with Mill and would be more likely to applaud him for the controversial passage, as they actually did, than to condemn it. But the *Record* was interested, one must infer, in its being able to list them as Reverends. And it was more interested still in listing Roundell Palmer and Gladstone, whose names it emphasized with italics. When the *Record* repeated the accusation on 14 June, Palmer responded quickly with a plea of not guilty as charged: he had not subscribed to

73 *An Examination of Sir William Hamilton's Philosophy*, ed. John M. Robson (Toronto: University of Toronto Press, 1979), *CW*, vol. IX, p. 103.

74 *Spectator*, 27 May 1865, p. 585.

75 *Record*, 2 June 1865, p. 3. Defensively, *The Record* later averred that the account had been supplied by a correspondent.

Mill's campaign, he urged; finally Beal, for Mill's committee, apologized, saying they had given the name of "R. Palmer" because a subscription under that name had been ascribed to his address.[76]

The *Morning Advertiser*, omitting reference to Palmer and Gladstone, was even more explicit about the practical consequences of the obnoxious passage, which it too quoted, saying: "we have no hesitation in saying that we not only have never, in the whole course of our reading, met with ranker Atheism, but never anything equal to it as regards the revolting form into which that Atheism is put." Then, after listing the clergymen whose names the *Record* had given as Mill's supporters, it concluded:

> It therefore behoves them, and, indeed, all of Mr. Mill's supporters in Westminster, who believe in a *Supreme Being*, to ascertain from Mr. Mill himself whether or not he ever penned the passage in question [the *Advertiser* did not have the work to hand]; and if he should admit that he did, then we leave it to the consciences of all such persons to decide whether they are acting right in supporting him in his efforts to obtain a seat in Parliament.[77]

The *Spectator* was incapable of letting such slanders pass in silence, asserting that "nothing can be more ludicrous than to accuse Mr. Mill of atheism on the score of a passage which expresses the faith of thousands, theologians, mystics, practical men, both in the past and the present, who have deeply considered and passionately rejected Mr. Mansel's peculiar heresy." What Mill asserted actually enforces "the teaching of some of the highest and most orthodox theologians of every Church."[78]

We know of no way of accurately assessing the effect of this controversy on Mill's attractiveness as a candidate in the election of 1865. Reading the arguments on both sides over a century later—and being biased towards Mill—we are tempted to believe that he was in fact aided by the row over the passage. There were two issues: as to the first, the accusation of atheism in the abstract, it seems likely that the electors of Westminster would be more influenced by the judgment of Connop Thirlwall, Bishop of St. David's,[79] who asserted that the passage "breathes

76 *The Times*, 17 June 1865, p. 12; *Record*, 14 June 1865, p. 2. We regret to say that we know no more about the pseudo-Palmer.

77 3 June 1865, p. 5.

78 *Spectator*, 10 June 1865, p. 631.

79 Readers of Mill's *Autobiography* will recall that on their first encounter in debate, in 1825, Mill judged him to be "the best speaker" he had ever heard. *CW*, vol. I, p. 129.

the purest spirit of Christian morality,"[80] than by the fiercely sectarian *Record* or by "its clumsy attendant spirit," the "organ of the licensed victuallers," as the *Spectator* called the *Morning Advertiser*.[81] Nonetheless, both the charge of atheism and the licensed victuallers were to be heard again in 1868, in changed circumstances.

The second issue connected with the *Examination* affair is easier to deal with: the *Spectator* said in attacking the *Record* that it was unlikely that those whose names were cited gave a thought to Mill's religious opinions when they supported him as a candidate.[82] In fact, it is quite likely that they knew more about Mill's opinions than did the public at large, or even the readers of his books, for it is not really probable that they gave no thought to the matter; their view was that Mill's appropriateness should be judged on other grounds—what the *Spectator* called "moral and political principles stricter than nine-tenths of our members of Parliament could afford to adopt."[83] And it is likely also that they approved of the policy of "reserve" concerning the expression of religious opinions that Mill, like his father, generally followed. Mill took this line throughout the campaign, refusing to answer questions about his religious beliefs on the grounds that they were not germane to his political behaviour.

Other attempts to show that Mill was a dangerous influence were no more successful, so far as the public record shows. A letter in *The Times* attacking Mill's "revolutionary" views in his *Principles* elicited no more than a mere denial by a supporter who signed himself "Barrister."[84] More dangerous potentially, and expressed more savagely, was the attack in the *Standard*, just before nomination day, on Mill's views about population control. The writer, it is obvious, knew little about Mill and his writings, but must have known, though he did not dare openly assert, that Mill was a Neo-Malthusian. The attack merits quotation as indicating, more than does any other record of the election of 1865, the kind of accusation that probably was being made much more explicitly by canvassers. Mill is described as "the idol of the Westminster Radicals, the pet of the advanced Liberal press, the chosen of Knightsbridge booksellers [Charles Westerton] and Piccadilly auctioneers [James Beal]," who would, if elected, "as certainly bring in a bill to enforce this 'legal obligation' " to abstain from having children beyond one's means "as he will introduce a measure for giving votes to the fair sex, and for making sundry other

80 Letter to the Editor, *Spectator*, 17 June 1865, p. 668.
81 *Spectator*, 10 June 1865, p. 631.
82 Ibid., pp. 631–2.
83 Ibid.
84 *The Times*, 5 June 1865, p. 9; 7 June 1865, p. 12; 8 June 1865, p. 8.

fanciful alterations in our constitution." If the voters consider Mill's theories on population, concludes the *Standard*,

> morally wrong, politically unsound, repulsive to contemplate, wicked to practise, shocking to natural feeling, offensive to true notions of political science, insulting to the people among whom they are broached, and degrading to the man by whom they are propounded, they will not hesitate to record their votes for the Conservative candidate. He may not have written books, but neither has he advocated measures which it is a disgrace even to name. He may not be puffed into notice as an original thinker, but he has not come forward to advocate a dangerous and disgusting theory. He may value Liberty and esteem Representative Government, but he loves the first too well to make it a pretext for unnatural licence, and he regards the second too highly to allow its honour to be compromised by an attempt to legislate in favour of a policy which commences in crime, and which can end only in national discredit and disgrace.[85]

There seems little indication that this issue took on anything like the proportions it might have, perhaps because, in spite of what the *Standard* tried to draw out of Mill's remarks in his *Principles* (not properly attributed in the article),[86] his reserve on this matter was at least equal to that he employed on religion—and with even more reason: in 1873 Gladstone withdrew his support from the committee planning a memorial to Mill on being informed by Abraham Hayward that Mill had been arrested for distributing birth-control literature in his youth.[87]

Of all these matters, probably only the first, the religious one, was causing Mill's committee much anxiety, nor does it appear that what were already being called his "crotchets"[88]—such as women's suffrage, proportional representation, and limitations on the right of bequest—were greatly troublesome to those of his supporters who did not agree with them. At the beginning of June their spirits were high. Despite

85 *Standard*, 10 July 1865, pp. 5–6; mostly reprinted after the election in *Public Opinion*, 15 July 1865, pp. 55–6.

86 The salient passages in *Principles of Political Economy* [PPE], ed. John M. Robson, CW, vols. II–III (Toronto: University of Toronto Press, 1965), are in bk. I, chap. x, sect. 3; bk. II, chap. xii, sect. 2; bk. II, chap. xiii, sect. 1 (CW, vol. II, pp. 156–7, 358, 368n).

87 See Francis E. Mineka, "John Stuart Mill and Neo-Malthusianism, 1873," *Mill News Letter*, 8 (fall 1972), 3–10.

88 See *Spectator*, 10 June 1865, p. 632.

the inclement weather, *The Times* reported that many were turned away from a meeting in St. James's Hall on 1 June. Mill's views on several subjects were outlined and praised, and his absence explained rather than defended. Cheers greeted the announcement by Malleson that at a meeting of Shelley's supporters earlier that day "it had been unanimously agreed to support Mr. Mill."[89] He also remarked that the "little differences of opinion which existed in regard to certain views entertained by Mr. Mill should subside before the unanimous concurrence expressed in favour of his general principles," and met with renewed enthusiasm when he asserted that Mill's election would remove the stain on large constituencies of "electing men who had more money than wits." Evidently no express attacks on Grosvenor were made, although Dr. Lankester, from the chair, invited comparisons, knowing they would speak for themselves.[90]

Smith's supporters were now ready publicly to join the battle of the halls, announcing on the 7th a meeting for 13 June; Mill's responded on the 8th by advertising one on the same day; Grosvenor's remained silent. The Conservative meeting in Willis's Rooms, St. James's, was much more impressive than the Liberal's in the Polygraphic Hall, Charing Cross: the former featured the candidate himself for the first time, while the latter, expressly held for the electors of St. Anne's and St. Martin's parishes, was again without its celebrated hero. Smith, "hailed with repeated shouts and hurrahs" on his appearance, presented himself as not a party man, the reason being not irresolution but a determination to maintain independence. In fact, there was no leader to whom he could give undivided allegiance. His remarks were clearly designed to attract floating Liberal votes rather than to consolidate Tory support, and indeed there was no other candidate likely to attract any significant number of Tory votes. He presented himself as against "class" representation, being himself a member of the "working classes," and in favour of a £6 franchise, administrative reform, financial economy, and social reforms in education and in "the streets." In indirect though obvious allusion to Mill, he said that although opposed to pledges, he would pledge himself to pay attention to local issues. Little opposition to Smith was expressed, and the vote approving his candidature carried with only four negatives, though

89 This vote may well confirm the Radicals' statement that Grosvenor's supporters had forced Shelley's hand; however, the report in the *Daily News* of the Liberal Registration Society's meeting in Caldwell's Rooms indicates that what was pledged was support to *both* Grosvenor and Mill.

90 2 June 1865, *The Times*, p. 8, and *Daily News*, p. 3.

one spectator strove against considerable interruption to advocate Grosvenor's claims.[91]

Perhaps Mill's supporters were busy at their own meeting, which was slightly reported and seems to have been almost perfunctory in matter and manner.[92] In any case, another Liberal meeting on the 22nd for the electors of those parishes, at the Pimlico Rooms, was quickly advertised, with the named speakers including Lord Hobart and Professor Beesly.[93]

Probably in response to these two meetings, Grosvenor's committee finally decided to renew their efforts, private and public.[94] The candidate had been silent since the fiascos of early April and obviously needed to reassert his claim on the electors' franchises. A meeting in the heart of Grosvenor land, in the Hanover Square Rooms, was advertised for 20 June, and secret consultations with Mill's supporters began. In the words of *Mr. J.S. Mill and Westminster*,

> Strong efforts were now made by members of Captain Grosvenor's committee, although not sharing the confidence of his more select adherents, to effect co-operative action, without a junction with Mr. Mill's committee. To Mr. Prout and Mr. Sainsbury the credit of this effort is due. It was violently opposed by those members of the decaying "Rump," whose presence in the committee was tolerated.[95]

The first effect of these efforts was seen at a meeting of Mill's committee on 19 June, presided over by Brewer, at which a resolution was made to arrive at an agreement with Grosvenor's committee, so that the Liberal interest would not be divided, though perfect independence should be preserved.[96] At Grosvenor's meeting on the 20th, which was well attended though slightly reported and at which Grosvenor seems to have been better in control of his rhetoric, Brewer announced that Mill's committee wished to amalgamate with Grosvenor's,[97] and accommodation was reached before the meeting on Mill's behalf on the 22nd.

91 *Daily News*, 14 June 1865, p. 3.

92 See ibid.

93 Ibid., 17 June 1865, p. 4.

94 The need was constantly before them of dispelling the dismissive attitude evident in a squib in the *Daily News*, 19 June 1865, p. 3: "A Candidate 'in the Wood.'—In the window of a public-house in the Strand might have been observed last evening the following announcement:—'Captain Grosvenor's Committee *on draught.*' "

95 *Mr. J.S. Mill and Westminster*, p. 11.

96 20 June 1865, *The Times*, p. 7, *Daily News*, p. 3.

97 *Daily News*, 21 June, 1865, p. 3.

But pressures and anxieties were building up and, much as Mill's committee respected Mill's decision to remain aloof, they had begun to feel very strongly that he was needed on the spot to establish himself, even if merely by his presence, as a serious candidate and to answer specific questions about practical political matters. Unlike him, they had much to lose if he were defeated: they had invested much energy, hope, rhetoric, and money,[98] and were becoming concerned about growing support for Smith and the continuing animosity between them and Grosvenor's supporters despite the "accommodation." Increasingly even the favourable portion of the press suggested that his absence was a liability. The public accusations that Mill was an atheist seem finally to have decided them:

> The vehemence of the onslaught satisfied the committee that Mr. Mill must appear in person. This was opposed to the whole principle of the contest, and was debated with vigour. The common-sense of Mr. Westerton, Mr. Beggs, Mr. Ellis and Mr. Storr, intent on victory, overcame the scruples of Dr. Brewer and Mr. Beal, who ventured to prefer defeat to a departure from the great principles asserted in the candidature.[99]

So they increased their pressure on Mill, but he continued to insist, in two letters of 21 June, that they should act on their own and that he would meet with them only after his planned arrival in England.[100] At the meeting on the 22nd this difficulty asserted itself awkwardly. Brewer, lauding Mill as one whose principles would be to the "benefit of mankind," said that it was a mistake to think of him as "a mere thinker," because "from personal knowledge . . . he could assure the meeting that Mr. Mill was a most eloquent speaker." The *Daily News* reports at this point: "A Voice.—'He will not give us a specimen.' " Brewer's vague if

98 In spite of their pride at Mill's principled refusal to contribute, his committee's advertisements hint at this anxiety: "Subscriptions to defray the necessary outlay for securing Mr. Mill's return, free of all expense to him, are received by Mr. C. Westerton, St. George's-place, Knightsbridge; Mr. James Beal, No. 209, Piccadilly; and Mr. J.S. Storr, King-street, Covent-garden; or may be paid to the City Bank, Old Bond-street." This appears just above a two-and-a-half column list of his committee, which in turn is followed by the announcement of a meeting on 1 June to help secure Mill's return. *Daily News*, 31 May 1865, p. 4.

99 *Mr. J.S. Mill and Westminster*, p. 9.

100 *LL*, *CW*, vol. XVI, pp. 1069–71. In a letter to Chadwick of the next day he reported these matters, and promised Chadwick support if he decided at this late date to run as an independent. One can hardly imagine what his committee's response would have been had they known of this offer.

hopeful response, "He would very shortly appear among the electors," was greeted with cheers that probably were elicited by relief. More than one speaker felt compelled to refute the charge of atheism against Mill, and, on the positive side, his claim to be a friend to the working classes was asserted and it was announced that contributions to his election fund had passed £1000. However, an amendment to the conventional motion was offered, to the effect that Mill was not a fit and proper person to represent Westminster, and a "terrific uproar ensued, which lasted half an hour. At length the resolution in favour of Mr. Mill was declared carried."[101] Such confusion operated strongly on the committee's nerve, reinforced by the repetition of the suggestion that Mill should appear in a generally supportive leader in the *Daily News* of 24 June,[102] and they again increased their pressure on Mill, which finally became irresistible. On 26 June he reluctantly agreed to return to London,[103] where he arrived on the 30th, a week before the meeting of the Political Economy Club and just twelve days before polling day.

What met him immediately was the problem that had been much troubling his supporters—the competition between them and Grosvenor's supporters for Liberal votes. His committee had agreed to an amalgamation with Grosvenor's, on the condition that Grosvenor and five of his supporters would meet with Mill and five of his supporters, but when, on the day of his arrival in London, Mill was informed of the arrangement, he declined:

> . . . I beg to say, that I can have no objection whatever to a conference between the two Committees for the proposed purpose [of cooperation between them], but that I cannot personally take any part in it. I have from the first declared that I am not a candidate, in the ordinary sense of the term; that I do not offer myself to the electors, but that, if thought worthy of the honour of being elected, I will do my best to serve them. To engage personally in a negociation with another candidate, would be not only to assume the character which I have disclaimed but to take into my own hands, in a certain degree, the management of the election. That management must rest, as it has hitherto done, wholly with your Committee; with whose judgment respecting the mode of conduct which most conduces to the

101 23 June 1865, *The Times*, p. 7, *Daily News*, p. 3.

102 *Daily News*, 24 June, 1865, p. 4. The leader also urged full cooperation between Mill's and Grosvenor's committees.

103 See his letter to Westerton, *LL*, *CW*, vol. XVI, p. 1073.

furtherance of the liberal interest, I have neither the wish nor the right to interfere.[104]

The self-satisfaction behind this response from the heights is better displayed in a letter of 2 July to Lady Amberley from Helen Taylor, residual legatee of her mother's power and not shy about its use:

> Mr. Mill has undergone a sort of persecution from his Committee to show himself and speak at meetings, which, in moderation, however, he is willing to do; but others want him to combine with Captain Grovesnor [sic] which he thinks quite out of the question. He has no objection to the Committee's Cooperating with Captain Grovesnor's Committee if they themselves think fit, since he leaves the conduct of the election in their hands, but any personal combination between himself and a man who (as well as the Tory candidate) is employing all the old corrupt practices would be an utter dereliction of the principles on which he declared himself willing to stand. The fact is that the Committee who are in the midst of the fight fancy they see a chance of success and are stimulated to leave no means untried at the last moment. We, who are in the position of cool lookers-on, think the probability of success is so faint as to amount to none, and do not lose sight of the original plans.[105]

In any case, his supporters must have been pleased that the negotiations with Grosvenor's committee could be advanced. Not that doubts about the captain's liberalism were removed. Some of Mill's committee were obsessed by the part played by Grosvenor's family in the Rump, and continued to see him as fundamentally a "Conservative Whig," representing him (wrongly) as an opponent of the ballot[106] and mistrusting his declarations in favour of limited parliamentary reform.[107] And all of them could see the likelihood of Tory as well as Whig votes going to him, and the power of his connection thus being thrown behind Smith as well. Grosvenor's supporters, however, were exaggerating the meagre Tory support for Mill, and Grosvenor himself had written to Mill's chairman, Westerton, to protest that Mill's promoters seemed to be joining the

104 To Westerton, 30 June 1865, *LL*, *CW*, vol. XVI, pp. 1073–4. This letter was printed in *Mr. J.S. Mill and Westminster*, pp. 11–12.
105 Russell Archives, McMaster University.
106 But of course Mill was no comfort to them on this issue.
107 See *Morning Advertiser*, 3 June 1865, p. 5.

Tories in attacks on him in the press.[108] Mill's response was typically abstract, and not conciliatory; though Tory support for him was only nominal, the Tories were likely to be more favourably disposed to anyone other than a "regular government man, as they suppose Grosvenor to be."[109]

For the practically minded, however, the obvious solution was a coalition, in spite of the perceived difficulties on the Radical side which centred on two issues—Grosvenor's political principles and his electioneering practices. The first was surprisingly easy to overcome: his supporters had already argued that he had been misrepresented, for he favoured substantial reform and supported the ballot, as his electoral speeches revealed. About the second issue little is known. Mill's supporters made a great fuss about walking to the polls rather than being conveyed thither in carriages, for which Grosvenor presumably paid, although three years later it was asserted that Mill's followers had indeed used the carriages. In any case, the combined expenditures of the Grosvenor and Mill committees were probably lower than those of Smith's.[110]

The anxiety in Grosvenor's group may have been even greater than in Mill's, and they, less ideologically hampered, seem not to have made any conditions. The process moved smoothly and quickly. There was some public encouragement, undoubtedly prompted by Grosvenor supporters, such as a letter in the *Daily News* on 1 July 1865 and an advertisement in the same paper on 3 July, both urging cooperation between the committees and both from a "liberal elector." By 5 July the two committees had agreed to cooperate, and Mill concurred in the arrangement.[111] A small but revealing window onto the resolving tension is provided by the eight advertisements pertaining to the Westminster election in *The Times* of 7

108 *LL*, *CW*, vol. XVI, p. 1059n.

109 Ibid., p. 1059.

110 Mill's supporters admitted to expenditures of "over £2,200, all raised from admirers of the distinguished writer, or from friends favourable to the mode of election persevered in," and accepted the estimate of Grosvenor's as being £5000. They mentioned that Smith's had been estimated as between £10,000 and £16,000, but thought perhaps they did not exceed £7000 or £8000. (*Mr. J.S. Mill and Westminster*, p. 23.) In the election of 1868, as indicated below in chapter 8, the imbalance was greater.

111 To Chadwick, 6 July 1865, *LL*, *CW*, vol. XVI, pp. 1075–6. In that letter Mill says that his committee seemed to have complete confidence in the *bona fides* of Grosvenor's, and so there "was nothing" for him to do "but acquiesce" in the agreement; since he had agreed in advance, the best interpretation to be put on this comment is that he was trying to soften what may have looked to Chadwick like betrayal of support for his still not abandoned candidacy.

July. First appears a statement by Grosvenor's committee[112] publicly announcing that the meeting of five (unnamed) members of each committee had taken place to ensure that the "party question" would not divide Liberal votes. The injunction, one that was to mark all the joint efforts henceforward and through the 1868 election, was—don't plump.[113] Second comes another Grosvenor notice, merely announcing that his committee was meeting daily at 14 Waterloo Place.[114] Next come two Mill advertisements, inviting electors to meetings on the 8th and 10th. These are followed by the first appearance of an advertisement headed "Mill and Grosvenor for Westminster," in which Mill's committee, responding to the invitation signalled in the first advertisement above, ask their supporters not to plump for one candidate.[115] Then the opposition enters, with two notices: in the first Smith urges his supporters to keep up their good work; and in the second daily committee meetings at 1 Cockspur St. are announced. Then, below an irrelevant notice, appears an advertisement that somewhat undermines the coalition: "Metropolitan Elections.—All earnest Liberal Reformers who wish to see the metropolis properly represented are requested to vote for Goschen, for City; J. Stuart Mill, for Westminster; Hughes, for Lambeth; and Phillips, for Finsbury."[116]

Whatever the qualms on the Liberal side about the coalition, there can be no doubt that Smith's supporters were much disturbed by it: an advertisement on 8 July comments on what it sees as a strange alliance, and asks whether the two Liberals could possibly agree on political issues. The answer (in case anyone did not perceive the rhetorical nature of the question) was given: no.[117]

But, at least as far as the election was concerned, this was whistling in the dark. While there was insufficient time for elaborate cooperation by that late date (on 7 July, when all the cited Liberal advertisements appeared, the election was only five days away, the meetings with electors had been planned, and halls rented), both Liberal groups must have felt considerably happier and more confident. Indeed it is now hard to see

112 We do not know how the order of advertisements in *The Times* was determined.

113 The term used for voting for only one candidate in a constituency where two or more candidates were to be elected and each voter had as many votes as there were seats.

114 This is the most frequent kind of electoral advertisement in the papers.

115 It also appeared in the *Daily News*, as did the two Mill ones.

116 *The Times*, 7 July 1865, p. 5; cf. *Daily News*, 7 July 1865, p. 4.

117 *The Times*, 8 July 1865, p. 5.

why Grosvenor's supporters were jittery at all, for the strength of his family connection was still evident to all observers. Meanwhile the case for Mill continued to build: De Lacy Evans, the retiring member, made a public contribution to Mill's fund on 5 July and explained his reasons for support, and the Rev. Charles Kingsley followed the lead of his fellow clergymen[118] by stating that he had preached a sermon in the Chapel Royal, Whitehall, on the text of Mill's *Examination*, though not specifically on what he refers to as "the now famous passage," which he describes as both true and startling.[119]

And Mill had agreed to meet the electors. As Helen Taylor indicated in her letter to Lady Amberley:

> Mr. Mill has consented to address two meetings, one of which is to be of working men, and I am glad of this last especially. I like him to address the working men and I think his doing so will produce impressions on them that will be of use in the future. Altogether this contest seems to me to have been satisfactory and to have drawn out a good deal of hidden liberal opinion from the press. We are surprised at the advanced ideas expressed in many of the country papers which we have seen on the occasion.[120]

Most commentators go astray here, following Mill's account in the *Autobiography*, which, like Helen Taylor's letter, implies that he met the electors only twice. In fact, pressure on him was such that, whatever the limitations of his promise and expectations on his return, he spoke at four meetings prior to the nomination meeting on 10 July; he also spoke at it, and at another in the evening of that day.[121]

The first meeting, on 3 July, was planned merely as a meeting with the committee, but they "resolved on the bold step of hiring the large room at St. James's Hall," giving "at one bound a prominence and importance to the contest not anticipated by Mr. Mill," who, in

118 Dean Stanley had written a second letter, strongly anti-Mansel, published, undoubtedly through the committee's efforts, in *The Times*, the *Daily News*, and the *Morning Star* on 1 July 1865.

119 *Daily News*, 5 July 1865, p. 3, and *The Times*, 5 July 1865, p. 14, for Evans; *Daily News*, 1 July 1865, p. 5, and *The Times*, 1 July 1865, p. 5, for Stanley; *Daily News*, 4 July 1865, p. 6, for Kingsley.

120 Russell Archives.

121 The last reported only in the *Daily Telegraph*; see *Public and Parliamentary Speeches* [*PPS*], *CW*, vols. XXVIII–XXIX (Toronto: University of Toronto Press, 1988), vol. XXVIII, pp. 42–3.

> his practical ignorance of public meetings, . . . wandered through the building to the platform without his committee, and sat alone, looking upon the scene, until a zealous friend withdrew him to the room in which his committee were assembled. Long before the hour announced, anxious throngs, grouped in twos and threes, wended their way through the borough to the hall. It quickly filled. No other candidate could have secured such an array of earnest friends.[122]

In short, the private discussion Mill expected had been transformed into a triumphant public opportunity to get a first view of the famed philosopher willing to stand for principle in practical political life. As many as 600 persons were present,[123] including on the platform "most of the leading Reformers not only of the city of Westminster but of the metropolis at large."[124] The committee was delighted: here were

> Westminster men who remembered Burdett; old leaguers who rejoiced in the memory of Covent Garden gatherings; literary friends, Radicals of every hue; Conservatives who admired, and others who came wondering at the reputation and power of the man who could thus gather his countrymen as O'Connell, or Bright, or Cobden alone had done, a brilliant array of beauty, in galleries set apart for ladies, swelled the numbers, until every foot of space was closely occupied. Mr. Mill's formal entry was the signal for applause, again and again renewed, lasting for some minutes; and throughout the proceedings, the cheers which instantaneously greeted each noble sentiment, testified the high tone and importance of the men assembled.[125]

Mill, it must be remembered, had not anticipated this occasion and spoke impromptu.[126] It seems certain, however, that had he been far less effective than he was, the occasion would still have been triumphant. Certainly he was not experienced in addressing mass audiences, but his whole career prepared him to speak his mind coherently and precisely whatever the circumstances, and so he did. "Unused to a public appearance, a slight nervousness was apparent in him, but his manner was calm

122 *Mr. J.S. Mill and Westminster*, p. 13.

123 That is the figure given ibid.; the *Daily News* in its report on 4 July estimated 300–400.

124 *The Times*, 4 July 1865, p. 14.

125 *Mr. J.S. Mill and Westminster*, p. 14. The press reports are hardly less restrained in bearing out this account.

126 He had worked on a speech, but withheld it until the next meeting, the one he had anticipated as public, on 5 July.

and appreciative; the delivery quick; the words terse, incisive; the matter, condensed philosophy."[127] In fact, there was little "condensed philosophy" on this occasion; Mill limited himself mainly to a brief summary of his attitude to his own candidacy, noting that his election would not be the conferring of an honour but the imposing of an onerous duty, which he feared he could not fulfil totally. However, his candidature, in the special circumstances, was valuable in demonstrating the utility of "purity of election." His supporters—unlike their Conservative foes—deserved great praise for abstaining from "the illegitimate expenses" and bearing "the burden of the legitimate." He then went on to a remarkable eulogy of his father, to whom in his early life he owed everything, and who laboured mightily for liberalism when to do so was personally damaging as well as difficult. His having grown up among reformers in Westminster had, he thought, helped determine his own career from the time when their numbers were few until the present when thousands rallied behind reform.[128] He also here revealed what was later to appear in his *Autobiography* as a post facto justification of his parliamentary behaviour:

> I have never been one of those who have left things alone when they have been an uphill fight, but I have left them when the fight was no longer difficult. . . . I have left that prosperous thing, and have turned to something else—to something that was still a crotchet, still an abstraction, still something that no practical person would battle with. . . . For I have been accustomed . . . to see that the crotchet of to-day, the crotchet of one generation, becomes the truth of the next and the truism of the one after. (*Cheers.*)

Having introduced the issue of his "crotchets," Mill did not specify them, but invited questions on his views. This audience did not much respond, although one question was asked on church and state in Ireland, and the meeting concluded with great applause and the announcement of the other meetings that Mill would address on the 5th (also in St. James's Hall), the 6th (at the Regent Music Hall, Vincent Square), and the 8th (in the Pimlico Rooms—this the one specifically for the working classes).[129]

Mill's second public meeting, on 5 July, was also an enormous success

127 *Mr. J.S. Mill and Westminster*, p. 14.

128 Here, perhaps prompted by reports of Roebuck's eulogy of him, he introduced some rare remarks in his praise.

129 For a collated version of this speech, with details about the meeting, see *PPS*, *CW*, vol. XXVIII, pp. 13–18. The further meetings were also, of course, advertised widely in the press.

from the moment of his introduction by Edwin Lankester, surgeon and Middlesex coroner, as "the great philosopher of the day," who would be shown not to be "an advocate of chimerical theories . . . , but a man of large and practical views . . ., a great political and a great practical philosopher"; "though some of his ideas were termed crotchets, they would turn out to be the seed from which they would hereafter have abundant results."[130] Characteristically, Mill's interpretation of the contest at hand focused on issues of principle and morality, not personality, as he opened with an assertive reiteration of the platform outlined in his letters to James Beal of 7 March and 17 April 1865, though he added a strong claim to "practical knowledge of business" on the basis of his thirty-five years in the "actual business of government" in the East India Company. Alluding to reported sarcasm about his unusual refusal to woo the electors, Mill told his audience that if the choice were offered, he "would rather be honest than be elected": this comment drew forth "loud cheers, which continued for several minutes." Indeed, the meeting's initial enthusiasm grew, with more and more responsive endorsement and laughter—the conventional view of Mill as humourless is simply wrong—and undoubtedly encouraged a slight heightening of his platform rhetoric. The heart of his speech was an explanation of his adherence to "advanced" liberalism that more than anything in his first speech justifies both the appellation "condensed philosophy" and the further comment: "High politics were being uttered; a noble regard to truth—a higher regard for truth than for the honour of winning suffrages—stamped, beyond recall, the popular belief that, before all competitors, John Stuart Mill was to be Westminster's chosen representative."[131] His principles, of course, fortunately made appropriate his attack, reiterated in all his election speeches, on the venal influence of wealth and position. The question period this time was more active, though no serious challenge was mounted, and the meeting ended, after an intervention by an unidentified woman who made some pungent comments in favour of "womanhood suffrage," in unanimous endorsement of Mill's candidacy.

The third of Mill's meetings, on 6 July, not surprisingly repeated, in content and procedure, the earlier ones. But an interesting diversion in the question period can undoubtedly be attributed to Smith's workers. An unnamed auditor quoted the passage in Mill's *Principles* that had appeared on a Tory placard: "As soon as any idea of equality enters the mind of an uneducated English working man, his head is turned by it. When he

130 For this speech, see ibid., pp. 18–28.
131 *Mr. J.S. Mill and Westminster*, p. 14.

ceases to be servile he becomes insolent."[132] Mill's response, which detailed his views of the necessary educational qualifications for the suffrage and included praise of the Lancashire operatives for their support of the North in the American Civil War, won, the papers reported, "Loud applause," and "Cheers."[133]

The next meeting, on 8 July, a Saturday, was the one alluded to by Helen Taylor as involving "working men"—the advertisement alluded to "electors and non-electors"—and was for that reason viewed as special. Mill perhaps tailored his remarks slightly to the occasion, concentrating on the corrupting influence of money, which he adroitly tied to support for the South in the Civil War, but he made no strong move towards demagoguery. It may also be that he introduced specially for the non-electors a promise to remain a liberal independent except on issues directly between the government and the Tories. Perhaps recalling Smith's stated allegiance to administrative reform, Mill declared himself as sharing the "general conviction" that "most of the departments of public affairs—almost all the public business—was either badly done or done not nearly so well as it ought to be done." What was needed was "skilful management of public affairs by trained and specially qualified people with the preservation and extension of their local liberties and the responsibility of all public functionaries to the people. In short, they wanted a system of administration which should at once be skilful and popular." Such comments, however admirable and typical of Mill, are not rabble-rousers, but cheers were elicited by them.

The question period once more featured a quotation from his writings, like the one on the 6th almost certainly inspired by Smith's agents: "How do you explain your writing that the upper classes are liars, and the lower classes—the working classes—habitual liars?"[134] The newspapers do not exactly record the sequence that Mill describes in his *Autobiography*—when he instantly acknowledged authorship of the words, he was cheered to the echo, and George Odger said that this was the kind of man to represent the interests of the working class.[135] However, the more extended answer reported in the press at least won "Applause," "cheers," and a final "Hear, hear":

> Mr. Mill said such was his writing. He thought so, and so did the most intelligent of the working classes themselves, and the passage applied

132 *PPE*, bk. I, chap. vii, sect. 5 (*CW*, vol. II, p. 109).
133 For a full report of the speech, see *PPS*, *CW*, vol. XXVIII, pp. 28–31.
134 Cf. *Thoughts on Parliamentary Reform*, *CW*, vol. XIX, p. 338.
135 *CW*, vol. I, pp. 274–5.

> to the natural state of those who were both uneducated and subjected. If they were educated and became free citizens, then he should not be afraid of them. Lying was the vice of slaves, and they would never find slaves who were not liars. It was not a reproach that they were what slavery had made them. But those persons who quoted this passage were not candid enough to read on. . . . He said that he was not speaking of the vices of his countrymen, but of their virtues, and that they were superior to most other countrymen in truthfulness . . . and that the lower classes, though they did lie, were ashamed of lying, which was more than he could venture to say of the same class in any other nation which he knew.

Another Tory-inspired question raised Mill's views on family size, attributing to him the opinion that working-class parents should have fewer children than the wealthy.[136] Mill replied that he had said only that the working classes had no more right than others to large families, and that no people had "a right to have more children than they could support and educate," and then went on to a more open statement of Malthusianism than he ever made elsewhere publicly, one far more direct than was customary among politicians. All "morality," he remarked, "was a triumph over some . . . natural propensities." Continuing in what may be a unique example of an aspiring politician answering a question by dismissing nature as an ethical norm, Mill added: "The strongest of their natural propensities had been overcome by the various inducements that had been addressed to mankind—by public opinion, by education, by religion, none of which influences had ever been sufficiently or satisfactorily brought to bear on this particular end." Perhaps realizing that his condensed philosophy needed some political dilution, he finished his long answer by saying: "No class who might be called rich had a right to have more sons and daughters than they could provide for, because if they could not leave them well off they might be quartered on the public. (*Cheers.*)" At this point, rather surprisingly, an unnamed person on the platform continued the theme by asking: "How can Mr. Mill reconcile his doctrine with the Scriptural injunction, that we are to increase and multiply?" Mill's reply, which was heard through "Much laughter" and responded to with "Cheers and laughter," demonstrated again his quick wit as he capped Genesis with Ecclesiastes: "It says we are to eat and drink, but not to over-eat and over-drink ourselves."

136 The passage in question (one of those cited in n17 above) is in *PPE*, bk. II, chap. xii, sect. 2 (*CW*, vol. II, p. 358).

The question session continued at length, with some sharp queries and many thoughtful replies about proportional representation, Romanism in the Church of England, sabbatarianism, the value of the franchise to working people, non-intervention, electoral bribery, and primogeniture. Worth noting are two specific questions and answers, with the audience's responses. The first of these revealed openly the tender religious nerve: "Has Mr. Mill any confidence in and sympathy with the religion taught by Jesus Christ and his apostles; and does he believe that a State Church is a benefit to this nation or otherwise?" This was met with "Cries of Don't answer," and Mill responded to the first part of the question as the loudest part of the audience urged: "He had already declared that he could not consent to answer any questions about his religious creed." The general response was: "Loud applause, and 'Quite right,' " and then Mill answered the second part of the question by saying that though he believed having an Established Church was a mistake, the time was not right for disestablishment. The second interchange was over the ballot and is interesting, if the report is taken as accurate, in its quiet reception. Question: "The ballot?" Answer: "Mr. Mill did not think it was now necessary, especially to the working classes, and that if it was necessary it was amongst shopkeepers."[137]

On the whole, this last pre-nomination meeting, like all of the preceding ones, was considered a great success by Mill's supporters, as their retrospective account indicates:

> These meetings . . . roused an enthusiasm, cheering to those who had dared to undertake the doubtful task of summoning a philosopher from his study to introduce him to the arena of excitement, which only an election can invoke, and to the higher eminence of the Senate. They did more. They spoke to all England, and aided the Reform cause in many a doubtful field. Europe and the new world were watching the contest. Representatives of the United States, Italians, and Germans attended the meetings.[138]

In summary, one may say of Mill's election speeches that he not only expressed his views openly and fairly, with the exception of reserve on religion, but adopted a rhetorical stance appropriate to the circumstances, unusual as they were. In parliament, as we shall see, he was certainly not devious, but he phrased his thoughts with a judiciousness that, appropri-

137 For the reports, see *PPS*, *CW*, vol. XXVIII, pp. 31–40.
138 *Mr. J.S. Mill and Westminster*, p. 15.

ate to the Commons, was not needed before other audiences. His relish for polemical combat had, of course, been evident long before his candidature, but he had no time for polemic for its own sake. While he seems not to have regretted the opportunity to pitch his message at a lower level than that suitable for the printed page or (in those days) for the House of Commons, he did not blunt the moral intent of his message. Indeed it exactly matched that of his main supporters, whose scheme, however modified in the course of the election, still was based on one (though not the only possible) noble view of the political process. Consequently the philosophical level sometimes attained in his speeches was apt, as he set forth with clarity and directness the method of his politics and offered his prospective constituents a line of vision that passed beyond the pressures, constraints, and opportunities of the moment. He would readily confess that good will and altruistic motives in themselves did not make the ideal politician—a realistic grasp of immediate difficulties, limitations, and contingencies was essential to working a representative system to progressive advantage. In effect, Mill argued that the best politician was one who used the possibilities inherent in a particular context to further ultimate objectives favourable to the public interest.

In the nature of things, however, many could not see what the future required of the present. Even well-intentioned and liberal-minded politicians could all too easily succumb to the demands, details, and routines of day-to-day political life and conclude that acting upon principle was a luxury they could ill afford. Progress could not result from subordinating principle to practice, but from seeking the maximum good in each specific set of circumstances. Mill had, in fact, laid out the essence of his political method in his speech of 5 July:

> Believing as I do that society and political institutions are, or ought to be, in a state of progressive advance; that it is the very nature of progress to lead us to recognise as truths what we do not as yet see to be truths; believing also that . . . it is possible to see a certain distance before us, and to be able to distinguish beforehand some of these truths of the future, and to assist others to see them—I certainly think there are truths which the time has now arrived for proclaiming, although the time may not yet have arrived for carrying them into effect. That is what I mean by advanced Liberalism. But does it follow that, because a man sees something of the future, he is incapable of judging of the past? . . . I venture to reverse the proposition. The only persons who can judge for the present . . . are those who include

> to-morrow in their deliberations. We can see the direction in which things are tending, and which of those tendencies we are to encourage and which to resist. . . . But while I would refuse to suppress one iota of the opinions I consider best, I confess I would not object to accept any reasonable compromise which would give me even a little of that of which I hope in time to obtain the whole.[139]

One could compromise one's principles or one could compromise in the interest of one's principles.

Even in Westminster, even among the radical high-minded who so enthusiastically advanced his name and supported him, it is unlikely that many could appreciate fully the implications of this position. But its high-mindedness was apparent, as well as its obvious direction towards the ultimate public good. The campaign was proving wonderfully successful, with the press, apart from the Tory papers that kept up the sniping on specific issues, generally supportive.[140] One would expect, however, some criticism on the pragmatic level, and on the eve of the election *The Times* typically sounded a note of caution:

> In this instance [Westminster] the usual fault of the Liberals, the disregard of prudent party tactics, has brought into the field a Conservative, for whom his friends confidently predict success. It would be, indeed, creditable to the electors of Westminster to choose a man of Mr. Mill's mental powers and faculty of lucid exposition, even though they might not agree with his opinions; but it may unfortunately prove that not even in Westminster, with its traditions of Fox and Hobhouse and Burdett, and many another worthy, is a utilitarian philosopher able to stand against those practical utilitarians who know that the greatest happiness of the greatest number in a borough at election time is promoted by putting a round sum into the hands of an active agent.[141]

This concentration on Mill may well appear unfair to the other

139 *PPS*, *CW*, vol. XXVIII, p. 23.

140 See, for example, leading articles in the *Daily Telegraph*, 5 and 7 July 1865, and the *Morning Star*, 5 July 1865 (dissenting on the ballot issue), and in both on 11 July 1865, just before the poll. For the tone of Tory attacks, see, for example, two letters in the *Standard*, 8 July 1865, p. 5, its leading article on 10 July 1865, pp. 4–5 (where Mill's Malthusianism is thoroughly condemned), and three more letters on 11 July 1865, p. 5, one of which is discussed below in reference to Grosvenor.

141 *The Times*, 11 July 1865, p. 11.

candidates, but it well matches the contemporary public interest. Judged by press coverage, Smith and Grosvenor were not doing well in the final days of the campaign. Smith's meetings on 23 and 26 June were reported briefly in *The Times*,[142] and his candidature, like Grosvenor's, was normally mentioned when Mill's was being celebrated. The *Standard* was not silent, but its advocacy continued to concentrate on adversarial comment on Smith's opponents rather than on praise of him. For instance:

> upon Westminster the Conservative party have every possible claim. In fact, these claims appear to be warmly acknowledged by the constituency, notwithstanding the boastful candidature of Mr. Mill, who hardly thinks a Westminster elector worth speaking to, who would associate with him, in the exercise of the suffrage, a class of voters of midnight-meeting celebrity, and whose general philosophy is an impeachment of Providence. We say little of Captain Grosvenor. He is likely, if returned, to prove harmless and useless. But Westminster needs, in Parliament, an active, intelligent, business representative, faithful to Conservative principles, and, provided that its Conservative electors do not sleep over their duties, will surely have one.[143]

Advertisements for Smith of course continued to appear,[144] but his committee's main endeavours were going into the canvassing, about which no specific details are known though the general outline is clear from the records of the 1868 election.[145]

Grosvenor seems not to have made any public appearances at this stage in the campaign, though he was undoubtedly much in evidence in the West End. The early attacks on him as at best a lukewarm reformer had been rebutted in a circular letter dealing with the two main issues, parliamentary reform and the ballot. As to the first, he said:

> . . . I have explained that I desire to see a general but constitutional reconstruction of our representative system, in which all towns with more than 5,000 inhabitants should be taken from the county constituencies, and given a share in the borough representation. . . . The right of voting might then, I think, fairly be extended to every £10 occupier in counties. . . . With regard to the borough franchise,

142 Ibid., 24 June 1865, p. 5, and 27 June 1865, p. 7.

143 *Standard*, 10 July 1865, p. 4.

144 For a specially detailed one, see ibid.

145 See chapter 8 below.

> I would extend it to every householder bearing the local and public burthens, at the same time including a properly adjusted lodger franchise.

His comment on the second matter was straightforward and unambiguous, if ungrammatical: "Adoption of the Ballot would have my support, knowing that in many constituencies it is needed to secure the free and independent exercise of the franchise, and therefore the voter is justly entitled to it."[146]

The *Daily News*, staunchly Liberal but not unqualifiedly Millian in this period, had done its best for Grosvenor, saying he "is understood to have prosecuted a highly successful canvass. He is conducting his election by the methods to which the electors are accustomed. He shows himself freely, speaks with courage, and employs the established organization of election contests. His opponents have not been able to fasten upon any salient point in his life or opinions which can be turned to his disadvantage." The continuation of the account, however, again suggests how lightly Grosvenor's qualifications were rated even by those favourably disposed:

> Fortunately for him, the most serious mishap which has yet befallen him is his encounter with Dr. Tweedie. This gentleman, having heard that he was infected with the damnable heresy of Homoeopathy, came forward and tendered the new British Pharmacopoeia to the Captain, requiring his unfeigned assent and consent to all things therein contained. The gallant candidate was ready to declare that "he alloweth" the said book, but not that he will use no other prescriptions than are set forth in it by authority. Whereupon the orthodox Tweedie saith, "Let him be excommunicated, *ipso facto,* and not restored until he repent and publicly revoke . . . his senseless error." We have heard complaints of electors who, by asking pledges, are said to have encroached upon the freedom and independence of the candidate's mind, but this is the first time the public has heard of an elector laying claim to the regulation of a candidate's bowels. If Captain Grosvenor, in the course of this election, should come as well

146 Quoted in a letter from "A Westminster Reformer and a Member of Captain Grosvenor's Committee" to the editor of the *Morning Advertiser* (3 June 1865, p. 5), which, although viciously opposed to Mill (an attack on his irreligion immediately precedes this letter), was generally more on the Liberal than the Conservative side.

> out of all encounters as he has done out of this ludicrous one with the irrepressible Dr. Tweedie, he will head the poll.[147]

Such was the perception of Mill's running-mate, and it cannot have done Mill much good, though perhaps little harm. And while the manifest qualifications of the philosopher candidate may have made Grosvenor more attractive to Liberals who were persuaded not to plump, some of Mill's opinions might well have damaged Grosvenor's chances. One voice at least sounded this note:

> As a Liberal elector of Westminster I gave my promise to Captain Grosvenor, and having something approaching a repugnance to the mountebank nonsense promulgated by Mr. Mill I felt no qualms of conscience in according my second vote to Mr. Smith, the manly tone of whose address could not fail to satisfy any reasonable elector; for in his address, independently of his avowed intention to vote for measures, and not for a party, I discovered the ring of the true English metal. Such a man, I thought, could not desert his expressed principles.
>
> Now, however, the case, as far as I am concerned, is altogether altered; for such is my opinion of the impracticability and uselessness of Mr. Mill's advocacy of any cause that I could not be a party, even indirectly, to his becoming the representative of the city of Westminster; I shall, therefore, without hesitation, plump for Mr. Smith. In this determination I am joined by several of my friends.

Though signed "A Liberal Elector" and accompanied (so the letter concludes) by his card, this evidence would be less suspect if it had not appeared in the *Standard* on 11 July 1865.

Perhaps this letter had been prompted by anxieties roused on the previous day, 10 July, when the electors—and non-electors—gathered at the hustings for the ritual nomination meeting, which was held in front of St. Paul's Church, Covent Garden. Mill had actually gone the length of saying as late as the evening of the 8th (a Saturday) that he would not attend, and was only persuaded by the dedicated efforts of Westerton and Storr.[148] The Tories had used his known reluctance to put the rumour about that he had retired from the contest. So the usual excitement was heightened, and the unruly crowd expressed itself in loud and partial

147 *Daily News*, 24 June 1865, p. 2. These remarks preceded the favourable assessment of Mill that nonetheless insisted that it was time for him to face the electors.

148 *Mr. J.S. Mill and Westminster*, p. 16.

howls as Mill, having made his way there from the committee rooms, met the other candidates in the vestry of St. Paul's and then appeared with them. In that setting for that purpose the candidacy of the country's leading philosopher did nothing to spoil the "fun," as Matthew Arnold might have said about this ritual of the period. The *Morning Star* (Mill's most enthusiastic supporter) commented:

> throughout the whole proceedings, a continuous volley of yells and howls, mingled with cheers for the respective candidates, was kept up. The speeches of neither proposers, seconders, nor candidates could be heard except by those close beside them, and in most cases the speakers wisely addressed their remarks to the reporters, and made them as brief as possible. It is right to state that the uproar came chiefly, not from the respectable portion of the electors and non-electors, but from bands of ruffianly lads, who seemed to be organised for the purpose.[149]

Mill's reported remarks bear out that account, indicating that he began by saying it would be "entirely useless . . . to attempt to make a speech, which it would be impossible that [anyone] . . . could hear," but he went on to assert that the very conditions of his candidature justified his election. It seems one young man was able to hear something, as well as to see much, for forty years later he recalled the occasion vividly:

> It was a day in 1865, about 3 in the afternoon, during Mill's candidature for Westminster. The hustings had been erected in Covent-garden, near the front of St. Paul's Church; and when I—a young man living in London—drew near to the spot, Mill was speaking. The appearance of the author of the treatise "On Liberty" (which we students of that date knew almost by heart) was so different from the look of persons who usually address crowds in the open air that it held the attention of people for whom such a gathering in itself had little interest. Yet it was, primarily, that of a man out of place. The religious sincerity of his speech was jarred on by his environment—a group on the hustings who, with few exceptions, did not care to understand him fully, and a crowd below who could not. He stood bareheaded, and his vast pale brow, so thin-skinned as to show the blue veins, sloped back like a stretching upland, and conveyed to the observer a curious sense of perilous exposure. The picture of him as

149 11 July 1865, p. 2; for a full account, see *PPS*, *CW*, vol. XXVIII, pp. 40–1.

> personified earnestness surrounded for the most part by careless curiosity derived an added piquancy—if it can be called such—from the fact that the cameo clearness of his face chanced to be in relief against the blue shadow of a church which, on its transcendental side, his doctrines antagonized. But it would not be right to say that the throng was absolutely unimpressed by his words; it felt that they were weighty, though it did not quite know why.[150]

Thomas Hardy did not bother to recall, nor did the reporters record, any substantive contributions by Grosvenor or Smith on that occasion, both being apparently unhearable. Much more excitement was occasioned by the high bailiff declaring, on the show of hands, that it went for Smith and Grosvenor, when other observers saw about an equal number for Mill and Smith, with a very much smaller number for Grosvenor. This declaration was met, the *Daily Telegraph* reported, by "Hisses, laughter, and It's a lie," and the *Morning Star* expressed some concern over the "functionary's organs of vision."[151] These proceedings were, of course, merely a formality, and Mill's supporters called for the poll to be held, as arranged, on 12 July.

Mill, however, unexpectedly spoke again on the evening of the 10th, in response to his committee's assessment of the electoral mood. He was greeted enthusiastically by a large assembly in St. Martin's Hall, including—as the papers had noted of his other meetings—a large number of ladies, and—as the papers and his supporters also noted enthusiastically—the Comte de Paris on the platform.[152]

Reading these reports consecutively with the growing lists of subscribers published by Mill's committee almost daily during the latter stages of the campaign, and noting the absence in the dailies of serious coverage of Smith's and Grosvenor's campaigns, it is difficult to believe that Mill's committee can have been anything but confident on the 12th. But indeed all was somewhat uncertain, with three untried candidates vying for

150 Michael Millgate, ed., *The Life and Work of Thomas Hardy* (London: Macmillan, 1989 [1984]), pp. 355–6.

151 For these reports, see *PPS*, *CW*, vol. XXVIII, pp. 40–2.

152 The tone of the report in *Mr. J.S. Mill and Westminster* (p. 15) reminds one that, as Mill had much earlier averred, even Radicals can love a lord: "He [the Comte] had proposed to himself the pleasure of meeting Mr. Mill on the hustings; but the *fête* of the Queen Marie Amélia interposed an obstacle. No special reception was arranged, and his presence was unknown to the audience. He was received, on his arrival, by the chairman (Mr. James Beal), and introduced by him to Mr. Mill, and engaged in conversation with him until the meeting commenced."

support in an election not run on strict party lines. So Mill's supporters tried to leave nothing undone at the last moment:

> Arrangements had been made by the committee to fill each post of importance, as inspectors at booths, representative, and, where possible, check-clerks, by volunteer friends. The list of eminent men sharing in the close and harassing work of the day was highly complimentary. Young barristers deemed it a privilege to attend to bear their part in the struggle; solicitors either attended in person or sent able representatives; City merchants in person acted as check-clerks, ignoring Mincing-lane and the Jerusalem Coffee-house in their zeal for a glorious result; eminent writers, like H.D. McLeod and William Galt, shared the representative labours at the booth, and the chairmen of local committees, such as Mr. Ellis, Mr. Edwards, Mr. Saphin, Mr. Ogden, Mr. Malleson, Dr. Brewer, Mr. Westerton, Mr. Elsworth, Mr. Pratten, and Mr. Jobson, were untiring in their efforts. . . .
>
> The excitement was not personal. No ill-feeling was engendered. Each side strove to the utmost to vindicate the cause it espoused. No ladies, like Mrs. Carew, who gave to the Liberals of Westminster their party cry of "buff and blue, and Mrs. Carew," or the beautiful Duchess of Devonshire, shared in the canvass, or in elegant chariots escorted humble voters to the poll, save Miss Isa Craig and Mrs. Westerton, each of whom gracefully entered into the contest, and aided the fortunes of the day in Mr. Mill's behalf.[153]

One of the 1865 carriages has entered history in another guise (and with another hirer) as part of the story of women's suffrage.

153 *Mr. J.S. Mill and Westminster*, p. 17. The account continues with an explanation of the way the agreement between the two Liberal camps worked: "The compact made between Mr. Mill's and Captain Grosvenor's committee that 'no plumping' but divided Liberal votes should be the order of the day, required unceasing attention. It was feared that many like Lord Ernest Bruce, Granville Berkeley, and Hon. F. Byng, who had openly avowed (as good spaniels of Whiggism) a contempt for Mr. Mill, would induce friends of the same place-hunting stamp to ignore the compact and plump for Grosvenor. . . . Arrangements had been made in the event of any sign of treachery being apparent, that every plump for Grosvenor should have a corresponding plump for Mill; but, on the whole, the committee of each may honourably congratulate the other that no feelings were allowed to operate, but that an alliance made in honour was gallantly maintained, the performance being to many in each camp a most extreme yielding of inclination to principle."

> Barbara [Bodichon], Bessie [Rayner Parkes], Isa Craig, and Emily Davies . . . as four of the leading suffragists were active on behalf of Mill. . . . Barbara hired a carriage, draped it with placards calling for Mill's election, and the four of them drove about Westminster—a sight then strange indeed. Marian [Evans] took no part in the election. She had "been going through many *actions de grace* towards him" as she re-read Mill's works, but [said:] "I am not anxious that he should be in Parliament; thinkers can do more outside than inside the House." She did not think he would be elected.[154]

However, he was. The polling began slowly, but gradually built up. The running record shows: 9 o'clock, Grosvenor, 782; Mill, 764; Smith, 711; 12 o'clock, Grosvenor, 2772; Mill, 2767; Smith, 2574. Smith's consecutive notes to his sister show his early recognition of the outcome: "Things are looking a little badly for us—not very much so, but enough to render it very possible that we may be beaten. You must prepare Father for it." And later, in spite of his continued support in the districts "contiguous to the colossal establishment" over which he presided,[155] he wrote again: "I think you may have a disappointment. Men have broken their promises to a considerable extent, and we are dropping behind. Don't be discouraged; it is all for the best."[156]

Certainly the Liberals thought it all for the best when at 4 o'clock the poll closed and the result was given as Grosvenor, 4544; Mill, 4539; Smith, 3832.[157] The next day, at the official declaration of the poll in Covent Garden, the "dense mass of people" crowded around the hustings had their zeal temporarily cooled—whether intentionally or not—by a shower from a watering cart. But the fun was resumed when Beal announced (undoubtedly sending more than a shiver down the spine of Colonel

154 Lawrence and Elisabeth Hanson, *Marian Evans and George Eliot* (London: Oxford University Press, 1952), p. 252. George Eliot's words come from a letter to Clementia Taylor of 10 July 1865. The reference to the election carriage derives from Emily Davies's manuscript "Draft of a Family Chronicle," p. 427. Emily Davies Papers, Girton College.

155 *Mr. J.S. Mill and Westminster*, p. 19. This pamphlet supplies at this point an interesting account of the voting in each of the parishes. See appendix A.

156 Akers-Douglas, *Smith*, pp. 51–2; Maxwell, *Smith*, pp. 125–6.

157 Smith's final letter to his sister on that day gave the close of poll figures (not quite accurately: Grosvenor, 4384; Mill, 4379; Smith, 3812), and added: "So I was 572 behind [Grosvenor] and am left out in the cold; but although disappointed, I am not at all castdown about it." (Ibid.) The official result was declared the next day: Grosvenor, 4534; Mill, 4525; Smith, 3824 (now 710 behind Grosvenor).

"Westminster Election: The Nomination in Covent-Garden," *Illustrated London News*, 22 July 1865

Taylor and the Hon. Bob Grimston) that "'the unredeemed Conservative pledges would be offered to auction the next day,' by his friend Mr. Storr (of the firm of Debenham and Storr), so honourably known as the auctioneers of property of that and other descriptions"; an announcement "received with great glee, and thoroughly relished."[158] In that mood the crowd greeted Mill with "a most enthusiastic ovation," and he spoke to them once more in a distinctly political tone, again extolling the virtuous defeat of the money interests supporting the Conservatives.[159] It was reported that he "looked upon the exciting scene before him with that quiet, benign, and thoughtful expression of countenance for which he is so remarkable under all circumstances, and seemingly not the least moved or discomposed, except what was denoted by a pleasing smile which his intellectual features could not conceal, however desirous their owner may have been to so do."[160] He and Grosvenor (Smith did not put in an appearance) then retired in triumph, though still not as one.[161]

If there is anything surprising in the result, one might instance the closeness of the contest between Mill and Grosvenor for the head of the poll, and the size of the vote for Smith—who at least on the evident record did very feeble running—as well as the relatively small total vote.[162] That last observation reflects a general perception: in the words of the *Annual Register*, the general election "took place under circumstances of as little excitement as can perhaps ever be expected to attend the choosing by a great nation of its representative body." It was—until after the election—still the era when it could be said that Lord Palmerston's government had "done that which it is most difficult and most salutary for a Parliament to do—nothing."[163]

There was in those circumstances no reason for Westminster to elect its second Tory in thirty-five years. Indeed, had Mill headed the poll there would have been no astonishment, for at least publicly Grosvenor had a

158 *Mr. J.S. Mill and Westminster*, p. 22. For an explanation, see p. 255 below.

159 *PPS*, *CW*, vol. XXVIII, pp. 43–5.

160 *Morning Star*, 13 July 1865, p. 2. For a full account, see *PPS*, *CW*, vol. XXVIII, pp. 43–5.

161 "[It] is worthy of record that the Whig elect made no overture to meet Mr. Mill, and retired as complete a stranger to the great body of electors as a scion of the house of Westminster is likely to be. It is recorded by the biographers of the governing families, 'That, as a family, they have, in their long career, done few striking acts, have furnished no great statesmen, yielded no orators, or generals, or admirals, or men of the highest rank in any one department of life.'" So, unforgivingly, *Mr. J.S. Mill and Westminster*, pp. 22–3.

162 For the polling by district, see appendix A.

163 Robert Cecil, "The House of Commons," *Quarterly Review*, 126 (July 1864), p. 245.

difficult time, if the press bears honest witness. As to Mill's election, it was seen as a matter for general celebration and self-congratulation (Tory qualms aside); not only in Westminster, but among the literate throughout the country (and even abroad) it was thought that the right thing had been done, and a surge of quiet satisfaction was felt. Not perhaps a philosopher-king, but the thinking man's thinking moralist and logician had joined the legislators, and nothing but good could come of the induction. Of all the eulogies published at the time, that in *Punch*, England's premier comic weekly, speaks best when, under the title "Philosophy and Punch," it greeted the election of J.S. Mill as MP for Westminster:

> Logic's in Parliament with Mill. Hurrah!
> Deep from the well of Truth a bucket draw,
> But the pure crystal, ere you quaff it, boil.
> The generous fire, that warms it, will not soil.
> Imparting strength, add spirits, which will come,
> For brandy if you call, and summon rum.
> Withal let lemon, deftly squeezed and peeled,
> Flavour and fragrance, sugar sweetness, yield.
> Mingle, and pour; the brimming goblet fill:
> That *Punch* in punch may drink, "Success to Mill."[164]

164 22 July 1865, p. 32.

THREE

Parliamentary Reform and the Radicalization of the Liberal Party

In the interval between Mill's triumph at the polls in July 1865 and his entrance into the House of Commons in February 1866, the political environment was transformed. The death of Lord Palmerston in October removed from the scene the guardian of the somewhat stagnant political pool that had accumulated during the preceding decade. The ministry that was then formed, led by Russell in the Lords (as prime minister), was unquestionably a new Liberal force, with Gladstone, the leader in the Commons, as its major propeller. The parliament that assembled in early 1866 understood that the new government intended to take up the question of parliamentary reform. Palmerston had done everything in his power to scuttle such attempts during his premiership, and his efforts had not been unavailing. Now he was no longer in the way of Russell, whose commitment to a further instalment of parliamentary reform dated from 1849, or of Gladstone, whose recent adherence to the cause made up in fervour what it lacked in pedigree.

That government, in leaping over Palmerston's coffin, did not take sufficient note of the ditch being dug to receive them by the Tories and anti-Reform Whigs. From 1859 through 1865, Lord Derby, leader of the Conservative party, had conducted a nominal opposition to Palmerston, a prime minister who had done for the Tories what they could not do themselves. Meanwhile his restless lieutenant in the Commons, Benjamin Disraeli, became increasingly impatient with treading water when he much preferred making waves. With Palmerston gone and a Liberal ministry in office pledged to an extension of the franchise, Tory passivity could no longer be taken for granted. Given the prospect of dissension within Liberal ranks over a reform bill and the misgivings shared by a number of Palmerstonian Liberals concerning Gladstone's enhanced status, the Conservatives would not be loath to bring down the government when they had a favourable opening.[1] The future of prominent parties (individual and collective) was highly uncertain. Mill could not afford to be indifferent to the struggle for power that was about to ensue, for its outcome would inevitably influence profoundly his means if not his ends. His response to the decisive issue of parliamentary reform would be moulded by the personal and party context from which the issue emerged.

Mill, welcomed in the House as a distinguished thinker and author, was of course an unknown quantity as a member of the "exclusive club" of the Commons. It appears likely that he had not well thought out his precise role as participant in the various stages of legislation, but the responses to his first appearances and his own habit of careful analysis led him to alterations in his behaviour, including his propensity to offer public advice. Brief as his parliamentary career was, it shows a four-part pattern: his first unreflective steps; his role as a radical supporter of the Liberal government; his less constrained advocacy of independent personal positions during the Conservative ministry of Derby and Disraeli; and, finally, his reassertion of support for Gladstonian Liberalism during the election campaign of 1868, when it appeared (correctly) that the Liberals would be returned to power. Through these stages, while his tactics shifted with his immediate goals, his primary commitment to long-range strategy remained: as always when ethical precepts rub into practice, the accusation of casuistry becomes tenable. The moralist in parliament must beg for a view from the gallery of the future, not the floor of the present; the improvement of humankind is not an available platform for amendments to legislation. In the aftermath of Palmerston's death, Mill's mission in the House of Commons took on dimensions absent from the 1865 campaign and undisclosed in the account of his parliamentary career presented in the *Autobiography*.[2]

In discussing Mill's thought and practice in relation to political issues in the parliament of 1866–8, through the first three of his parliamentary stages, several particular episodes call for special attention. Stage one saw his initial actions and his first major speech, on the cattle plague; stage two, his part in the debate on the Liberal Reform Bill, the defeat of which brought the Conservatives into office; stage three, his stance in relation to

1 For analyses of the personal and party stakes in the struggle over parliamentary reform, see Maurice Cowling, *1867: Disraeli, Gladstone and Revolution: The Passing of the Second Reform Bill* (Cambridge: Cambridge University Press, 1967); and F.B. Smith, *The Making of the Second Reform Bill* (Cambridge: Cambridge University Press, 1966).

2 For that account, see *Autobiography* [A], in *Autobiography and Literary Essays*, ed. John M. Robson and Jack Stillinger, *Collected Works* [CW], vol. I (Toronto: University of Toronto Press, 1981), pp. 272–90.

the Hyde Park riots and the Reform League, his participation in the debate on the Conservative Reform Bill, leading to the Second Reform Act,[3] and his advocacy during the Conservative ministry of particular measures, such as women's suffrage, proportional representation, and reform of the law on electoral corruption.

There can be no question that Mill's first actions were, in the strict sense, impolitic. Anyone wishing then (or at subsequent periods) to enter gently into the consciousness of the House would avoid expressing any opinion on Irish affairs, but Mill almost as soon as he was graciously received, voted with only five other non-Irish members for an amendment to the speech from the throne.[4] And his first speeches (14 and 16 February) on the cattle plague[5] did not much impress the House. Kate Amberley learned of Mill's maiden speech soon after it was delivered, from G.O. Trevelyan, Liberal MP for Tynemouth, and one of the few Liberal academics sitting in the House. She reports that Mill had spoken "rather inaudibly," and that Trevelyan "thought it a failure and that he wd. never get the ear of the house."[6]

Three days after this entry in Kate Amberley's journal, Mill gave a brief speech that greatly displeased the House. The occasion was the introduction of the government's bill for suspension of habeas corpus in Ireland, a measure devised in response to the Fenian threat.[7] Unlike the cattle plague, the condition of Ireland evoked deep feeling in Mill. He did not, strictly speaking, oppose the habeas corpus bill (he did not vote in the division in which an overwhelming majority of the House carried the measure) but much of what he said on the 17th angered many honourable members.[8] His remarks dwelt much less on Fenian violence than on the tragically flawed character of English government in Ireland. He considered the bill "a cause for shame and humiliation to this country." Cries of "no, no!" greeted his observation that every "foreigner, every continental writer, would believe for many years to come that Ireland was a country on the brink of revolution, held down by an alien nationality,

3 The most important of his contributions in this debate, his amendment to give the franchise to women on the same basis as men, is discussed in chapter 4.

4 *Parliamentary Debates* [*PD*], 3rd ser., vol. 181, col. 273 (8 Feb. 1866). For a full discussion of Mill and Ireland, see chapter 5 below.

5 See pp. 84–6 below.

6 *Amberley Papers*, vol. I, p. 468.

7 For a full discussion of this occasion, see chapter 5.

8 *Public and Parliamentary Speeches* [*PPS*], ed. John M. Robson and Bruce L. Kinzer, *CW*, vols. XXVIII–XXIX (Toronto: University of Toronto Press, 1988), vol. XXVIII, pp. 52–4.

and kept in subjection by brute force."[9] His account in the *Autobiography* indicates that he was immediately made aware of having damaged his opportunities of influencing the House, though in retrospect he takes the opportunity of defending both his principles and his subsequent tactics:

> In denouncing, on this occasion, the English mode of governing Ireland, I did no more than the general opinion of England now admits to have been just; but the anger against Fenianism was then in all its freshness; any attack on what Fenians attacked was looked upon as an apology for them; and I was so unfavourably received by the House, that more than one of my friends advised me (and my own judgment agreed with the advice) to wait, before speaking again, for the favourable opportunity that would be given by the first great debate on the Reform Bill.[10]

Not only the substance but the form of Mill's performance was questionable on grounds of political expediency. On that subject Henry Lucy's opinion has weight. New members, he says, must realize "that the House will not brook a lecture or advice from a member whose face and figure are not so familiar that they seem to have become as much a portion of the Chamber as the clock over the gangway or the canopy over the Speaker's chair. Whether the advice be sound or empty, the counsellor eminent or obscure, does not matter. Mr. John Stuart Mill and Mr. Fawcett when they first entered Parliament fell into the besetting sin of young members"—and paid the penalty.[11]

But Mill (and Fawcett) learned the lesson, thanks to native intelligence and, as his account in the *Autobiography* indicates, to sound advice. The principal aid in this respect seems to have been J.A. Roebuck who, having aided the campaign to get Mill into the House, must have keenly awaited the first speech from his old friend and debating companion, and as keenly felt disappointment over it. Not wishing to address Mill directly, Roebuck wrote on 9 March to Chadwick, who passed on the advice, which, basically, was to wait before speaking again until the debate on the second reading of the Reform Bill. Then, "Mill if he pleases, may make what ought to have been his début. If he will speak as a philosopher putting Bright and all paltry influences on one side, coming forth in his own great strength aye majesty, depend upon it, the House would listen and be

9 Ibid., pp. 52, 53.

10 *A*, *CW*, vol. I, p. 277. For other contemporary judgments of Mill's success and failure in the House, see chapter 1, pp. 7–12 above.

11 Henry Lucy, *Men and Manners in Parliament* (London: T. Fisher Unwin, 1919), p. 140.

delighted. Let him be himself, clear bold and *understandable* (there is a new word) and he will put his mark upon the debate." The advice turned to what Roebuck, now a thirty-year veteran, knew well:

> Having determined what to say, he ought to plant himself steadily on his feet, give the right pitch and tone of voice, then earnestly and with perfect simplicity make his opening statement—The House will be anxious to hear him—Let him show, that he is no mere puppet, that he is no man's follower—but one possessed by strong opinions fairly and honestly laid before his country—he with his great powers, will be able to captivate his country and to lead them in the course he desires. . . . If he follows these badly expressed counsels he will succeed.[12]

After the speech from the throne, as indicated above, the first item on the government's, but not Mill's, agenda was the cattle plague. The official figures, which may significantly underestimate the magnitude of the devastation,[13] indicate that by the end of 1865 some 73,000 animals had been infected. To prevent its further spread, livestock farmers and their representatives in parliament (landlords whose incomes were also threatened) wanted a prohibition on the movement of cattle and compulsory slaughter of diseased animals and their contacts, with adequate compensation being paid to the owners of such animals.[14] Within a week of the opening of parliament, the government presented to the House of Commons a bill incorporating these principles.[15]

The most notable participants in the debate on the Cattle Diseases Bill were Robert Lowe, Lord Cranborne, John Bright, and Mill, making his maiden speech. Lowe and Cranborne criticized the government for having failed to act with a swiftness and energy commensurate with what they deemed to be a crisis of national proportions. The plague's impact on the supply of healthy meat and milk, they claimed, affected

12 Yale University.

13 On 9 February Lord Spencer declared that 120,000 deaths of cattle could be attributed to the plague. *PD*, 3rd ser., vol. 181, cols. 295–9.

14 For the agricultural and veterinary context of the cattle plague, see Arved B. Erickson, "The Cattle Plague in England, 1865–1867," *Agricultural History*, 35 (1961), 94–103, and Sherwin A. Hall, "The Cattle Plague of 1865," *Medical History*, 6 (1962), 45–58. For a brief account of the administrative and parliamentary response to the plague, see W.L. Burn, *The Age of Equipoise* (London: Allen and Unwin, 1964), pp. 212–16.

15 The bill was introduced by the home secretary, Sir George Grey, on 12 February; see *PD*, 3rd ser., vol. 181, cols. 355–82.

consumers as well as producers.[16] Generous provision for compensation would have to be made so that it would be in the farmers' interest to slaughter animals that might otherwise spread the disease. Bright vehemently disagreed. "Nothing can be more monstrous than the notion that the public ought to be called upon to make up to private persons all losses in consequence of accident, or, as it is called in this case, of a visitation of Providence."[17]

Mill in truth had no particular interest in the subject itself, remarking to Edwin Chadwick on 10 February that he would be happy to see the latter at the House in a couple of days' time "as the debate being on the Cattle Plague, I shall not feel bound to pay any special attention to it."[18] But he used the debate as an opportunity to establish for himself a presence in the Commons, serving notice on the House of his determination to take an active part in its proceedings. Therefore he entered on Bright's side, although Mill did not object to the principle of compensation.

He argued that the amount provided by the bill was excessive and would induce the farmer "to be careless as to the spread of the disease; because if his animals on becoming infected were ordered to be slaughtered, he knew he should get an exaggerated compensation for them."[19] Mill also objected to the source of the compensation. The bill stipulated that the burden should fall chiefly upon the county rate. According to Mill, it proposed to compensate "a class for the results of a calamity which was borne by the whole community," whereas it should have required "farmers who had not suffered . . . to compensate those who had."[20]

The debate on the cattle plague was not what it seemed on the surface, and the argument and alliances it spawned were heavily condi-

16 For Lowe's speeches on the cattle plague, see ibid., cols. 484–8 (14 Feb. 1866) and 618–20 (16 Feb. 1866); for Cranborne's, see ibid., cols. 492–7 (14 Feb. 1866).

17 Ibid., col. 474. The Bill proposed that the farmer should receive for his slaughtered animal two-thirds of its market value when healthy.

18 *Later Letters* [*LL*], ed. Francis E. Mineka and Dwight N. Lindley, *CW*, vols. XIV–XVII (Toronto: University of Toronto Press, 1972), vol. XVI, p. 1147.

19 *PPS*, *CW*, vol. XXVIII, p. 48 (14 Feb. 1866); for Mill's speech on the second reading of the Bill, see ibid., pp. 47–9. To the chagrin of the Tories, Gladstone, apparently only too happy to make use of the arguments Bright and Mill presented to the House, acknowledged that they had identified a blemish in the bill. He thereupon proceeded to move that the level of compensation be reduced from two-thirds to one-half the value of the animal when healthy, an amendment accepted by the House. See *PD*, 3rd ser., vol. 181, cols. 527–9 and 540–1 (14 Feb. 1866).

20 *PPS*, *CW*, vol. XXVIII, p. 49; for Mill's response during committee stage to an attack launched upon his position by Lowe, see ibid., pp. 51–2 (16 Feb. 1866).

tioned by the extraneous issue of parliamentary reform. Lowe and Cranborne would be among the first hounds in the anti-reform pack in 1866 and 1867; Bright and Mill would be among the keenest advocates of franchise extension. Two complementary objectives shaped the attitude of Lowe and Cranborne to the Cattle Bill: first, to show that the government that was about to sail on hazardous seas in the ship of reform had reacted tardily and feebly to a national emergency; second, to demonstrate that, however unsatisfactory the ministry might be, the House of Commons as at present constituted was fully capable of dealing promptly, decisively, and constructively with the matter at hand. Bright and Mill, conversely, had to hammer away at the question of compensation to expose the tendency of a House of Commons controlled by the landed classes to legislate in their interest at the expense of the rest of the community. In drawing the attention of the House to the unfairness inherent in the bill's compensation provisions, Mill confessed that he did not blame the government for proceeding as it had, "considering the way in which the House was constituted."[21] He also treated his colleagues to a brief disquisition on the disparity between aristocracy as it should be and as it was:

> An aristocracy should have the feelings of an aristocracy, and inasmuch as they enjoyed the highest honours and advantages, they ought to be willing to bear the first brunt of the inconveniences and evils which fell on the country generally. This was the ideal character of an aristocracy; it was the character with which all privileged classes were accustomed to credit themselves; though he was not aware of any aristocracy in history that had fulfilled those requirements.[22]

Thus Mill used the compensation issue to illustrate the self-serving nature of aristocratic government and the need for a thorough reform of parliament.[23]

Once Mill's intention to take an active part in the proceedings of the House had been made clear, his interventions in the 1866 parliamentary reform debate were awaited with considerable interest by the other members and the public. As an eminent political philosopher who in the recent past had given much thought to the subject—in *Thoughts on Parliamentary Reform* (1859), "Recent Writers on Reform" (1859), and *Considerations on Representative Government* (1861)—he could claim to speak with a

21 Ibid., p. 49.

22 Ibid.

23 For a fuller discussion of Mill's response to the Cattle Diseases Bill, see B.L. Kinzer, "Mill and the Cattle Plague," *Mill News Letter*, 19 (1984), 2–12.

measure of authority. He could not assume, however, that many members of the House were favourably disposed towards the specific recommendations he had formerly made. A reform package that included adult suffrage limited only by an educational qualification, plural voting (based not on property but on mental fitness), and Thomas Hare's scheme of personal representation could expect to find few friends in the House, even among Radicals. The initiative in any case, as Mill well knew, did not lie with him but with the Russell-Gladstone government, and everyone understood that the author of *Representative Government* would not be the leaders' prompter.

Nonetheless, Mill cared a great deal about the content of a reform measure. In February 1865, five months before his triumph at Westminster and eight months before Palmerston's death, he took a decidedly gloomy view of the prospects for parliamentary reform. He told Max Kyllman: "no Reform Bill which we are likely to see for some time to come, will be worth moving hand or foot for."[24] By the end of the year he had come to see things somewhat differently, explaining to Chadwick: "The whole of our laws of election from top to bottom require to be reconstructed on new principles: but to get those principles into people's heads is work for many years, and they will not wait that time for the next step in reform. . . . And perhaps some measure of reform is as likely to promote as to delay other improvements in the representative system."[25]

Mill could reasonably suppose that the "next step" would in some fashion take up not only the suffrage question but also the redistribution of seats. He acknowledged that a bill dealing solely with the former would jeopardize the progress he wished to make on the latter. The proposal and passage of such a limited bill now, Mill warned Hare, would exclude the subject of personal representation from the sphere of parliamentary discussion for some time. Once a reform bill had been enacted, "the whole subject of changes in the representation will be tabooed for years to come."[26] Mill did not expect the Liberal administration to bring in a bill that incorporated the views he and Hare held, nor did he hope to bring the House around to their way of thinking. The most he could hope for was that the measure would be sufficiently broad in scope to allow consideration of the views. For this achievement it was necessary that he be listened to in debate; he had learnt, especially from his Irish intervention, how easily he could alienate the members on both sides of the House by displays of what they saw as intemperate radicalism.

24 *LL*, *CW*, vol. XVI, p. 997 (15 Feb. 1865).
25 Ibid., p. 1129 (29 Dec. 1865).
26 Ibid., pp. 1138–9 (11 Jan. 1866).

This elasticity did not signify a waning allegiance to the reform programme delineated in *Representative Government.* Mill's assessment reflected an important shift in political context that was both personal and parliamentary. Mill was now member for Westminster; Palmerston was dead; Russell and Gladstone had left no doubt that parliamentary reform would be the centrepiece of their 1866 legislative endeavours. Mill could either separate himself from Gladstone by refusing to support the Liberals' bill and argue for what was (at present) impossible—quite probably before a deaf House; or he could pragmatically offer support for a moderate but achievable step in the right direction. Mill chose to follow where Gladstone led on this critical question; by following he would, when he could without hindering the more immediate good, introduce the future best to an attentive House.

There was more than just hope of immediate or future franchise reforms determining Mill's behaviour. He had formulated a political strategy which could not be separated from Gladstone's political fortunes. For some time before 1866 Mill had admired Gladstone, to whom he had sent a complimentary set of *Dissertations and Discussions* seven years earlier. Mill informed the grateful recipient that "in venturing to send you my last publication, I intended a mark of respect to one of the very few political men whose public conduct appears to me to be invariably conscientious, and in whom desire of the public good is an active principle, instead of at most, a passive restraint."[27] Mill appreciated Gladstone's earnestness, his restless and powerful intelligence, his prodigious administrative capacity. In 1866 Mill associated his own presence in parliament with a project for the construction of an advanced Liberal party. To Theodor Gomperz he wrote: "One ought to be very sure of being able to do something in politics that cannot be as well done by others, to justify one for the sacrifice of time and energies that might be employed on higher work. Time will show whether it was worth while to make this sacrifice for the sake of anything I am capable of doing towards forming a really advanced liberal party which, I have long been convinced, cannot be done except in the House of Commons."[28] As Mill saw it, Gladstone alone had the experience, stature, and ability necessary to lead a radicalized Liberal party. Yet the parliamentary sessions of 1866 and 1867 brutally exposed Gladstone's political vulnerability. Mill was determined to do whatever he could to assist the man whom he believed indispensable to the achievement of the fundamental political realignment Mill sought to facilitate.

27 Ibid., vol. XV, p. 632 (6 Aug. 1859).
28 Ibid., vol. XVI, pp. 1196–7 (22 Aug. 1866).

The radicalization of the Liberal party, however, would require more than a Gladstonian ascendancy. No less needful was the effective integration of the working classes within a transformed Liberal party if it was to be more interested in accelerating progress than in congratulating itself on what had already been accomplished. "Land and money," Mill declared in an extraparliamentary speech delivered one day before his oration on the second reading of the 1866 Reform Bill, were "the leading powers in this country."[29] Aristocratic and middle-class prejudices retarded social and political improvement. Only a sizeable injection of working-class influence could make the Liberal party a dynamic instrument of political progress. One of Gladstone's principal merits, from Mill's vantage point, was his sympathy for the aspirations of the working classes. In the same speech, occasioned by a reform meeting held in St. James's Hall on 12 April, Mill paid tribute to the service Gladstone had rendered the working classes:

> Every year of his official life had been marked by a succession of measures—no year being without them—some great, some small, but all aiming at the public good—to the good of the people of this country, and especially of the poorer classes. These measures were not even suggested to him; they were the offspring of his own mind, will, and purpose—the free gift from him to his country-men, unprompted, unsuggested. . . . Was it not Mr. Gladstone who first broke silence on the subject of reform after the ridiculous failure of 1860? and he was the man who made that celebrated declaration that every human being, inasmuch as he had an interest in good government, had a *prima facie* cause for admission to the suffrage.[30] If we do not stand by him as he is doing our work—if he fails from any defect of ours, from the want of encouragement to go on—the consequence will be that we shall richly deserve to suffer, for we shall not easily find another to serve us in the same way.[31]

Mill put together Gladstonian leadership, franchise extension, and the growth of working-class activism (already exhibited in the Reform League) to come up with a new and better political order. At the beginning of 1866 he told H.S. Chapman: "English statesmanship will have to assume a new character, and look in a more direct way than before to the interests of posterity. We are now . . . standing on the very boundary

29 *PPS*, *CW*, vol. XXVIII, p. 55 (12 April 1866).

30 See *PD*, 3rd ser., vol. 175, col. 324 (11 May 1864).

31 *PPS*, *CW*, vol. XXVIII, p. 58.

line between this new statesmanship and the old; and the next generation will be accustomed to a very different set of political arguments and topics from those of the present and past."[32] To understand Mill's involvement in the combat over parliamentary reform, therefore, it is not to the *Autobiography* (or to *Considerations on Representative Government*) that we must turn; rather it is to the parliamentary situation, to the combat itself, and to Mill's interpretation of its significance.

The Reform Bill Gladstone introduced on 12 March provided for a reduction in the borough household qualification from £10 to £7 and for a county occupation franchise of £14. It was a franchise bill pure and simple.[33] Had it passed, working-class voters would have constituted approximately a quarter of the total electorate of England and Wales. The Tories were not inclined to mount a frontal assault on the measure, preferring to let Robert Lowe and the band of Liberal renegades hostile to parliamentary reform (designated the "Adullamites" by Bright) make the running. Although the bulk of Mill's fine speech on 13 April focused on the need for working-class enfranchisement, the occasion for it was a motion tabled by Lord Grosvenor (an Adullamite) and seconded by Lord Stanley (a Conservative for whom Mill had considerable respect) that called for a postponement of the bill's second reading until a redistribution scheme had been presented. Mill, knowing that the Adullamites and their Tory sympathizers wanted to wreck the bill, apprehended that from such a wreckage Gladstone would not emerge without serious injury. That Mill must have agreed with the substance of Grosvenor's motion did not move him to support it. The preface to his elegant argument on behalf of parliamentary reform was devoted to a defence of the ministry's exclusive concentration on the franchise. Mill insisted that the bill, though "far more moderate than is desired by the majority of reformers," significantly enlarged working-class electoral power and was therefore "not only a valuable part of a scheme of Parliamentary Reform, but highly valuable even if nothing else were to follow."[34]

Mill's eloquent contribution to the debate on the second reading of the Reform Bill entailed more than mere partisan support. It was the work

32 *LL*, *CW*, vol. XVI, p. 1137 (6 Jan. 1866).

33 For the cabinet's decision not to take up redistribution, see Cowling, *1867*, pp. 99–100. After indicating in March that it would offer a Seats Bill only after the second reading of the Franchise Bill, the government introduced the measure on 7 May. On 31 May Mill spoke on this bill and briefly argued the case for personal representation. He did not oppose Gladstone's redistribution scheme.

34 *PPS*, *CW*, vol. XXVIII, pp. 60–1. Gladstone's diary entry for 13 April includes: "Reform Debate. Mill admirable." *Gladstone Diaries*, ed. H.C.G. Matthew, vol. VI: *1861–1868* (Oxford: Clarendon Press, 1978), p. 430.

of a political prospector staking out politically important ground that he considered himself especially fit to mine. Recognizing that Gladstone's bill could be headed for trouble, Mill urged that debate not focus on the pros and cons of democracy, for "this is not a democratic measure."[35] Opponents of democracy had no cause to oppose the bill. Its principle, Mill maintained, involved not the representation of individuals, but of the class to which those individuals belong: "The opponents of reform are accustomed to say, that the constitution knows nothing of individuals, but only of classes. Individuals, they tell us, cannot complain of not being represented, so long as the class they belong to is represented. But if any class is unrepresented, or has not its proper share of representation relatively to others, that is a grievance. Now, all that need be asked at present is that this theory be applied to practice."[36]

The great merit of the bill, he argued, was that it would make the working classes "a substantial power in this House" without making them the predominant power. No one need fear the consequences, which would be wholly salutary. The franchise extension proposed could not give the labouring classes a controlling influence over legislation; it would merely ensure that the working classes be heard in the House of Commons. That they be heard was essential to their protection and to the nation's future well-being. "Every class knows some things not so well known to other people, and every class has interests more or less special to itself, and for which no protection is so effectual as its own. . . . I claim the benefit of these principles for the working classes."[37] Conceding adequate representation to the working classes would serve an educative no less than a protective function. "I can hardly conceive a nobler course of national education than the debates of this House would become, if the notions, right or wrong, which are fermenting in the minds of the working classes, many of which go down very deep into the foundations of society and government, were fairly stated and genuinely discussed within these walls."[38]

These assertions, of course, are entirely consistent with the arguments presented in *Thoughts on Parliamentary Reform* and *Considerations on Representative Government.* What is new is that they are employed on behalf of a measure that in detail had little in common with Mill's preferences. Mill strongly endorsed the bill because it was Gladstone's. If passed under Gladstone's auspices, even this "moderate" bill could do much to further

35 *PPS*, *CW*, vol. XXVIII, p. 61.
36 Ibid.
37 Ibid., p. 65.
38 Ibid., p. 66.

Mill's political objectives. Its success would strengthen Gladstone's hold over the party and give the working classes a real presence within the system. Such success, however, depended in part upon persuading cautious members of parliament that they should encourage rather than resist this presence. Thus Mill adopts a conciliatory tone, acknowledging the "good sense and good feeling which have made the governing classes of this country ... capable of ... advancing with the times."[39] Mill showed a modicum of respectfulness towards the establishment and affirmed the non-radical character of the proposed change with a view to maximizing his usefulness both to Gladstone and to the advancement of working-class interests.

The bill, and the government whose child it was, survived for another two months. On 18 June Lord Dunkellin's amendment to substitute a rating for a rental franchise in the boroughs was carried against the ministry by a vote of 315 to 304.[40] A week later the Russell-Gladstone government resigned. Throughout its difficulties over the reform question, Mill had steadfastly adhered to the Gladstonian line.[41] In the aftermath of the bill's defeat, Mill spoke to a meeting of Westminster electors on 23 June. He denounced the Tories and eulogized Gladstone, "the greatest parliamentary leader which the country had had in the present century, or, perhaps, since the time of the Stuarts."[42]

The balance Mill showed at this time is most impressive. While doing what he could to give Gladstone a boost, he in no way jeopardized his own standing with the politically aware members of the labouring classes. He announced his belief that "the educated artisans, those especially who take an interest in politics, are the most teachable of our classes. They have much to make them so; they are, as a rule, more in earnest than any other class; their opinions are more genuine, less influenced by what so greatly influences some of the other classes—the desire of getting on; their social position is not such as to breed self-conceit."[43] The cause of popular

39 Ibid., p. 67.

40 A rating value of £7 was approximately equal to an £8 rental value. The intent of the amendment was to restrict the extent of working-class enfranchisement. Mill's prediction that the bill would be "carried by increasing instead of diminishing majorities" proved mistaken. *PPS, CW,* vol. XXVIII, p. 57 (12 April 1866).

41 Kate Amberley recorded in her journal on 23 June a conversation with Gladstone: "I told him that Mill was so grieved at the Govt. going out, and said that ... he had never hoped to be under a leader with whom he could feel so much sympathy and respect as he did for Gladstone, and Gladstone answered 'Poor fellow, he has all through been most kind and indulgent to me.'" *Amberley Papers,* vol. I, p. 516.

42 *PPS, CW,* vol. XXVIII, p. 89.

43 Ibid., p. 66.

education, Mill contended, "would be most forwarded by the presence of working people's representatives in this House. . . . Unless I am mistaken . . . very few years of a real working-class representation would have passed over our heads, before there would be in every parish a school-rate, and the school doors freely open to all the world; and in one generation from that time England would be an educated nation."[44] Mill's sympathies penetrated far below the upper crust of the labouring classes. His zeal for improvement embraced the suffering masses of mid-Victorian England:

> Are there not all the miseries of an old and crowded society waiting to be dealt with—the curse of ignorance, the curse of pauperism, the curse of disease, the curse of a whole population born and nurtured in crime? (*Cheers.*) All these things we are just beginning to look at—just touching with the tips of our fingers; and by the time two or three more generations are dead and gone, we may perhaps have discovered how to keep them alive, and how to make their lives worth having. I must needs think that we should get on much faster with all this—the most important part of the business of government in our days—if those who are the chief sufferers by the great chronic evils of our civilisation had representatives among us to stimulate our zeal, as well as to inform us by their experience.[45]

In Mill's attempt to smelt the ore of party Liberalism to obtain the metal, working-class agitation and participation were to be the key agents. Mill's conduct inside and outside the House of Commons in relation to both Gladstone's position and the aspirations of the politically conscious members of the working classes resonates with an acute sensitivity to new forces at work and their potential for constructive political engagement.

That conduct, however, wore a somewhat different public face following the resignation of Russell and Gladstone in late June 1866. The formation of a minority Conservative government headed by Derby and Disraeli told Mill that he need no longer eschew aggressive advocacy of radical views to which he had usually given but circumspect expression while Gladstone was leader of the House of Commons. Although Mill remained as committed as before to avoiding actions that might create difficulties for Gladstone, this determination now required a much less severe self-restraint than had the circumstances of the first half of 1866.

44 Ibid., pp. 67, 68.
45 Ibid., p. 67.

Having no sympathy whatever for the Tory government, Mill felt himself able to adopt an expansive interpretation of his political independence. Yet it would be misleading to suggest that he saw himself as an entirely free agent. He had by no means given up on Gladstone, and the intensification of the extraparliamentary agitation in the summer of 1866 reinforced his adherence to a strategy whose goal was the radicalization of the Liberal party.

That those who had contributed to the defeat of the Liberal Reform Bill should now sit on the government front benches aroused the forces out of doors for whom parliamentary reform was the first order of business. Both the Manchester-based Reform Union, dominated by the middle class, and the metropolitan-based Reform League, dominated by artisan groups, went on the offensive.[46] The League, eager to impress upon the new government the earnestness of the labouring classes on the question of the franchise, announced that a public demonstration would be held in Hyde Park on 23 July. The right to hold mass public meetings had been one of the issues galvanizing those responsible for the foundation of the Reform League. The view of the Derby ministry, one that was not contradicted by Sir George Grey, a former Liberal home secretary, was that royal parks were not appropriate locations for public meetings and that such gatherings were prohibited by law.[47] The Tory home secretary, Spencer Walpole, authorized Sir Richard Mayne, metropolitan police commissioner, to promulgate an order forbidding the meeting.[48] At about 6 p.m. on 23 July the Leaguers, led by their president, Edmond Beales, arrived at the locked gates of Hyde Park and were confronted by a police barricade. Beales did not mind the government thinking he carried the match that could ignite an agitation of truly menacing proportions, but he had no intention of striking that match. On being informed that the demonstrators would not be admitted to the park, Beales (a barrister, it should perhaps be noted) marched his legions off to Trafalgar Square. The confusion arising from the shift, aggravated by the turbulence of a crowd that apparently included more than a few ruffians out for a bit of fun, resulted in the felling of the Hyde Park railings. Three days of commotion in the Hyde Park area ensued. Damage

46 For the public agitation, see Cowling, *1867*, pp. 242–86; Frances Elma Gillespie, *Labor and Politics in England, 1850–1867* (Durham, NC: Duke University Press, 1927), pp. 235–88; and Royden Harrison, *Before the Socialists: Studies in Labour and Politics, 1861–1881* (London: Routledge & Kegan Paul, 1965), pp. 78–136. Both the Union and the League had endorsed Gladstone's Reform Bill.

47 For Grey's speech, see *PD*, 3rd ser., vol. 184, cols. 1074–5 (19 July 1866).

48 See ibid., cols. 1073–4 (19 July 1866).

to the grounds was fairly extensive and some two hundred people were injured.[49]

Mill participated in the 24 July debate in the House sparked by the Hyde Park imbroglio. His speech, delivered in a House where many members felt they had good cause to be alarmed at the recent (and continuing) turn of events, was remarkably bold. Laying responsibility squarely at the government's door, Mill declared they had attempted to enforce an exclusion for which there could be no justification. In doing so, they had precipitated the disturbance and heightened bad feeling between the governing classes and the masses. "Noble Lords and right honourable Gentlemen opposite may be congratulated on having done a job of work last night which will require wiser men than they are, many years to efface the consequences of."[50]

Disraeli, cognizant that Mill's opinions on this matter were shared by few MPs on either side of the House, rose when Mill resumed his seat. He opened with a remark calculated to accentuate Mill's isolation: "I take it for granted . . . that the speech we have just heard is one of those intended to be delivered in Hyde Park, and if I may judge from it as a sample, we can gather a very good idea of the rhetoric which will prevail at those periodical meetings we are promised." Brilliantly highlighting the contrast, as he would have it, between the responsible conduct of ministers of the crown and the irresponsible language of the eminent member for Westminster, Disraeli vigorously rejected Mill's imputations. He denied that the government was opposed to working-class political meetings, but insisted that such meetings should be held "at the proper time and place." The 23rd of July at Hyde Park, Disraeli implied, was neither, as the "riot, tumult, and disturbance" unleashed by the League's initiative unhappily demonstrated.[51]

Mill devotes more than a page of the *Autobiography* to the curious and rather enigmatic dénouement of the Hyde Park affair. The Reform League, claiming the right of free assembly, announced plans to hold a

49 Henry Broadhurst, who was present, gives a useful account of the riots in his autobiography, *The Story of His Life from a Stonemason's Bench to the Treasury Bench* (London: Hutchinson, 1901), pp. 33–40; for a contemporary press report, see the *Daily News*, 24 July 1866, p. 5; see also Donald C. Richter, *Riotous Victorians* (Athens, Ohio: Ohio University Press, 1981), pp. 51–61.

50 *PPS*, *CW*, vol. XXVIII, p. 100. Matthew Arnold's linking of Mill and Jacobinism in *Culture and Anarchy* derived at least in part from Arnold's hostile reaction to the Hyde Park riots and Mill's defence of the Reform League. See *Culture and Anarchy*, R.H. Super, ed., *Complete Prose Works of Matthew Arnold*, vol. V (Ann Arbor: University of Michigan Press, 1965), pp. 111, 132–3.

51 *PD*, 3rd ser., vol. 184, cols. 1412–14.

meeting in Hyde Park on 31 July in defiance of the government. Mill shared the common perception that serious violence would erupt from such a confrontation, without any benefit. Having successfully persuaded leading members of the League to cancel the plan, he agreed to address a League meeting at the Agricultural Hall on the 30th.[52] He believed that he had been "the means of preventing much mischief." A trace of bitterness can be detected in this account, a bitterness directed not against the League but against certain elements of the metropolitan press that at the time had accused him of being "intemperate and passionate." "I do not know," he says, "what they expected from me; but they had reason to be thankful to me if they knew from what I had in all probability preserved them. And I do not believe it could have been done, at that particular juncture, by anyone else."[53]

The object of reviewing this well-known episode is not to assess the accuracy of Mill's claims, but to understand the motives that moved him to act as he did. What Mill reported no doubt did occur, but his version perhaps assigns too much weight to his intervention. It may be that he exaggerates the effectiveness of his pacifying role in the rough-and-tumble of late July.[54] Whatever the practical import of Mill's involvement with the League at the end of July 1866, the whole business usefully illuminates the purposeful intent that fashioned his response to the reform crisis of 1866–7. Mill cast himself as the unofficial (and unappointed) mediator between Gladstone and the Reform League. Through Gladstone, he reasoned, the working classes could be integrated into the political process. The mode of achieving this worthy end could also contribute to a transmutation of the Liberal party, making it an effectual instrument of social and political reform.[55] For Gladstone to surmount his current political problems and secure the ascendancy Mill wished him to have, he had to maintain a respectable distance between himself and the radicalism of the Reform League. Mill, and in this he resembled Bright, tried to hold

52 *PPS*, *CW*, vol. XXVIII, pp. 102–5.

53 *A*, *CW*, vol. I, pp. 278–9.

54 Evelyn L. Pugh, "J.S. Mill's *Autobiography* and the Hyde Park Riots," *Research Studies*, 50 (1982), 1–20.

55 A statement in a letter Mill wrote to Fawcett at the beginning of the year reveals something of what he had in mind: "One of the most important consequences of giving a share in the government to the working classes, is that there will then be some members of the House with whom it will no longer be an axiom that human society exists for the sake of property in land—a grovelling superstition which is still in full force among the higher classes." *LL*, *CW*, vol. XVI, p. 1130 (1 Jan. 1866).

for Gladstone strategically significant territory that Gladstone himself could not afford to occupy.[56]

Not much should be made of Mill's refusal to join the Reform League. Given the strong exception he took to its programme of manhood suffrage (on which Mill may have believed at the time the League to be wavering—towards universal suffrage)[57] and the ballot, his association with its struggle is impressive. In declining an invitation to join the League, Mill observed that "the general promotion of the Reform cause is the main point at present, and ... advanced reformers, without suppressing their opinions on the points on which they may still differ, should act together as one man in the common cause."[58] The Leaguers surely could not find fault with the case Mill stated in his major speech in the Commons on the 1866 Reform Bill, or with the manner of his stating it. His performance in the debate on the second reading had shown him ready and willing to act "in the common cause." In the controversy over Hyde Park, Mill not only defended the League's right to meet there, but also sent in a £5 donation to assist those who had been arrested by the police on 23 July.[59] Six months later Mill participated in a delegation that put before Walpole a formal request for the appointment of a working man to the Royal Commission on Trades Unions.[60] In the summer of 1867 he subscribed to a Reform League fund created to organize the newly enfranchised electors on behalf of advanced Liberalism.[61] He eagerly lent his voice to the talking-out of the 1867 Parks Bill, the Tory government's restrictive legislative answer to the demand for access to Hyde Park.[62] And in 1868 he contributed financially to the needy campaign chests of a number of League-connected working-class candidates.[63]

In late July 1866 Mill had used what influence he had with the League to urge caution. An easing of the war of nerves between the authorities and the agitators was necessary if violence were to be prevented. Mill asserted himself not merely for the sake of peace. Indeed, he had no wish

56 For a stimulating discussion of Bright, Mill, and the emergence of the Gladstonian Liberal party, see John Vincent, *The Formation of the Liberal Party, 1857–1868* (London: Constable, 1966), pp. 149–211.

57 *LL*, *CW*, vol. XVI, p. 1151 (26 Feb. 1866).

58 *LL*, *CW*, vol. XVII, pp. 2010–11 (to [George Howell?], 22 July 1865).

59 *LL*, *CW*, vol. XVI, p. 1186 (to Beales, 26 July 1866).

60 See *PPS*, *CW*, vol. XXVIII, pp. 133–4, and letter to George Jacob Holyoake, *LL*, *CW*, vol. XVI, pp. 1242–3 (16 Feb. 1867).

61 *LL*, *CW*, vol. XVI, pp. 1291–2 (to Beales, 22 July 1867).

62 *PPS*, *CW*, vol. XXVIII, pp. 215–17, 236–8.

63 See Vincent, *Formation of the Liberal Party*, p. 159.

for the conflict between the government and the League to disappear; rather, he sought to enclose the League's expression of that conflict within bounds prescribed by the goal of building and sustaining an unofficial and necessarily unacknowledged alliance between Gladstone and the working-class reform movement.

The same concern prompted Mill in early 1867 to call upon the League to exercise self-restraint. In late February delegates representing the League and the trade unions met to remind the government that the working classes were not to be trifled with. This conference resulted in the adoption of an unmistakably militant resolution. In the event of governmental resistance to working-class enfranchisement, the conference proclaimed, it would "be necessary to consider the propriety of those classes adopting a universal cessation from labour until their political rights are conceded."[64] The *Morning Star* reported that the speeches given at the conference were demagogic.[65] Disturbed by what he read of the meeting, Mill wrote to William Randal Cremer, a leading figure in trade union and radical political circles, to protest against the extreme rhetoric employed on the occasion. Any reform bill acceptable to parliament, Mill argued, would in the nature of things have to be a compromise. Menacing language hinting at "revolutionary expedients" should be avoided by those leading the agitation. He unequivocally stated that in England the conditions that might justify a revolution did not exist.[66] Although League members had been given "ample provocation and abundant excuse" for their "feelings of irritation," they ought not to allow such irritation to rob them of their sense of proportion. Imprudence would harm the cause of reform. Especially arousing Mill's displeasure was evidence "of a determined rejection beforehand of all compromise on the Reform question, even if proposed by the public men in whose sincerity & zeal as reformers you have repeatedly expressed the fullest confidence."[67] Mill feared that the tenuous line joining Gladstone to the working-class reform movement was beginning to fragment. The course

64 Quoted in Gillespie, *Labor and Politics*, p. 284.

65 *Morning Star*, 28 Feb. 1867, p. 2.

66 What conditions could justify revolution? "One is personal oppression & tyranny & consequent personal suffering of such intensity that to put an immediate stop to them is worth almost any amount of present evil & future danger. The other is when either the system of government does not permit the redress of grievances to be sought by peaceable & legal means, or when those means have been perseveringly exerted to the utmost for a long series of years, & their inefficacy has been demonstrated by experiment." Letter to Cremer, *LL*, *CW*, vol. XVI, p. 1248 (1 March 1867).

67 Ibid., pp. 1247–8.

pursued by Derby and Disraeli in 1867 further jeopardized the enterprise to which Mill had committed himself.

From their accession, the Conservatives had been concerned over parliamentary reform, approaching the issue with more indecisiveness than enthusiasm. When the parliamentary battle was joined, it centred on attempts to finesse details of qualifications of the borough householders. Offering borough household suffrage, the bill produced by Derby and Disraeli also stipulated that only male heads of households who paid their rates directly should be eligible for the franchise. In the interest of convenience, 171 boroughs practised the composition of rates, whereby the local authorities compounded with the landlords for the payment of the occupiers' rates.[68] The names of compound householders did not appear on the rating book and they therefore would be excluded from the vote under clause 3 of the Tory bill. However flexible in committee Disraeli would show himself to be, he rigidly insisted that the bill would stand or fall on the personal ratepaying requirement.[69]

Calculation and conviction led Gladstone to denounce the bill as arbitrary and fraudulent. Early in the debate on clause 3 he moved to eradicate for electoral purposes the distinction between direct ratepayers and compounders, although holding no brief for household suffrage "pure and simple." Still sore from the bruising he had taken the previous session, he now acted to restore his authority by attacking that aspect of the Tory bill that he found most objectionable. The outcome he looked for was defeat of the government and settlement of the question on terms that satisfied his own preferences. He got neither. In the division of

68 There were approximately 486,000 compound householders in parliamentary boroughs. The system spared the occupier the bother of putting aside money to meet his quarterly rating obligations. What was in it for the landlord and local authority? "A deduction of twenty or twenty-five per cent was allowed when the rate was compounded, so that the owner of fifty or a hundred small houses derived no small profit by calling on his tenants to pay the full rate in their rent, while he had a discount in paying it over to the parish. Naturally it was convenient for the parish to be saved the trouble of collecting from the small occupiers." Charles Seymour, *Electoral Reform in England and Wales: The Development and Operation of the Parliamentary Franchise, 1832–1885* (New Haven: Yale University Press, 1915), p. 149.

69 "The bill as it went into committee included no lodger franchise. . . . The Act enfranchised all £10 lodgers in parliamentary boroughs. The county occupation franchise in the bill began at £15 p.a. In the Act it was lowered to £12 and supplemented by a £5 franchise for copyholders. The period of qualifying residence was two years in the bill, one in the Act. The provision to allow voters to vote by voting papers, which was included in the bill, was removed by the time it was passed." Cowling, *1867*, p. 223.

12 April, forty-seven Liberals, a number of Radicals among them, rejected Gladstone's leadership. The amendment went down by a vote of 310 to 289. Disraeli, it was abundantly clear to all, would do no business with Gladstone. The Radicals who did not answer Gladstone's call figured that Disraeli would, in the end, find it necessary to do business with them. They put the survival of the bill before a parliamentary victory for Gladstone. In his diary Gladstone tersely recorded: "A smash perhaps without example."[70] Mill, voting with the minority, stayed in Gladstone's company.[71]

Mill's only substantive speech on the ratepaying issue was given in the debate that saw Gladstone up his bid in a final attempt to stop Disraeli in his tracks. On 6 May Disraeli told the House that the government could not accept the amendment of J.T. Hibbert, Radical MP for Oldham, that would allow those compounders choosing to opt out of composition to pay the reduced (composite) rate. The government, Disraeli indicated, would instead introduce an amendment permitting such compounders to deduct the rate, to be paid in full, from the rent received by their landords.[72] Disraeli added that the administration would regard the matter as a question of confidence. Gladstone took up the challenge, advising the House to reject Disraeli's amendment.[73]

Mill's correspondence of the 6th reveals the gravity with which he approached the debate that he joined on the 9th. Explaining to Thomas Hare his inability to attend Max Kyllman's funeral service in Manchester on the 7th, Mill cited "the absolute necessity of my being present at a most critical debate and division on the Reform Bill."[74] The tone and content of his speech issued from his reading of what was at stake. He criticized Disraeli for politicizing the ratepaying question and for recommending an amendment that would increase electoral corruption. Mill did not expect the government to attend to his complaints; his words were aimed at those Radicals who previously had disregarded Gladstone's counsel. "I hope that honourable Gentlemen on this side of the House, who loving household suffrage not wisely but too well, have brought matters to this state, intend to come down handsomely to the registration societies in

70 *Gladstone Diaries*, vol. VI, p. 513.

71 For the division, see *PD*, 3rd ser., vol. 186, col. 1700 (12 April 1867).

72 Robert Blake, Disraeli's most authoritative modern biographer, states that this counter-amendment "would in practice have been either legally meaningless or administratively unworkable." *Disraeli* (New York: St. Martin's, 1967), p. 470.

73 See Cowling, *1867*, pp. 269–71.

74 *LL*, *CW*, vol. XVI, p. 1267; to Edward Kyllman, Max Kyllman's brother, Mill wrote of this debate and division as "unhappily among the most critical in the whole progress of the Reform Bill." Ibid., 1268.

their own neighbourhoods; for the registration societies are destined henceforth to be one of the great institutions of the country."[75] Shortly thereafter Mill warned those Radicals who had evinced a tendency to act on the supposition that more of what they wanted could be had from Disraeli than from Gladstone that a heavy price (monetarily and politically) would be exacted at the polls for their determination "to outwit the Chancellor of the Exchequer, and make his Bill bring forth pure and simple household suffrage, contrary to the intentions of everybody except themselves who will vote for it."[76] Fifty-eight Liberals (advanced and otherwise), refusing to heed Gladstone or Mill, voted with the government, whose amendment carried by a majority of sixty-six.

The sentiments Mill expressed on 9 May did not originate in a conviction that household suffrage was a bad idea in itself. His objective was to make his free-wheeling Radical colleagues realize that whereas they reckoned Disraeli could be made to play their game, they might very well be playing his. If that were so, they could wind up swallowing a brand of household suffrage that would not easily go down even Radical throats. More importantly, Mill wanted them to understand that purchasing any bill of goods from Disraeli at Gladstone's political expense could severely harm the prospects for the formation of a powerful advanced Liberal party.

Gladstone could scarcely seek out of doors the comfort Disraeli denied him within. The stepped-up pace of the extraparliamentary agitation in the spring of 1867 did nothing to strengthen Gladstone's hand. In 1866 the Leaguers might have thought a £7 franchise bill more attractive than anything the Tories were likely to offer. By April 1867 they could not be at all sure of this and "utterly denounced" Gladstone's proposal of a £5 rating franchise.[77] On 6 May the League defied the government and held a demonstration in Hyde Park. Feelings were running high inside and outside the House. Gladstone could make no overt move towards the League. Mill had to take up ground distinct from that claimed by the League while looking for openings to convince its supporters that Gladstone was the statesman to whom they must turn for leadership.

Gladstone made that search somewhat easier after the stinging defeat of 9 May. His "reaction to this second defeat was to abandon the £5 rating line altogether . . . and to deliver a sarcastic address to the Reform Union on 11 May in which he attacked the Adullamite Whigs for the first time in

75 *PPS*, *CW*, vol. XXVIII, p. 147.
76 Ibid.
77 *Labor and Politics*, p. 278n.

public . . . and went as near as a responsible politician could to committing himself as soon as he returned to office to reject the personal payment principle."[78] This was the sort of Gladstonian muscle-flexing that Mill could unreservedly endorse.

On 17 May Disraeli made his stunning announcement to the House that the government intended to accept the principle of Grosvenor Hodgkinson's amendment for the abolition of composition. Such acquiescence did not entail a repudiation of the principle of personal payment, but it did sweep away the restrictive effects of the bill's distinction between direct ratepayers and compounders.[79] Disraeli's prestigious (a most apt word etymologically) performance on 17 May obviated Radical obstruction and ensured the passage of the bill. Again he had caught his leading rival (and just about everybody else) off guard and made it appear that the House could carry on very well without any help from Gladstone. In his speech to a London meeting of the Reform Union on 25 May, Mill strove to undo this impression. He complained of the government's indefensible treatment of the compounder and suggested that Disraeli had been consistent only in his unwillingness to play straight:

> This is very like all that has been going on ever since the beginning of these reform discussions. It has been a succession—I will not say of tricks, because I do not like to use hard words, especially when I cannot prove them, but of what is called in the vernacular, trying it on. The object is just to see what you will bear, and anything that you will bear you shall have to bear, but if you show that you will not bear it, then perhaps it may not be required of you.[80]

No better, perhaps, could be expected of Disraeli, but for Mill it was imperative that his audience understand who had done what for whom in 1866 and 1867. Reformers should be indignant when the leader of the House of Commons

> gibes at those to whom we really owe all this, when he . . . talks of their "blundering hands," and gives it to be understood that they have not been able to carry reform and he can, and that it is not their measure. He is quite satisfied if he can say to Mr. Gladstone, "You did not do

78 Cowling, *1867*, p. 272.

79 In the end the 1867 act abolished composition in parliamentary boroughs. The confusion and inconvenience caused by this change, however, led to the passage in 1869 of a measure (32 & 33 Victoria, c. 41) that reinstated composition and also provided that compound occupiers have their names recorded in the ratebook.

80 *PPS*, *CW*, vol. XXVIII, p. 169.

D'ISRAEL-I IN TRIUMPH; OR, THE MODERN SPHYNX.
(*Suggested by* Mr. Poynter's *admirable Picture of "Israel in Egypt."*)

> it." But Mr. Gladstone did do it. He could not carry his measure last year because Mr. Disraeli and his friends opposed it; Mr. Disraeli can carry his Reform Bill because Mr. Gladstone will not oppose anything but that which is not real reform, and will support to the utmost that which is. I have no objection to thank everybody for their part in it when once we have got it. The people of England know that but for the late government this government would have gone one hundred miles out of their way before they would have brought in any Reform Bill at all. And every good thing we have got in this bill, even that which seems to be more than Mr. Gladstone was prepared to give, has only been given for the purpose of out-bidding Mr. Gladstone.[81]

Mill's freedom from direct party obligations during the Conservative regime allowed him to concentrate on what were variously perceived as crotchets and bravely principled ideals. In the *Autobiography* he accentuates his independent advocacy of fundamental principles concerning women's suffrage and the representation of minorities. "In the general debates on Mr. Disraeli's Reform Bill, my participation was limited to the one speech [9 May] already mentioned; but I made the Bill an occasion for bringing the two greatest improvements which remain to be made in representative government formally before the House and the nation."[82] Mill invariably stressed the non-party character of these initiatives, though the "occasion" for bringing them forward was of course coloured by party considerations. Of women's suffrage more will be said elsewhere.[83]

Thomas Hare's proposal for personal or proportional representation answered Mill's earnest search for the means to obtain a legislature that was truly representative of the breadth of views, interests, and abilities embodied in the electorate. On 31 May 1866 Mill had introduced the plan in his remarks on the redistribution scheme that the Liberal government had been pressured into introducing. On this occasion he had not opposed Gladstone, though the measure conceded nothing to his or Hare's views.[84] But the changed circumstances provided an opportunity. In November 1866 Mill wrote to Hare: "There will, in all probability, be a Tory Reform Bill, and whatever may be its quality, no moving of amendments or raising of new points will in the case of a Tory bill be regarded by Liberals as obstructiveness, or as damaging the cause. Then will be the

81 Ibid., pp. 170–1.
82 *A*, *CW*, vol. I, p. 284.
83 See below, chapter 4.
84 *PPS*, *CW*, vol. XXVIII, pp. 83–6.

very time to bring forward and get discussed, everything which we think ought to be put into a good Reform Bill."[85]

Mill's speech on personal representation should be seen as a continuation by other means of a mission that had begun in 1859 with his highly laudatory review of Hare's scheme in "Recent Writers on Reform" in *Fraser's* and then expanded in *Considerations on Representative Government.*[86] Hare's proposal called for a system of balloting that would enable voters to list in order of preference the candidates they wished to support. The quota of votes necessary to secure election was to be determined by dividing the number of valid ballots by the number of seats in the House of Commons. Those candidates obtaining the requisite number of votes once the first-place preferences were counted would be declared elected, and their surplus would be distributed to the candidate listed second on each of the surplus ballots. The process would continue until the number of seats available had been filled. In a letter to George Cornewall Lewis written shortly after the publication of Hare's *A Treatise on the Election of Representatives, Parliamentary and Municipal* (1859), Mill remarked: "I think it both a monument of intellect, and of inestimable practical importance at the present moment."[87] To Hare himself Mill observed: "The more I think of your plan, the more it appears to me to be *the* great discovery in representative government."[88]

In Hare's scheme Mill saw the most practicable means of reconciling democracy with competence, diversity, and liberty. Conditions prevalent within the existing electoral system discouraged men of ability and independent mind from seeking seats in the House of Commons, and when such men did seek election the same conditions usually stood in the way of their success. The implementation of Hare's scheme would in essence create a national constituency for men of talent and integrity and greatly enhance their electoral prospects. Under Hare's plan, each member of the legislature could justifiably claim to represent a virtually unanimous constituency, the relation between representative and elector being founded on shared conviction and mutual respect. The influence of money at elections would be considerably reduced; the influence of principles would be notably enhanced. The vista of universal suffrage itself did not give Mill pause, provided that the electoral system gave the educated minority representation in the House of Commons commensurate with their numbers in the country. "The cause of the minority would

85 *LL*, *CW*, vol. XVI, p. 1215 (18 Nov. 1866).
86 *EPS*, *CW*, vol. XIX, pp. 358–67, 448–65.
87 *LL*, *CW*, vol. XV, p. 608 (20 March 1859).
88 Ibid., p. 653 (19 Dec. 1859).

be likely to be supported with such consummate skill, and such a weight of moral authority, as might prove a sufficient balance to the superiority of numbers on the other side, and enable the opinions of the higher and middle classes to prevail when they were right, even in an assembly of which the majority had been chosen by the poor."[89]

Mill's motion on behalf of personal representation, and his lengthy and lofty speech supporting it,[90] were presented to an audience for whom castles in the sky seemed decidedly inferior to country and town houses on the ground. Mill did not delude himself into thinking that his motion had the slightest chance of passing. Indeed, he did not even press it to a division. He acted as the eminent philosophical sponsor of a plan whose great merits, he trusted, would come to be better understood and appreciated as public opinion matured. His initiative was intended to elucidate those merits, and thereby to contribute to that maturation. If there was one message above all others that he wished to convey to the House, it was that Hare's plan possessed a moral and political significance that entirely transcended party loyalities:

> The plan I propose ensures this variegated character of the representation in a degree never yet obtained, and guarantees its preservation under any possible extension of the franchise. Even universal suffrage, even the handing over of political predominance to the numerical majority of the whole people, would not then extinguish minorities. Every dissentient opinion would have the opportunity of making itself heard, and heard through the very best and most effective organs it was able to procure. We should not find the rich or the cultivated classes retiring from politics, as we are so often told they do in America, because they cannot present themselves to any body of electors with a chance of being returned. Such of them as were known and respected out of their immediate neighbourhood would be elected in considerable numbers, if not by a local majority, yet by a union of local minorities; and instead of being deterred from offering themselves, it would be the pride and glory of such men to serve in Parliament; for what more inspiring position can there be for any man, than to be selected to fight the uphill battle of unpopular opinions, in a public arena, against superior numbers? (*Cries of Agreed, agreed.*) All, therefore, which the best Conservatives chiefly dread in the complete ascendancy of democracy would be, if not wholly

89 *EPS*, *CW*, vol. XIX, p. 364.
90 See *PPS*, *CW*, vol. XXVIII, pp. 176–87 (30 May 1867).

removed, at least diminished in a very great degree. These are the recommendations of the plan when looked at on its conservative side. Let us now look at it in its democratic aspect. (*Agreed, agreed.*) I claim for it the support of all democrats, as being the only true realization of their political principles. What is the principle of democracy? Is it not that everybody should be represented, and that everybody should be represented equally? Am I represented by a member against whom I have voted, and am ready to vote again? Have all the voters an equal voice when nearly half of them have had their representative chosen for them by the larger half? In the present mode of taking the suffrages nobody is represented but the majority. But that is not the meaning of democracy. . . . [T]he majority should be represented by a majority, and the minority by a minority.[91]

Were proportional representation to be adopted, Mill's task of radicalizing the Liberal party would have been vastly lightened. A truly radical minority—not too minor—would, he was sure, have found its way into parliament. Mill, however, was a pragmatist and his immediate role had to be investing the better part of his energies in the challenge of shaping a radicalized Liberal party that would be receptive to personal representation and to much else that he wanted for his country.

The quality and character of the men returned to the House of Commons at future general elections would be determined as much by the unspoken assumptions of candidates and electors regarding appropriate electoral conduct as by the qualifications for the vote. In 1865 changing those assumptions was the central purpose of Mill's campaign. In 1868 he took a leading part in the debates on the government's Election Petitions and Corrupt Practices at Elections Bill. His predominant concern during what would be his last session in parliament was to make a mountain of this legislative molehill.

Before the 1867 session was out, the Conservative government had indicated that a bill on the subject would receive high priority in 1868.[92] Mill, thinking that a number of advanced Liberals shared his interest in the matter, began to lay the groundwork for a concerted effort in the autumn of 1867. In November he wrote to Chadwick: "The great question of next session will be the promised bill against electoral corruption. The

91 Ibid., vol. XXVIII, pp. 183–4.

92 The ministry had actually introduced a bill in 1867, which had been referred to a select committee of the House. It was, however, withdrawn on 29 July and on 16 August Disraeli informed the House of the government's intention to deal with the matter early in the following session. See *PD*, 3rd ser., vol. 189, col. 1606.

advanced Liberals must have *their* bill, and I am anxious that all who have thought on the subject . . . should put down, as heads of a bill, all that has occurred to them as desirable on this subject. When all suggestions have been put together, the most feasible may be selected, and the best radicals in and out of the House may be urged to combine in forcing them on the government."[93] Later that month Mill was in touch with W.D. Christie, whom he regarded as the principal authority on the subject.[94] He proposed that Christie draft a measure that could serve as an instrument of discussion for advanced Liberals, who might gather on the reassembling of parliament "and produce an outline of a Bill which might be circulated among the party. It might be possible to prevail on Mr. Gladstone to introduce it: but . . . the bill will only be a rallying point: the fight will . . . be . . . on the attempt to engraft its provisions on the bill of the Tory Government."[95] Mill thus displayed a readiness to direct and coordinate the Radical initiative on electoral corruption, with which he clearly wished to associate Gladstone.

Christie promptly answered Mill's request. The points he emphasized concerned the need to include municipal elections within the bill's purview and to provide for a post-election enquiry into all the contests without regard to whether a complaint had been lodged. Mill acknowledged that corruption at parliamentary elections often fed off unsavoury practices resorted to at the municipal level; a satisfactory bill would encompass both parliamentary and municipal elections. As for a universal and systematic process of enquiry, Mill confessed that the idea was new to him. "One can at once see many reasons in its favour, but it will be a difficult thing to get carried, owing to the habitual objection to 'fishing' enquiries, and to enquiries when there is not complaint. It is, however, evident that the absence of complaint, is, in such a case, no evidence of the absence of mischief." Mill also put other questions to Christie: What penalty should be imposed on the convicted briber? Should all money spent by candidates and their agents at elections "pass through a public officer, so that the mere fact of incurring expenditure in which he is passed over should be legal proof of an unlawful purpose?"[96] Mill's

93 *LL*, *CW*, vol. XVI, p. 1325 (4 Nov. 1867).

94 In February 1864 Christie had read a paper, "Suggestions for an Organization for the Restraint of Corruption at Elections," before the Jurisprudence Department of the National Association for the Promotion of Social Science. Less than two months later Mill attended a meeting of the Law Amendment Society, at which Christie's paper "Corruption at Elections" was discussed. For Mill's brief remarks on this occasion, see *PPS*, *CW*, vol. XXVIII, pp. 9–11.

95 *LL*, *CW*, vol. XVI, p. 1331 (20 Nov. 1867).

96 Ibid., p. 1337 (28 Dec. 1867).

absorption in such details reflects his judgment that only stringent and comprehensive action could subdue the corruption that contaminated the British electoral system.

Shortly thereafter Mill received and read Christie's 1864 pamphlet *Electoral Corruption and Its Remedies*, whose recommendations he considered "excellent." Central to Christie's scheme was the appointment of an official in each constituency to oversee all aspects of the electoral process. Mill concurred.[97] In mid-January Christie learned of Mill's disposition to move forward with Christie's plan "of an investigation after every election, parliamentary or municipal, by a special officer, with the addition of an appeal from that officer to one of the Judges."[98]

Disraeli did not look to Christie for guidance on the subject of electoral corruption. The bill introduced by the government primarily concerned jurisdiction over controverted elections.[99] The measure proposed to transfer the trial of election petitions from Election Committees of the House of Commons to a judicial tribunal.[100] The principle of the bill did not meet with much opposition. Gladstone accepted the need for such a change and did not take a prominent part in the debates. Mill allowed that though the bill "does in reality only one thing, that thing is a vigorous one, and shows an adequate sense of the emergency."[101] He would not criticize the bill for what it did, but for what it failed to do. The magnitude of the problem posed by the corrupt influence of money at elections, Mill believed, demanded action across a broad front. He applied himself to the task of persuading the House to expand substantially the scope of the bill.

Had the House of Commons in 1868 been inclined to follow Mill's lead, the Election Petitions and Corrupt Practices at Elections Act would have been a very much larger measure than it turned out to be. Mill urged the House to establish the enquiry mechanism devised by Christie.[102] He strenuously argued for extending the bill's provisions to municipal elections.[103] He called upon the House to limit each candidate to one

97 Ibid., p. 1348 (8 Jan. 1868).

98 Ibid., p. 1353 (17 Jan. 1868).

99 Cornelius O'Leary provides a good account of the content and passage of the Election Petitions and Corrupt Practices at Elections Bill in *The Elimination of Corrupt Practices in British Elections, 1868–1911* (Oxford: Clarendon Press, 1962), pp. 27–43.

100 The act called upon the justices of each of the three superior courts at Westminster to select annually one of their members to try election petitions.

101 *PPS*, *CW*, vol. XXVIII, p. 262 (26 March 1868).

102 Ibid., pp. 263–4 (26 March 1868).

103 Ibid., p. 264 (26 March 1868), pp. 307–8 (14 July 1868), pp. 311–12 (17 July 1868), pp. 316–17 (22 July 1868).

paid agent and to prohibit the payment of canvassers.[104] He recommended that in those instances where the evidence pointed towards "general and extensive bribery" in a constituency, those responsible for the petition should not be held accountable for its costs.[105] He supported Henry Fawcett's effort to transfer official election expenses from the candidates to the rates, a change advocated by Mill in *Thoughts on Parliamentary Reform* and in *Representative Government.*[106] Mill lost every point.

The discussion in the *Autobiography* of this failed parliamentary campaign carries the full weight of Mill's disappointment (his experience of the 1868 general election did nothing to diminish the strength of his feeling on the subject). Referring to the "fight kept up by a body of advanced Liberals," he blames the Liberal party for the futility to which that fight was condemned:

> The Liberal party in the House was greatly dishonoured by the conduct of many of its members in giving no help whatever to this attempt to secure the necessary conditions of an honest representation of the people. With their large majority in the House they could have carried all the amendments, or better ones if they had better to propose. But it was late in the Session; members were eager to set about their preparations for the impending General Election: and while some . . . honourably remained at their post . . . a much greater number placed their electioneering interests before their public duty. . . . From these causes our fight . . . was wholly unsuccessful, and the practices which we sought to render more difficult, prevailed more widely than ever in the first General Election held under the new electoral law.[107]

Implicit in this passage is a criticism of Gladstone's leadership. Any

104 Ibid., pp. 317–18 (22 July 1868).

105 Ibid., pp. 279–80 (21 May 1868), pp. 309–10 (14 July 1868), pp. 318–19 (22 July 1868).

106 Ibid., pp. 327–8 (24 July 1868); *CW*, vol. XIX, pp. 320, 496. Fawcett's amendment was actually carried in a small House by a vote of 84 to 76. On the third reading, however, the government managed to reverse this decision, defeating Fawcett's amendment 102 to 91. Mill's correspondence amply confirms the vigilance he displayed in the House in connection with the corrupt practices legislation; see his letters to Christie in 1868: *LL*, *CW*, vol. XVI, pp. 1381–2 (31 March), pp. 1383–4 (3 April), p. 1397 (8 May), p. 1398 (11 May), pp. 1399–400 (20 May), p. 1405 (25 May), p. 1409 (6 June), and p. 1425 (27 July).

107 *A*, *CW*, vol. I, pp. 283–4.

qualms Mill might have had about the quality of that leadership were not expressed in 1868.

Coming from a well-known proponent of purity of election, Mill's earnest activity during the 1868 session could have caught no one by surprise. That he should identify the cause so exclusively with a group of advanced Liberals reveals something of his underlying hopes for political realignment. To be sure, in the House he tactfully avoided declarations that could be construed as "party" motivated. Yet the relevant material in his correspondence and in the *Autobiography* attests to his supposition that action in parliament, having as its aim a comprehensive assault on corrupt practices, would necessarily be Radical-inspired. Such a supposition was not entirely warranted. Dissatisfaction with the modest scope of Disraeli's bill was not restricted to Radicals. Beresford-Hope, a Tory, proposed an amendment to forbid the use of public houses as committee rooms. The *Saturday Review*, which took particular delight in excoriating advanced liberalism, regretted that the bill did not go further. "The truth is that the Government Bill is only a half-measure. The whole of our election system requires overhauling. It is better to do what is proposed than to do nothing, but far more will yet have to be done before we have exhausted all reasonable legal efforts to put down or to detect bribery."[108] *The Times*, not one of Mill's favourite newspapers, could write that "the great increase in the number of the moneyed class is as threatening a spring of danger as the adoption of Household Suffrage."[109] Misgivings about the influence of money at elections were not the monopoly of Radicals. An aristocratic bias and a democratic bias occasionally produced similar conclusions.

Mill's bias was emphatically of the latter sort. In *Considerations on Representative Government* he had written:

> There has never yet been, among political men, any real and serious attempt to prevent bribery, because there has been no real desire that elections should not be costly. Their costliness is an advantage to those who can afford the expense, by excluding a multitude of competitors; and anything, however noxious, is cherished as having a conservative tendency, if it limits the access to Parliament to rich men. . . . They care comparatively little who votes, as long as they feel assured that none but persons of their own class can be voted for.[110]

108 Quoted in O'Leary, *Elimination of Corrupt Practices*, pp. 39n–40n.
109 Quoted in ibid., p. 38.
110 *EPS*, *CW*, vol. XIX, pp. 497–8.

Mill's aversion to the Palmerstonian ascendancy arose from his conception of what politics ought to be about. Palmerston's House of Commons, Mill tended to think, operated as a club of comfortable gentlemen who wanted nothing more than to preserve an order of things that had treated them well. The Palmerstonian Liberal party stood for an ill-defined "progress" in general and nothing very much in particular. Complacency and obtuseness rendered it unfit to erect the scaffolding of principle that Mill considered essential for coherent and cogent party action. Politics without principle might serve nicely the interests of the rich; it could not foster the social and moral improvement that Mill prized.

The transformation of the Liberal party into a vehicle of radical reform was inseparable from the creation of a politics of principle. The entry into the political arena of men of intelligence wedded to ideas and ideals was to be encouraged. Working-class participation in an advanced Liberal party purged of Palmerstonians was also requisite. The securing of these objectives would make of the Liberal party something far better than the loose combination of individuals that had followed Palmerston. They could not be secured in the absence of a dramatic reduction in the cost of contesting elections. Each of the amendments put forward by Mill to the Election Petitions and Corrupt Practices at Elections Bill was directed to this end. He had no wish to humble the aristocracy only to find a snobbish philistine plutocracy in its place. "They desired to diminish the number of men in this House, who came in, not for the purpose of maintaining any political opinions whatever, but solely for the purpose, by a lavish expenditure, of acquiring the social position which attended a seat in this House, and which, perhaps, was not otherwise to be attained by them."[111] Be it the struggle over franchise extension or the debate on corrupt electoral practices, Mill forged for himself a plan of campaign that was decisively shaped by his commitment to the radicalization of the Liberal party.

111 *PPS*, *CW*, vol. XXVIII, p. 280 (21 May 1868).

FOUR

Women's Suffrage

> Of all my recollections connected with the H of C that of my having had the honour of being the first to make the claim of women to the suffrage a parliamentary question, is the most gratifying as I believe it to have been the most important public service that circumstances made it in my power to render. This is now a thing accomplished & the cause has a sufficient number of supporters among the best men in the H of C. to carry on as much of the contest as can be conducted there. It remains for the intelligent women of the country to give their moral support to the men who are engaged in urging their claims, & to open the minds of the less intelligent to the fact that political freedom is the only effectual remedy for the evils from which most women are conscious that women suffer.[1]

In a letter written to the sister of John and Jacob Bright and the organizer and president of the recently formed Edinburgh Branch of the National Society for Women's Suffrage, one could expect and accept a little hyperbole on Mill's part, especially in response to a fulsome letter expressing her and her Society's deep regret at his defeat in the recent election for Westminster and their inexpressible gratitude for all he had done for the cause. Hyperbole can express sincere feelings; Mill expressed the same sentiments in his *Autobiography* the next year, where it is hard to think of any ulterior motives:

> the . . . motion which I made in the form of an amendment to the Reform Bill . . . was by far the most important, perhaps the only really

1 To Priscilla McLaren, *Later Letters* [*LL*], ed. Francis E. Mineka and Dwight N. Lindley, *Collected Works* [*CW*], vols. XIV–XVII (Toronto: University of Toronto Press, 1972), vol. XVI, p. 1521 (12 Dec. 1868).

important public service I performed in the capacity of a Member of Parliament: a motion to strike out the words which were understood to limit the electoral franchise to males, thereby admitting to the suffrage all women who as householders or otherwise possess the qualification of male electors.[2] For women not to make their claim to the suffrage at the time when the elective franchise was being largely extended, would have been to abjure the claim altogether; and a movement on the subject was begun in 1866, when I presented a petition for the suffrage signed by a considerable number of distinguished women. But it was as yet uncertain whether the proposal would obtain more than a few stray votes in the House: and when, after a debate in which the speakers on the contrary side were conspicuous by their feebleness, the votes recorded in favour of the motion amounted to 73—made up by pairs and tellers to above 80—the surprise was general and the encouragement great: the greater too because one of those who voted for the motion was Mr. [John] Bright, a fact which could only be attributed to the impression made on him by the debate, as he had previously made no secret of his non-concurrence in the proposal.[3]

The actual record of his activities during his election campaign and in the House on behalf of the women's cause seems surprisingly meagre after Mill's claims. He mentioned it twice during his campaign speeches in the summer of 1865 and not at all during his second unsuccessful campaign. In the House during the debate on the Russell-Gladstone Reform Bill, he presented a petition on behalf of Barbara Bodichon et al., and asked leave to bring in a motion for a return of the number of persons fully meeting the qualifications for the vote who were excluded by their sex. During the debate on Disraeli's Reform Bill, he introduced his motion for the return, presented more petitions and moved his well-known amendment on 20 May 1867, of which result he was justly proud. In contrast, on the presumably less significant matter of corrupt practices at elections, Mill spoke, or intervened in debate, thirteen times. There are two explanations—there are undoubtedly more—which reconcile this meagre amount of activity with his recognition that its

2 For the motion, see *Parliamentary Debates* [*PD*], 3rd ser., vol.187, cols. 817–29, 842–3 (20 May 1867); also *Public and Parliamentary Speeches* [*PPS*], ed. John M. Robson and Bruce L. Kinzer, *CW*, vols. XXVIII–XXIX (Toronto: University of Toronto Press, 1988), vol. XXVIII, pp. 151–62, "The Admission of Women to the Electoral Franchise," 20 May 1867.

3 *Autobiography* [*A*], in *Autobiography and Literary Essays*, *CW*, vol. I (Toronto: University of Toronto Press, 1981), p. 285.

object was the most significant one he undertook. The first is his shrewd understanding of the art of the immediately possible,[4] and the second his perhaps visionary hope for a parliamentary party led for the first time by a true man of movement, W.E. Gladstone, and of a possible role for himself within it. The two are complementary.

Although Mill includes the belief in the suffrage for women as one of his "crotchets,"[5] the epithet should in no way be taken to imply that it was a recent whim and certainly not of passing importance. He had held the belief, as he himself records in the *Autobiography*,[6] from his earliest rational days—which was very early indeed. It was certainly not from his father that he received the opinion; it may have been from Bentham, but most likely it was his own logical reasoning on the question that convinced him. Certainly there is no reason to doubt his remark that it was his belief in the need to advance the position of women in society that attracted Harriet Taylor to him.[7] The circle around W.J. Fox,[8] in which Mill first met the Taylors, held radical views on the subject of love, marriage, divorce, and political rights (roughly in that order). And although many of the writings in the *Monthly Repository* exalted the role of women in the home, rocking the cradle and cultivating small minds, some went so far as to envisage a future in which women were speaking with silver tongue in silken senatorial robes in the parliament of the noblest.[9]

Mill's feelings for Harriet would have done nothing to weaken his

4 "There are only two things worth working for—a practical result or a principle: if a practical result it sh[d] be one which is attainable; if a principle, not to go the whole length of it is to sacrifice it. I look upon agitation for manhood as distinguished from universal suffrage as decidedly mischievous." To Max Kyllmann, *LL*, *CW*, vol. XVI, p. 998 (15 Feb. 1865—just before he was asked to stand as a candidate).

5 Mill uses the term, which others had obviously already attached to radicals' ideas, in "Westminster Election 1865 [1]," his campaign speech on 3 July 1865 (*PPS*, *CW*, vol. XXVIII, p. 16), and again half-humorously, putting it in quotation marks, in a letter to Edwin Chadwick, *LL*, *CW*, vol. XVI, p. 1458 (9 Oct. 1868).

6 *A*, *CW*, vol. I, p. 253n.

7 Ibid.

8 In the early 1830s Fox was the minister of the Unitarian Chapel at South Place.

9 Mrs. Mary Leman Grimstone wrote: "'All that is custom now was innovation once;' all that is innovation now will be custom by-and-by. . . . But I will ask the thinking, the informed, the liberal man . . . whether a woman, so armed and animated, though a *new*, would be a ridiculous sight in Parliament, or in a nobler assembly still, that of the enlightened of all classes of her country people? If nature has endowed her with eloquence, and study possessed her with knowledge to serve the cause of her country, should she be declared incompetent, because she were wrapped in a silken shawl instead of a senator's robe? because she spoke with a voice of silver instead of brass?" *Monthly Repository*, 9 (1835), p. 34.

belief in women's equality or, possibly more accurately, superiority. At least they were superior in the areas most needing improvement if mankind (Mill's word) was to step forward into a better world. In the *Autobiography*, Mill explains, in a lengthy footnote to his disclaimer of having learnt his views about the position of women from Taylor, what it was that he did learn from her:

> What is true is, that until I knew her, the opinion was, in my mind, little more than an abstract principle. . . . But the perception of the vast practical bearings of women's disabilities which found expression in the book on *The Subjection of Women*, was acquired mainly through her teaching. But for her rare knowledge of human nature and comprehension of moral and social influences, though I should doubtless have held my present opinions I should have had a very insufficient perception of the mode in which the consequences of the inferior position of women intertwine themselves with all the evils of existing society and with all the difficulties of human improvement.[10]

His interest emerges publicly again in mid-century. Between October 1846 and August 1851 a series of articles jointly authored with his wife[11] appeared in the newspapers, prompted by reports from the magistrates' courts of cases of domestic brutality.[12] At first glance these seem odd subjects for a renowned philosopher and political economist to be spending his time on with his new—in only one sense—bride. They seem almost as odd for a radical reformer, and still quite strange for a strong feminist, particularly for one in the mid-nineteenth century. But their interest is not eccentric. Mill believed what he wrote about her influence on him and, whether or not later scholars believe it, the grounds of her influence that Mill himself provides cannot be ignored. It was the "perception of the vast practical bearings" that he learnt from her, and the lesson was applied at the time when Mill was looking for an explanation for the failure of English society to evince signs of movement following the introduction of such signal fuels as a Reform Bill, a new Poor Law, the

10 *A*, *CW*, vol. I, p. 253n.

11 To be accurate, they were not actually married until April 1851; John Taylor died in 1849.

12 *Newspaper Writings* [*NW*], ed. Ann P. and John M. Robson, *CW*, vols. XXII–XXV (Toronto: University of Toronto Press, 1986), vol. XXIV, nos. 318, p. 916; 329, p. 952; vol. XXV, nos. 389, p. 1151; 390, p. 1153; 392, p. 1164; 393, p. 1167; 395, p. 1172; 396, p. 1176; 400, p. 1183.

Repeal of the Corn Laws, the rise of cooperatives and of trade unions, the struggles of the Ten Hours men and the Chartists, and the influence of the liberal uprisings in Europe. His wife's intuition found the answer that had evaded his logical analysis: tyranny was embedded in the English home.

Far from the hearths of England producing gentle, caring people, quite the reverse was true at all levels of society, particularly at the lowest. Here was the explanation for the failure of the working class to improve, and it was an explanation of the problem that allowed for a solution. The subjection of one half of the human race to the other, a subjection that entailed the subjection of all the world's children as well, meant that democracy and democratic tendencies were smothered in the cradle. That society was largely indifferent to disgusting acts of brutality within the home (and some of the cases they commented upon had been reported with a truly appalling relish for the details of hideous acts of mistreatment—for instance, the man who "hanged [his wife] only in jest"[13]) was shown by the incredibly light punishments meted out by judges and the law's failure to provide any protection for the wives of England who were subsumed legally under their husbands' identity (*sous couverture*).[14] To impress upon the public's consciousness the consequences of the legal subjection of women to men, later quite specifically and narrowly the subject of *The Subjection of Women*, was the purpose of the letters to the newspapers:

> The great majority of the inhabitants of this and of every country—including nearly the whole of one sex, and all the young of both—are, either by law or by circumstances stronger than the law, subject to some one man's arbitrary will [and] it would show a profound ignorance of the effect of moral agencies on the character not to perceive how deeply depraving must be the influence of such a lesson given from the seat of justice. It cannot be doubted that to this more than to any other single cause is to be attributed the frightful brutality which marks a very large proportion of the poorest class, and no small portion of a class much above the poorest.[15]

13 *NW, CW*, vol. XXIV, p. 1183 (*Morning Chronicle*, 28 Aug. 1851).

14 Enough members of society shared the Mills' feelings to have passed through parliament 16 & 17 Victoria, c. 30, An Act for the Better Prevention and Punishment of Aggravated Assaults upon Women and Children (14 June 1853). Support for this bill provided part of the motivation for their articles.

15 *NW, CW*, vol. XXV, p. 1156. For a fuller discussion of these letters, see the introduction to *NW, CW*, vol. XXII, pp. xciii–xcix.

Mill, with Taylor Mill's encouragement, was continuing his lifelong practice of testing abstract ideas, or deductive principles, against actual cases. He came to believe firmly that "the legal subordination of one sex to the other ... is ... now one of the chief hindrances to human improvement."[16]

One of the manuscripts Mill worked on in 1860–1, after recovering from the immediate overwhelming grief on his wife's death in 1858, was that of *The Subjection of Women.* In the *Autobiography* he says:

> It was written at my daughter's suggestion that there might, in any event, be in existence a written exposition of my opinions on that great question, as full and conclusive as I could make it. The intention was to keep this among other unpublished papers, improving it from time to time if I was able, and to publish it at the time when it should seem likely to be most useful. As ultimately published it was enriched with some important ideas of my daughter's, and passages of her writing. But in what was of my own composition, all that is most striking and profound belongs to my wife; coming from the fund of thought which had been made common to us both, by our innumerable conversations and discussions on a topic which filled so large a place in our minds.[17]

The reference to his wife's contribution is well known and no further comment need be made except, perhaps, to stress the importance given to these beliefs by their being his wife's. The first draft was written in the house overlooking her grave, which he purchased immediately after her death. The cause of women's suffrage was part of the sacred memory of his beloved Harriet.

This house he gave to his step-daughter Helen Taylor in 1869. Taylor had joined Mill in Avignon twenty-four hours after her mother's death[18] and together they built a new life founded on their shared grief. Her voice became as important, or nearly so, as her mother's had been. Over the

16 *The Subjection of Women,* in *Essays on Equality, Law, and Education,* ed. John M. Robson, *CW,* vol. XXI (Toronto: University of Toronto Press, 1984), p. 261.

17 *A, CW,* vol. I, p. 265.

18 When after Mill's retirement from the East India Company, he and his wife left for the continent, Helen Taylor had taken the opportunity to continue her longtime ambition and had returned to the provincial stage, this time in Newcastle. On receiving a telegramme from Mill, she had immediately left but had not arrived in Avignon until "too late too late too late." Mill-Taylor Collection [M-T], British Library of Political and Economic Science, London School of Economics, vol. XXIV, 708, Taylor to Algernon Taylor (Nov. 1858).

years the voice sounds strident and, at times, unreasonable if not irrational. But there is no doubt that for Mill it sounded wise and fulfilled both emotional and intellectual needs. Her influence was profound and must be considered in any attempt to understand his parliamentary career. As with the question of his wife's influence, any assessment of Taylor's influence has to be based on Mill's beliefs about her, not on history's judgment. Mill's praise of her in the *Autobiography* is nearly as fulsome as that of her mother; she was

> the inheritor of much of her wisdom, and of all her nobleness of character, whose ever growing and ripening talents from that day to this have been devoted to the same great purposes, and have already made her name better and more widely known than was that of her mother, though far less so than I predict that if she lives, it is destined to become. Of the value of her direct cooperation with me, something will be said hereafter: of what I owe in the way of instruction to her great powers of original thought and soundness of practical judgment, it would be a vain attempt to give an adequate idea. Surely no one ever before was so fortunate, as, after such a loss as mine, to draw another such prize in the lottery of life—another companion, adviser, and instructor of the rarest quality. Whoever, either now or hereafter, may think of me and of the work I have done, must never forget that it is the product not of one intellect and conscience but of three, the least considerable of whom, and above all the least original, is the one whose name is attached to it.[19]

Mill became genuinely fond of Helen Taylor and valued her companionship very highly. He wrote daily and affectionately on the infrequent occasions when they were apart. For example, when he had returned briefly to Blackheath alone in January 1860:

> Dearest Lily—I arrived here about nine this morning. . . . I found Hadji [the family name for Algernon Taylor, Helen's brother] looking pale but, I thought, with a more animated (or rather less dead) expression of countenance than usual. He seems disposed to be amiable. Puss (who seems to have entirely forgotten me) quite startled me by her size—rather bulk than stature. It may be an illusion, from having been used to a little puss & little doggy (to whom remember me) especially as the teapot also looked as if it had grown.[20]

19 *A*, *CW*, vol. I, pp. 264–5.
20 *LL*, *CW*, vol. XV, p. 659.

There are many other indications of the pleasant home she created for him. They travelled together, several times in the Pyrenees and once, having decided to ignore the threat of brigands, on a long and highly successful trip through the interior of Greece, using donkeys, carriages, and their own feet.[21]

The collaboration was so productive because Taylor was well read, knowledgeable, and sympathetic to his ideas; Mill found in her an intellectual companion. She was able to share in most of his pursuits and take an interest in them all; according to Mill, "we always agree in sentiments."[22] In a letter to F.D. Maurice, he spoke of his good fortune:

> In our age & country, every person with any mental power at all, who both thinks for himself & has a conscience, must feel himself, to a very great degree, alone. I sh[d] think you have decidedly more people who are in real communion of thoughts, feelings & purposes with you than I have. I am in this supremely happy, that I have had, & even now have, that communion in the fullest degree where it is most valuable of all, in my own home. But I have it nowhere else.[23]

On another occasion, Mill refers quite unconsciously to their "working hard and efficiently for [their] opinions."[24] He valued highly her advice and criticism and took it without offence. When he was somewhat disingenuous in answering a question about his religious beliefs in the 1868 election campaign, Taylor sent him a scorching rebuke, one which could only be sent and received by two people who were very sure of their mutual confidence and respect: "I cannot tell you how ashamed I feel. . . . Do not disgrace yourself as an open and truthful man; do not shut the door to all future power of usefulness on religious liberty by such mean & wretched subterfuges as this letter."[25] Mill understood her feelings and approved; he wrote in a letter to George Grote, explaining their contentment after Mill's failure in the election of 1868, "she is very deeply imbued with the conviction that one true principle set afloat in the world does more for progress than a hundred points of practical detail."[26] He had himself many years earlier written something very similar:

21 For Mill's description of the trip's success, see ibid., pp. 779–81 (to George Grote, 11 June 1862), and for Taylor's, see Mill/Taylor Collection, XXIII, 660 (draft to Fanny Stirling, 6 July 1862).

22 *LL*, *CW*, vol. XVII, p. 1540 (to Duncan McLaren, 3 Jan. 1869).

23 Ibid., vol. XVI, p. 1048 (11 May 1865).

24 Ibid., p. 1511 (to Henry Fawcett, 7 Dec. 1868).

25 M-T, vol. LIII, 53, 12 Nov. 1868.

26 *LL*, *CW*, vol. XVI, p. 1502 (11 Dec. 1868).

> A solemn declaration of opinion from an authoritative quarter, going the full length of a great principle, is worth ten paltry practical measures of nibbling amendment. The good which any mere enactment can do, is trifling compared with the effect of whatever helps to mature the public mind . . . and we always find the *gradual* reform proceeds by larger and more rapid steps, when the doctrines of radical reform are most uncompromisingly and intrepidly proclaimed.[27]

The continuation of the letter to Grote shows how much he appreciated the support that she had given him—and makes it easier to understand why he accepted her strong criticism:

> I am not sure whether she did not dislike my being in Parliament more than I did myself, as she certainly suffered more from it in health: but she would not give in, and made it a point of pride to encourage me to stay at the post as long as there seemed any chance of my doing anything at it. On the whole, we both feel that circumstances have decided well for us. We think I was able to do some good work while I was in the House, and we look forward with delight to being able now to work in a much pleasanter manner.[28]

As well as the enormous moral support, there was Taylor's "direct cooperation" with Mill; they indeed laboured together. He wrote in his *Autobiography* that when he became a member of parliament:

> The general mass of correspondence . . . swelled into an oppressive burthen. At this time, and thenceforth, a great proportion of all my letters (including many which found their way into the newspapers)* were not written by me but by my daughter, at first merely from her willingness to help in disposing of a mass of letters greater than I could get through without assistance, but afterwards because I thought the letters she wrote superior to mine, and more so in proportion to the difficulty of the occasion. Even those which I wrote

27 *NW*, *CW*, vol. XXIII, p. 589 (*Examiner*, 11 Aug. 1833).

28 *LL*, *CW*, vol. XVI, p. 1502 (11 Dec. 1868). And again to Cairnes: "Helen is in at least her usual health, and is likely to get much better now, for the relief to her from our return to more healthy circumstances is such as any one would hardly believe possible. She bore up most heroically and wished me to remain in harness while it seemed a duty to do so, but it was at the cost of gradually drying up her springs of life." Ibid., p. 1507 (4 Dec. 1868).

> myself were generally much improved by her, as is also the case with all the more recent of my prepared speeches, of which, and some of my published writings, not a few passages, and those the most successful, were hers.[29]

Much, if not most, of the correspondence touching on the arguments for, and the organization of, the women's movement outside parliament bears her hallmark. She made abstracts of his letters when he was away, drafted suggested replies, and, on occasion it appears, wrote to his dictation.[30]

Taylor also made possible both a politically and personally significant aspect of his life by supervising the houses both at Blackheath and Avignon and acting as hostess. Without her it would not have been easy, maybe not even possible, for him to invite people to Blackheath to discuss plans or to be converted gently to a cause. A typical invitation is in a letter to Henry Fawcett, member of parliament and Liberal in good standing; the letter begins with congratulations on his marriage to Millicent Garrett and easily continues:

> It will give me great pleasure to repeat my congratulations personally. Would it be convenient and agreeable to you and Mrs Fawcett to dine with us here on Sunday the 12th at five?
>
> The Liberal party is at sixes and sevens, but things are not, I think, so bad as they look. The women's suffrage question may perhaps come on as early as Monday.[31]

It would have been possible for some Victorian bachelors to entertain in this fashion with the aid of a good housekeeper, but it is hard to imagine John Stuart Mill managing and it would not have been easy for anyone accepting the conventions of the time to invite the Frances Power Cobbes of that world to dine and be wooed to the cause.

There was already a small but very influential and experienced group of women who did not need wooing for the suffrage cause, although they

29 *A*, *CW*, vol. I, pp. 286–7. Mill's asterisked note reads: "One which deserves particular mention is a letter respecting the Habitual Criminals Act and the functions of a police generally, written in answer to a private application for my opinion, but which got into the newspapers and excited some notice. This letter which was full of original and valuable thoughts was entirely my daughter's. The fertility and aptness which distinguishes her practical conceptions of the adaptation of means to ends is such as I can never hope to rival." There is ample proof of Mill's claim, at least the part about authorship, in the handwriting of the surviving drafts. In *Letters*, ed. Hugh S.R. Elliot, 2 vols. (London: Longmans, Green, 1910), the editor assigns many to Taylor, although much of his evidence no longer seems to exist.

30 *LL*, *CW*, vol. XVI, p. 1084 (to Helen Taylor, 2 Aug. 1865).

31 Ibid., p. 1266 (1 May 1867).

had largely up until the mid–1860s been occupied with other aspects of the women's movement. Not a small service that Taylor rendered Mill was providing him with a link to this capable group of ardent supporters. They had a central office in Langham Place at the top of Regent's Street and there, on a regular basis, came together a remarkable group of women: Barbara Bodichon (née Leigh Smith), Bessie Rayner Parkes (later Belloc), Jessie Boucherett, Adelaide Proctor, Emily Davies, Elizabeth and Millicent Garrett (who was shortly to marry Henry Fawcett, thereby prompting Mill's invitation to dinner).

These women were not without connections and they had for a decade been working with some success to advance the position of women. They had begun a campaign for a married women's property bill, temporarily scuppered by the passing of the Matrimonial Causes Act in 1857. Significantly for the future tactics of the movement, during the passage of the latter bill, they had been encouraged by the courageous stand taken by Gladstone for equal grounds for divorce for men and women. During the early 1860s, the same group, spearheaded by Emily Davies, had supported Elizabeth Garrett (later Anderson) in her attempt to gain the right, finally achieved in 1865, to practise medicine with a licence from the Apothecaries' Society. They had also with considerable support from male colleagues managed to gain the right for girls to sit the lower examinations for Oxford and Cambridge and were advancing along the first steps towards the founding of Girton College at Cambridge in 1869. The Society for the Employment of Women, of which the Earl of Shaftesbury was honorary president, operated from Langham Place and published the *Englishwoman's Journal*, the first paper dedicated to a serious, continuous discussion of women's issues. It was printed by the Victoria Press, organized by Emily Faithfull, staffed only by women and appointed printers to Her Majesty the Queen. Helen Taylor knew these women through her membership in the Kensington Society, a group that met each month for papers and discussion.

When the invitation to be a candidate came from James Beal, the practical side of Mill must have immediately seen the possibilities for furthering women's suffrage. He was in an admirable position to do so given his reputation, his widespread acquaintance among liberals as well as radicals, his connection with the Langham Place group through Taylor, and her passionate as well as capable support for all his causes but especially the women's cause.

On women's suffrage of all his crotchets, Mill knew caution was necessary; ridicule was the women's worst enemy, and their elation and interest in his campaign made his circumspection all the more necessary.[32] Fortunately another of Mill's crotchets—a disapproval of campaigning—allowed him to avoid to a large extent bringing the question of votes for women to public notice. His presence was enough, however, to encourage the women to put their case forward indirectly by attending his meetings in large numbers and, in at least one case, to press their case directly. The press reported, without ridicule, the presence of women at Mill's open meetings and on one occasion an unidentified lady spoke "in a vigorous and well-finished style of public speaking"[33] at the end of the meeting.

In his letter to Beal—the letter not written for publication but allowed to be made public—outlining his views on many subjects, Mill had mentioned that he would "open the suffrage to all grown persons, both men & women, who can read, write, & perform a sum in the rule of three, & who have not, within some small number of years, received parish relief."[34] He also mentioned women's votes in his second speech to his prospective constituents, a great many ladies being present in the galleries, although only in passing; he included it as one of his less widely known crotchets:

> It would have been as easy for me, as it is for many others, to have put forth a plausible profession of political faith. . . . I might have made out a long bona fide list of political questions on which I have the high satisfaction of believing that I entirely agree with you. I might have passed gently over all subjects of possible difference and observed a discreet silence about any opinion that might possibly have startled any body. Did I do this? I did the very reverse. I put forth no address, but instead I undertook that whatever questions you put to me concerning my political opinions I would answer fully. The questions that you did put to me I answered with a degree of unreserve which has been a sort of scandal in the electioneering world. What compelled me to say anything about women's votes or the representation of minorities? Is it likely that any one would have

32 Emily Davies reminiscing about hiring carriages during the 1865 election and covering them with placards for Mill expressed doubts, perhaps prompted by hindsight, about the helpfulness of such an action. "Family Chronicle," p. 427. There was, however, no contemporary reference to this audacious move, not even in *Punch*. Possibly Davies's memory took the thought for the deed.

33 *Daily Telegraph*, 6 July 1865, reprinted in "Westminster Election 1865 [2]," *PPS*, *CW*, vol. XXVIII, p. 27.

34 *LL*, *CW*, vol. XVI, p. 1031 (17 April 1865). This letter was published in the *Daily News*, the *Morning Advertiser*, and *The Times*. Cf. p. 41 above.

> questioned me upon those points? Not one of you probably would, but you asked what my opinions on Reform were, and being asked, I did not think it consistent with plain dealing to keep back any of them.[35]

Plain dealing was a virtue highly prized by Harriet Taylor Mill, Helen Taylor, and Mill himself. But there was no need to overdo it; the subject was not mentioned in any of the other half dozen speeches he gave—except in answer to a question after his speech on 8 July.[36] Mill had no reason to elaborate on his crotchets from the public platform; quite the reverse. In doing so, he would only invite trouble and might well do more harm by such advocacy than by the much more controllable and temperate advancement of his views on less volatile occasions. Mill was well aware that his views were known and talked about and that his books were selling; much of his influence came from the moderation with which the most advanced of all the respected radicals put forward his views. He had no desire to enter parliament to any more laughter than was unavoidable for a known advocate of votes for women; for all his reticence, *Punch* was quick to leap when a chance appeared.[37]

There is another illuminating attitude revealed in these speeches that throws light on his advocacy at this time of women's suffrage. Mill described with some self-satisfaction the radical role he had played:

> I have sat by the cradle of all the great political Reforms of this and the last generation; and I have not only sat by the cradle of these reforms, but before I was out of my teens I was up and stirring, and writing about them. I have stood by these reforms, which now count followers by millions when their followers did not count tens of thousands, nay, not thousands nor hundreds. When they only counted tens I was amongst them. Nay, I may say, when their followers only counted units. . . . I have said this for the purpose of showing I have never been one of those who have left difficult things for others. I have never been one of those who have left things alone when they have been an uphill fight, but I have left them when the fight was no longer difficult. When the thing was prosperous I have left it for a time, and have said, "This matter no longer requires me," and I have therefore transferred my services to those who did. I have left that

35 "Westminster Election 1865 [2]," *PPS, CW*, vol. XXVIII, p. 18 (5 July 1865).

36 "Westminster Election 1865 [4]," ibid., p. 39 (8 July 1865).

37 As early as 10 June 1865, *Punch* had published a set of "inedited correspondence" on "Spinster Suffrage" (p. 233).

> prosperous thing, and have turned to something else—to something that was still a crotchet, still an abstraction, still something that no practical person would battle with. For I have been accustomed even in my life—and all history confirms the same thing—I have been accustomed to see that the crotchet of to-day, the crotchet of one generation, becomes the truth of the next and the truism of the one after.[38]

The belief that his main duty in life was to promote in their infancy unpopular ideas, lending his support to a proposition at the time when no one else would espouse it, is important in his approach to the advocacy of the women's cause in the House. He expected little, no more than the introduction of the question. He was very aware, perhaps not quite correctly as events were to prove, that votes for women was still only a smirk on most men's faces.

The sparseness of Mill's allusions to women's suffrage in his campaign was to avoid the smirks becoming laughter; in any case there were already many who were aware of his views and of his intention to act to further the women's cause. His successful election did not change his policy; he became if anything more cautious publicly, although very outspoken in private. During and after the campaign, he and Taylor insinuated the question every chance they had both in conversation and in his wide correspondence; Fawcett, Amberley, Holyoake, Chadwick, Plummer, Cairnes, Hare, Kyllman—all of whom undoubtedly already knew his views—were reminded of his (and by implication, their) commitment to universal, rather than manhood, suffrage. He responded promptly and warmly when the Reform League informed him of its espousal of universal suffrage.[39] The Kensington Society under Emily Davies's guidance had chosen as their resolution for discussion at the meeting in the November after Mill's election, "Should women have the franchise?" Taylor drafted a paper on the question (one cannot help but wonder if she was asked to do so—Emily Davies was a shrewd woman), but in the event she and Mill did not return from Avignon until it was time for Mill to take his seat.

After he had taken his seat in the House in February, Mill bided his time. The context for his public advocacy of votes for women has to be kept in mind. It is hard to recapture the uncouth nature of the House when in a boisterous mood, and both he and his crotchets, especially votes for women, could become the objects of ribaldry unstoppable if Mill took

38 "Westminster Election 1865 [1]," *PPS*, *CW*, vol. XXVIII, pp. 15–16 (3 July 1865).

39 *LL*, *CW*, vol. XVI, p. 1151 (to Leverson, 26 Feb. 1866).

a wrong step. He believed (quite possibly wrongly) that if there was any chance of women gaining the suffrage in the future, it was going to be through the good offices of the Liberal party. He also believed in June 1866 that the gaining of the suffrage was a matter of years, maybe decades, certainly not months.[40] He knew he was considered by many as a great thinker, but one who thought dangerously radical thoughts. What he first needed to do to promote this cause and his other crotchets was to gain the ear of the House and support from the Liberals. He tried to establish himself as a considerate party man, prepared to consider Liberal needs as well as his own interests. This is not to say that he did not genuinely come to believe that Gladstone deserved his support as the potential leader of a party of movement.

The choice of diseased cattle for the maiden speech of a wild radical has more than a touch of sly humour to it, even if his point dealt with landlord compensation. He was forcefully reminded how easy it was to lose the House's goodwill when he spoke on the suspension of *habeas corpus* in Ireland; for two months he remained sitting down until he rose to speak effectively in support of Gladstone and the Reform Bill on 13 April thus gaining, according to the *Autobiography*, "the ear of the House."[41] He did not mention universal suffrage.[42] But in May 1866 when the Reform Bill was before parliament, Caroline Liddell, a friend and neighbour, must have approached him, because he wrote what was obviously a reply encouraging her to circulate a petition and offering to present it.[43] Two days later on 8 May, Taylor received a letter from Barbara Bodichon asking if her stepfather would present a petition for women's suffrage.[44] Taylor replied that her "father" would present any petition and enclosed £20.[45] They helped to gather signatures because, as Taylor explained to Kate Amberley, although they thought it would be mischievous to ask for votes for women while the Reform Bill was before the House, they thought that women should express their desire to be included.[46]

40 Ibid., vol. XVII, pp. 1727–8 (to Dilke, 28 May 1870).
41 *A*, *CW*, vol. I, p. 275.
42 *PPS*, *CW*, vol. XXVIII, pp. 54 and 58.
43 *LL*, *CW*, vol. XVI, p. 1163 (6 May 1866). She does not appear to have done so, but she did sign one Taylor sent her. Caroline E. Liddell to Helen Taylor, 28 May 1866, M-T, vol. XXI, 48.
44 M-T, vol. XII, 40 (8 May 1866).
45 Ibid., 41 (9 May 1866).
46 Bertrand Russell Archives, McMaster University, Hamilton, Ont., Helen Taylor to Kate Amberley, [29 May] 1866. At the same time, the same women, including Taylor, were circulating a petition in support of Elizabeth Garrett.

PUNCH, OR THE LONDON CHARIVARI.—March 30, 1867.

MILL'S LOGIC; OR, FRANCHISE FOR FEMALES.

"PRAY CLEAR THE WAY, THERE, FOR THESE—A—PERSONS."

Mill was obviously not anxious to upset the Reform Bill and the Liberal government with it. But on 7 June he introduced the question into the House—though not into the debate—for the first time since he took his seat, openly associating himself with the women's cause; he presented, without speaking, the petition containing 1521 signatures[47] that the women under Barbara Bodichon's leadership had garnered in two weeks. The signers were unexpectedly numerous and impressive. Mill had told the petitioners, through Helen Taylor, that he would need at least one hundred signatures;[48] when the petition was handed to him in the lobby of the Commons, he is said to have "brandished" it, saying he could certainly make an effect with it now.[49] And he did, not only within the House but also outside it. The presentation provoked no hilarity in the

47 *PPS, CW,* vol. XXIX, p. 575.

48 M-T, vol. XII, 41. Helen Taylor to Barbara Bodichon, 9 May 1866 (draft).

49 For more details, see Anna J. Mill, "The Ladies' Petition," *University Women's Review,* May 1964, pp. 10–13.

House and it received straightforward reporting in the newspapers. For example, the *Daily News*, the *Morning Advertiser*, the *Evening Standard*, and the *News of the World* all gave Mill a sober paragraph mentioning the number of signatures and reporting that they were all gathered—according to Mr. Mill—by the ladies unaided, and that they included those of Mrs. Somerville and Harriet Martineau. The *Evening Standard* dubbed him "the ladies' man," but none of the papers reported laughter in the House or tried to raise any itself.[50]

The strength and weight of the support for the petition suggested that the best tactic would be to give notice immediately of a motion requesting the tabling of figures indicating how many voters with the requisite property qualifications were unable to exercise the franchise because of their sex.[51] The petition's reception by the press would not discourage such a move. Mill tried to persuade Russell Gurney to ask for the return, but he shrank "from identifying himself with our movement just at the beginning of his parliamentary life."[52] Gurney may have decided wisely because, in spite of Mill's stature as a thinker, the notice of motion, unlike the petition, aroused "Cheers and laughter" in the House according to the *Daily News*—the *Morning Star* said "Laughter and cheers," *The Times* "laughter," and the *Manchester Guardian* "Great laughter." The papers' own reports, if they had a slant, were still respectful of Mill.[53]

The publicity was good but the House unpredictable. Laughter could at any moment shake the ground on which "the ladies' man" stood. The petition and the notice of his intention to request the numbers of women affected were, therefore, as far as it was wise to take the House. He explained to a fellow MP why he was asking for so little at this time:

> The notice which I gave in the House yesterday goes as far as I think it prudent to go, on this subject, in the present session. As there is no chance that we can succeed in getting a clause for admitting women to the suffrage introduced with the present Reform Bill, it seems to me and to other friends of such a proposal desirable merely to open the subject this year, without taking up the time of the House and increasing the accusation of obstructiveness by forcing on a discussion

50 The reports all appeared on 8 June 1866, except that in the *News of the World* which appeared on 10 June 1866.

51 "An Address for the Return of the number of Freeholders, Householders, and others in England and Wales who, fulfilling the conditions of property or rental prescribed by Law as the qualification for the Electoral Franchise, are excluded from the Franchise by reason of their sex." *PPS*, *CW*, vol. XXVIII, pp. 91–3.

52 Quoted from a copy of a letter from Helen Taylor to Barbara Bodichon, 7 June 1866, supplied by Barbara McCrimmon.

53 All the accounts appeared on 9 June 1866.

which cannot lead to a practical result. What we are now doing will lay the foundation of a further movement when advisable, and will prepare for that movement a much greater amount of support in the country than we should have if we attempted it at present.[54]

By the middle of June the Liberal Reform Bill was taking a beating under the combined attack of the Tories and the Adullamites. Gladstone had been unable to keep control in the House of Commons and the initiative over the bill had escaped him. To introduce a chimera, a wild scheme that might well envelope him, the party, and the cause in ridicule when the Liberals were already floundering, would be to lose what influence he had with Gladstone and the House. On 12 June he postponed even his prudent motion for a week; before the week was up, the government was defeated in the House of Commons on the Reform Bill.

The assumption of office by Derby and Disraeli put Mill with the Liberals on the opposition side of the House. Now his motion could in no way be thought by the Liberal party to be a fly in their jar of reform ointment because the jar had slipped from their grasp. The Conservatives were a minority government, so they were unlikely to give the Liberals a chance to defeat them in the House over such a moderate request. When Mill's first opportunity came on 17 July 1866, the moment was a good one for the avoidance of both irritation and hilarity. He spoke briefly and explicitly,[55] placing "the expediency of the particular measure upon the narrowest grounds upon which it can rest," to quote more of his words from his description of how to persuade an Englishman.[56] He was, of course, always a utilitarian; at no time and in no place did he ever put a toe, much less take a stand for women's suffrage, on the ground of natural rights or natural justice:

> Sir, I rise to make the Motion of which I have given notice. After the petition which I had the honour of presenting a few weeks ago, the House would naturally expect that its attention would be called, however briefly, to the claim preferred in that document. The petition, and the circumstances attendant on its preparation, have, to say the least, greatly weakened the chief practical argument which we have been accustomed to hear against any proposal to admit women to the electoral franchise—namely, that few, if any, women desire it.

54 *LL*, *CW*, vol. XVI, p. 1175 (to Christopher Darby Griffith, 9 June 1866).

55 "Electoral Franchise for Women," *PPS*, *CW*, vol. XXVIII, pp. 91–3 (17 July 1866).

56 "Comparison of the Tendencies of French and English Intellect," *NW*, *CW*, vol. XXIII, p. 445 (*Monthly Repository*, Nov. 1833).

> Originating as that petition did entirely with ladies, without the instigation, and, to the best of my belief, without the participation of any person of the male sex in any stage of the proceedings, except the final one of its presentation to Parliament, the amount of response which became manifest, the number of signatures obtained in a very short space of time, not to mention the quality of many of those signatures, may not have been surprising to the ladies who promoted the petition, but was certainly quite unexpected by me. I recognize in it the accustomed sign that the time has arrived when a proposal of a public nature is ripe for being taken into serious consideration—namely, when a word spoken on the subject is found to have been the expression of a silent wish pervading a great number of minds, and a signal given in the hope of rallying a few supporters is unexpectedly answered by many.

Mill's claims in these opening remarks both that the matter was commonly discussed and that at least one of the grounds of objection (that "the chief practical argument") was removed could hardly be true in 1866, but they show clever debating technique. His opponents were left to argue that women's suffrage was not commonly discussed, and so defeat their own position by their very discussion, or they had to accept—and perhaps be convinced by—Mill's claim. His second claim appealed to the practical man of business. Not for his opponents arguments from theory; they were not philosophers or speculators. The Englishman in the House of Commons had more than a gene or two from Mr. Gradgrind, and Mill attempted to establish from the beginning the practicality of this issue on a pragmatic basis: the petition showed that the time had come when a "proposal of a public nature is ripe for being taken into serious consideration." This was no laughing matter. Mill's delighted surprise at the number and quality of the signatures was genuine, but he used it also to stress the practicality of the question. He was assuring the House that he was pursuing a desirable and desired reform. He continued in the same reasonable vein: when a complaint is made by a number of persons, "the least we can do is to ascertain what number of persons are affected by the grievance"—an obviously practical proposal. The request also had the additional advantage of setting the parameters of the discussion for the future—or at least it tried to.[57]

57 In view of Mill's care in attempting to restrict the subject of debate to those sharing the qualifications of male voters—and up until the Married Women's Property Act of 1870 (indeed really up until that of 1882) the debate would be restricted technically to widows and spinsters—it is a little surprising that Mill and

The rest of this brief, unemotional speech concentrated on the denial of any party intent behind the move. Mill said that he would have moved for this information, and for no greater concession from the House, regardless of which party had been in power; he would not have asked for anything more had there still been a reform bill under discussion. He pointed out, however, that his motion could not at any time have been construed as a motion for an additional lowering of the franchise or for a move to garner more Liberal voters. He very nearly allowed his wit to lighten the matter-of-fact tone: "hon. Gentlemen opposite seem to think, and I suppose they are the best judges" that qualified women voters would vote Conservative; the hon. Member for Dublin University, Mill pointed out, "in his humorous manner, advised me on that ground to withdraw this article from my programme."[58] Very briefly, at this point Mill touched on ground that might not be considered practical in the eyes of all his listeners:

> I entertain the firmest conviction that whatever holds out an inducement to one-half of the community to exercise their minds on the great social and political questions which are discussed in Parliament, and whatever causes the great influence they already possess to be exerted under the guidance of greater knowledge, and under a sense of responsibility, cannot be ultimately advantageous to the Conservative or any other cause, except so far as that cause is a good one.

He had prepared a telling last sentence:

> I listened with pleasure and gratitude to the right hon. Gentleman who is now Chancellor of the Exchequer [Disraeli], when in his speech on the second reading of the Reform Bill, he said he saw no reason why women of independent means should not possess the electoral franchise, in a country where they can preside in manorial courts and fill parish offices—to which let me add, and the Throne.

Taylor would have dismissed out of hand Langham Place's practical suggestion to make it clear in the next petitions that they were asking for the suffrage only for widows and spinsters and not for wives. They knew full well that their opponents would concentrate on married women and the havoc to be wreaked upon the happy couple. Possibly the answer lies in Taylor's belief in floating a principle, or, more unkindly, possibly it lies in her seeming determination to assert herself and her power as Mill's stepdaughter behind the scenes. See Ann P. Robson, "The Founding of the National Society for Women's Suffrage 1866–67," *Canadian Journal of History*, 8 (March 1973), pp. 1–22.

58 James Whiteside, speech on the Elective Franchise Bill (30 May 1866), *Parliamentary Debates*, 3rd ser., vol. 183, col. 1509.

The conclusion reminded the Conservative leader in the Commons of his willingness to consider far more than Mill himself was asking for, and reminded the Tories that a laugh at Mill was a laugh at their leader. To give his last word to the Throne was very canny; not many in the House would have dared to associate their sovereign, however indirectly, with ribald repartee. The House appears to have kept its countenance; *Hansard* reported no disturbance and the newspapers, after their interest a month earlier in the notice of motion, paid little attention to the actual moving of it.[59]

Mill might well be satisfied with his tactics in this his first session; the idea of votes for women had been insinuated into the consciousness of the House and he had avoided the dreaded ridicule. The women's cause had been placed where it might well get support from members on either or both sides of the House. His request, agreed to by the home secretary Spencer Walpole, could in no way be considered as impractical or obstructive. Gladstone was consulting him; Earl Grey had asked for his participation in a proposal for cumulative voting;[60] and he felt he had shown himself to both Liberals and Conservatives—at least to those who did not read only *The Times*[61]—to be a moderating force in the wake of the Hyde Park riots that had taken place the week after his motion.[62] It was as an established parliamentarian that he left with Helen Taylor for six months in Avignon, from where he wrote to Theodor Gomperz: "I am indeed reduced to wondering whether I shall ever be able to resume those quiet studies which are so prodigiously better for the mind itself than the tiresome labour of chipping off little bits of one's thoughts, of a size to be swallowed by a set of diminutive practical politicians incapable of digesting them."[63] Satisfaction is a sometime thing.

It is quite clear that the next parliamentary move in the women's cause was already decided upon and that they were continuing to pave the way for it with considerable care and effort. In November he wrote in reply to Thomas Hare, whose plan for proportional representation was high on, if not at the top of, Mill's list of next-steps-to-the-earthly-heaven:

59 Helen Taylor reported to Barbara Bodichon: "The report in the 'Times' is a good one, the 'Daily News' the best." Quoted from a copy of a letter, 18 July 1866, provided by Barbara McCrimmon. The *Manchester Guardian* reported without comment on 19 June 1866, and the *News of the World* on 22 July 1866.

60 *LL*, *CW*, vol. XVI, p. 1171 (to W.E. Gladstone, 25 May 1866); p. 1169 (to Earl Grey, 21 May 1866). On 21 July 1866, Mill spoke at the inaugural dinner of the Cobden Club at which Gladstone presided. *PPS*, *CW*, vol. XXVIII, pp. 96–8.

61 *A*, *CW*, vol. I, pp. 278–9.

62 Ibid., p. 278. See above, chapter 3, pp. 95–6.

63 *LL*, *CW*, vol. XVI, p. 1196 (22 Aug. 1866).

"There will, in all probability, be a Tory Reform Bill, and whatever may be its quality, no moving of amendments or raising of new points will in the case of a Tory bill be regarded by Liberals as obstructiveness, or as damaging the cause. Then will be the very time to bring forward and get discussed, everything which we think ought to be put into a good Reform Bill."[64] Their immediate activity for the women's question was to stimulate public opinion outside the House in order to bring pressure to bear. The women in London made attempts, with mixed results, to found a national society for women's suffrage. They felt they must constantly consult with Mill through Taylor, both of whom were in Avignon.[65] While they were there Taylor prepared an article, which Mill offered to John Chapman:

> My daughter, from whom you have already more than once accepted articles, has written one on the claim of women in independent circumstances to the suffrage, which she sends by this post and places at the service of the Westminster Review if you are disposed to insert it. It is written, as you will see, with a practical object, to aid the parliamentary movement which will probably be made in the next session, and it takes, therefore, mainly the constitutional ground and that of analogy to English institutions, taking only incidental notice of the broader and higher principles on which the claim may be rested. It is desirable that the article, if accepted, should be in the January number, as the number following may perhaps be too late for the immediate occasion.[66]

Chapman agreed (he owed Mill),[67] and the article appeared in the January number.[68] The running head referred to the Ladies' Petition presented by Mill the previous June, and the thesis was, as Mill indicated

64 Ibid., p. 1214 (18 Nov. 1866). Mill's and Hare's hopes for proportional representation are discussed above in chapter 3, pp. 104–7.

65 It was unfortunate that Taylor proved herself (and she was, as always on the suffrage question, speaking for both of them) more of a hindrance than a help in the valiant efforts being made by Emily Davies, Clementia Taylor, and others to establish a national committee to work for women's suffrage. See Robson, "Founding of the National Society for Women's Suffrage."

66 *LL*, *CW*, vol. XVI, p. 1216 (21 Nov. 1866).

67 For all the debts, monetary and otherwise, that Chapman owed Mill, see ibid., pp. 1226, 1227, 1228, 1230, 1245 (Mill to John Chapman, 1, 8, 13, 29 Jan. and 20 Feb. 1867).

68 "The Ladies' Petition presented to the House of Commons by Mr. J. Stuart Mill, June 7th, 1866," *Westminster Review*, n.s. 31 (Jan. 1867), 63–79.

to Chapman, directed towards the kind of arguments that would keep the discussion on a practical, factual level. As soon as they returned to London, Mill was in touch with Chapman to arrange for a reprint of Taylor's article for distribution.[69]

They increased their widespread correspondence urging support for the question. Mill's influence with all classes was considerable and most of the letters went out over his name, although it is quite clear that the burden of this correspondence was borne by Taylor.[70] The amount of time given to the nurturing of opinion is quite remarkable. People of quite insignificant influence are taken on by Taylor as though she could not bear to lose an argument or leave unconverted a mind she had encountered. To Richard Russell she wrote three long letters refuting his position and belabouring him with sarcasm, although it is clear from the first that her tolerance for his attitude was limited.[71] After patiently refuting, with examples, his position that the sexes should not intermingle—the higher the civilization the fewer the objections—and that gaining the vote would not mean gaining admission to a seat in parliament, her patience wore thin and her sharp turn of phrase cut through:

> As to the objection that men & women might on some occasions differ collectively, and that the women might have their own way, it has much less force than the similar objection to the working classes, because men and women are much more likely to be evenly balanced in number than the poor & the rich. I cannot see how arranging that men shall always have their own way in everything can in justice be the proper way to prevent women from occasionally having theirs.[72]

The letters went out over Mill's name.

Mill was using his personal influence on his radical admirers. The Fawcetts were not the only newlyweds invited to dine at Blackheath; the highly and advantageously connected Amberleys also came.[73] And there

69 *LL*, *CW*, vol. XVI (6 Feb. 1867).

70 Her authorship, which can frequently be identified by the acid turn of phrase, can be attached to much of the correspondence at this time beyond that concerning women's suffrage.

71 Since Francis Mineka could give no more about him than his address, it may be taken that Russell was not a burning light in Islington, never mind London. *LL*, *CW*, vol. XVI, pp. 1251, 1257, and 1261 (6, 20 March and 2 April).

72 Ibid., p. 1252 (6 March 1867).

73 He was Lord John Russell's son and she was a daughter of the Stanleys of Alderley. Kate Amberley became Taylor's closest friend until her tragic early death from diptheria in 1874, caught while nursing her daughter Rachel. Mill and Taylor stood *in loco deus parentis* to young Bertrand.

were others, some long-time friends, all influential in their spheres, such as Thomas Hare, George Grote, and Herbert Spencer. Their activity seemed to be paying dividends; the movement seemed to be gaining recognition. To those not near to London, Mill wrote. He was quite gleeful in a letter to John Elliot Cairnes: "My daughter is very much pleased that you think favourably of what she has been doing. We have been made very happy by the adhesion of the Daily News, in an admirable article for which the cause is evidently indebted directly to Mr Hill, and indirectly to you."[74] And a few days later: "The progress of the cause of women's suffrage, both here and in the United States, is indeed wonderful. It is a great encouragement to those who have been working uphill."[75]

It was in this optimistic frame of mind that Mill began to turn his attention seriously to the preparations for moving his amendment to substitute the word "person" for "man" in the Reform Bill Disraeli introduced on 18 March 1867. He was expecting his opportunity to come around the middle of April—considerably earlier than was to be the case. On 15 March he presented a petition for the suffrage on behalf of Mrs. French; on 19 March he gave notice to the House of his amendment. On 26 March he wrote to Thomas Hare for help:

> I understood you to say one day in conversation, that the majority of the old deeds of endowment of schools included girls as well as boys, but that this part of the original design has been allowed to fall into desuetude. Am I right as to the fact? If so, I shall make use of it in my speech on the representation of women.
>
> ... Helen asks me to beg you to be kind enough to tell Miss Hare that there is now no chance of the women's suffrage debate coming on next Thursday, and it is not likely even for next week.[76]

Mill presented another petition on 5 April, obviously doing more spade work. His supporters were helping dig by circulating petitions in their own constituencies; the networking was amazingly successful particularly around Manchester, where Lydia Becker and Jacob Bright had collected the majority of the over 13,000 names.[77] On 8 April Mill was showing a little of the anxiety that one would expect when a speech of such momentous personal importance was in the offing with the date

74 *LL*, *CW*, vol. XVI, p. 1235 (9 Feb. 1867).
75 Ibid., p. 1239 (to Cairnes, 13 Feb. 1867).
76 Ibid., p. 1260 (26 March 1867).
77 Ibid., p. 1283 (to Cairnes, 30 June 1867).

uncertain. The debate that day was on the scheduling of the Reform Bill's going into committee:

> there was a great deal of inconvenience in leaving a matter of so much importance in vagueness and uncertainty. He spoke feelingly on the subject, as he had a Motion on the paper which would be the first Amendment on the Reform Bill when they got into Committee, and he was naturally anxious therefore to know whether the Bill would come on on Thursday. He was perfectly ready to bring forward his Motion on that day, or later if the House thought fit; but it was extremely important that he should know on what day he would be called upon to bring it forward.[78]

Mill was anxious also for strategic reasons. It was vitally important that when he introduced the amendment he have his own troops in attendance. He needed to have a reasonable debate with speakers who had the ear of the House, filling that ear with prepared, thoughtful arguments. Being also very anxious that it not be an irritated ear, on 11 April he very graciously, almost too graciously, gave way to Gladstone. It was not for Mill to put forward women's suffrage over the possibility of bringing down the government; the House would not have listened.

> Sir, I confess I attach the highest importance to the Amendment which stands on the paper in my name. Nevertheless, I shall waive my right to proceed with it now, entertaining as I do a confident hope that the distinguished supporters and sympathizers, will with one consent allow me at some early period an opportunity for a full discussion upon a proposal which I can assure hon. Gentlemen is a most serious one, and is becoming every day more serious from the number as well as the quality of its supporters. I should not for a moment think of interposing this Motion in the way of anything so important as the Amendment of my right hon. Friend the Member for South Lancashire, upon which the House is desirous, no doubt, of coming to a decisive judgment before we either adjourn or are dissolved.[79]

The early period was not as early as Mill might have hoped; he continued to maintain his reasonable voice in the House for another six

78 "The Reform Bill [1]," *PPS*, *CW*, vol. XXVIII, p. 143 (8 April 1867).
79 "The Reform Bill [2]," ibid., p. 145.

FUN.—May 4, 1867.
THE "MILL"-ENNIUM.
The Honourable Member for Westminster.—"I BEG TO PROPOSE—THE LADIES!"

weeks. He spoke with moderation and precision twice more on the Reform Bill,[80] both speeches upholding Gladstone and both speeches having to do with the endlessly vexed question of the compound householders.

Luck was, appropriately, a lady on the evening of 20 May when Mill's opportunity finally came to introduce his amendment. He rose to address the House at a tolerably early time of the evening when the members were in a reasonably good frame of mind.[81] The supporters whom he had counted upon were in their seats, their speeches at the ready. He had little difficulty in gaining the ear of the House in spite of, perhaps because of, a long tense moment when he first stood up: he faltered and hesitated and seemed to pull himself together.[82] His speech, however, once he was fairly launched, was a model of dispassionate reasoned argument.[83] There were no carelessly provided opportunities for derogatory laughter, but he kept the interest of the House with a debater's light touch, throughout the body of his speech using his customary rhetorical technique of responding to his opponents' presumed objections.

He began on the same ground as he had ten months previously when moving his earlier motion; his amendment had no bias of class, or party, or privilege:

> There is nothing to distract our attention from the simple question, whether there is any adequate justification for continuing to exclude an entire half of the community, not only from admission, but from the capability of being ever admitted within the pale of the Constitution, though they may fulfil all the conditions legally and constitutionally sufficient in every case but theirs. Sir, within the limits of our Constitution this is a solitary case.

He proceeded to set as narrow a base for the discussion as he could, a base

80 "The Reform Bill [3]" and "The Reform Bill [4]," ibid., pp. 146–9 and 150–1 (9 and 17 May 1867). Compare chapter 3, pp. 100–4 above.

81 Evelyn L. Pugh gives a good description of the circumstances in "John Stuart Mill and the Women's Question in Parliament, 1865–1868," *The Historian*, 41 (May 1980), p. 408, although contemporary accounts on the whole give a picture of greater success.

82 Michael St. J. Packe in *The Life of John Stuart Mill* (London: Secker and Warburg, 1954) implies considerable boisterousness in the House (p. 492) but gives no reference; the newspaper reports stressed the respect with which the speech was heard.

83 "The Admission of Women to the Electoral Franchise," *PPS*, *CW*, vol. XXVIII, pp. 151–62 (20 May 1867). The following quotations are all from this speech.

which would totally exclude married women—only single women had the qualifications necessary—and thus reduce the chances for jokes and innuendos about married couples. (Either intentionally or not, Mill rarely uses the word "sex.") He next laid out the philosophical grounds for his belief and drew the parallel with Gladstone's position, thus, presumably, giving pause to the Gladstonians in the House who were not certain of their leader's position on this matter:[84]

> Now, Sir, before going any further, allow me to say, that a *primâ facie* case is already made out. It is not just to make distinctions, in rights and privileges, without a positive reason. I do not mean that the electoral franchise, or any other public function, is an abstract right, and that to withhold it from any one, on sufficient grounds of expediency is a personal wrong; it is a complete misunderstanding of the principle I maintain, to confound this with it; my argument is entirely one of expediency. But there are different orders of expediency; all expediencies are not exactly on the same level; there is an important branch of expediency called justice; and justice, though it does not necessarily require that we should confer political functions on every one, does require that we should not, capriciously and without cause, withhold from one what we give to another. As was most truly said by my right honourable friend the Member for South Lancashire, in the most misunderstood and misrepresented speech I ever remember; to lay a ground for refusing the suffrage to any one, it is necessary to allege either personal unfitness or public danger. Now can either of these be alleged in the present case?

The answer quite obviously was "no," an answer that Mill clearly illustrated by worthy examples. He was sufficiently in control of the House to risk a glimmer of humour with one of his quiet sarcasms, using as one of his examples capable women schoolmistresses, who "teach much more than a great number of the male electors have ever learnt." Mill's last argument from principle reflected the concern that Taylor had addressed in her article for the *Westminster*: it was "repugnant to the particular principles of the British Constitution" that taxation and representation should not be co-extensive.

Mill then turned to his opponents' objections. The development of his argument strongly suggests that in preparing this speech he had

84 For a discussion of the uncertainity about Gladstone's position, see Ann P. Robson, "A Birds' Eye View of Gladstone," in Bruce L. Kinzer, ed., *The Gladstonian Turn of Mind* (Toronto: University of Toronto Press, 1985), pp. 63–96.

referred back to the manuscript for *The Subjection of Women* (although with his remarkable memory the referral may not have involved actually reading it). He started on a light topical note with another quiet display of humour at his opponents' expense. He would, he said, be expected to address the practical arguments against his proposition: "Now, there is one practical argument of great weight, which, I frankly confess, is entirely wanting in the case of women; they do not hold great meetings in the parks, or demonstrations at Islington. How far this omission may be considered to invalidate their claim, I will not undertake to decide." (Future proponents of votes for women were to answer that question in a way totally unforeseen by Mill, his friends, and his opponents.) However most "practical objections," he contended, were not really such: "The difficulty which most people feel on this subject, is not a practical objection; there is nothing practical about it; it is a mere feeling—a feeling of strangeness; the proposal is so new; at least they think so, though this is a mistake; it is a very old proposal. Well, Sir, strangeness is a thing which wears off."

Mill was ably removing from under his opponents' feet the ground upon which to stand for a reply. And again the sly humour—not enough to encourage heckling:

> And as for novelty, we live in a world of novelties; the despotism of custom is on the wane . . . and in this House at least, I am bound to believe that an appeal lies from custom to a higher tribunal, in which reason is judge. Now, the reasons which custom is in the habit of giving for itself on this subject are usually very brief. That, indeed, is one of my difficulties; it is not easy to refute an interjection; interjections, however, are the only arguments among those we usually hear on this subject, which it seems to me at all difficult to refute.

Indeed enough to discourage heckling. He then went on referring to his opponents' arguments as aphorisms. He came dangerously near to loosening his control when he outlined the argument that women have power enough already. Laughter broke out, showing how carefully he had to tread to avoid mirth. To answer the objection that politics were not a woman's business, Mill argued that they were not most men's. But a man was not a worse lawyer for voting. Mill discreetly referred to voting only, not to legislating—not that he was able to prevent his opponents from arguing in their response that women should not be in the House any more than he was able to prevent their harping on wives rather than independent women. For this latter harp, Mill himself was partly responsible as he could not avoid refuting the argument "that those who are principally charged with the moral education of the future generations of men, cannot be fit to form an opinion about the moral and educational interests of a people." But any little that was lost was surely more than compensated for by his in-House joke: "It is thought, perhaps, that those ... whose chief daily business is the judicious laying-out of money, so as to produce the greatest results with the smallest means, cannot possibly give any lessons to right honourable gentlemen on the other side of the House or on this, who contrive to produce such singularly small results with such vast means. (*Ironical cheers.*)"[85]

Mill then proceeded to some positive practical arguments. There had been a social revolution that had weakened the boundaries separating men's and women's spheres; as a result, "women and men are, for the first time in history, really each other's companions" and share each other's interests. Again can be seen the strong influence of the ideas that he and Harriet Mill had discussed and that he had set down in the draft of *The Subjection of Women.* Mill talked of the wife now being the man's "chief associate, his most confidential friend, and often his most trusted adviser." And he asked: "Is it good for a man to live in complete communion of thoughts and feelings with one who is studiously kept inferior to himself. . .? Does any one suppose that this can happen without detriment to the man's own character? Sir, the time is now come when, unless women are raised to the level of men, men will be pulled down to theirs."

Mill must almost have been able to hear the inflection of his beloved wife's voice as he argued that if women were not encouraged to interest themselves in public affairs, they would continue to interest themselves in private advancement and would always be urging men to pursue the selfish interests of personal and family advancement. It could not be expected that women should themselves make or encourage others to make altruistic sacrifices if they had no understanding of or role to play in the public good. If women were frivolous, men would be frivolous. And although it was undoubtedly true, as many women had proved, that it was possible to take a broad view of the public interest without having the vote, the denial of the vote told them that such interest was outside their province.

Mill then dissected the argument that women did not want the suffrage. If the claim were true, it would be proof that denial of the

85 Could Mill possibly have realized he was inverting Gladstone's scathing rejection ten years earlier of the possibility of women giving the House advice on money matters? *PD*, 3rd ser., vol. 138, col. 276 (9 May 1855).

privilege had had its expected effect and numbed their inclinations. However, the number of petitions showed that many, many women wanted the right to vote. The number of signatures was all the more revealing because few women wanted to make themselves conspicuous by speaking out—all their breeding inclined them to the opposite. They had been brought up to make a virtue of necessity and in this case that meant not asking for what they thought they could not have. That all women did not want the vote was no reason to deny it to those who did. Those who did not want it did not have to exercise it, or they could do as they were advised by a male relative. Such behaviour would undoubtedly be distributed quite evenly throughout the classes, not advantaging any particular group. Those who did want it would use it and benefit from the use. Indeed the whole sex would benefit by no longer being classed with children, idiots, and lunatics (he might have added peers), even if only one in 20,000 actually cast a vote.

Mill's response to the next argument—that women did not need direct power because they had sufficient indirect power—was particularly clever and redirected the laughter that the idea caused. Not only did he seek a startling analogy and an appealing one, but in so doing he deflected onto quite a different target any potential sarcasm about coquettish or manipulating women:

> I should like to carry this argument a little further. Rich people have a great deal of indirect influence. Is this a reason for refusing them votes? Does any one propose a rating qualification the wrong way, or bring in a Reform Bill to disfranchise all who live in a £500 house, or pay £100 a year in direct taxes? Unless this rule for distributing the franchise is to be reserved for the exclusive benefit of women, it would follow that persons of more than a certain fortune should be allowed to bribe, but should not be allowed to vote.

He admitted that women had a great deal of power over men; that fact strengthened his argument. This power they exercised under the worst possible conditions; it was irresponsible. If women had a public voice, then their influence would be a healthy one.

For his refutation of the next common assertion of his opponents, Mill drew on the articles he and Harriet Mill had written together in the 1850s. These arguments too were already in the draft of *The Subjection of Women*. His opponents said that women suffered no practical inconvenience from being denied the suffrage, because their interests were safely in the hands of their fathers, husbands, brothers, or other male relatives, safely since their interests were identical and the males' knowledge greater. After pointing out that this argument had been perennially used about all unrepresented classes—operatives represented by manufacturers, agricultural labourers by farmers—Mill turned to the specific question of women:

> I should like to have a return laid before this House of the number of women who are annually beaten to death, kicked to death, or trampled to death by their male protectors: and, in an opposite column, the amount of the sentences passed, in those cases in which the dastardly criminals did not get off altogether. I should also like to have, in a third column, the amount of property, the unlawful taking of which was, at the same sessions or assizes, by the same judge, thought worthy of the same amount of punishment. We should then have an arithmetical estimate of the value set by a male legislature and male tribunals on the murder of a woman, often by torture continued through years, which, if there is any shame in us, would make us hang our heads.

He continued with a devastating attack on the laws in other areas—although here he was talking of laws in a looser sense, many of them being, in fact, by-laws in royal charters of self-governing bodies. Education showed that women were not given favourable treatment. Where were the universities? the high schools? the schools for governesses, if it were to be argued that home education were more suitable? Where were the endowments left for poor children of both sexes? One expert, Mill reported, said that Christ's Hospital School had 1100 boys and 26 girls.[86] In employment, nearly all the professions, except governessing, were closed to the educated woman. The Apothecaries had just closed the narrow gap through which Miss Garrett had squeezed and the Royal Academy had retracted the privilege of associate membership when female artists proved highly successful.[87]

He ended his disquisition on the practical inconvenience of the laws supported by a male legislature by cutting loose on the subject of married women's property, a bill concerning which he was shortly to support. By law a wife owned nothing and unless she were judicially separated—still

86 Presumably Thomas Hare.

87 Mill was referring to the Apothecaries' Society's amending their by-laws to make compulsory the attendance at public lectures (Elizabeth Garrett had had private classes); it is not clear what action of the Royal Academy he had in mind. The latter point is discussed, though not settled, in *PPS*, *CW*, vol. XXVIII, p. 160n.

a difficult process in 1867—her earnings and savings gained "by heroic exertion and self-sacrifice" could be "pounced upon" at any time by an errant husband. The richer classes knew full well the inequity of the law and contrived by marriage settlements "to make a private law for themselves":

> Why do we not provide that justice for the daughters of the poor . . . so that a poor man's child, whose parents could not afford the expense of a settlement, . . . may have a voice in the disposal of her own earnings, which, in the case of many husbands, are the best and only reliable part of the incomings of the family? I am sometimes asked what practical grievances I propose to remedy by giving women a vote. I propose, for one thing, to remedy this. I give these instances to prove that women are not the petted children of society which many people seem to think they are . . . and are not sufficiently represented by the representation of the men who have not had the heart to do for them this simple and obvious piece of justice.

His peroration—he had taken just over half an hour of the members' time—is moving even on the page; charged with vocal emotion, the effect must have been considerable:

> We ought not . . . to withhold from a limited number of women that moderate participation in the enactment and improvement of our laws, which this motion solicits for them, and which would enable the general feelings of women to be heard in this House through a few male representatives. We ought not to deny to them, what we are conceding to everybody else—a right to be consulted; the ordinary chance of placing in the great Council of the nation a few organs of their sentiments—of having, what every petty trade or profession has, a few members who feel specially called on to attend to their interests, and to point out how those interests are affected by the law, or by any proposed changes in it. No more is asked by this motion; and when the time comes, as it certainly will come, when this will be granted, I feel the firmest conviction that you will never repent of the concession.

His summation at the end of the debate, after others had spoken and before the question was put, was lighter. Following the debater's book of rules, he wittily put down his opponents' general performance, then referred slightingly to their arguments; he introduced no new arguments, but repeated briefly his own arguments, and sat down:

> I will merely say, in answer to the noble Lord who requested me to withdraw the Motion,[88] that I am a great deal too well pleased with the speeches that have been made against it—his own included—to think of withdrawing it. There is nothing that has pleased me more in those speeches than to find that every one who has attempted to argue at all, has argued against something which is not before the House: they have argued against the admission of married women, which is not in the Motion; or they have argued against the admission of women as Members of this House; or again, as the hon. Member for the Wick boroughs (Mr. Laing) has done, they have argued against allowing women to be generals and officers in the army; a question which I need scarcely say is not before the House. I certainly do think that when we come to universal suffrage, as some time or other we probably shall come—if we extend the vote to all men, we should extend it to all women also. So long, however, as you maintain a property qualification, I do not propose to extend the suffrage to any women but those who have the qualification. If, as is surmised by one of the speakers, young ladies should attach so much value to the suffrage that they should be unwilling to divest themselves of it in order to marry, I can only say that if they will not marry without it, they will probably be allowed to retain it. As to any question that may arise in reference to the removal of any other disabilities of women, it is not before the House. There are evidently many arguments and many considerations that cannot be overlooked in dealing with these larger questions, but which do not arise on the present Motion, and on which, therefore, it is not necessary that I should comment. I will only say that if we should in the progress of experience—especially after experience of the effect of granting the suffrage—come to the decision that married women ought to have the suffrage, or that women should be admitted to any employment or occupation which they are not now admitted to—if it should become the general opinion that they ought to have it, they will have it.

How carefully Mill had had to tread was shown again when his passing mention of universal suffrage brought an "Oh, oh"—a good instance of his "unanswerable interjections"; he had hitherto kept other aspects of his advanced radicalism out of sight (or hearing). The House divided "amid much merriment" and the amendment was lost, 196 to 73; but the

88 George Edward Arundell Monckton-Arundell, Viscount Galway, in *PD*, 3rd ser., vol. 187, cols. 841–2 (20 May 1867).

merriment was amongst the minority. It was the "announcement of the number voting for the amendment [that] was greeted with cheers and laughter."[89] "The minority," reported the *Morning Advertiser*, "cheered the unexpectedly large number voting on their side."[90] Mill, being one of the tellers, would have been in the midst of the elation.

Mill was a little taken aback and disappointed that the lack of opposition brought an early conclusion to the debate; he obviously felt that he had a powerful team, a team likely to persuade many who were doubtful, some who had never given the matter consideration, and even some who had been opposed. He would have preferred more time for his proselytizing. Nonetheless he was vastly pleased at the outcome: "You will have seen the debate on the representation of women. The minority of 73 (which would have been near 100 if the division had not taken place unexpectedly at a bad time of the evening) is most encouraging, and has put its members and many other supporters in great spirits. The greatest triumph of all is getting [John] Bright's vote: ten days before, he was decidedly against us."[91] His careful planning had gained him an unexpected success in parliament, removing the smiles from the faces of the opponents of women's suffrage onto those of its supporters.

Equally impressive was the response of the newspapers. The coverage of the debate was extensive and serious. *The Times* gave it over two columns[92] and that was not unusual for the coverage; those who summarized were fair. All reported the merriment in the division but none tried to turn it into ridicule of the debate—in most cases quite the contrary, as when the *Morning Advertiser* make it clear where the glee lay. And there is no indication of barracking during the speech. The laughs Mill got, and the reports show there were many, were those he solicited. The *Yorkshire Post and Leeds Intelligencer*, taking a full column to refute a proposal it said was too silly to need refutation, bemoaned the fact that "the wags of the House of Commons threw away the best chance that had been open to them this session" and concluded that the "introduction of the subject by so grave a philosopher as Mr Mill alone saved it from being laughed out of the House of Commons. Indeed, only the high reputation of Mr Mill could be sufficient to gain for so preposterous a proposal, a moment's serious consideration."[93]

89 *Morning Star*, 21 May 1867.

90 21 May 1867.

91 *LL*, *CW*, vol. XVI, p. 1271 (to Cairnes, 26 May 1867). Keeping John Bright's name on the side of the ayes was to influence the parliamentary tactics of the women's supporters for the next few sessions.

92 21 May 1867.

93 22 May 1867.

But Mill got it many, many more than one such moment. Nearly all the major papers in the following days carried lengthy editorials. *The Times*, also opposed, gave a full column to serious argument.[94] The *Leeds Mercury*, whose publisher Edward Baines voted with Mill, also gave, not surprisingly, a full column but of well-argued support for this new political issue.[95] The *Manchester Weekly Times* began its editorial: "Mr Mill made his greatest parliamentary speech on Monday evening" and castigated the silliness of his opponents.[96] The *Morning Herald* disagreed: the speech was in its view poor and halting and as ridiculous as the proposal, but the editorialist did not himself use ridicule.[97] The *Evening Standard* interpreted Mill's halting delivery at the beginning as deliberation that resulted in a very careful speech.[98] It was; Mill had taken great care not only with the content but also with the preparation of the House and of the public in order to have the matter taken seriously. And he succeeded: what the House took seriously, the press took seriously, and, perhaps more importantly, what the press took seriously, so did the members of parliament.

Mill did not raise the question of women's suffrage again in the House beyond the presentation of petitions,[99] but his contribution to the women's movement cannot be overestimated. The fact of his presence in parliament had given enormous encouragement to the many women working in separate fields to improve their position in society. The fact that he had made "the claim of women to the suffrage a parliamentary question" gave the movement a national focus. Throughout the country, from Bristol to Edinburgh, the work of petitioning parliament went on—and on and on. Not until 1928[100] was Dame Millicent Fawcett to lead a celebratory delegation of newly enfranchised women to lay a wreath at the base of the statue of John Stuart Mill on the Embankment. It is to his credit, however, that through all those years the question of the removal of women's political disabilities was never, well hardly ever, treated as a laughing matter in the House of Commons.

94 22 May 1867

95 22 May 1867.

96 25 May 1867.

97 21 May 1867.

98 21 May 1867.

99 For a list of the petitions Mill presented, including those on women's suffrage, see *PPS*, *CW*, vol. XXIX, appendix C, pp. 272–93.

100 Mill would have been dismayed by the date. See *LL*, *CW*, vol. XVII, p. 1727 (to Charles Dilke, 28 May 1870).

FIVE

Ireland

If few members sitting in the House of Commons from 1866 through 1868 can have given more thought to the subjects of parliamentary reform and sexual equality than had J.S. Mill, the same (Irish MPs excepted) may be said about the Irish question. Over the preceding four decades Mill had intermittently responded to the Irish problem as it intruded upon the consciousness of England. His 1825 article "Ireland" offered a vigorous political and legal defence of Daniel O'Connell's Catholic Association.[1] In the 1830s Mill incorporated the condition of Ireland into his assault on aristocratic government without, however, presenting any sustained treatment of the subject. The 1840s found him grappling with the practical and theoretical sides of the Irish land question, an exercise prompted both by the calamity of the famine and by his work on the principles of political economy.[2] In the seventeen years before Mill entered parliament the *Principles of Political Economy* went through six editions. The revisions he made in the sections of the *Principles* pertaining to Ireland reveal the change and continuity in his views on the land question. Consistently supporting the principle of peasant proprietorship, Mill nonetheless acknowledged the difficulties of its application to Ireland and displayed varying degrees of commitment with respect to action by the state.[3] (The fluctuations in part reflect changing English perceptions

1 "Ireland," in *Essays on England, Ireland, and the Empire* [*EEIE*], ed. John M. Robson, *Collected Works* [*CW*], vol. VI (Toronto: University of Toronto Press, 1982), pp. 59–98.

2 From October 1846 to January 1847 Mill contributed forty-three leading articles to the *Morning Chronicle* on the condition of Ireland. See *Newspaper Writings* [*NW*], ed. Ann P. and John M. Robson, *CW*, vols. XXII–XXV (Toronto: University of Toronto Press, 1986), vol. XXIV.

3 The secondary literature on Mill and the Irish land question is sizeable: E.D. Steele, "J.S. Mill and the Irish Question: The Principles of Political Economy,

of Irish circumstances.) Mill's parliamentary career is full of interest, not least because his years in the House coincided with a critical juncture in the history of the Union. Irish land, Irish nationalism, and the Irish university question combined to make Ireland one of Mill's central preoccupations during his Westminster years.

For reasons that will be made clear, Mill's response to the Irish university question did not become a matter of public record, save for a brief allusion to the subject in his pamphlet *England and Ireland.* It is through his correspondence, not his speeches or public writings, that we learn of his politically charged engagement with the issue during his first session in the House of Commons. An investigation of that engagement offers a distinctive angle of vision on the dilemmas of liberalism when confronted with the problem of Ireland, and also illuminates, with an intense if narrow ray, the character of Mill's parliamentary politics at this time.

In 1845 the government of Sir Robert Peel moved to augment higher educational opportunities for the middle-class Catholic laity of Ireland. Until then, Irishmen eager to obtain a university degree in their own country had but one choice: Trinity College Dublin, founded in the late sixteenth century. Although a 1793 act of the Irish parliament had enabled this amply endowed Anglican institution to award degrees to non-Anglicans, its identification with the Protestant establishment in Ireland remained palpable. Non-Anglicans were excluded from professorships, fellowships, scholarships, and prizes—proscriptions that would not be lifted until the early 1870s. The number of Catholics taking degrees at Trinity was small during the first half of the nineteenth century. Peel did not deny the legitimacy of the Catholic grievance in the sphere of higher education. Protestant frenzy over the building grant and annual subsidy provided to the Catholic seminary at Maynooth, however, argued against an attack upon the Anglicanism of Trinity College. Instead, Peel's government proposed to set up three nondenominational Queen's Colleges, in Belfast (primarily for Presbyterians), Cork, and Galway.

1848–1865," *Historical Journal,* 13 (1970), 216–36, and "J.S. Mill and the Irish Question: Reform, and the Integrity of the Empire," *Historical Journal,* 13 (1970), 419–50; R.N. Lebow, "J.S. Mill and the Irish Land Question," in *John Stuart Mill on Ireland,* ed. R.N. Lebow (Philadelphia: Institute for the Study of Human Issues, 1979), pp. 3–22; Lynn Zastoupil, "Moral Government: J.S. Mill on Ireland," *Historical Journal,* 26 (1983), 707–17; T.A. Boylan and T.P. Foley, "John Elliot Cairnes, John Stuart Mill and Ireland: Some Problems for Political Economy," *Hermathena,* 135 (1983), 96–119; B.L. Kinzer, "J.S. Mill and Irish Land: A Reassessment," *Historical Journal,* 27 (1984), 111–27.

Together these colleges, opened in 1849, formed the Queen's University, chartered in 1850.[4]

The Queen's colleges did not have a sufficient number of powerful friends within the Catholic hierarchy either in Ireland or in Rome to save them from papal condemnation. Fearing for the "faith and morals" of Irish Catholic youth, Pope Pius IX issued rescripts against the colleges in 1847, 1848, and 1850. A national synod of the Irish Catholic hierarchy, convened at Thurles in 1850 and assiduously managed by Paul Cullen, apostolic delegate and soon to become archbishop of Dublin, censured the Queen's University plan and instructed Catholics to keep clear of the Queen's colleges.[5] Not long thereafter Cullen spearheaded the drive to found an independent Catholic university in Dublin, which opened its door in 1854, John Henry Newman sitting (very occasionally) in the rector's office.[6]

By the mid-1860s neither the Catholic University nor the Queen's colleges (except that at Belfast, which enjoyed the support of a substantial Presbyterian constituency) were prospering. Both lacked adequate funding, the predicament of the Catholic University being by far the more serious. Lacking government charter and endowment, the Catholic University on average had only 125 students in attendance during the 1860s. The mission of the Queen's colleges was hampered by the hostility of the bishops, though there were Catholic families prepared to ignore the injunctions of the hierarchy.[7] The advocates of the Queen's University

4 For the establishment of the Queen's Colleges, see T.W. Moody, "The Irish University Question in the Nineteenth Century," *History*, 43 (1958), 90–109; T.W. Moody and J.C. Beckett, *Queen's Belfast, 1845–1949: The History of a University*, 2 vols. (London: Faber and Faber, 1959); Donal A. Kerr, *Peel, Priests and Politics: Sir Robert Peel's Administration and the Roman Catholic Church in Ireland* (Oxford: Clarendon Press, 1982), pp. 290–351.

5 The key votes on the subject of cooperation with the government on the university proposal were only narrowly carried by Cullen, whose uncompromising stance met with the disapproval of Daniel Murray, then archbishop of Dublin. For a full account of the synod, see Emmet Larkin, *The Making of the Roman Catholic Church in Ireland, 1850–1860* (Chapel Hill: University of North Carolina Press, 1980), pp. 3–57.

6 For the establishment of the Catholic University, see F. McGrath, *Newman's University: Idea and Reality* (Dublin: Browne and Nolan, 1951). The lectures and essays that make up Newman's *The Idea of a University* originated in his association with the Catholic University.

7 From 1862 to 1867, 725 students entered the Cork and Galway colleges, of whom 311 (or just over 40 per cent) were Roman Catholic. See K. Flanagan, "The Godless and the Burlesque: Newman and the Other Irish Universities," in *Newman and Gladstone: Centennial Essays*, ed. J.D. Bastable (Dublin: Veritas Publications, 1978), pp. 244–6.

system, concerned to protect the struggling colleges at Cork and Galway from the enmity of an increasingly confident and aggressive ecclesiastical power, were alert to the need for political vigilance.

Among those advocates was John Elliot Cairnes, professor of jurisprudence and political economy at Queen's College Galway, and friend of J.S. Mill. Mill and Cairnes first met in 1859, at a gathering of the Political Economy Club in London.[8] They corresponded frequently in the first half of the 1860s. In the summer of 1861 Mill read the manuscript of Cairnes's *The Slave Power*, a work that dissected the economic dynamics of American slavery and its expansionist tendencies, and he strongly encouraged Cairnes to publish it.[9] When the book appeared, Mill wrote an appreciative article for the *Westminster Review*.[10] The high value Mill placed upon this developing friendship was expressed to Cairnes in June of 1862: "I do not think there is an opinion or a sentiment in the book with which I substantially disagree; and this is so very generally the case when I read anything you write, that I feel growing up in me, what I seldom have, the agreeable feeling of a brotherhood in arms."[11] Mill conveyed his esteem for Cairnes in a letter to Henry Fawcett: "He has one of the clearest intellects I know, combined, I think, with an excellent moral nature, and is capable, if he has anything like fair play, of doing great things."[12]

Cairnes had been raised and educated in Ireland (he was a graduate of Trinity College) and Mill did not hesitate to draw upon his friend's knowledge of that country. In late 1864 Mill sought from Cairnes information and elucidation on agrarian conditions in Ireland for the sixth edition of the *Principles*.[13] Cairnes answered with his "Notes on the State of Ireland," which Mill acknowledged to be "a complete Essay on the state and prospects of Ireland, and are so entirely satisfactory that they leave me nothing to think of except how to make the most of them."[14] In the summer of 1865 Cairnes, much encouraged by Mill's recent triumph,

8 See Boylan and Foley, "John Elliot Cairnes, John Stuart Mill and Ireland," p. 98.

9 *Later Letters* [*LL*], ed. Francis E. Mineka and Dwight N. Lindley, *CW*, vols. XIV–XVII (Toronto: University of Toronto Press, 1972), vol. XV, pp. 738–9 (18 Aug. 1861).

10 *Westminster Review*, LXXVIII (1862), 489–510; reprinted in *Essays on Equality, Law, and Education*, *CW*, vol. XXI, pp. 143–64.

11 *LL*, *CW*, vol. XV, p. 785 (24 June 1862).

12 Ibid., p. 787 (21 July 1862).

13 Ibid., pp. 959 (3 Oct.), 964–5 (8 Nov.), 967 (1 Dec.).

14 Cairnes's essay is printed as appendix H of the *Principles of Political Economy* [*PPE*], ed. John M. Robson, *CW*, vols. II-III (Toronto: University of Toronto Press, 1965), vol. III, pp. 1075–86. For Mill's response, see *LL*, *CW*, vol. XVI, p. 985 (5 Jan. 1865).

would turn to his friend for political assistance on the Irish university question.

As the holder of a chair at Queen's College Galway, Cairnes had a personal professional stake in the defence of an institution striving to prevail in an inhospitable environment. Yet the strength of Cairnes's convictions on the issues raised by the university question reflects a depth of principle that goes far beyond material and career considerations. For Cairnes the Irish counterpart of the slave power in America was the Roman Catholic hierarchy, whose noxious ambitions it was the responsibility of liberalism to contain. Cairnes did not doubt that Cullen and his cohorts wished to destroy the nondenominational Queen's colleges; the vital principle of unsectarian education was endangered by the insatiable bigotry of Rome.[15]

The chief problem, as Cairnes saw it in the summer of 1865, concerned an apparent dearth of backbone in Palmerston's Liberal government under pressure from the Catholic hierarchy. A charter for the Catholic University in a form acceptable to Cullen was not a practical political option for this government. But before the 1865 session of parliament wound up its business, the government did imply that Irish Catholics had cause for complaint. In June of that year Sir George Grey, speaking on behalf of the Palmerston administration, announced that the government contemplated presenting a scheme that would permit Catholics to acquire a Queen's University degree without being obliged to attend one of the nondenominational Queen's colleges.[16] Cairnes feared that the government was about to descend the slippery slope of

15 Although the leading historian of the Roman Catholic church in Ireland in the nineteenth century would not urge the hierarchy to enter a plea of guilty to the charge of bigotry, he does not deny that Cullen and his associates sought the destruction of all unsectarian education in Ireland. "They refused to give an inch on what they regarded as being fundamental—a complete system of denominational education on all levels absolutely under their control." Emmet Larkin, *The Consolidation of the Roman Catholic Church in Ireland, 1860–1870* (Chapel Hill: University of North Carolina Press, 1987), p. 492.

16 See *Parliamentary Debates* [*PD*], 3rd ser., vol. 180, cols. 541–90 (20 June 1865) for the debate on a motion offered by Daniel O'Donoghue ("The O'Donoghue," MP for Tipperary) calling for a charter for the Catholic University. Presumably, the government's inclination to appease the hierarchy on the higher education question had its roots in political calculation of a mundane nature: at the 1859 general election Tories won 55 of the 105 seats, the high-water mark of Conservative success in Ireland in the post–1832 era. Irish Catholic electoral preference for Liberals over Tories could no longer be taken for granted by Palmerston and his colleagues. See K.T. Hoppen, "Tories, Catholics, and the General Election of 1859," *Historical Journal*, 13 (1970), 48–67.

concession. Such a descent, he believed, would ultimately undermine the integrity and purpose of the Queen's colleges and render them entirely unfit to execute the solemn and essential charge with which they had been commissioned at their foundation.

Cairnes sounded the alarm in a letter to Mill of August 1865, two months after Grey's statement in the House of Commons. He remarked on the success of the Queen's colleges, "which is now imperiled by the disposition to conciliate a party who in the name of freedom of education are seeking to get the control of the education of the country into their own hands in order to corrupt and pervert it."[17] The tone of Mill's reply was much less fierce. He observed that, undesirable though it was to open up Queen's University degrees to non-Queen's college students, Grey's speech virtually committed the government to that course and there did not seem to be much anyone could do to stop it. That being so, the main objective should be to keep the opponents of the Queen's colleges off the senate of the Queen's University: "The great point is, to insist that the particular scheme of education which the British nation has instituted because it thinks that (for Ireland) it is the best, shall continue to have fair play; and that the enemies of the scheme shall have no voice in deciding how it shall be carried out."[18]

Determined to enlighten Mill respecting the gravity of the threat and to recruit him into the ranks of the activists who deplored any tampering with the Queen's University charter to curry favour with Catholic bishops, Cairnes would not let the matter rest. His reply of late August noted that the government had in mind an affiliation of Catholic educational institutions with the Queen's University in an arrangement that would enable their candidates to obtain Queen's University degrees. Should this be consummated, Catholic institutions could not be denied representation in the Queen's University senate. Cairnes had learned "that one half the whole body is the Government's notion of what would constitute 'due' representation": a sectarian Catholic presence of this magnitude would make unachievable the aims for which the Queen's colleges were established.[19] As it was, students from Irish Catholic colleges (and from anywhere else) in pursuit of a degree could present themselves for the

17 Mill-Taylor Collection [M-T], British Library of Political and Economic Science, London School of Economics, vol. LVI [i], fols. 177–8 (20 Aug. 1865).

18 *LL*, *CW*, vol. XVI, pp. 1094–5 (22 Aug. 1865).

19 For the government's draft memorandum on the projected organization of the "Queen's Irish University," see Larkin, *The Consolidation of the Roman Catholic Church in Ireland*, pp. 474–5.

London University examinations.[20] Cairnes thought it far better that the "Irish ultramontane party" be given representation in the London University senate, where it could never exercise a dominant voice, than be admitted to the senate for the Queen's University, "with which it has no affinity." This alternative, Cairnes allowed, "would fail to satisfy the expectations of the party, but so would any concession which fell short of transferring the education of the people of Ireland into their hands."[21]

Mill remained less than keen to join the fray. An expansion of the London University senate to conform with Cairnes's suggestions would not answer the government's problem. Political constraints being what they were, Mill put forward the idea of a Queen's University board that would confer degrees but have no governing authority over the Queen's colleges. In appointing the members of this board, the government should give places to the ultramontane element, "but not to the extent of half. . . . They are not entitled to half. The Catholic religion is entitled to half, but not any particular section of the Catholic body." Mill was not optimistic about procuring even this degree of protection for the Queen's colleges, though he assured Cairnes he would do what he could to help in his new capacity as a member of parliament.[22]

In the autumn Cairnes drafted a lengthy article on university education in Ireland, which the *Theological Review* published in January 1866.[23] This essay forcefully defended the Queen's colleges and, with equal force, exposed and condemned the methods and aims of the Catholic hierarchy in Ireland. After reading this article, Mill informed Cairnes that he would take his "stand against the denominational system in any form for Ireland." He echoed Cairnes on the importance of a collegiate education that brought together Catholic and Protestant youth—a cause that warranted "almost any encouragement to the system of the Queen's University, except that of actually refusing degrees to those who have studied elsewhere." Coupled with the proclamation of his strong support was the observation that the behaviour of the Catholic prelacy might give the government a pretext for abandoning the stance it had adopted just prior to the general election. Members of parliament loyal

20 London University was an examination-administering, degree-granting institution prepared to recognize evidence of qualification for a university degree regardless of a candidate's educational background. See Negley Harte, *The University of London 1836–1986: An Illustrated History* (London: Athlone Press, 1986).

21 M-T, vol. LVI [i], fols. 179–84 (28 Aug. 1865).

22 *LL*, *CW*, vol. XVI, pp. 1101–2 (2 Sept. 1865).

23 "University Education in Ireland," *Theological Review*, 3 (1866), 116–49; reprinted as "Thoughts on University Reform," in John Elliot Cairnes, *Political Essays* (London: Macmillan, 1873), pp. 256–314.

to the Queen's University system should endeavour to persuade the Russell-Gladstone ministry that a retraction was both possible and desirable. Mill also asked Cairnes whether he had given any thought as to who should initiate the parliamentary defence of the Queen's colleges. Mill seemed to be gearing up for battle in the expectation that significant damage could be averted. "Any tolerable stand made in the House will have powerful support outside, from the mass of feeling in the country always ready to be called forth against any new concession to Catholics."[24]

Mill's adherence to the cause greatly pleased Cairnes, who readily agreed that the contest was not yet lost. He confessed, however, to some anxiety about the leadership question. The "general indifference of English liberals" to the subject meant that the lead might fall to Sir Robert Peel (son of the former prime minister), "who is pretty certain to do us mischief."[25] Cairnes understandably interpreted Mill's query as signalling a willingness to take up a front-line position in the anticipated clash, and he plainly wished to press Mill forward. Peel's unsuitability for leadership, Cairnes pointedly observed, made Mill's "adhesion—I hope I am not too sanguine in thus understanding you—of simply inestimable value."[26]

Towards the end of January a worried Cairnes wrote to Mill concerning a statement by Lord Wodehouse (lord lieutenant of Ireland) to the effect that the government intended to affiliate the Catholic University and other colleges to the Queen's University and to reconstitute the governing body of the Queen's University in accordance with this change.

24 *LL*, *CW*, vol. XVI, pp. 1133–4 (6 Jan. 1866). E.D. Steele maintains that Mill's view of the education issue was narrow and short-sighted. Stating that Mill shared the Nonconformists' "obdurate resistance to the educational concessions persistently sought by the Catholic Church in Ireland," he concludes that Mill showed himself "to be as righteously unsympathetic as any Orangeman to the sentiments of the majority of the Irish population." "J.S. Mill and the Irish Question: Reform, and the Integrity of the Empire," p. 434. Whatever the "sentiments of the majority of the Irish population" may have been, Mill believed that an educational system entirely controlled by the Catholic church could not be in the best interests of Irish society. The outcome of the church's eventual victory in this sphere would not have convinced Mill that he had been mistaken. For a further exposition of Mill's attitude, see B.L. Kinzer, "John Stuart Mill and the Irish University Question," *Victorian Studies*, 31 (1987), 71–7.

25 Cairnes was not impugning Peel's motives but his temperament and abilities. K.T. Hoppen says that Peel's tenure of the Irish chief secretaryship "between 1861 and 1865 was marked by choleric intemperance, lack of application, and burst blood vessels all round. That Palmerston should have kept so manifestly absurd a man in so important an office . . . suggests a profound contempt, not only for most things Irish, but for the Irish Liberal Party in particular." *Elections, Politics, and Society in Ireland, 1832–1885* (Oxford: Clarendon Press, 1984), p. 261.

26 M-T, vol. LVI [i], fols. 187–90 (9 Jan. 1866).

Cairnes had feared as much; what especially perturbed him was the implication that the government might not bother to consult parliament about the restructuring, since it did not propose to endow the Catholic University. Both Mill and Cairnes reasoned that their best hope lay in the House of Commons, whose participation the ministry must not be allowed to circumvent. Cairnes reported that he had communicated with Thomas Hughes and Henry Fawcett, Radical MPs sympathetic to the Queen's colleges, and they were prepared to ensure that Russell and Gladstone not pursue such a course without incurring the public wrath of some Liberals in the House.[27]

On the last day of January 1866 Mill, lately returned from Avignon to take his seat in the House, expressed his desire to discuss with Cairnes "the critical state of things respecting the education question." Mill was much troubled. "If the ministry does not take care, they will commence the breaking up of their party by this measure."[28] Mill's earnestness and his ascription of such significance to the matter reinforced Cairnes's sense of his friend's commitment.

Encouraged by a conversation with George Goschen, a member of the Liberal cabinet, to think that the government had not yet made a "definitive bargain" with the Irish bishops, Cairnes expanded his lobbying efforts, which now involved not only Hughes and Fawcett, but also Charles Neate, P.A. Taylor, G.J. Shaw-Lefevre, and a number of Scottish MPs. Furthermore, he had let it be known that Mill "would be happy to consult with them on the subject." Casting his most distinguished ally in a leadership role, Cairnes urged Mill to consider reaching an understanding with Sir Hugh Cairns and Sir Robert Peel, who would probably want to share in the defence of the Queen's colleges, although neither was accustomed to cooperating with Radicals. Cairnes desired that Sir Hugh and Sir Robert be relegated to supporting parts, recognizing that Liberals would be reluctant to follow their lead.[29]

Mill's answer may have caused Cairnes to ponder the quirkiness of political life. Mill had been taking soundings of his own. Having been assured by Grant Duff, an experienced Scottish MP, that the weight of Scotland in the House of Commons would come down against any government move to favour the Catholic hierarchy at the expense of the Queen's colleges, Mill now became skittish at the prospect of the Tories exploiting the issue to topple a fragile Liberal ministry pledged to parliamentary reform. Vigorous opposition to an attack on the existing

27 Ibid., fols. 194–6 (25 Jan. 1866).

28 *LL*, *CW*, vol. XVI, p. 1143 (31 Jan. 1866).

29 M-T, vol. LVI [i], fols. 200–5 (10 Feb. 1866).

Queen's University system was perfectly justifiable; a joint operation embracing enemies of the Russell-Gladstone government Mill could not sanction. Robert Lowe, an ardent opponent of parliamentary reform and a staunch friend of the Queen's colleges, had told Mill of his intention to draw out the government on the education issue by putting a question in the House. Lowe had not requested assistance from Mill and the latter was disinclined to associate himself with an initiative emanating from this source. "It is most clear to me that we, meaning myself and the other liberal members you mention, should endeavour to act directly on the members of the Government, and should avoid even the appearance of concert with any of those who would like to do them an ill turn." Mill also scolded Cairnes for his unauthorized use of Mill's name: "I am very anxious not to be held out to any one, even to sincere liberals, and much less to false liberals and Tories, as desiring to communicate with them on the subject."[30]

By the time Cairnes received Mill's disquieting missive, he had discovered from Thomas Hughes that the government did not plan to retreat from the policy announced the previous summer. Whatever Mill's misgivings, Cairnes would not countenance any swerving action designed to avert a collision with the ministry. Sorry though he was to have taken undue liberty with Mill's name—"My wishes must have in some degree misled my attention and led me to attribute more to slight words than I was warranted in doing"—Cairnes contended that a government averse to doing its duty by the Queen's colleges deserved no quarter. Perhaps more confident of victory than he had been heretofore, Cairnes accepted Mill's view that Radical and Conservative opponents of the government scheme, though they might vote together, should act independently. Who set the ball rolling in the House mattered less to him than Mill's public endorsement of the principles governing their cause. "I believe that a speech from you on the subject would produce a moral effect of the highest value; for it would show that, while the true liberals of England were prepared to make any concession which the claims of justice most liberally construed would prescribe, they were not prepared to sacrifice their principles for any amount of parliamentary support."[31]

On 20 and 23 February Peel and Lowe put their questions to the government.[32] In response, Gladstone offered vague assurances, the ambiguity of which was more real than apparent: "It will be perfectly

30 *LL*, *CW*, vol. XVI, pp. 1148–9 (13 Feb. 1866).

31 This paragraph has conflated the substance of two letters written by Cairnes to Mill on 14 Feb. 1866; see M-T, vol. LVI [i], fols. 206–9.

32 *PD*, 3rd ser., vol. 181, cols. 811–12, 967–8.

practical, right, and convenient that no definite proceeding shall be taken by the Crown before the House has an opportunity of expressing its opinion."[33] Gladstone deftly warded off motions and speeches that might embarrass the government. Mill and other interested members were persuaded that the time for parliamentary action had not arrived.

Mill must have been relieved upon hearing Gladstone's avowal of respect for the dignity and claims of the Commons. Had he grasped that what could be described as "perfectly practical, right, and convenient" in February might later strike the government as not only highly inexpedient but unnecessary, he would have been less pleased. Gladstone had said that the House should be consulted prior to any definitive step being taken; he had not said that it would be. He could not have known at this juncture just how precarious his political position would become. It is probable that in February the cabinet had not yet decided precisely how it would handle the Irish university question. Gladstone expected the matter to be laid before the House in some form, but he could not foresee the impact of the reform struggle on the rest of the government's programme. Between February and June that struggle would put the ministry in jeopardy and accentuate its general vulnerability. To have put the university question into play in the House of Commons under such conditions would have been foolhardy. Gladstone, as was his wont, chose his words with care in February 1866. The dénouement, one he had not scripted, left little doubt that he had misled the House. He had not lied to it. The absence of parliamentary consent notwithstanding, the Russell-Gladstone administration issued, by royal patent, a supplemental charter to the Queen's University the day before it resigned near the end of June. That supplemental charter invested the Queen's University with the authority to set a matriculation examination, passage of which would entitle the candidate to a Queen's University degree though he might never have had any connection with one of the Queen's colleges.[34]

33 Ibid., col. 968 (23 Feb. 1866).

34 The promulgation of the supplemental charter did not guarantee its implementation. The Queen's University senate, enlarged by the government's appointment of six new senators, accepted the supplemental charter by a vote of eleven to nine. Three Queen's University graduates, however, challenged the supplemental charter in the courts. Following the dismissal of their suit on technical grounds, the petitioners launched a class action that ultimately succeeded in preventing the senate from giving effect to the supplemental charter. For the sporadic negotiations between the Tory administration and the Irish hierarchy on the university question from the summer of 1866 until the summer of 1868, see Larkin, *The Consolidation of the Roman Catholic Church in Ireland,* pp. 493–532.

When in late June Cairnes caught scent of the supplemental charter, his disgust was extreme, his anger profound. Snubbing party and parliament, the Russell-Gladstone government had opened the Queen's University to all comers, "an act of great treachery."[35] Mill, though very disappointed, was less indignant. He acknowledged that had the defenders of the Queen's colleges, "who were holding back on account of the Reform Bill," known of the ministry's intent, they would "have brought the matter before the House at once, which would have been very disagreeable to the Government" (exactly the reason Russell, Gladstone, and the Irish chief secretary, Chichester Fortescue, held their respective tongues). Mill, however, preferred to leave open the possibility that something other than rank duplicity lay behind what had transpired: "Whether treachery or misunderstanding, the fact is most unfortunate both in its direct and its indirect consequences."[36]

Mill was very much on Cairnes's side, but the politician in him precluded the sort of commitment Cairnes wanted. The contours of his parliamentary career were largely defined by his investment in Gladstone's leadership of a radicalized Liberal party. Whereas Cairnes was at this time consumed by Irish subjects, and the Queen's University struggle especially, Mill was pursuing a political strategy of sizeable proportions. That strategy, made plausible by the unsettled parliamentary climate in the years following Palmerston's death and by the ostensible emergence of a dynamic strain of working-class political activism, prescribed that Mill show Gladstone every courtesy and consideration. He wanted to stand up for the Queen's colleges, but he did not want to step on Gladstone in the process. Writing to Cairnes, Mill had not ruled out "treachery." Writing to Gladstone a day later, he conveyed his displeasure in words that could not remotely suggest anything of the kind. Mill put the whole thing down to an

> unfortunate misunderstanding. . . . Whose fault it was I am unable to say; very probably ours. But the fact is that many Liberals who were opposed to the changes fully believed that . . . in some shape (such as the notice of the introduction of the intended Bill) they should be . . . warned before the last moment arrived; being anxious not to stir until the last moment, on account of the Reform Bill. I am afraid that the consciousness of having, or being thought to have, partly themselves

35 M-T, vol. LVI [i], fols. 214–15 (28 June 1866).
36 *LL*, *CW*, vol. XVI, pp. 1177–8 (3 July 1866).

to blame, will not tend to soften their feelings, or disincline them to blame others.[37]

Only after Gladstone had fallen from office did Mill make a public statement on the Irish university question. In *England and Ireland* he briefly delineated Ireland's requirements in the educational sector, advocating "a complete unsectarian education" for "the entire people, including primary schools, middle schools, high schools, and universities, each grade to be open free of cost to the pupils who had most distinguished themselves in the grade below it."[38] Cairnes would like to have had such a statement sooner. Mill, for whom the question of timing always figured prominently, was as punctual as he could be given his perception of the political problems raised by the Irish university question.

Mill's years in parliament were also the years of the Fenian challenge to the Union. That challenge would make a deep impression on Mill and impel him to reassess Ireland's needs.

The Irish Republican Brotherhood, more commonly referred to as the Fenian organization, was a revolutionary body established in 1858. Dedicated to the expulsion of British power from Ireland through force of arms, the Fenian movement embodied the most militant expression of Irish nationality of the nineteenth century.[39] In Ireland, Britain, and the United States, Fenian cells laid plans for the liberation of Ireland. (In the aftermath of the American Civil War, many Irish-Americans with military experience were eager to use the skills they had recently acquired in a struggle against British rule.) Attempts were made to coordinate the wings of this transatlantic movement. However ineffectual their actions might appear in retrospect, the Fenians would both puncture English complacency and profoundly affect the Irish revolutionary tradition. In September 1865 the British government showed that it took the threat seriously by raiding the offices of the *Irish People*, the Fenian newspaper founded in 1863. British forces in Canada were alerted to the likelihood of a Fenian

37 Ibid., p. 1180 (4 July 1866). Mill remained silent on 16 July when some supporters of the Queen's Colleges in the House of Commons rebuked Gladstone and his former colleagues for their part in the supplemental charter affair. See *PD*, 3rd ser., vol. 184, cols. 842–910.

38 *EEIE*, *CW*, vol. VI, p. 531.

39 The most important recent study of the Fenians is that of R.V. Comerford, *The Fenians in Context: Irish Politics and Society 1848–82* (Dublin: Wolfhound Press, 1985); for the Anglo-American dimension, see L. O Broin, *Fenian Fever: An Anglo-American Dilemma* (London: Chatto & Windus, 1971); important aspects of the movement are also treated in T.W. Moody, *Davitt and Irish Revolution 1846–82* (Oxford: Clarendon Press, 1982).

invasion, and when the Irish-American contingent crossed the border into Canada in June its members were rounded up with little difficulty. The uprising in Ireland finally came in early March 1867. Poorly organized and miserably supplied with men and weapons, the revolt was easily suppressed by police and troops. Arraignments and heavy sentences ensued. The scene of action then shifted to England. In September 1867 two prominent Fenians were seized in Manchester. The van carrying them to prison was assaulted by a group of their associates, who secured their escape. A police-guard lost his life in the incident, a crime for which three Fenians would eventually go to the gallows. And at the end of the year a Fenian gunpowder explosion at London's Clerkenwell prison resulted in six fatalities and numerous injuries, many of the victims being residents of the district in which the prison was located.

Mill's attitude towards these extreme manifestations of Irish nationalism was reflected in his parliamentary behaviour, as well as in his approach to the land question.[40] In his third speech in the House of Commons, on the Liberal government's 1866 Habeas Corpus Suspension Bill (Ireland), he repudiated the self-satisfaction with which England had tended to look upon Ireland during the preceding decade:

> England had for a considerable number of years been flattering itself that the Irish people had come to their senses; that they were now sensible that they had got Catholic Emancipation and the Incumbered Estates Bill, which were the only things they could possibly want; and had become aware that a nation could not have anything to complain of when it was under such beneficent rulers as us, who, if we do but little for them, would so gladly do much if we only knew how.[41]

40 Mill himself had evinced a relatively optimistic view of Ireland's future in the pages of *Considerations on Representative Government* (1861): "There is now next to nothing, except the memory of the past, and the difference in the predominant religion, to keep apart two races, perhaps the most fitted of any two in the world to be the completing counterpart of one another. The consciousness of being at last treated not only with equal justice but with equal consideration, is making such rapid way in the Irish nation, as to be wearing off all feelings that could make them insensible to the benefits which the less numerous and less wealthy people must necessarily derive, from being fellow-citizens instead of foreigners to those who are not only their nearest neighbours, but the wealthiest, and one of the freest, as well as most civilized and powerful nations of the earth." *Essays on Politics and Society*, ed. John M. Robson, *CW*, vols. XVIII–XIX (Toronto: University of Toronto Press, 1977), vol. XIX, p. 551.

41 *Public and Parliamentary Speeches* [*PPS*], *CW*, vols. XXVIII–XXIX (Toronto: University of Toronto Press, 1988), vol. XXVIII, pp. 52–3.

POOR IRELAND!

Members of parliament were "present at the collapsing of a great delusion."[42] Unequivocally clear in this speech is Mill's recognition that the condition of Ireland was not what many had believed, and that the current troubles in that country had occurred not because something had gone wrong, but because deep-seated problems had never been put right. Mill did not offer remedies on this occasion: he did, however, suggest that when order had been restored the imperial parliament would have to embark upon constructive solutions. "When . . . the immediate end had been effected, he hoped that we should not again go to sleep for fifty years, and that we should not continue to meet every proposal for the benefit of Ireland with that eternal '*non possumus*' which, translated into English, meant, 'We don't do it in England.' "[43]

In light of what has previously been said about the Gladstonian imprint on Mill's politics at this time, it is important to note that his general condemnation of English government in Ireland did not extend to a criticism of the particular Liberal administration then in office. That suspension of habeas corpus should be necessary pointed to the inadequacy of what had hitherto been done for Ireland, but Mill did not question the necessity. A feature of the speech is his disentangling of Russell and Gladstone from the causes that had brought Ireland to the edge of rebellion: "He was not prepared to vote against the granting to Her Majesty's Government the powers which, in the state to which Ireland had been brought, they declared to be absolutely necessary. . . . They did not bring Ireland into its present state—they found it so, through the misgovernment of centuries and the neglect of half a century."[44] Such words gave Gladstone more cover than they did Russell.

With the Fenian threat of early 1866 turning into a Fenian uprising in March 1867, the developing image of Ireland in Mill's mind rapidly came into sharper focus. That the Fenians had done wrong he did not deny, but they had done so in the belief that they were doing right. The desperation of these men, and the acts born of that desperation, had more to do with the failure of the British government than with the wickedness of the men who had bound themselves to smite British power. Mill took a leading part in the 25 May delegation to Lord Derby that called on the Tory government to spare the life of Thomas F. Burke, a Fenian sentenced to be hanged for his part in the March uprising.[45] On the evening of the 25th

42 Ibid., p. 52.

43 Ibid., p. 54.

44 The third reading of the Habeas Corpus Suspension Bill passed the House by a vote of 354 to 6. Mill abstained.

45 *PPS*, *CW*, vol. XXVIII, pp. 165–7. The next day Mill wrote to Cairnes: "We are not yet

Mill spoke to a large reform meeting at St. James's Hall. When he turned to Ireland the rhetoric invoked revealed the depth of the passion aroused in him:

> I should like to know . . . whether you think that we have any right to hold Ireland in subjection unless we can make Ireland contented with our government? (*Cries of No, no.*) . . . Do you think the Irish people are contented with our Government? (*Cries of No, no.*) . . . Do you think those men who have been driven desperate by the continuance of what they think misgovernment . . . who do not understand the English people, and do not understand that you are determined to do them justice, and do not know that you are going soon to be strong enough to do it—(*cheers*)—and because they do not know this, their patience is worn out, and in most desperate circumstances they endeavour to get rid of what they think misgovernment at the risk of their lives—do you think, I say, that those men are not fit to live for that reason? (*Cries of No.*)

Mill admitted that the Fenian leaders had undertaken to raise civil war and had put at risk the lives of their fellow citizens. They merited punishment, but should not be executed. "Political malcontents," he observed, "are very seldom bad men; they are generally better than average." Imprisonment was sufficient punishment. "They should not be treated like the scum of the earth; and we would always hope that the time would come, and we would do our utmost to make the time come, when an amnesty would let them all out of prison."[46] Had Gladstone

---

safe from the gross blunder as well as crime of shedding the blood of Fenian prisoners. The Government had decided by a majority, to hang Burke. About 50 M.P.'s, of which I was one, went as soon as possible to intercede with Lord Derby, and at this time of writing I do not yet know what is the result. If they have not given in we shall attack them furiously in the House tomorrow." *LL*, *CW*, vol. XVI, p. 1272 (26 May 1867). The government did give in. Lord Stanley, son of the prime minister and a member of the Conservative cabinet, recorded in his diary: "after much discussion it was decided in deference to the generally expressed feeling, to commute the sentence of Burke, the Fenian left for execution." *Disraeli, Derby and the Conservative Party: Journals and Memoirs of Edward Henry, Lord Stanley, 1849–1869*, ed. John Vincent (Hassocks, Sussex: Harvester Press, 1978), p. 310.

46 *PPS*, *CW*, vol. XXVIII, pp. 172–3. On 14 June Mill again dealt sympathetically with the Fenians, this time in the House of Commons. "Do I exculpate their conduct? Certainly not. It was greatly culpable, because it was contrary to the general interests of society and of their country. Still, errors of this character are not errors which evince a vulgar mind—certainly not a mind likely to be guilty of ordinary crime and vice—rather a mind capable of heroic actions and lofty virtue." Ibid., p. 189.

been in office in 1867, Mill would have been disinclined to give such a speech.

It should not be inferred from the foregoing discussion that Mill had excessively tender feelings for Irish nationalism. Although he understood the sources and justification of Irish nationalism and recognized its growing strength, he did not see it as an agency of moral development. There is no evidence to suggest that Fenianism led Mill to find progressive elements in Irish nationalism. In his pamphlet *England and Ireland* he would assert that the indelible Catholicism of the Irish masses would ineluctably associate an independent Ireland with the forces of reaction. "In any Continental complications, the sympathies of England would be with Liberalism; while those of Ireland are sure to be on the same side as the Pope—that is, on the side opposed to modern civilization and progress, and to the freedom of all except Catholic populations held in subjection by non-Catholic rulers."[47]

Fenian violence would move Mill to re-examine his position on the Irish land question. From this re-examination would emerge a highly controversial policy proposal directed at removing what Mill held to be the chief cause of Irish disaffection and desperation. That policy recommendation would make some of his fellow MPs wonder whether they might have less to fear from the Fenians than from the Radical member for Westminster.

Most of what Mill had written on Ireland prior to his becoming an MP concerned the land question. Given the extent to which the land question was generally understood to constitute the heart of the Irish problem, and the fact that when writing on Ireland Mill often did so as a political economist, there is nothing at all mystifying about this preponderance.[48] That Mill's Irish interventions during his years in the House of Commons similarly should concentrate on the land question is equally unremarkable. The substance of these interventions, however, sparked a lot of remarks at the time and has kindled not a few since.

At the end of April 1866 the already beleaguered Russell-Gladstone ministry brought forward an Irish Land Bill.[49] Endeavouring to encourage improvements and discourage evictions, the government proposed to invest Irish tenants with a legal claim to compensation for improvements

47 *EEIE*, *CW*, vol. VI, p. 523.

48 For an excellent study of the political economists and the Irish question during Mill's lifetime, see R.D. Collison Black, *Economic Thought and the Irish Question 1817–70* (Cambridge: Cambridge University Press, 1960).

49 The bill was introduced by Chichester Fortescue, Irish chief secretary, on 30 April; see *PD*, 3rd ser., vol. 183, cols. 214–22. It was not enacted.

in those instances where no written contract between landlord and tenant denied the latter's right to such compensation. On the second reading of this "extremely mild measure," Mill "delivered one of [his] most careful speeches . . . in a manner calculated less to stimulate friends, than to conciliate and convince opponents." So Mill states in the *Autobiography*.[50]

Mill's opponents could be forgiven for wondering what it was he was trying to convince them of in this speech of 17 May. He began with an assertion that may have inadvertently done the government more harm than good. "I venture to express the opinion that nothing which any Government had yet done, or which any Government has yet attempted to do, for Ireland . . . has shown so true a comprehension of Ireland's real needs, or has aimed so straight at the very heart of Ireland's discontent and of Ireland's misery."[51] Such a ringing endorsement from Mill in a House of Commons that had its full complement of landlords was perhaps something the Liberal ministry might have rather done without. Be that as it may, Mill meant to do well by the government, and the oddness of the speech he gave on this occasion is in part a consequence of that intention. Mill professed to find in the bill a principle to justify his extravagant praise. "It is a fulfilment of the promise held out by the Chancellor of the Exchequer [Gladstone] at the beginning of the Session[52] . . . to legislate for Ireland according to Irish exigencies, and no longer according to English routine."[53] In fundamental respects Irish society differed from English society, and Englishmen had too long been blind to the fact that what worked for England might not work for Ireland. Indeed, it was English experience that had been unique, not Irish. "Irish circumstances and Irish ideas as to social and agricultural economy are the general ideas and circumstances of the human race; it is English circumstances and English ideas that are peculiar."[54] British legislators should turn to the continental system of agriculture if they wanted guidance for framing Irish land reforms.[55] The assessment Mill then offered of the European agricultural experience probably persuaded most of his listeners that they had been wise to pay as little attention to this aspect of continental experience as they did to most others:

50 *Autobiography*, in *Autobiography and Literary Essays*, ed. John M. Robson and Jack Stillinger, *CW*, vol. I (Toronto: University of Toronto Press, 1981), p. 279.

51 *PPS*, vol. XXVIII, p. 75.

52 See Gladstone's speech on the Habeas Corpus Suspension Bill (Ireland), *PD*, 3rd ser., vol. 181, cols. 721–2 (17 Feb. 1866).

53 *PPS*, *CW*, vol. XXVIII, p. 75.

54 Ibid., p. 76.

55 Ibid., p. 77.

> It tells us that where this agricultural economy in which the actual cultivator holds the land directly from the proprietor, has been found consistent with the good cultivation of the land or with the comfort and prosperity of the cultivators, the rent has not been determined, as it is in Ireland, merely by contract, but the occupier has had the protection of some sort of fixed usage. (*Hear, hear.*) The custom of the country has determined more or less precisely the rent which he should pay, and guaranteed the permanence of his tenure as long as he paid it.[56]

Unrest and agitation in Ireland, Mill maintained, should be seen as the product of an agricultural system that could never achieve a just equilibrium without tenant-right and fixity of tenure.

Having said all of this, Mill did *not* proceed to make a practical case for fixity of tenure. Instead, he defended the ministerial measure on the supposition that it would contribute to accomplishing the aim supported by the English governing class: the creation in Ireland of a facsimile of the English agricultural economy. Such a goal, whose wisdom Mill openly questioned, entailed making prosperous farmers of the most capable of the Irish tenantry. Indispensable to this process was the provision of compensation for improvements, without which Irish tenants would lack the incentive to act the part of Anglicized tenant farmers: "Give the tenant compensation, awarded by an impartial tribunal, for whatever increased value—and only for the increased value—he has given to the land. Do not use the fruits of his labour or of his outlay without paying for them, or without giving him assurance of being paid for them."[57]

What is one to make of this curious speech? On the one hand, Mill announces that at last a government has recognized the need to treat Irish problems within an Irish context. On the other, he recommends the bill because its content was consistent with the resolve of his audience to establish in Ireland a system of agriculture resembling that of England. In that the bill would have invested Irish tenants with rights not possessed by English tenants, Mill's initial point carries some weight. But in adopting exceptional means to achieve the same old ends, had the ministry really shown "a comprehension of Ireland's real needs"? One may doubt whether Mill thought so. He welcomed the measure not in the expectation that, if implemented, it would do much to put the land question to rest. He appreciated that only through the failure of such a modest scheme would English politicians reach the realization that a far more

56 Ibid.

57 Ibid., p. 79.

radical path had to be taken. He gave the bill his approbation in 1866 in the belief that circumstances still allowed some time to bring home to the British public the necessity for a fresh approach. Explaining why he did not ask the House to establish fixity of tenure, Mill stated: "It is perhaps a sufficient reason that I know you will not do it (*laughter*); and I am also aware that what may be very wholesome when it grows up as a custom, approved and accepted by all parties, would not necessarily have the same success if, without having ever existed as a custom, it were to be enforced as a law."[58]

Within eighteen months of this speech Mill would say farewell to such circumspection and restraint. The inflection and articulation of the 1866 speech were heavily modulated by English political circumstances no less than by Irish agricultural conditions. Mill could not remain silent when the opportunity arose to tell the House that Ireland needed fixity of tenure. He would not, however, move from there to a criticism of the Liberal government's lame proposal. On the contrary, he would bestow copious praise upon it. His admission that fixity of tenure would not fly in the House served to justify a course of action that chimed with an allegiance to political ends inseparable from the fate of Gladstone.

By late 1867 Mill's perspective had changed dramatically. The intervening year and a half had seen the fall of the Russell-Gladstone ministry, the uprising in Ireland, and the Fenian incidents at Manchester and Clerkenwell. The time for experimentation had expired. Further postponement of radical action, Mill would now decide, was tantamount to an abdication of British authority in Ireland, the consequences of which would be highly inauspicious for both the English and the Irish. Mill's trenchant pamphlet *England and Ireland*, published in February 1868, emanated from his conviction that to delay much longer a conclusive settlement of the Irish land question was to invite irreparable damage to the British body politic (and moral).[59]

Mill begins *England and Ireland* with a sketch of the historical association between the two nations. Exploring the ancient roots of Irish disaffection, the level of which, he avers, had never been higher than at present, he goes on to suggest that the Irish question had entered a new phase. Fenianism was the extreme expression of a prevalent feeling among the Irish people that English rule must end. The governors of

58 Ibid., p. 77.

59 In fact the first two editions of *England and Ireland* (each 1500 copies) appeared in February, the third in April (250 copies), the fourth in May (250 copies), and the fifth in October of 1869 (250 copies). The fifth was reissued in April 1870. Information from the Longman Archive, Reading University.

Ireland had "allowed what once was indignation against particular wrongs, to harden into a passionate determination to be no longer ruled on any terms by those to whom they ascribe all their evils."[60] The English governing class had repeatedly failed to grasp that there could be no "English" solutions for Irish problems. Disabled by an insular belief in the superiority of all things English, they had, in framing Irish policy, given no thought to the relevance of Ireland's history, traditions, customs, and institutions. Sowing English seeds in Irish soil, they had reaped a bitter harvest.

England could yet salvage her position in Ireland provided she produce a comprehensive settlement of the land question. Only repudiation of the English doctrine of "absolute property in land" could bring about such a resolution.[61] Land is a thing "which no man made, which exists in limited quantity, which was the original inheritance of all mankind, and which whoever appropriates, keeps others out of its possession."[62] The English doctrine of landed property, Mill observes, entered Ireland with the conquest of that country. From that time forward this idea had been linked with alien spoliation and domination, and its legitimacy had never been accepted by the Irish people. Unlike the English, the Irish assumed that "the right to hold the land goes, as it did in the beginning, with the right to till it."[63] The exportation of English bias to Ireland had created an idle parasitical landlord class whose consumption of rent fuelled an often reckless extravagance. Endemic agrarian outrage bore witness to Irish rejection of a land system that betokened values foreign to their experience and incompatible with their aspirations.

Having sketched in the historical background, Mill turns to a comparative treatment of the social economies of England and Ireland. Whereas England had become a predominantly industrial society, Ireland remained almost wholly agricultural. In a mixed economy, with a

60 *EEIE*, *CW*, vol. VI, p. 510.

61 Ibid., p. 512.

62 Ibid.

63 Ibid., p. 513. To what extent, if any, this portion of *England and Ireland* owes something to the publication in 1865 of the first volume of the Brehon law tracts is impossible to say (Mill does not refer to them). This volume included an editorial introduction that offered a reconstruction of early Irish society that could easily have been the source of Mill's views on primitive Celtic society. For a discussion of the Brehon law tracts, see Clive Dewey, "Celtic Agrarian Legislation and the Celtic Revival: Historicist Implications of Gladstone's Irish and Scottish Land Acts," *Past and Present*, no. 64 (1974), 43–55.

substantial commercial and factory sector, "a bad tenure of land, though always mischievous, can in some measure be borne with. But when a people have no means of sustenance but the land, the conditions on which the land can be occupied, and support derived from it, are all in all."[64] Yet in Ireland, where the particulars of landed tenure were of the utmost consequence for the welfare of the bulk of the population, the "terms are the very worst in Europe."[65] England's capitalist farmers had little in common with the Irish peasantry. The former farmed for profit, while the latter farmed for survival. Differing from the capitalist tenant, "the peasant farmer will promise any amount of rent, whether he can pay it or not."[66] English landed proprietors also differed considerably from their Irish counterparts. Imbued with the commercial spirit, most English landlords sought to improve their property; the average Irish landlord did virtually nothing to better his estate. With no security for compensation, and little capital to spare, the Irish peasant had no incentive to make improvements that would ultimately benefit the landlord in the form of an enhanced property valuation.

What, then, is to be done for the Irish tenant? Leaving behind the ambivalence and hesitation characteristic of the *Principles of Political Economy* on this subject, Mill declares unreservedly for fixity of tenure. "When . . . the land of a country is farmed by the very hands that till it, the social economy resulting is intolerable, unless either by law or custom the tenant is protected against arbitrary eviction, or arbitrary increase of rent."[67] Perhaps less could have been offered in the past, but now the inescapable choice for England lay between granting the peasantry "permanent possession of the land" and abandoning the Union.[68] England must give satisfaction to the Irish masses or face the prospect of future insurrection of ever-increasing magnitude and intensity that would in the end bring about a sundering of the Union. Mill admits that his proposals "may be revolutionary; but revolutionary measures are the thing now required. . . . In the completeness of the revolution will lie its safety. . . . If ever, in our time, Ireland is to be a consenting party to her union with England, the changes must be so made that the existing generation of Irish farmers shall at once enter upon their benefits. The rule of Ireland now rightfully belongs to those who, by means consistent with justice, will make the cultivators of the soil of Ireland the owners of

64 *EEIE*, *CW*, vol. VI, p. 514.
65 Ibid.
66 Ibid., pp. 515–16.
67 Ibid., p. 517.
68 Ibid., p. 518.

it; and the English nation has got to decide whether it will be that just ruler or not."[69]

Justice, Mill holds, demands that England do right by Ireland. If brute force alone keeps the Irish in the Union, then England has forfeited her claim to govern that country. The moral sanction for English governance has to rest with its voluntary acceptance by the Irish people. The last opportunity to gain that acceptance had presented itself; England must answer the needs of the Irish people or acknowledge the moral bankruptcy of her rule.

Much of the second half of *England and Ireland* finds Mill arguing that expedience and morality point to the same conclusion. Neither the people of England nor the international community would tolerate government by martial law in Ireland. Rejection of radical land reform would lead to a rupture of the Union and Irish independence. Mill clearly regards such an outcome as objectionable on numerous counts, and he outlines the drawbacks of separation for both countries. Anarchy and civil war might ensue in Ireland, rendering that nation highly vulnerable to foreign invasion and thereby weakening England's capacity to defend herself. The financial burdens on an independent Irish state responsible for its own security would be ruinous. Assaying the various forms of association short of independence that might be applied to the English-Irish connection, Mill discards each in turn as impracticable. The autonomy conceded to Canada could not safely be given to Ireland because of the latter's geographical proximity to England. A partnership of equals, such as that attempted by Austria and Hungary, could not succeed where the power of one was vastly superior to that of the other, and where the relations between the masses of each country were coloured by a legacy of bitterness and animosity. Separation, Mill sums up, would be detrimental to both England and Ireland and no form of federal union between the two could long endure.[70]

However much Ireland might lose by separation, she would be better off in one vital matter. An independent Ireland "would convert the peasant farmers into peasant proprietors: and this one thing would be more than equivalent for all that she would lose."[71] The securing of this essential reform need not be left to an independent Irish government. "This benefit . . . she can receive from the Government of the United Kingdom, if those who compose that government can be made to perceive

69 Ibid., pp. 518–19.
70 Ibid., pp. 520–6.
71 Ibid., p. 526.

that it is necessary and right. This duty once admitted and acted on, the difficulties of centuries in governing Ireland would disappear."[72]

Mill then proceeds to put forward a simple scheme by which that can be accomplished. He calls upon parliament to appoint a commission to assess the rental value of all land held by tenants in Ireland. On the basis of this valuation, the commission would determine the tenant's annual financial obligation and this amount would be guaranteed to the landlord by the state. Assuming the tenant paid the fixed rent each year, he would in effect become the permanent occupant of the holding.[73]

Not trusting to his readers' familiarity with his previous defences of peasant proprietorship, Mill furnishes an abridged version of the case he had tried to make in his *Morning Chronicle* articles of 1846–7 and in the *Principles of Political Economy*.[74] He insists that experience elsewhere had shown the capacity of peasant proprietorship to generate a prosperous agriculture and a contented peasantry. Such a system, moreover, supplied an important check to overpopulation, "because it is much more obvious how many mouths can be supported by a piece of land, than how many hands can find employment in the general labour market."[75] Give the Irish tenant something to gain through industriousness and frugality, and he will not be slow to display these qualities.

In his peroration Mill returns forcefully to the requirements of justice. The "superstitions of landlordism" must now be surmounted and the distinction between the essentials and accidentals of landed property firmly grasped.[76] If England could not raise her understanding to this level, she would have no option but "to retire from a country where the modification of landed property is the primary necessity of social life."[77] The final paragraph of *England and Ireland* brings together the moral and expedient strands of his argument in a passage loaded with rhetorical power:

> Let our statesmen be assured that now, when the long deferred day of Fenianism has come, nothing which is not accepted by the Irish tenantry as a permanent solution of the land difficulty, will prevent Fenianism, or something equivalent to it, from being the standing

72 Ibid.

73 Ibid., pp. 526–7.

74 These arguments have been lucidly expounded by Zastoupil in "Moral Government: J.S. Mill on Ireland."

75 *EEIE*, *CW*, vol. VI, p. 529.

76 Ibid., p. 530.

77 Ibid.

> torment of the English Government and people. If without removing this difficulty, we attempt to hold Ireland by force, it will be at the expense of all the character we possess as lovers and maintainers of free government, or respecters of any rights except our own; it will most dangerously aggravate all our chances of misunderstandings with any of the great powers of the world, culminating in war; we shall be in a state of open revolt against the universal conscience of Europe and Christendom, and more and more against our own. And we shall in the end be shamed, or, if not shamed, coerced, into releasing Ireland from the connexion; or we shall avert the necessity only by conceding with the worst grace, and when it will not prevent some generations of ill blood, that which if done at present may still be in time permanently to reconcile the two countries.[78]

The reception given *England and Ireland* in the London press was generally unfavourable (Mill would have been surprised had it been otherwise).[79] Only the *Spectator* categorically endorsed Mill's remedy.[80] The *Daily News* declared that Mill had never written "with more judicial calmness, gravity, and luminosity," but expressed doubts about the wisdom of his plan.[81] Respectful yet critical, the *Pall Mall Gazette* gave the pamphlet a mixed review, entering practical objections to Mill's proposal while conferring high praise on his treatment of the evil consequences that would issue from a breakup of the Union.[82] The *Saturday Review*, running true to form, vehemently denounced Mill "as the most recent and most thoroughgoing apostle of Communism."[83]

The Times devoted a review and a couple of leading articles to *England and Ireland.* The reviewer described the tone of the pamphlet as "irritated and impatient," its author seeming "to express a supercilious contempt for everyone who is not a philosopher, or has not had the experience of an Indian official." It might have been thought that Mill "would have set the example of impartial and calm discussion. Instead of this he has produced what we must needs characterize as the most ill-conditioned political essay which has yet appeared on the subject."[84] A leading article

78 Ibid., p. 532.

79 This reception is amply documented by E.D. Steele in "J.S. Mill and the Irish Question: Reform, and the Integrity of the Empire," pp. 437–44.

80 Ibid., p. 441.

81 Ibid., p. 439.

82 Ibid., p. 440.

83 Ibid.

84 "Mr. Mill on Ireland," *The Times*, 20 Feb. 1868, p. 10.

on 21 February insisted that "Parliament will have better advisers than those who first encourage discontent by representing political anomalies and large defects as systematic oppression, and who then use that discontent as a menace to the British people."[85] A leader of the following day divulged an anxiety that disturbed the equanimity of more than a few English landed gentlemen in the aftermath of the reform agitation and the passage of the 1867 Reform Act. It observed that "any legislation which should establish the right of the Irish occupier to the permanent ownership of the land merely by reason of his occupation must necessarily apply equally to the English occupier." Referring to Mill's "mischievous schemes," *The Times* set forth its hope and belief "that the most eminent men in both Houses will at once repudiate these fantastic doctrines, and bring the discussion of Irish affairs once more within the bounds of practical good sense."[86]

In his article, "Mr. Mill on Ireland," which appeared in the *Economist* on 22 February, Walter Bagehot also asserted that Mill had exceeded "the bounds of practical good sense."[87] The gravamen of Bagehot's case was that the forces shaping the historical experience of Ireland had rendered the Irish character unfit for such a plan as Mill had put forward: "The successful cases of land legislation have been the gift of a property completely fixed, in lieu of one partially, but incompletely, fixed; it has been a gift to persons prepared by a fitting experience, not to persons spoiled by a degrading past."[88] Like the reviewer in *The Times*, Bagehot complained of the pamphlet's tone: "Mr. Mill relies, too, more than he should upon a sort of intellectual terror; he tries to frighten us into his plan by hinting, or even saying, that we shall be thought fools if we do not agree with him."[89] The originality of Bagehot's treatment lies in his attempt to explain how it was that a thinker of Mill's great distinction could have been responsible for such a piece of work. To those who thought that his exposure to the political arena had drastically upset Mill's intellectual and moral balance, and made him into a demagogue, Bagehot answered:

> An honester or a more simple-minded man than Mr. Mill—a man more ready, in season or out of season, to maintain an unpopular doctrine—does not live. But the fact is, he is easily excitable and suscep-

85 *The Times*, 21 Feb. 1868, p. 9.

86 Ibid., 22 Feb. 1868, p. 9.

87 Reprinted in Norman St. John Stevas, ed., *Historical Essays*, vols. III–IV of *Collected Works of Walter Bagehot* (London: The Economist, 1968), vol. III, pp. 547–53.

88 Ibid., p. 553.

89 Ibid.

> tible; the evil that is in his mind at the moment seems to him the greatest evil,—for the time nearly the only evil,—the evil which must be cured at all hazards. . . . Fenianism, he admits, is only a form of the same discontent which Ireland has so long nurtured. . . . But this sober consideration has not steadied Mr. Mill's thoughts; the sudden flaring evil has excited his mind, as such evils so often do.[90]

Bagehot does not here tell us everything we need to know about the impulse driving *England and Ireland*, but he has told us much.

There is no indication that the storm in the press gave Mill second thoughts about the soundness of his judgment. Writing to Cairnes shortly after the reviews appeared, he observed that he had "met with more approbation, and not more abuse," than he had anticipated. He had indubitably succeeded in attracting plenty of attention to his bold plan, a result that had value in itself. He commented to Cairnes:

> all the public signs, and all the authentic private information I have access to, tend to shew that nothing short of what I propose would now tranquilize Ireland, or reconcile the Irish people to the Union. And I am sure that nothing less than some very startling proposal would have any chance of whipping up the languid interest of public men in the subject, and making them feel the critical nature of the situation, or exert their minds to understand it.[91]

Mill offered a similar estimate in the *Autobiography*, where he acknowledged that the

> pamphlet was not popular, except in Ireland, as I did not expect it to be. But, if no measure short of that which I proposed would do full justice to Ireland, or afford a prospect of conciliating the mass of the Irish people, the duty of proposing it was imperative; while if on the other hand, there was any intermediate course which had a claim to a trial, I well knew that to propose something which would be called extreme was the true way not to impede but to facilitate a more moderate experiment.[92]

The assumptions on which this political strategy was predicated must be kept in view when considering Mill's part in the major debate on the

90 Ibid., pp. 547, 548.
91 *LL*, *CW*, vol. XVI, p. 1369 (1 March 1868).
92 *A*, *CW*, vol. I, p. 280.

condition of Ireland that occupied the House of Commons in mid-March, less than a month after the publication of Mill's pamphlet. Just as the participants in this debate could not ignore *England and Ireland*, however much they might regret its existence, so Mill, in his speech of 12 March, could not ignore the charges that had been levelled against it both in the press and in parliament. Early in the debate Charles Neate, member for Oxford City and himself a political economist, compared Mill to Jack Cade, denounced "the rashness of his scheme," and urged the House to do nothing for Ireland that was "at variance with those principles of political economy and political wisdom under which England had grown great and prosperous."[93] The most formidable parliamentary assault on Mill's pamphlet was launched by Robert Lowe. Lowe, claiming that Mill had greatly exaggerated the Fenian threat, asserted that Ireland's difficulties were the consequence of rural overpopulation and uneconomic holdings, and maintained that the infusion of British capital needed for Irish agricultural improvement depended on the creation of a stable and secure social environment that assured adequate protection for person and property. Taking up the specific parts of Mill's plan, Lowe rejected each in turn as unsound in theory and unworkable in practice.[94]

On 12 March, using the occasion of the debate to reply to the objections that had been raised against the plan outlined in *England and Ireland*, Mill made no apology for the views expressed in it.[95] Answering Neate's charge that the "real obstacle to the peace and prosperity of Ireland is the proposal of extravagant and impossible remedies," Mill declared that "the real obstacle is . . . the persistent unwillingness of the House even to look at any remedy which they have pre-judged to be extravagant and impossible. . . . Great and obstinate evils require great remedies."[96]

Mill's general strategy was to claim that his scheme had been

93 *PD*, 3rd ser., vol. 190, cols. 1316–17 (10 March 1868).

94 Ibid., cols. 1483–1503 (12 March 1868); cols. 1492–9 contain the remarks specifically directed against Mill.

95 E.D. Steele argues that "Mill retracted much that was really challenging in the pamphlet when he addressed the Commons a month after it had appeared" ("J.S. Mill and the Irish Question: The Principles of Political Economy," p. 217). He suggests that the adverse press commentaries on *England and Ireland* persuaded Mill that he had placed himself outside the field of play on which the issue would be taken up, and sees the speech of 12 March as a rather feeble attempt to put himself back into the game ("J.S. Mill and the Irish Question: Reform, and the Integrity of the Empire," pp. 437–8). We consider Steele's reading of this speech to be seriously flawed.

96 *PPS*, *CW*, vol. XXVIII, p. 248.

misrepresented and misunderstood. Some people, for example, had the impression that he had urged the state to buy the land to sell or lease to the tenants. This, he assured his listeners, was not part of his plan.[97] Another misapprehension was that he wished to compel unwilling tenants to accept perpetuity of tenure. Many Irish tenants, Mill conceded, did not pay a full rent, and some of these might prefer to retain their present arrangement.[98] He also granted that there were patriotic landlords in Ireland whose inclination to enter into an agreement with their tenants more favourable than the valuation would provide need not be interfered with.[99] As for his proposal that the government could, if the landlord liked, assume responsibility for collecting the annual rent charge and distributing an annual dividend in its place to the landlord, Mill indicated that this option had been inserted for the convenience of the landlords and did not figure as an essential component of his plan.[100] Taking up the objection that the holdings in Ireland were too small to accommodate this scheme, Mill contended that the virtual cessation of the consolidation movement, together with the fact that the number of individual holdings had not declined over the preceding decade and a half, confirmed that most were of sufficient size to support the occupant.[101]

Once Mill had, in his view, disposed of the criticisms of his proposal, he went on to present a strong defence of the principle of peasant proprietorship, closing with an appeal to the House for consideration of the plan he had advanced.[102] The House could modify his scheme without vitiating its essence. For instance, members might prefer to withhold the guarantee of perpetuity from tenants of holdings below a certain size, whose eligibility for fixity of tenure would be conditional upon improvement of the land. The immediate application of the principle could be confined to arable land. Mill made it clear he might not be prepared to support such "temperaments" of his plan. He simply wished to emphasize that the House could limit the employment of the principle without crippling its fundamental usefulness. Ending his speech on a hopeful note, Mill expressed his conviction that "as the plan comes to be more considered, its difficulties will, in a great measure, disappear, and the House will be more inclined to view it with favour than at present."[103]

97 Ibid., p. 254.
98 Ibid., pp. 254–5.
99 Ibid., pp. 255, 260.
100 Ibid., pp. 257–8.
101 Ibid., p. 258.
102 Ibid., pp. 259–61.
103 Ibid., p. 261.

To what extent did Mill's qualifications and elaborations of 12 March represent a retreat from the position taken in *England and Ireland*? His speech differs from his pamphlet, but the difference does not come from his having had second thoughts about fixity of tenure for Irish tenants. Rather, it arises from the distinct roles Mill assigned the pamphlet and the speech in his campaign for reform. The purpose of *England and Ireland* was to rivet public attention on the need for radical action and to state boldly the form this action ought to take. Mill next had to obtain a hearing in the House of Commons. The pamphlet had deliberately set forth his proposal in the simplest of terms, with a bare minimum of detail; in his speech it was incumbent on him to show an unfriendly House that room existed for a flexible implementation of that proposal. The relation of the pamphlet to the speech was plainly laid out by Mill in a letter to Cairnes, written only hours before the opening of the debate on Ireland: "The object [of *England and Ireland*] was to strike hard, and compel people to listen to the largest possible proposal. This has been accomplished, and now the time is come for discussing in detail the manner in which the plan, if adopted, would work."[104] Designed to complement and amplify his tract, the speech endeavoured to put his plan before the House in such a way as to shed light on its practicability as an instrument of legislation.

Tactical considerations, therefore, obliged Mill to focus on the mechanics of his plan rather than on the essentially moral motive that powered it. Mill grasped that the politics of moral suasion could not do without a quantity of practical hard-headedness. In *England and Ireland* that hard-headedness had occupied a conspicuous place in his discussion of the Union. Yet any interpretation of *England and Ireland* that leaps from such a recognition to a judgment that the pamphlet was shaped chiefly by the author's imperial mentality necessarily misses the heart of the matter.[105] Like his contemporaries, Mill accepted as a given that different societies were at different stages of development and that the

104 *LL*, *CW*, vol. XVI, p. 1373 (10 March 1868).

105 Steele contrasts the moderation of the 1862 and 1865 editions of the *Principles of Political Economy* with the sweeping exhortations of *England and Ireland*, and argues that in the latter Mill recommends fixity of tenure as the antidote for Irish nationalism. Fenianism, he contends, placed the Irish problem squarely within Mill's comprehension of imperial requirements. *England and Ireland*, Steele concludes, was the work of a "patriot and . . . a convinced 'imperialist' " ("J.S. Mill and the Irish Question: Reform, and the Integrity of the Empire," p. 450). Although Steele has drawn attention to a side of Mill that ought not to be glossed over, he neglects to give due consideration to other important sides and thereby does Mill a disservice.

civilization of England was socially, economically, and politically among the most advanced the world had yet seen. He perceived nothing illiberal in the proposition that imperial authority exercised by an advanced civilization over "backward populations" could serve well the interests of the latter. It was not a question of the Englishman possessing an innate superiority over the Irishman. The consequential point was that the societies of which each was a part were notably different, one being far more developed than the other. A union of the two, *if* used effectively by the dominant force, could accelerate the progress of the less advanced. Ireland, of course, had a special place within the empire as a constituent member of the United Kingdom. Nonetheless, her juridical status and her participation in the sovereignty of the imperial parliament could not disguise her political subordination. The duty of Westminster, Mill held, was to provide the Irish people with what they needed from government. And if imperial requirements could not be reconciled with moral requirements, it was the former that would have to give way. Of this, readers of *England and Ireland* were left in no doubt.

Although the practical complications likely to arise from Irish independence affected Mill's perspective, they were not crucial to his demand for radical land reform. Fenianism had raised the spectre of ultimate separation. Such a separation would signify English moral failure. In response to Fenianism, Mill's mind seized upon Irish land as a decisive test of English moral will. Only complete justice to Ireland could expiate English sins and save England from the humiliation and futility of a struggle to hold a people bent upon independence. The impassioned tone of *England and Ireland* derived from Mill's radical moral consciousness. In his mind the elevation of the Irish masses had become inextricably bound to the moral condition of England. The only Union worth having was one in which England exhibited a capacity for upright, responsible leadership. The time had come for England to supply that leadership or get out of Ireland.

Gladstone is not mentioned in *England and Ireland*, but there is reason to think that he was in Mill's mind when he wrote it. Internal evidence indicates that the pamphlet was not written until the very end of December 1867, at the earliest.[106] By this time Gladstone was beginning to recover some of the political ground he had lost in 1866–7. The controversy over parliamentary reform now behind them, the Liberals had every incentive to put their house in order in preparation for doing electoral

106 The pamphlet includes an indirect reference to the Clerkenwell blast of 13 December and to the "Limerick declaration" of 23 December. See *EEIE*, *CW*, vol. VI, pp. 508, 509.

GLADSTONE'S DREAM!

battle with the Tories. For leadership they could not go elsewhere than to Gladstone.[107] On 19 December, only days after the Clerkenwell explosion, Gladstone gave a speech at Southport that had the Irish problem at its centre. He told his audience that the grievances of Ireland had to be addressed. Only after acceptable answers had been found for Irish questions would the British people "instead of hearing in every corner of Europe the most painful commentaries on the policy of England towards Ireland . . . be able to look our fellow Europeans in the face."[108] In searching for these answers, Gladstone implied, parliament would need to take into account Irish ideas as to what should be done: "There are certain matters in which the very effect of a Union requires that the three should have a common opinion and a common policy. So far as that goes I would not for a moment listen to any plans whatever for separate institutions and a separate policy for England, Scotland or Ireland; but this I venture to say that in all matters except that, no man ought to be able to say that any of these nations is governed according to the traditions, the views or the ideas of another."[109] Gladstone also made specific reference to the land question. Placing compensation for improvements at the forefront of any settlement, he acknowledged that the entire subject of Irish land reform was "of vast importance."[110]

Mill would not have missed the significance of this speech,[111] or been unaware of Gladstone's rising political fortunes. But he no longer had to tread softly for Gladstone's sake. In the drive towards a Liberalism more programmatic than anything yet seen, Mill would try to set a pace that he hoped would keep him within Gladstone's sight while helping the latter gain acceptance for measures that would have horrified Palmerston. And Gladstone did not seem unwilling to act the part Mill wished to assign him. In the same debate that occasioned Mill's parliamentary defence of his Irish land proposal, Gladstone committed himself to the disestablish-

107 At Christmas, 1867, Gladstone learned from Russell that the latter did not intend to lead the Liberal party into the next election. Russell's retirement would open the way for Gladstone to become sole leader of the party.

108 Quoted in J.L. Hammond, *Gladstone and the Irish Nation* (1938) (London: Frank Cass, 1964), p. 80.

109 Ibid., pp. 80–1.

110 Quoted in Steele, *Irish Land and British Politics* (Cambridge: Cambridge University Press, 1974), p. 63. Steele's monograph is a superb study of the making of the Irish Land Act of 1870.

111 From Avignon on 22 December Mill wrote Chadwick: "I infer from the newspapers that the public are half crazy about Fenianism. Gladstone's Lancashire speeches will, however, I hope have some effect in recalling some of them to common calmness and ordinary good feeling." (*LL*, *CW*, vol. XVI, p. 1335.)

ment of the Irish church. He also indicated that though he could not concur in Mill's conclusions regarding the land question, he had been impressed by the argument, which he had evidently followed with an appreciative attentiveness. Moreover, Gladstone pressed somewhat further the line he had taken in his speech at Southport:

> I own I am one of those who are not prepared—I have not daring sufficient—to accompany my hon. Friend the Member for Westminster . . . notwithstanding the powerful and weighty statement with which he supported—or rather introduced—his proposal, for what appeared to me to be the dismissal of the landlords of Ireland. Whether the Irish landlords have done their duty or not I will not undertake to say. But I will say I believe that false legislation, and the miserable system of ascendancy which has prevailed in Ireland have so distorted and disfigured the relations of class to class throughout that country, that, until the evil is effectively cured, we cannot pass a fair judgment upon any of them, or form a conclusion as to what we may reasonably hope to see effected in the future.[112]

Whatever it might mean, such language could scarcely have persuaded Mill that his shift into high gear on the Irish land question had been imprudent. That shift had reflected his sense that an anticipated Gladstonian surge would open up a fast lane to the leader's left, a lane that Mill moved to occupy with the publication of *England and Ireland.*

112 *PD*, 3rd ser., vol. 190, cols. 1758–9 (16 March 1868).

SIX

Jamaica

Were a book to be written on the subject of J.S. Mill and the problem of empire, one could reasonably expect to find in it chapters on both Ireland and Jamaica. Yet Ireland and Jamaica figure in a study of Mill's parliamentary career not because his politics were generally dominated by imperial preoccupations, but because his years in the House of Commons coincided with events that gave Ireland and Jamaica a central place in English public debate. Much that Mill said and did in response to the issues raised by these events occurred outside the walls of the Palace of Westminster. When Mill takes up Ireland and Jamaica in his *Autobiography*, he does so within the larger context of his parliamentary career, albeit without suggesting that the political opportunities and constraints arising from his position as an MP governed in any fundamental way his behaviour on these issues. Membership in the House of Commons was not a prerequisite for writing *England and Ireland* or chairing the Jamaica Committee. It is nonetheless arguable that Mill would not have written the former or chaired the latter had he not been in parliament at the time. Ireland and Jamaica turn up where they belong in the *Autobiography*, though not because political calculations of a parliamentary sort were prime determinants of the role Mill chose to play on these great questions. His prominence in the controversies over Ireland and Governor Eyre was conditioned to a marked extent by his presence in parliament, because he then was prominent, and because the incidents that triggered these debates touched in him a political nerve and moral sensibility that conceivably were more exposed between 1865 and 1868 than at any other time. Mill's activism across a multitude of fronts in these years derives in large measure from that exposure, and the public brawl over the events in Jamaica shows that activism to excellent advantage—or disadvantage, depending on the observer's point of view.

Nothing Mill did in or out of parliament during the second half of the 1860s aroused such strong feeling as his conduct as a member of the Jamaica Committee. In all probability, Mill himself felt more strongly about the conduct of the authorities in Jamaica in the autumn of 1865 that led to the formation of the Jamaica Committee than he did about anything else in his entire public life. The same might be said of other people, since the public controversy arising from the actions of Governor Eyre and some of his subordinates engaged the most fundamental moral and political convictions of its leading participants. Of none was this more true than of Mill.

The developments in Jamaica that engendered the controversy can be briefly summarized. Economic hardship, judicial inequities, political unrest, and seething racial tension had created acute discontent among the island's black population (about 440,000) and much fear among the white settlers (about 13,000). In October 1865 an uprising occurred at Morant Bay, St. Thomas-in-the-East, when a group of some four hundred black residents led by Paul Bogle, a native Baptist preacher, marched on the court house at Morant Bay and did battle with two-score volunteers assembled to defend the local magistrates within. On this day the mob would have its way, and when it was over a much-hated magistrate and a number of his associates lay dead, having been beaten to death. On learning of this confrontation and outcome, Edward John Eyre, governor of Jamaica, convened a Council of War and proceeded to declare martial law over the eastern third of the island (the town of Kingston excepted). Little more than a week was needed to suppress what Eyre saw as a rebellion with potentially frightening implications for the white minority. Martial law remained in effect for several weeks thereafter, during which the authorities had a near monopoly on the infliction of violence. A royal commission would subsequently establish that before the proclamation of martial law was lifted, those responsible for its implementation had put to death 439 Jamaicans, flogged at least 600, and burned a thousand dwellings.[1] (The troops charged with putting down the rising suffered no casualties.) Among those executed was George William Gordon, a mulatto politician with a large popular following. Gordon had vociferously criticized Eyre in the Jamaican Assembly and in a series of public meetings held in the spring and summer of 1865. Convinced that Gordon was the chief begetter of the rebellion, Eyre had him removed from Kingston to Morant Bay, where a dubiously constituted and managed court martial

1 "Report of the Jamaica Royal Commission," *Parliamentary Papers* [PP], 1866, XXX, 515.

found him guilty of high treason and sentenced him to be hanged. Gordon was executed on 23 October.[2]

On 3 November the first news of the uprising reached England. Not until the 13th did some of the details of the disturbance and suppression become available; fairly full accounts of what had transpired appeared in the press on the 17th. The earliest evidence of Mill's response is a letter of 15 November, written from Avignon. As of this date he could have known nothing about the execution of Gordon and probably very little about the terrible retribution exacted by the authorities. Mill's correspondent on this occasion was Rowland G. Hazard, a philosophically minded American woollen manufacturer. Hazard had alluded to the subject of political rights for blacks in the aftermath of the American Civil War. Mill wrote:

> I was happy to find, though it was no more than I expected, that we think exactly alike on the necessity of giving equality of political rights to the negroes. What had just taken place in Jamaica might be used as a very strong argument against leaving the freedmen to be legislated for by their former masters. . . .[3] It seems not at all unlikely that England will have to make a clean sweep of the institutions of Jamaica, and suspend the power of local legislation altogether, until the necessary internal reforms have been effected by the authority of the mother country.[4]

2 For the Royal Commission's conclusions respecting the Gordon case, see ibid., 518–28. An able general examination of the background and character of the uprising is provided by W.P. Morrell, in his *British Colonial Policy in the Mid-Victorian Age: South Africa, New Zealand, and the West Indies* (Oxford: Clarendon Press, 1969), pp. 399–427. For a modern and sympathetic biography of Eyre, see Geoffrey Dutton, *The Hero as Murderer: The Life of Edward John Eyre, Australian Explorer and Governor of Jamaica, 1815–1901* (London: Collins, 1967). For a leftish and Jamaican nationalist treatment of the causes of the uprising, see Don Robotham, *"The Notorious Riot": The Socio-Economic and Political Bases of Paul Bogle's Revolt* (Kingston: Institute of Social and Economic Research, University of the West Indies, 1984). In his account of the public struggle touched off by the events in Jamaica, Bernard Semmel also discusses the events themselves: *The Governor Eyre Controversy* (London: MacGibbon and Kee, 1962).

3 The Jamaica Assembly was elected on a high property qualification, thus ensuring the political domination of the planter class.

4 *Later Letters* [*LL*], ed. Francis E. Mineka and Dwight N. Lindley, *Collected Works* [*CW*], vols. XIV–XVII (Toronto: University of Toronto Press, 1972), vol. XVI, p. 1117. In 1866 Jamaica would indeed be made a crown colony, and important internal reforms would be carried out by Eyre's successor, Sir John Peter Grant, between 1866 and 1874. See Vincent John Marsala, *Sir John Peter Grant, 1866–1874* (Kingston: Institute of Jamaica, 1972).

Thus, in mid-November, Mill, aware that a revolt of some kind had occurred in Jamaica and little more, attributed the disturbance to planter misgovernment and oppression, and inferred that the upshot would be a reconstruction of imperial government in Jamaica. The sentiments he expressed on racial justice were no more (and no less) than might be expected from the author of "The Negro Question" (1850), "The Contest in America" (1862), and "The Slave Power" (1862).[5]

Mill had no connection with the initial phase of the anti-Eyre protest, which took the form of deputations to the prime minister and large meetings held mainly in urban centres of nonconformist strength in the weeks immediately following press revelation of the violent deeds perpetrated in the name of the British government.[6] In early December the Jamaica Committee was organized in London. Many of its leading members had been active on behalf of the Northern cause during the American Civil War. They now wanted the British government to disavow the actions of the authorities in Jamaica and to secure justice for those who had been victimized. Chairing the committee was Charles Buxton, MP, whose father, Thomas Fowell Buxton, had been a major figure in the crusade to abolish slavery in the British Empire. P.A. Taylor, a Unitarian and Radical member of parliament for Leicester, became treasurer. Serving as secretary was Frederick William Chesson, who wrote for the *Morning Star*, a radical London newspaper. Both Taylor and Chesson had been officers of the London Emancipation Society, an organization formed in 1862 to persuade the English public that at the heart of the Civil War was the conflict between freedom and slavery. Other members of the Jamaica Committee who had vigorously advocated the cause of the North included John Bright, Thomas Hughes, J.M. Ludlow, and Goldwin Smith.[7]

Precisely when Mill became a member of the Jamaica Committee is

5 For these essays, see *Essays on Equality, Law, and Education* [*EELE*], ed. John M. Robson, *CW*, vol. XXI (Toronto: University of Toronto Press, 1984), pp. 85–95, 125–42, 143–64.

6 Meetings of protest took place in Blackburn, Bradford, Brighton, Derby, Leeds, Manchester, Newcastle, Plymouth, Reading, Rochdale, Shields, and York. See *The Times* , 22 Nov., p. 7; 28 Nov., p. 7; 29 Nov., p. 6; 2 Dec., p. 9; 4 Dec., p. 5; 12 Dec., p. 5; 13 Dec., p. 12; 15 Dec., p. 5.

7 See Semmel, *Governor Eyre Controversy*, pp. 58–65. In addition to Taylor, Smith, and Chesson, Mill, in the *Autobiography*, would mention the following as having been especially active on the Jamaica Committee: Frederic Harrison, Louis Alexis Chamerovzow, Henry James Slack, and William Shaen. *Autobiography* [*A*], in *Autobiography and Literary Essays*, ed. John M. Robson and Jack Stillinger, *CW*, vol. I (Toronto: University of Toronto Press, 1981), pp. 281n–2n.

unclear; he did so while still in Avignon.[8] It may have been as early as the middle part of December, by which time he certainly had read the reports in the press of the executions, floggings, and destruction of property. Burning with indignation, he wrote to a correspondent on 14 December:

> There seems likely to be enough doing in Parliament, this session to occupy all one's thoughts. There is no part of it all, not even the Reform Bill, more important than the duty of dealing justly with the abominations committed in Jamaica. If England lets off the perpetrators with an inadequate punishment, no Englishman hereafter will be entitled to reproach Russia or the French Revolutionists with any massacres, without at the same time confessing that his own country has done worse.[9]

Speaking for Mill and herself in a letter to Harriet Grote of 20 December, Helen Taylor declared: "we hope there will be a reaction. It is much to be desired that an example of legality may now be given, whatever its consequences, which will impress the lesson deeply on the English mind for some time to come."[10]

Lord Russell's Liberal ministry did not need the Jamaica Committee to make them mindful of the grave issues raised by the happenings in the West Indies. Cardwell, the colonial secretary, received Eyre's first dispatch on 16 November. Emphasizing the seriousness of the insurrection and the loss of life and property it had caused, Eyre reported on the proclamation of martial law, the shooting of "a large number of rebels," and the hanging, shooting, and flogging of "a great many prisoners," adding that "a considerable number of prisoners are still on hand." He also told of the arrest and court martial of Gordon.[11] In reply, Cardwell commended Eyre for his resourcefulness in rapidly quelling the rebellion. Nonetheless, Cardwell was troubled by a number of the officers' reports that Eyre had enclosed in his despatch. Some passages in these documents suggested that too much satisfaction had been obtained from the imposition of punishment by those administering it. Cardwell stated that the authors of

8 "I was abroad at the time but I sent in my name to the Committee as soon as I heard of it." *A*, *CW*, vol. I, p. 281.

9 *LL*, *CW*, vol. XVI, p. 1126 (to William Fraser Rae, 14 Dec. 1865).

10 *Amberley Papers*, ed. Bertrand and Patricia Russell, 2 vols. (London: Hogarth, 1937), vol. I, p. 438.

11 See *PP*, 1866, LI, 151; for an excellent article on the British government's handling of the Eyre controversy, see B.A. Knox, "The British Government and the Governor Eyre Controversy, 1865–1875," *Historical Journal*, 19 (1976), 877–900.

those reports "must say much more in order to justify the course pursued."[12] The colonial secretary requested more in the way of both information and explanation. Cardwell and his colleagues, conscious of the heavy burden of responsibility borne by a governor on an island such as Jamaica, were disposed to defend Eyre. Yet the reports in the press, together with the unforthcoming attitude of Eyre with respect to explanations, worried them a good deal. Gladstone pressed for a thorough enquiry.[13] In early December the government decided to relieve Eyre of his duties in Jamaica and to appoint a three-member royal commission, headed by Sir Henry Storks, governor of Malta.[14]

During the first half of 1866 the difficulties encountered by the Liberal government over parliamentary reform would constrain the behaviour of Mill and other Radical MPs who supported the Jamaica Committee. Before the opening of parliament, however, neither the government nor the Radicals could foresee the political riptide that would later carry off the Russell-Gladstone ministry. In January Mill put the Jamaica question right at the top of his agenda. To Henry Fawcett he wrote: "The two great questions of the year will be Jamaica and Reform, and there will be an immensity to be said and done on both subjects."[15] The grip Jamaica held on Mill's conscience at this time was fiercely displayed in a letter he penned to Edwin Arnold, a leader writer for the *Daily Telegraph*. Invited by Arnold to use the newspaper for a purpose regrettably left unspecified in his response, Mill informed Arnold that the *Daily Telegraph*, its vigorous backing of Mill's Westminster candidacy notwithstanding, had forfeited its claim upon his good will. He could not associate himself "with a paper which takes the part the Telegraph does on the Jamaica question. Not only every principle I have, but the honour and character of England for generations to come, are at stake in the condign punishment of the atrocities of which, by their own not confession, but boast, the Jamaica authorities have been guilty; and I cannot, while that question is pending, select as my official organ on another subject, a paper with which, in a matter of such transcendant importance, I am at open war."[16] Mill evidently did not require any royal commission

12 Knox, "The British Government and the Governor Eyre Controversy," p. 879.

13 Ibid., pp. 879–80.

14 Storks was at the same time appointed acting governor of Jamaica. The other two members of the commission were Russell Gurney, member of parliament and recorder of the City of London, and J.B. Maule, recorder of Leeds.

15 *LL*, *CW*, vol. XVI, p. 1131 (1 Jan. 1866).

16 *Additional Letters*, ed. Marion Filipiuk, Michael Laine, and John M. Robson, *CW*, vol. XXXII (Toronto: University of Toronto Press, 1991), pp. 160–1 (31 Jan. 1866).

report to tell him what had occurred in Jamaica or who ought to be held accountable for it. In light of this attitude, his public reticence on the issue throughout the life of the Liberal government is all the more striking.

The government did not want Jamaica to become a matter for parliamentary discussion while the royal commission took evidence and deliberated. It was clearly not an issue that any ministry could work to its own political advantage. Such considerations, however, could not have counted for much with Mill. And in his 17 February speech on suspension of habeas corpus in Ireland, he sounded like a man who would not hold his tongue for long on the Jamaica question. He told the House that he did not fear the government "would make a Jamaica in Ireland; and, to say truth, the fountains of his indignation had been so drained by what had taken place in that unfortunate island that he had none left for so comparatively small a matter as arbitrary imprisonment."[17] Yet Mill said nothing more on the subject until July, after the Russell-Gladstone government had fallen from office.

It would be foolish to suppose that Mill kept quiet out of respect for the task of the commissioners, whose report would not be released officially until 18 June. Well before then the English press and the Jamaica Committee had access to the evidence taken by the royal commission in the early months of 1866. Formally signed on 9 April, the report was received by Cardwell at the end of that month. On 1 May *The Times* carried a leading article summarizing the key facts established by the investigation.[18] At any rate, Mill had made up his mind about Eyre before the commission had begun its work. However strongly Mill felt about the matter, he abstained from venting his feelings in the Commons while the fragile Russell-Gladstone ministry struggled to keep its Reform Bill afloat. Had a perfectly secure Liberal government been in office he surely would not have held back. The spectacle of a vulnerable Gladstone harassed by anti-reform forces persuaded Mill that the assertion of principles dear to him had to be subordinated, at least temporarily, to political exigencies.

The royal commission report was the product of three months' intensive investigation in Jamaica. It has been aptly described by one imperial historian as "a masterly and notably impartial document."[19] Neither the proponents nor the detractors of Eyre would take serious

17 *Public and Parliamentary Speeches* [*PPS*], ed. John M. Robson and Bruce L. Kinzer, *CW*, vols. XXVIII–XXIX (Toronto: University of Toronto Press, 1988), vol. XXVIII, p. 54.

18 *The Times*, 1 May 1866, p. 11.

19 Morrell, *British Colonial Policy in the Mid-Victorian Age*, p. 418.

issue with its conclusions. The commissioners found that the "disturbances in St. Thomas-in-the-East had their immediate origin in a planned resistance to lawful authority" (they rejected the notion of a general conspiracy aimed at subverting the government). The threat posed by these disturbances was such that the authorities would have been derelict had they not responded energetically to them. The commissioners ascertained that "the disorder in fact spread with singular rapidity over an extensive tract of country, and that such was the state of excitement prevailing in other parts of the Island that had more than a momentary success been obtained by the insurgents, their ultimate overthrow would have been attended with a still more fearful loss of life and property." They consequently praised Eyre "for the skill, promptitude, and vigour which he manifested during the early stages of the insurrection; to the exercise of which qualities its speedy termination is in a great degree to be attributed." What they could not praise, however, the commissioners did condemn. They unequivocally declared that "by the continuance of martial law in its full force to the extreme limit of its statutory operation the people were deprived for a longer than the necessary period of the great constitutional privileges by which the security of life and property is provided for." Moreover, they forthrightly concluded that "the punishments inflicted were excessive," stating that "the punishment of death was unnecessarily frequent"; "the floggings were reckless, and at Bath positively barbarous"; "the burning of 1,000 houses was wanton and cruel."[20]

The commissioners reviewed the case of G.W. Gordon in a section of the report separate from their conclusions.[21] Without taking a position on the procedural irregularities of Gordon's court martial and execution, they did comment on the evidence relating to his involvement in the uprising. Gordon's conduct, they deduced, had markedly contributed to the poisoning of the political atmosphere in Jamaica. Nonetheless, the evidence was wholly insuffcient to justify conviction on a charge of high treason. "On the assumption that, if there was in fact a wide spread conspiracy, Mr. G.W. Gordon must have been a party to it, the conclusion at which we have arrived in his case is decisive as to the non-existence of such a conspiracy."[22]

A meeting of the Russell-Gladstone cabinet on 16 June accepted the conclusions of the royal commission.[23] Eyre was officially recalled. A

20 "Report of the Jamaica Royal Commission," *PP*, 1866, XXX, 530–1.

21 Ibid., pp. 518–28.

22 Ibid., p. 528.

23 The members of the government who seemed most disturbed by the repression

week later the Liberal government, defeated on parliamentary reform, resigned. For all their misfortune, they had been spared a debate on Jamaica. Instead, Derby and Disraeli would have to face the political battle that could not be long postponed now that the report of the royal commission had been released. The time had arrived for the Jamaica Committee to settle the terms on which it intended to fight that battle.

The executive of the Jamaica Committee met on 26 June, the day the Liberal government resigned from office. Charles Buxton was unable to attend, but he sent along a letter to the secretary that he wished to be conveyed to the executive. A previous meeting had considered the advisability of urging upon the government the necessity of prosecuting Eyre for the murder of Gordon, or supporting Gordon's wife in launching a prosecution, on the same charge, should the government refuse to act. Buxton did not care for either of these alternatives, and in his letter he explained why.

Acknowledging that the deeds done in Jamaica "must cover the name of Mr. Eyre with infamy," Buxton nonetheless was not persuaded that the governor was guilty of "wilful murder." Eyre had acted on the belief that British rule in Jamaica was threatened by a general conspiracy whose existence owed more to Gordon than to anyone else. The gist of Buxton's argument was that, inasmuch as Eyre did not grasp that the execution of Gordon was in fact "illegal," he ought not to be charged with "wilful murder." But Buxton's primary concerns did not arise from the question of Eyre's culpability. Rather, he had concluded that practically speaking there was nothing to be gained from a prosecution and quite a lot to be lost. "There cannot, I suppose, be the least doubt that its result would be to give a triumph to Mr. Eyre and his advocates." Buxton held that should a grand jury find a "true bill" against Eyre, which he thought highly improbable, the jury receiving the case would assuredly not convict. And if it did, the crown would grant him a pardon. Meanwhile, public opinion would regard Eyre "as a martyr who had been vindictively and cruelly assailed; and his escape from danger would be hailed as a glorious triumph for himself and his partisans." With respect to Eyre, the Jamaica

---

were W.E. Forster and Gladstone. The former held Eyre responsible "for this disgraceful slaughter so dishonouring to our character—so unjust in itself and so fraught with difficulty . . . if we are to attempt to govern Jamaica as Christian rulers in the future." As for the latter, he alone could have written the following: "The truth is, it is a most great and grievous offence, tho' with great and indeed extraordinary palliation. But the scale turns, and even the turn of the scale seems I think to require a marked void." Quoted in Knox, "The British Government and the Governor Eyre Controversy," p. 887.

Committee had already accomplished all it could reasonably hope for. He had been removed from office for his misconduct and his career lay in ruins. Eyre's offences merited punishment far more severe, but what had befallen him was "sufficient to be a serious warning to others." A prosecution would win public sympathy for Eyre and thereby dilute the force of the needful lessons that the Jamaica Committee had sought to impart. It would also focus all attention on the execution of Gordon, to the neglect of the many other atrocities committed by officials other than Eyre. The Jamaica Committee had an obligation to press for the "dismissal and disgrace" of the naval and military officers responsible for these outrages. Buxton therefore recommended that parliament be asked to require the government to call to account those guilty of savagely abusing their authority, and to provide compensation for the victims or their families. In closing, Buxton indicated that a decision to prosecute Eyre would leave him with no choice but to give up the chairmanship of the Jamaica Committee.[24]

Buxton could not carry a majority of the executive committee with him (according to Buxton, eleven of the fourteen members participating voted to assist Mrs. Gordon with a prosecution if the government would not move).[25] Mill was one of those who argued against Buxton's position. He did so not because he took issue with Buxton's assessment of the probable judicial outcome of a prosecution, but because of his view of the fundamental principle being contended for and its overriding importance.

> The question was, whether the British dependencies, and eventually perhaps Great Britain itself, were to be under the government of law, or of military license; whether the lives and persons of British subjects are at the mercy of any two or three officers however raw and inexperienced or reckless and brutal, whom a panic-stricken Governor or other functionary may assume the right to constitute into a so-called Court Martial. This question could only be decided by an appeal to the tribunals; and such an appeal the Committee determined to make.[26]

Refusing to have his name associated with the decision made on 26 June, Buxton went public with his opposition on 30 June, when the letter he had addressed to the secretary of the Jamaica Committee was printed

24 Letter published in *The Times*, 30 June 1866, p. 12.
25 "The Jamaica Committee," ibid., 10 July 1866, p. 5.
26 *A*, *CW*, vol. I, p. 281.

in *The Times*.[27] His colleagues were mightily displeased, especially when they learned of Mrs. Gordon's disinclination to prosecute, which they naturally attributed to Buxton's influence.[28]

The executive called a general meeting for 9 July at Radley's Hotel, to which they invited the press and the public. The meeting had a three-fold purpose: to upbraid Buxton for his conduct; to reaffirm the decision taken on 26 June; and to choose a new chairman. P.A. Taylor took the chair at Radley's and opened the meeting with a statement highly critical of Buxton, whose course of action had damaged "the prestige of the committee in a greater degree than its united enemies could accomplish." Buxton answered Taylor, expressing regret for the embarrassment he had caused the committee. That regret brought no recantation. "He entirely disapproved the course taken by the committee, and it was not to be supposed he was going to let the public lie under the impression that he approved it." When Buxton sat down, John Bright turned on him scathingly. Instead of simply withdrawing from the Jamaica Committee and issuing a statement to the effect that he could not support what it had determined upon, Buxton had written "a most hastily penned fulmination against the committee with which he had been acting, and of which he was chairman":

> Mr. Buxton had freely offered them his purse, and led them on to this point, and when they came to that point, which was the only one at which they could do any good, he backed out and left them all in the lurch. And not only did he back out, but fires on them with a most terrible cannonade, and embarrassed the committee to that degree that it became its duty, as soon as possible, to explain its true position to the public.

After Bright's salvo, Ludlow moved that the committee confirm the resolutions adopted by the executive committee on 26 June. Following a brief debate this resolution carried, "there being but one dissentient." Edmond Beales then proposed Mill for the chairmanship, to which he was unanimously elected.[29] Mill had remained silent throughout the meeting, no doubt considering it unnecessary for him to intervene and perhaps also unbecoming in one about to take Buxton's place. Nor did he say much upon accepting his new post:

27 *The Times*, 30 June 1866, p. 12.

28 See Semmel, *Governor Eyre Controversy*, p. 70.

29 "The Jamaica Committee," *The Times*, 10 July 1866, p. 5.

> I do so in the full conviction that the objects of this committee are simply to ascertain whether there exist in this country any means for making a British functionary responsible for blood unlawfully shed—(*applause*)—and whether that be murder or not. I believe it to be murder. (*Hear, hear.*) This committee ought not to rest until it obtains from the legislature the assurance that men like Mr. Eyre will be made responsible for their criminal actions. (*Hear, hear.*)[30]

To that legislature Mill and his associates would presently turn.

Ten days after the meeting at Radley's, Mill acted in his dual capacity as chairman of the Jamaica Committee and member of parliament to put ten questions to Disraeli, now chancellor of the exchequer and leader of the House of Commons. Notice of the questions had been given, and their content was known to Disraeli. Mill did not intend to read these questions in the House, "wishing to spare" its members "the monotonously painful details" they contained. Instead he simply asked "whether any steps had been or would be taken by Her Majesty's Government for bringing to justice those who had been concerned in the commission of various illegal acts in Jamaica?"[31] Disraeli, convinced that a recitation of the details would ultimately prove more painful to Mill than to the House or the government, insisted that Mill read the questions in their entirety.[32] Mill responded with a catalogue of "unlawful" acts committed in Jamaica by some thirteen officials—civil, military, and naval—and in each case asked the government whether steps had been or would be taken to bring those responsible to trial. Finally, he wanted to know whether the government intended to take legal action against Eyre "for complicity in all or any of the above acts, and particularly for the illegal trial and execution of Mr. George William Gordon: And, if not, whether Her Majesty's Government are advised that these acts are not offences under the Criminal Law?"[33]

Mill had unwittingly courted the parliamentary drubbing that Disraeli would administer in short order. The chancellor of the exchequer pointed out that in the very phrasing of his questions Mill had assumed a legal culpability that had yet to be established, thereby "trespassing in some degree upon the liberty and freedom of discussion" (one can imagine Disraeli's glee).[34] Mill had declared the unlawfulness of the acts

30 *PPS, CW*, vol. XXVIII, p. 91.

31 Ibid., p. 93; for the exchange between Mill and Disraeli, see *Parliamentary Debates* [*PD*], 3rd ser., vol. 184, cols. 1064–9 (19 July 1866).

32 *PD*, 3rd ser., vol. 184, col. 1064 (19 July 1866).

33 *PPS, CW*, vol. XXVIII, pp. 94–5.

34 *PD*, 3rd ser., vol. 184, col. 1066 (19 July 1866).

he had described, only to finish by enquiring if the government had been advised by their law officers "that these acts are not offences under the Criminal Law?" Disraeli questioned the propriety of proclaiming the guilt of those named *before* soliciting the opinion of the crown law officers on the matter. He took issue with the accuracy of some of Mill's statements, and reminded the House that the actions recounted had occurred "during the existence of martial law."[35] Conduct illegal under ordinary law, said Disraeli, was not necessarily unlawful under martial law. He praised the work of the royal commission, approved the decision of the late government to dismiss Eyre, and indicated that no further action on Eyre's case was contemplated. "Those who ask that further steps should be taken seem to me to confuse errors of conduct and errors of judgment with *malice prepense*."[36] As for the naval and military officers implicated by Mill, the Admiralty did not propose to pursue disciplinary action and the Horse Guards had not yet decided. "That being the state of the case, I am not prepared to offer any further information to the hon. Gentleman."[37] Disraeli had routed Mill,[38] but the government had yet to face the full-scale debate on the Jamaica question that would be occasioned at the very end of July by four resolutions moved by Charles Buxton.

That debate itself would be affected by a public statement of the Jamaica Committee that appeared in the London press a day before the House considered Buxton's four resolutions.[39] Defining its attitude in the wake of Mrs. Gordon's declared disposition not to initiate a prosecution and Disraeli's assertion of the government's refusal to institute legal proceedings against Eyre, the Jamaica Committee sought to explain the grounds upon which it felt compelled to act. The document affirmed that when there existed strong reason to believe that a British subject had been illegally put to death by a public official, the duty of the government was "to vindicate the law by bringing the offender to public justice."[40]

35 Ibid., col. 1067 (19 July 1866).

36 Ibid., col. 1069 (19 July 1866).

37 Ibid.

38 Taking up the matter in a leading article the following day, *The Times* said of Mill's question: "It is not easy to understand what good object could be served by shaping it in this way, instead of requesting the Government to state whether any criminal proceedings were to be instituted against the parties inculpated. As it is, exaggeration and inaccuracy have produced their ordinary effect, and the cause of the Jamaica Committee has been rather damaged than strengthened." *The Times*, 20 July 1866, p. 9.

39 This statement is included as part of appendix E of *EELE*, *CW*, vol. XXI, pp. 422–7; originally published in the *Daily News*, 30 July 1866, p. 3, and *The Times*, 30 July 1866, p. 5.

40 *EELE*, *CW*, vol. XXI, p. 422.

Although the reported conduct of the authorities in Jamaica had given rise to such a belief, the government had declined to recognize that duty. Consequently, the "duty now devolves upon private citizens of taking such measures as the constitution may point out for the defence of those legal and chartered rights which protect the lives and liberties of all."[41] The committee was in no way motivated by feelings of vindictiveness. "Their aim, besides upholding the obligation of justice and humanity towards all races beneath the Queen's sway, is to vindicate, by an appeal to judicial authority, the great legal and constitutional principles which have been violated in the late proceedings, and deserted by the Government."[42] The committee desired to establish "the principle that the illegal execution of a British subject by a person in authority is not merely an error which superiors in office may at their discretion visit with displeasure or condone, but a crime which will certainly be punished by the law."[43] This principle was deemed essential to the preservation of life and liberty, which could not safely be entrusted solely to "the Executive Government" but must be "under the guardianship of the law."[44] The committee also took up a question that would be central to the forthcoming debate and subsequent court proceedings: the validity of courts of martial law, which, in the committee's view, had in Jamaica been "made engines of indiscriminate butchery and torture."[45]

To the case of Gordon the statement of the Jamaica Committee devoted a lengthy paragraph, which sought to demonstrate that Gordon's path to the gallows was strewn with legal and ethical irregularities. Gordon's fate, the committee implied, had been sealed well before his court-martial tribunal assembled in Morant Bay.[46] "If the execution of Mr. Gordon was illegal, and, in the eye of the law, a murder, it was a murder of which Mr. Eyre was not only constructively but personally guilty; which was committed not only under his authority, but, to all intents and purposes, with his own hand."[47] The committee rejected Disraeli's contention that "proof of private malice is indispensable in order to make an illegal execution a murder"; acceptance of such judgment "would be to hold out impunity to the crime which is the most dangerous of all to the community—the crime of a public functionary who

41 Ibid., p. 423.
42 Ibid.
43 Ibid.
44 Ibid., pp. 423–4.
45 Ibid., p. 424.
46 Ibid., p. 425.
47 Ibid., p. 426.

abuses the power entrusted to him to compass, under the forms of justice, the death of a citizen obnoxious to the Government."[48]

Eyre sympathizers might find much to complain of in the statement of the Jamaica Committee, but the conjuring up of "butchery and torture" notwithstanding, the document speaks mainly to matters of law. As will shortly be seen, Mill's speech in the House debate on Buxton's resolutions would be highly legalistic in character. In seeking to bring Eyre before the bar of justice, the committee explicitly abjured any wish "to abet resistance to lawful authority or to weaken the arm of the magistrate in preserving public order."[49] At the core of the legal struggle waged by Mill and his colleagues was the issue of martial law and the use to which it had been put in Jamaica. A satisfactory rendering of Mill's major speech on the Jamaica question requires a perusal of the problem of martial law within the general context of the British constitutional tradition and with specific reference to the events in Jamaica.

A leading modern authority on the history of martial law as a legal concept and administrative device in Britain and the Empire from 1800 to 1940 delineates its standing in the following terms:

> All nineteenth-century commentators agreed that the Crown (and indeed all lawful citizens) had under common law the right and duty to repel force with force. . . . However, it was held that an executive officer was bound to use exactly the degree of force which was needed to terminate the danger—not a jot more or less. Any error in judgement of that exact degree would be justiciable in the ordinary courts after order was restored. . . . The whole drift of English legal thinking was towards banishing martial law from the confines of law properly understood—to say, in effect, as the duke of Wellington had said, that it was "no law at all." Its use was dependent on the existence of a state of open warfare: *inter arma silent leges.*[50]

The legal counsel employed by the Jamaica Committee, Edward James and James Fitzjames Stephen, were among those commentators. Shortly after the formation of the Jamaica Committee, James and Stephen were asked to submit their opinion respecting the constitutional purchase of

48 Ibid.

49 Ibid.

50 Charles Townshend, "Martial Law: Legal and Administrative Problems of Civil Emergency in Britain and the Empire, 1800–1940," *Historical Journal*, 25 (1982), 171, 172.

martial law and the bearing of that purchase on the conduct of the authorities in Jamaica. That opinion, dated 13 January 1866, formed the legal foundation of the case the Jamaica Committee thereafter attempted to make against Eyre.[51] The content of Mill's speech of 31 July in the House of Commons would not stray far from the findings of the royal commission and the judgments of James and Stephen in their capacity as legal counsel.

The opinion of James and Stephen maintained that insofar as the Petition of Right had pronounced martial law illegal, the term had no legal standing independently of the right and duty of the crown, as provided by common law, to employ military force "for the suppression of an insurrection and the restoration of order and lawful authority." Whatever was necessary to achieve this objective, not excluding "the destruction of life and property to any extent," constituted a legitimate, indeed obligatory, exercise of authority. Violations of individual rights not required by such necessity fell outside the scope of the excusable. Officers of the crown "are not justified in the use of excessive or cruel means, but are liable civilly or criminally for such excess. They are not justified in inflicting punishment after resistance is suppressed, and after the ordinary courts of law can be reopened." So-called courts martial were in fact not "courts," but "mere committees" set up to execute "the discretionary power assumed by the Government." The statute enacted by the legislature of Jamaica enabling the governor and his council to proclaim martial law did not (and could not) confer upon the representatives of the crown any power they did not already possess under common law. "The legality of the conduct pursued towards Mr. Gordon depends, they hold, on the question whether it was necessary for the suppression of open force, and the restoration of legal authority, to put him to death." Martial law was about "self-preservation," not about "punishment." James and Stephen concluded that nothing in the dispatch composed by Eyre for his superiors showed that the execution of Gordon was necessary either for the suppression of insurrection or the restoration of order. Eyre and those officers responsible for that execution were, accordingly, subject to a bill of indictment, which, in England, could be brought by any person.[52]

The founders of the Jamaica Committee shared the conviction that Eyre and other British officials were morally culpable; from the opinion of James and Stephen, it could reasonably be inferred that they were also

51 For that opinion, see "The Jamaica Committee," *The Times*, 16 Jan. 1866, p. 3.

52 Ibid. Stephen adhered closely to this opinion when he came to write the section on martial law for his three-volume work, *A History of the Criminal Law of England* (London: Macmillan, 1883), vol. 1, pp. 207–16.

legally culpable. They had committed murder. Mill firmly believed this to be so, and upon this belief he was ready to act.

The late rather than the current chairman of the Jamaica Committee, however, initiated the parliamentary debate. In view of what had recently passed within the Jamaica Committee, Buxton was all the more eager to express in the most public way possible the moral outrage that had moved him to assume the chairmanship in the first place. On 31 July 1866 he proposed four resolutions in the House of Commons. The first of these called upon the House to deplore "the excessive punishments which followed the suppression of the disturbances . . . and especially the unnecessary frequency with which the punishment of death was inflicted." The second resolution, quoting words from Cardwell, the former colonial secretary, asserted that public officials guilty of "great offences" should not go unpunished, and declared that "grave excesses of severity on the part of any Civil, Military, or Naval Officers ought not to be passed over with impunity." The third resolution urged the government "to award compensation to those whose property was wantonly and cruelly destroyed, and to the families of those who were put to death illegally." The last stated that those individuals serving sentences in Jamaica arising from their connection with the disturbances should have "all further punishment . . . remitted."[53]

To his resolutions Buxton appended an impassioned speech. Culling what suited his purpose from the evidence collected by the royal commission, he graphically recounted some of the horrifying details of what had been done to Jamaicans well after the necessity for repression had expired. Ignoring those findings that had led the commissioners to praise Eyre "for the skill, promptitude, and vigour which he manifested during the early stages of insurrection," Buxton belittled the peril to lawful authority embodied by Paul Bogle and his followers.[54] Given that no one was disposed to impugn the conscientiousness or impartiality that informed the work of the commissioners, Buxton's highly selective and unremittingly one-sided use of their report weakened somewhat the effect of what otherwise was a powerful denunciation of Eyre's fatally flawed (so it proved for many of its victims) handling of the Jamaica disturbances.

Charles Adderley, colonial under-secretary and, as such, leading for the government in this debate (Carnarvon, the colonial secretary, sat in the Lords), did not think much of Buxton's speech or resolutions. (Adderley's detractors occasionally wondered whether he thought much

53 For Buxton's four resolutions, see *PD*, 3rd ser., vol. 184, col. 1763.
54 For Buxton's speech, see ibid., cols. 1763–85.

at all.)[55] He took umbrage at Buxton's tone—"What right had he to consider himself the exclusive champion of the oppressed?"[56]—and claimed that the work of the royal commission had closed the case so far as the government was concerned. He criticized Buxton for making light of the very serious difficulties that had confronted Eyre, and drew attention to that portion of the commissioners' conclusions that had commended him. He did not consider the first resolution "inadmissible," but he did think it "unnecessary." "We all deplore the excesses that have been described by the Commissioners."[57] Adderley regarded the second resolution as inappropriate, since the government had acted and was acting in accordance with its substance.[58] The third resolution he dismissed as unwise. The government would consider claims for compensation where "it is shown that damage had been wantonly done by the agents of the Government," but passage of the resolution would "raise considerably higher and more extravagant expectations than those which are already rife there, and I think it would be an evil."[59] As for the last resolution, Adderley deemed it wholly unacceptable. He saw no reason why "the most atrocious scoundrels now being punished for the most bloody outrages should have their punishment remitted because others have been unjustly put to death."[60] He wound up with a recommendation "that this House should not pass any of these resolutions if they must all go together," and thereupon moved the previous question.[61]

It was less Buxton's resolutions than the behaviour of the Jamaica Committee that really irked Adderley. He reserved his harshest rhetoric for its members: "They saw but one side of the question; strong prepossessions, invincible prejudices incapacitated them from seeing more than one side, but it is remarkable that they prefer to range themselves on the side of those who are the disturbers of order, rather than on the side of those who have upheld it. And I must say that by their manner of proceeding in this case these gentlemen have forfeited for ever any title

55 Not all those detractors came from the Liberal end of the political spectrum. Carnarvon, Adderley's chief at the Colonial Office, complained of the latter's "incurable inaccuracy and confusion of mind." Quoted in Knox, "The British Government and the Governor Eyre Controversy," p. 894, and in Paul Smith, *Disraelian Conservatism and Social Reform* (London: Routledge and Kegan Paul, 1967), p. 41.
56 *PD*, 3rd ser., vol. 184, col. 1785.
57 Ibid., col. 1789.
58 Ibid., cols. 1794–5.
59 Ibid., col. 1796.
60 Ibid., col. 1797.
61 Ibid.

to be heard on any question that demands judicial calmness and impartiality for its consideration."[62] The latest evidence in Adderley's possession evincing the regrettable misapprehensions of the Jamaica Committee, as he thought, was an amendment of which its chairman had given notice. Buxton's resolutions made no specific reference to Eyre and said nothing about criminal indictments. Mill had informed the House of his intention to move an amendment calling upon the House to require that criminal charges be brought against Eyre. Failing this, of course, the Jamaica Committee had already made clear its determination to prosecute. Adderley argued that Mill ought to stay out of the debate on Buxton's resolutions. "It would be a monstrous thing in him to prejudge in debates here a case which he himself proposes to refer for decision to a judicial tribunal."[63] But Mill was not to be muzzled, and he rose to speak when Adderley finished.

In his *Autobiography* Mill says that "the speech I then delivered is that which I should probably select as the best of my speeches in Parliament."[64] Within the two weeks preceding this speech Mill had twice traded blows with Disraeli: first over the government's intentions respecting the acts of officials in Jamaica, and then over the responsibility of the government for the Hyde Park row. In both instances Disraeli had shown himself the far more telling puncher. Mill needed to make a good speech in the debate on Buxton's resolutions, for the sake of his own position in the House no less than for the cause in which he so fervently believed. If he could not realistically hope to persuade a majority to line up behind him on the Jamaica issue, he could at the very least put before the House and the country a cogent statement of his purpose and its justification. Knowing that he was saying what much of his audience did not want to hear, it was especially important that he say it well. He did. Mill would not have claimed this speech as his best had he not judged the manner of its presentation to have been worthy of its substance. There would be little applause, but the reported text is liberally sprinkled with shouts of "hear, hear." Throughout, Mill clearly held the respectful attention of the members. The satisfaction he felt with his performance, it may be surmised, also reflected his sense of the difficulty involved in conveying to the House that his conduct was governed by the facts of the case at hand. His interpretation of those facts, he would have his audience understand, was anchored in a reasoned conception of justice whose general acceptance was indispensable for sustaining civil society.

62 Ibid., col. 1793.

63 Ibid., col. 1792.

64 *A*, *CW*, vol. I, p. 281.

Mill's finely wrought speech opened, with a nice touch of irony, by welcoming Adderley's statement of the ministry's position: the Jamaica Committee "could have desired nothing better for their cause than that the speech which has just been delivered should go forth to the country as the defence of the Government for not taking any measures to bring those events under the cognisance of a judicial tribunal."[65] Mill, however, did not propose to speak to the particulars of Adderley's speech any more than he wished to endorse or oppose Buxton's resolutions. Instead, he felt obliged to avail himself of the present opportunity to argue for his view of what should follow from the report of the royal commission. "I . . . contend that the acts which have been committed demand the particular attention of the house, not however for the purpose of itself pronouncing any judgment on them, but for the purpose of requiring that they be referred to an authority more competent than this house—the only authority that is competent to pass a binding judgment on such acts—the authority of a judicial tribunal."[66] Mill then briefly summarized some of the key findings and conclusions of the commissioners, and observed that with regard to "the degree of culpability of these transactions there is a wide difference of opinion, but that there has been serious culpability no one now disputes."[67] Although the commissioners had been authorized to investigate and report on the events in Jamaica, they had not been "empowered to declare what is the character of those facts in the eye of the law."[68]

Mill did not focus on individual incidents. His approach was severely analytical: "The house has supped full of horrors throughout the speech of my honourable friend."[69] Throughout Mill's speech the House would sup upon a cold hard chain of reasoning, and it is possible they savoured Mill's fare even less than they liked that offered by Buxton:

> The taking of human lives without justification, which in this case is an admitted fact, cannot be condoned by anything short of a judicial tribunal. . . . I know not for what more important purpose courts of law exist than for the security of human life. It has been the boast of this country that officers of Government must answer for their acts to the same laws and before the same tribunals as any private citizen; and if persons in authority can take the lives of their fellow subjects

65 *PPS*, *CW*, vol. XXVIII, p. 106.
66 Ibid.
67 Ibid., p. 107.
68 Ibid.
69 Ibid.

> improperly, as has been confessedly done in this case, without being called to a judicial account, ... we are giving up altogether the principle of government by law, and resigning ourselves to arbitrary power.[70]

Mill also reiterated the Jamaica Committee's rejection of the argument made by Disraeli respecting *malice prepense.* A belief in the guilt of individuals executed without due process could not be admitted as a legitimate defence. Were it so admitted, excuse would be furnished for "actions of still greater atrocity than I claim any right to attribute to these. Did the perpetrators of the massacre of St. Bartholomew think their victims innocent? Did they not firmly believe them to be hateful to God and to all good men? Did the authors of the September massacres—did the French revolutionary tribunals and the Terrorist Government, believe in the innocence of those whom they put to death? Were they not fully persuaded that they were traitors and enemies of their country?"[71]

Mill reserved the last part of his speech for consideration of the issue of martial law. He did not challenge the notion that "the proclamation of martial law suspends all law so long as it lasts"; he did, however, "defy any one to produce any respectable authority for the doctrine that persons are not responsible to the laws of their country, both civil and criminal, after martial law has ceased, for acts done under it." What those with expert knowledge of the subject did agree upon was that "martial law is another word for the law of necessity, and that the justification of acts done under that law consists in their necessity. Well, then, we have a right to dispute the necessity."[72] Moreover, those administering martial law must recognize they have not a diminished but a heightened legal responsibility for their actions: "when there is absolutely no guarantee against any extremity of tyrannical violence, but the responsiblity which can be afterwards exacted from the tyrant ... it is indeed indispensable that he who takes the lives of others under this discretion should know that he risks his own."[73] Mill's final appeal was to the people of England rather than to a government he fully understood would in no way assist the efforts of the Jamaica Committee:

> It remains to be seen whether the people of this country will sustain us in the attempt to procure a solemn reassertion of the principle,

70 Ibid., pp. 107–8.
71 Ibid., p. 109.
72 Ibid., p. 110.
73 Ibid., p. 112.

that whoever takes human life without justification must account for it to the law. This great public duty may be discharged without help from the government, but without help from the people it cannot. It is their cause; and we will not be wanting to them, if they are not wanting to us.[74]

Despite securing some debating support from Thomas Hughes and A.S. Ayrton,[75] Mill could not expect to find much favour for the course he recommended with most members of the Commons. The speech best expressing the sense of the House was that delivered by Cardwell, colonial secretary in the Russell-Gladstone administration. Cardwell had given his assent to the findings of the royal commission. He now reminded the House of the conditions in Jamaica that had led the commissioners to praise Eyre for his initial response to the disturbances. The Liberal government had agreed "with the Commissioners in giving Governor Eyre credit for the vigour and promptitude with which he repressed the insurrection."[76] The unwarranted prolongation of martial law, however, and the floggings and executions carried out under the cover of martial law "were proceedings which it is certainly impossible to do other than in the strongest way to deplore and condemn. It was a grievous fault; and by the censure it has entailed, it has been answered grievously."[77] Cardwell spoke for most MPs in decisively distancing himself from the view of the matter taken by Mill:

I do not think that any one who has due regard to the truth can deny that Mr. Eyre really shared in the belief, universal at the moment among all the white and coloured men of the island, that a conspiracy for their destruction had existed, and that Mr. Gordon was to a great extent guilty of promoting it. We [the previous government] were of opinion . . . that it was not a case for a criminal prosecution, but was properly dealt with by the removal of Governor Eyre from his office.[78]

In the end, an arrangement worked out between Buxton and the Conservative government foreclosed action on the amendment of which Mill had given notice. Relying upon the opinion of Sir Hugh Cairns, the

74 Ibid., p. 113.
75 *PD*, 3rd ser., vol. 184, cols. 1827–30, and 1837–8.
76 Ibid., col. 1821.
77 Ibid., col. 1822.
78 Ibid., col. 1823.

attorney-general,[79] Disraeli placed an interpretation on the wording of the first resolution that allowed him to advise the House to accept it without a division. He claimed that in deploring "the excessive punishments which followed the suppression of the disturbances," the House would in actuality be avowing the legality of what they were lamenting, "because the use of the term 'punishment' is an acknowledgment that it was the result of a legal act."[80] Buxton demurred from the construction the government put on his terminology, and viewed adoption by the House of his first resolution as "a most decisive and emphatic condemnation upon excessive severity."[81] Disagreement over what it meant did not stand in the way of agreement that it be passed. Given vague assurances by Adderley that the issues raised in the other three resolutions would receive the attention of the government, Buxton withdrew them.

The parliamentary battle over Jamaica was over. The legal fight would now move into the narrow confines of the courts. The moral contest would be played out along a much broader front, the opposing sides each seeking to capture for their cause the mind and conscience of the English public.

The dynamics of the struggle changed somewhat with the return of Eyre to England in August 1866. Some local notables held a banquet in Eyre's honour shortly after his arrival in Southampton.[82] Eyre's supporters were ready to answer the campaign of the Jamaica Committee with one of their own. The Eyre Defence and Aid Fund Committee took shape in the late summer of 1866. Its more prominent members included the Earl of Shrewsbury, Lord Elcho, Sir Roderick Murchison, Thomas Carlyle, John Ruskin, and Henry Kingsley (contributions were received from Dickens and Tennyson). Hamilton Hume, whose hagiographic *Life of Edward John Eyre* would come out the following year, started up the committee and served as its secretary. His greatest catch was Carlyle. Responding to Hume's invitation to join the committee, Carlyle wrote a letter on 23 August that *The Times* published on 12 September. It was all that Hume could have hoped for.

> The clamour raised against Governor Eyre appears to me to be disgraceful to the good sense of England. . . . For my own share, all the light that has yet reached me on Mr. Eyre and his history in the world goes steadily to establish the conclusion that he is a just,

79 For Cairns's speech, see ibid., cols. 1816–19.

80 Ibid., cols. 1838–9.

81 Ibid., col. 1837.

82 See "Ex-Governor Eyre at Southampton," *The Times*, 23 Aug. 1866, p. 7.

humane, and valiant man, faithful to his trusts everywhere, and with no ordinary faculty of executing them; that his late services in Jamaica were of great, perhaps of incalculable value, as certainly they were of perilous and appalling difficulty . . . and, in short, that penalty and clamour are not the thing this Governor merits from any of us, but honour and thanks, and wise *imitation* (I will farther say), should similar emergencies rise, on the great scale or on the small, in whatever *we* are governing.[83]

If the existence of the Jamaica Committee persuaded Carlyle of his duty to enter the fray on Eyre's behalf when called upon, the creation of the Eyre Defence and Aid Fund and the publication of Carlyle's letter could only confirm Mill in his absolute determination to press forward.[84] In August the Jamaica Committee decided to launch a public subscription aimed at raising £10,000 to cover the costs of prosecution.[85] That decision was acted on in mid-October, when the committee issued a brief address that appeared in the *Daily News* and the *Examiner*.[86] Its authors,

83 This letter, together with other documents relevant to Carlyle's connection with the Eyre controversy, has been reprinted (with annotation) by Gillian Workman as an appendix to her article, "Thomas Carlyle and the Governor Eyre Controversy: An Account with Some New Material," *Victorian Studies*, 18 (1974), 77–90; appended material, 91–102. The above quotation is at pp. 91–2.

84 It must not be supposed that only members of the Jamaica Committee were appalled by Carlyle's rhetoric. Walter Bagehot wrote in the *Economist* (15 Sept. 1866) with reference to Carlyle's letter: "Is it possible to carry further the worship of brute force and of the sort of order in which brute force delights? If this is the authentic outcome of hero worship, it justifies, apart from other grounds, the distrust with which that new religion is regarded,—a religion which dethrones law in favour of caprice, and thrusts an usurping personal wilfulness into the seat of justice. . . . It is absolutely necessary in the interests of the highest as well as the meanest of Englishmen that the contemptuous disregard of the safeguards of personal liberty shown by Mr. Carlyle and his colleagues should receive public reprobation; and it is far more painful to witness their serious errors—because they ought to know better—than to read of the crimes and blunders of the poor coloured folk of Jamaica, whose very inferiority should have secured them the justest treatment." "Mr. Carlyle on Mr. Eyre," in *Historical Essays*, vol. III, pp. 563–4, 565.

85 See Mill's letter to Herbert Spencer, *LL*, *CW*, vol. XVI, pp. 1191–2 (15 Aug. 1866). As Mill later explained to Thomas Perronet Thompson: "The expensiveness of the attempt to get justice done in the Jamaica matter, arises from the necessity of bringing a number of witnesses from Jamaica to London, and maintaining them there until no longer required. Our lawyers' bills will doubtless be heavy, but will, for aught I know, not exceed as many hundreds as we are obliged to ask for thousands." *LL*, *CW*, vol. XVI, p. 1207 (10 Oct. 1866).

86 *Daily News*, 12 Oct. 1866, p. 3; *Examiner*, 13 Oct. 1866 (2nd ed.), p. 647; reprinted in *EELE*, *CW*, vol. XXI, pp. 427–9.

of whom Mill presumably was one, stated that the Jamaica Committee "will have to encounter a powerful resistance backed by all the resources of wealth."[87] Reference was made to the celebratory reception given Eyre by dignitaries at Southampton, and to the pronouncements issuing from representatives of the Eyre Defence and Aid Committee:

> The conduct of the ex-governor, so far from being repented or repudiated, is held up as a model for imitation; and the [Jamaica] committee submit that, as the matter at present stands, the public cannot feel assured that British subjects, who may have given offence to a party in power, will not again be put to death without lawful trial; or that those who have been concerned in such proceedings will not again be applauded, caressed, and marked out for future reward and honour by peers, members of parliament, chaplains of her Majesty [the reference is to Charles Kingsley, who spoke in praise of Eyre at the Southampton banquet], magistrates, and other persons in high station.[88]

They solicited public support for "an undertaking which they believe to be essential to the interests of public liberty and justice."[89] In their capacity as private citizens, members of the Jamaica Committee intended "to put the law into motion only on the positive and almost contumacious refusal of the government to do its duty."[90] The appeal did not fall on deaf ears, if the number of prosecutions instituted by the Jamaica Committee over the next eighteen months is anything to go by.[91]

The legal proceedings initiated by the Jamaica Committee targeted three individuals: Lieutenant Herbert Brand, who had presided at Gordon's court martial; Colonel Alexander Nelson (Brand's superior officer), who had commanded the troops at Morant Bay; and Eyre.[92]

87 *EELE*, *CW*, vol. XXI, p. 427.

88 Ibid., p. 428.

89 Ibid.

90 Ibid.

91 Even before the appeal made in October, the committee had managed to raise £3200. See Mill's letter to David Urquhart, *LL*, *CW*, vol. XVI, p. 1205 (4 Oct. 1866). At the end of 1867 the membership of the Jamaica Committee stood at 800, an increase of 500 over the previous year's total. See Semmel, *Governor Eyre Controversy*, p. 117.

92 For a narrative of the prosecutions, see Semmel, *Governor Eyre Controversy*, pp. 142–70; full contemporary accounts of the Eyre prosecutions, written from a perspective favourable to Eyre, were authored by W.F. Finlason, *Justice to a Colonial Governor; or Some Considerations on the Case of Mr. Eyre* (London: Chapman and Hall,

James Fitzjames Stephen, acting for the Jamaica Committee, with Mill and P.A. Taylor named as private prosecutors, filed an application for warrants against Nelson and Brand in the Bow Street Court in early February 1867. The charge was murder. Upon surrendering to the court, they were released on bail. A preliminary hearing led to the case being consigned to the Central Criminal Court.

Residing at this time at Adderley Hall in Shropshire, Eyre was excluded from this warrant on the premise that he was not subject to the jurisdiction of the Bow Street Police Court. In late March the solicitors of the Jamaica Committee, Shaen and Roscoe, requested from the bench of magistrates at Market Drayton (Shropshire) a warrant for the arrest of Eyre. The magistrates grudgingly met this request on 25 March. Two days later the case was heard, Stephen representing the Jamaica Committee and Hardinge Giffard (the future Lord Halsbury) representing Eyre. The accusation against Eyre concerned the murder (so it was characterized by the legal counsel of the committee) of Gordon, the charge being that he was an accessory before the fact. After hearing Stephen and Giffard, the magistrates unanimously decided that the evidence presented by Stephen had failed to establish a strong or probable presumption of guilt. Eyre was discharged.

The case against Brand and Nelson went before the London Grand Jury and Lord Chief Justice Cockburn on 10 April. The Jamaica Committee had reason to cheer the legal interpretation the lord chief justice placed on the evidence. In a massive charge, Cockburn insisted that martial law was military law and could not be validly applied to civilians, whatever the statutes of Jamaica might say; the proceedings against Gordon he described as "altogether unlawful and unjustifiable." He furthermore stated: "I come irresistibly to the conclusion that no jury, however influenced by prejudice or passion, arising out of local or other circumstances, if they had been guided by a competent, impartial, and honest judge, could, upon evidence so morally and intrinsically worthless . . . have condemned that man on the charges on which he was tried."[93] In gladdening the Jamaica Committee, Cockburn's charge occupied a category all its own. The Grand Jury disregarded the opinion of the lord chief justice, refusing to indict either Nelson or Brand.

In July 1867 the Jamaica Committee appealed to the Tory attorney-

---

1868), and *Report of the Case of the Queen v. Edward John Eyre, on His Prosecution in the Court of Queen's Bench* (London: Chapman and Hall, 1868).

93 Alexander James Edmund Cockburn, *Charge of the Lord Chief Justice of England to the Grand Jury at the Central Criminal Court, in the Case of the Queen against Nelson and Brand*, ed. Frederick Cockburn (London: Ridgway, 1867), pp. 114, 115.

general, Sir John Rolt (Cairns had vacated the post to take a lord justiceship), to review its case against Eyre and to commit him for trial.[94] The committee could not have been surprised by Rolt's refusal to act. Eyre moved to London in January 1868 and informed the Jamaica Committee of his presence, thereby seeming to thumb his nose at them. Stephen advised against any further legal action, but Mill prevailed on the committee to answer Eyre's challenge.[95] Sir Robert Collier replaced Stephen. In late February Collier sought to obtain a warrant for murder against Eyre. Sir Thomas Henry, chief magistrate in the Bow Street Court, denied the application, maintaining that the issues it raised had already been settled by the Grand Jury in the case of Nelson and Brand. Forced to recognize that securing an indictment for murder was out of the question, the Jamaica Committee had recourse to a different strategy. In April Collier successfully persuaded a Bow Street magistrate, James Vaughan, to grant a warrant against Eyre, under the 1802 Colonial Governors' Act, for "having issued an illegal and oppressive proclamation of martial law, and caused divers illegal acts to be committed under the same and . . . had unlawfully and oppressively caused the arrest, imprisonment and flogging of divers persons by virtue of the said illegal proclamation."[96]

In mid-May Vaughan determined that the evidence presented was sufficient to commit Eyre for trial. On 2 June Justice Blackburn of the Court of Queen's Bench gave his charge to the Middlesex Grand Jury. That charge diverged markedly from Cockburn's. The statutes of Jamaica, Blackburn stated, authorized the governor, on the advice of a Council of War, to proclaim martial law for a maximum of thirty days under special circumstances. If the Grand Jury should conclude that Eyre, using the best information available to him, had reasonably judged the danger to be so grave as to necessitate such a proclamation, then they should also conclude that he had legal justification for acting as he did. The same could be said of his conduct in relation to Gordon, Blackburn continued, if Eyre believed that Gordon had instigated the insurrection.[97] A day after hearing Blackburn's charge, the Grand Jury denied Collier and the Jamaica Committee the indictment they had asked for.

The legal remedies invoked by the Jamaica Committee had all proved

94 See "The Jamaica Committee and Mr. Eyre," *The Times*, 29 July 1867, p. 12.

95 See Mill's letter to Lindsey Middleton Aspland explaining this decision, *LL*, *CW*, vol. XVI, pp. 1364–5 (23 Feb. 1868).

96 For this phase of the proceedings against Eyre, see Finlason, *Report of the Case of the Queen v. Edward John Eyre*, pp. 59–87.

97 For Blackburn's charge, see "Ex-governor Eyre," *The Times*, 2 June 1868, pp. 9–10.

unavailing. There was no more to be done. A "Statement of the Jamaica Committee," signed by Mill, P.A. Taylor, and F.W. Chesson, was issued in mid-July.[98] It would serve as the committee's apologia. The opening paragraph announced the opinion of the executive "that the duty which they undertook of exhausting all the methods afforded by the criminal law of bringing the case under the cognizance of justice has now been performed."[99] Anxious to dispel the misconceptions "fostered by the language of those who were opposed to an inquiry," the authors of the "Statement" set forth yet again the "leading facts" respecting the events in Jamaica, the gravity of which had generated the moral and legal obligations that had shaped the committee's evolving mission. Aggravating that gravity, "in a constitutional point of view," was "the language of certain classes and of certain journalists . . . who applauded the arbitrary violence of Mr. Eyre."[100] Because the "duty of vindicating the law" had been "abandoned by the Government," the quest for that vindication, in accordance with "the principles of the English constitution," had devolved on private individuals; "if private citizens declined it, there would be no check on the illegal conduct of officers of the Crown."[101] The protractedness of the legal proceedings had been no fault of theirs, but had resulted from the character of the legal remedies available to them, from the delays incident on the need to transport witnesses from Jamaica, and from "the difficulty of finding Mr. Eyre within the jurisdiction of a professional minister of the law. Due allowance being made for these impediments, the proceedings have been carried on with all possible despatch."[102]

The last section of the "Statement" measured the committee's accomplishments against their aims. The latter were said to have been three in number: "to obtain a judicial inquiry into the conduct of Mr. Eyre and his subordinates; to settle the law in the interest of justice, liberty and humanity; and to arouse public morality against oppression generally, and particularly against the oppression of subject and dependent races."[103] On the first, the authors confessed failure. On the second, they claimed success, asserting their belief that Cockburn's "memorable charge" would be "a lasting barrier against the encroachment of martial law and its

98 See *EELE*, *CW*, vol. XXI, pp. 429–35.
99 Ibid., p. 429.
100 Ibid., p. 431.
101 Ibid., p. 433.
102 Ibid.
103 Ibid.

upholders on the rights and liberties of British subjects."[104] They went so far as to declare that "British jurisprudence . . . has been finally purged of martial law."[105] The fact that London magistrates had committed for trial Nelson, Brand, and Eyre "confirmed the principle that the officers of the Crown are responsible in the ordinary course of justice to the Courts of Law for acts done by them in the suppression, or alleged suppression, of insurrection."[106] As to the third object, the leaders of the Jamaica Committee covered their sores with an unguent whose composition betrayed more than a hint of smugness. Their labours had "been well repaid"; "A great amount of sound public opinion has been called forth."[107] Some credit was taken for the fact that the recent troubles in Ireland had not prompted a governmental response resembling that in Jamaica.[108] And discredit was given where discredit was due:

> That sympathy with Mr. Eyre and with his policy should . . . be exhibited in the quarters where it prevailed, was inevitable. It was inevitable also, that this sympathy should take the form of charges of vindictiveness, malignity and persecution against those who, without the slightest personal feeling, were endeavouring to discharge the unwelcome but indispensable duty of guarding public liberty and vindicating the law; nor was it unnatural that such charges should find acceptance among the unthinking, when, from the lapse of time, the agony of so many hundreds of sufferers has been forgotten, and the annoyance inflicted by legal proceedings on the author of the suffering alone remained present to the mind.[109]

104 Ibid., p. 434.

105 Ibid. This is a somewhat dubious reading of the status of martial law, once one moves beyond the sphere of "jurisprudence." The Jamaica calamity led Carnarvon to formulate a "Circular Despatch to Colonial Governors, Dated 30 January, 1867, on the Subject of Martial Law" (*PP*, 1867, XLIX, 395). This dispatch was devised to provide governors with a set of guidelines concerning the use of martial law. According to Charles Townshend, "The most important of these were that the governor had the responsibility for proclaiming and revoking martial law; that he must be satisfied that there was armed resistance which could not be dealt with by troops acting merely in aid of the civil power in the ordinary manner; and that martial law 'should not be proclaimed over a wider district than the necessities of public safety require.' " "Martial Law," p. 174.

106 *EELE*, *CW*, vol. XXI, p. 434.

107 Ibid.

108 These particular achievements are not mentioned among the claims Mill makes for the Jamaica Committee in the *Autobiography*; *A*, *CW*, vol. I, p. 282.

109 *EELE*, *CW*, vol. XXI, p. 434.

Having thus taken stock, the Jamaica Committee took their leave.

J.S. Mill was not a zealot; yet if he were to be judged solely on the basis of his part in the Eyre controversy, he could be mistaken for one. Deliberate in tone though his public utterances on the subject generally were, his correspondence displays a crackling vehemence that signals a passion bordering on the obsessive. To David Urquhart he wrote of "this Jamaica business the authors of which from the first day I knew of it I determined that I would do all in my power to bring to justice if there was not another man in Parl^{t} to stand by me."[110] The decision of February 1868, strongly backed by Mill, to press ahead with a prosecution of Eyre on his taking up residence in London occasioned an exchange with Lindsey Middleton Aspland, a member of the Jamaica Committee who disapproved of any further legal action. Mill told Aspland: "This protest and vindication must be made now or never: and to relinquish the effort while a single unexhausted chance remains would be, in my estimation, to make ourselves to some extent participants in the crime."[111] In June of this year Mill answered one of his Westminster supporters, who had reported that his conduct as chairman of the Jamaica Committee had alienated quite a number of those who had voted for Mill in 1865. That answer included the following statement:

> I cannot say that it is possible to me as a man to regard Mr. Eyre's conduct in Jamaica without the deepest indignation, or as an Englishman without a sentiment of humiliation: nor can I pretend that I can regard without abhorrence and contempt the man who knowing himself to be guilty in the eyes of many disinterested persons, of the wanton torture and death of many hundred men and women, can be content to shelter himself under any shield whatever against a judicial examination and does not eagerly challenge and earnestly invite the closest possible scrutiny into whatever justification he thinks he can offer.[112]

The feelings persisted. When he learned three years later that the Gladstone ministry intended to reimburse Eyre for his legal expenses, Mill was beside himself. "After this I shall henceforth wish for a Tory Government."[113]

A visceral response of intense moral revulsion, while perhaps vital to

110 *LL, CW*, vol. XVI, p. 1206 (4 Oct. 1866).

111 Ibid., p. 1365 (23 Feb. 1868).

112 *LL, CW*, vol. XVI, pp. 1410–11 (to Willam Sims Pratten, 9 June 1868).

113 Ibid., vol. XVII, p. 1829 (to Cairnes, 21 Aug. 1871).

the genesis of Mill's mission, was not of its essence. In his own mind Mill was able to distinguish between the force of his personal feelings and the requirements of principle, and it was his sense of the latter that determined his course on the Jamaica question. "Yet if all human sympathies could be cast aside altogether, the importance of instituting a judicial enquiry into the proceedings in Jamaica would still be paramount in the eyes of all thinking persons who look upon law and justice as the foundation of order and civilisation."[114]

In his major speech on Jamaica in the House of Commons Mill had laid particular stress on "the principle of government by law." To say that Eyre and his subordinates ought not to be answerable to a court of law, Mill admonished, meant "giving up altogether the principle of government by law, and resigning ourselves to arbitrary power."[115] The public statement issued by the Jamaica Committee underscored the same theme. Mill consistently made his commitment to the rule of law the nucleus around which he grouped the layers of his argument. Writing to Urquhart in October 1866, Mill remarked: "You approve of my speech [on Jamaica] because you see that I am not on this occasion standing up for the negroes, or for liberty, deeply as both are interested in the subject—but for the first necessity of human society, law."[116]

This view of government by law as the foundation on which the possibility of "human society" rested had been adhered to by Mill throughout his adult life. In a speech given to the London Debating Society in 1826, he had declaimed:

> Now a government of law is always preferable to a government of arbitrary will. However oppressive the laws might be, they might at any rate be known. . . . I can hardly imagine any laws so bad, to which I would not rather be subject than to the caprice of a man. . . . I would rather have every action controlled—every movement chained up by restrictive laws which iniquitous as they might be would not destroy my security, since I should only have to obey them and be safe: than lead a life of incessant anxiety lest by some acts I should unwittingly infringe against a will which had never been made known to me, and violate prohibitions which had never existed any where but in the royal bosom.[117]

114 Ibid., vol. XVI, p. 1411 (to Pratten, 9 June 1868).

115 *PPS*, *CW*, vol. XXVIII, pp. 107–8.

116 *LL*, *CW*, vol. XVI, p. 1205 (4 Oct. 1866).

117 *Journals and Debating Speeches*, *CW*, vols. XXVI–XXVII (Toronto: University of Toronto Press, 1988), vol. XXVI, p. 342.

Composed in a more philosophical vein for a more philosophical purpose, the following passage from *Utilitarianism* reveals much about why Mill responded as he did to the Jamaica question:

> Nearly all other benefits are needed by one person, not needed by another; and many of them can, if necessary, be cheerfully foregone, or replaced by something else; but security no human being can possibly do without; on it we depend for all our immunity from evil, and for the whole value of all and every good, beyond the passing moment; since nothing but the gratification of the instant could be of any worth to us, if we could be deprived of everything the next instant by whoever was momentarily stronger than ourselves. Now this most indispensable of all necessaries, after physical nutriment, cannot be had, unless the machinery for providing it is kept unintermittedly in active play. Our notion, therefore, of the claim we have on our fellow-creatures to join in making safe for us the very groundwork of our existence, gathers feelings round it so much more intense than those concerned in any of the more common cases of utility, that the difference in degree . . . becomes a real difference in kind. The claim assumes that character of absoluteness, that apparent infinity, and incommensurability with all other considerations, which constitute the distinction between the feelings of right and wrong and that of ordinary expediency and inexpediency. The feelings concerned are so powerful, and we count so positively on finding a responsive feeling in others (all being alike interested), that *ought* and *should* grow into *must*, and recognised indispensability becomes a moral necessity, analogous to physical and often not inferior to it in binding force.[118]

Another important, albeit less overt, influence on Mill's engagement with the Jamaica question sprang from an imperial ideal whose sustainability was conditional on the reality not falling too far short. In his chapter in *Representative Government*, "Of the Government of Dependencies by a Free State," Mill wrote: "This mode of government is as legitimate as any other, if it is the one which in the existing state of civilization of the subject people, most facilitates their transition to a higher stage of improvement."[119] Although the constitutional status of Jamaica had been different from that of India, Jamaica too was in effect a dependency

118 *Essays on Ethics, Religion and Society*, ed. John M. Robson, *CW*, vol. X (Toronto: University of Toronto Press, 1969), p. 251.

119 *Essays on Politics and Society* [*EPS*], ed. John M. Robson, *CW*, vols. XVIII–XIX (Toronto: University of Toronto Press, 1977), vol. XIX, p. 567.

of the British crown. The moral legitimacy of such imperial rule turned on the intent and capacity of the dominant country to provide the subject people with a government better—in the sense of promoting "the permanent interests of man as a progressive being"[120]—than they could provide for themselves. Great Britain, Mill believed, had performed this function in her dependent colonies, and could continue to do so. (The extent to which his service in the East India Company moulded or necessitated this belief is not the issue here.) The conduct of Eyre and his subordinates in Jamaica, if allowed to go unpunished, threatened to subvert this ideal and render it untenable.

The deeds done in Jamaica reminded Mill of the reaction to the Indian Mutiny. In a letter of October 1866 that addressed the Jamaica question, Mill observed: "my eyes were first opened to the moral condition of the English nation (I except in these matters the working classes) by the atrocities perpetrated in the Indian Mutiny and the feelings which supported them at home."[121] Lord Canning, the governor-general of India at the time of the Mutiny, had done his best to dam the flood of bloody revenge. Not only did Eyre fail in his obligation to do everything within his means to protect the lawful rights of the Queen's subjects in Jamaica; he had himself flagrantly violated those rights.

The quality of British imperial rule hinged on the quality of the men assigned responsibility for administering the colonies. Non-white populations must not be left to the mercy of English settlers, who had shown themselves to be pitiless enough. Referring to the problem New Zealand presented the British government, Mill wrote at the beginning of 1866: "Here, then, is the burthen on the conscience of legislators at home. Can they give up the Maoris to the mercy of the more powerful and constantly increasing section of the population? Knowing what the English are, when they are left alone with what they think an inferior race, I cannot reconcile myself to this."[122] Five years earlier he had asserted: "The government of a people by itself has a meaning, and a reality; but such a thing as government of one people by another, does not and cannot exist." By this Mill did not mean that imperial government could not exist. "But if the good of the governed is the proper business of a government, it is utterly impossible that a people should directly attend

120 *On Liberty*, *EPS*, *CW*, vol. XVIII, p. 224.

121 *LL*, *CW*, vol. XVI, p. 1206 (to Urquhart, 4 Oct. 1866). On 20 December 1865, Helen Taylor wrote to Mrs. Grote: "The Jamaica atrocities seem to me the natural consequence of those committed in India." *Amberley Papers*, vol. I, p. 438.

122 *LL*, *CW*, vol. XVI, p. 1136 (to H.S. Chapman, 7 Jan. 1866).

to it. The utmost they can do is to give some of their best men a commission to look after it."[123] Lord Canning had been one of "their best"; Eyre and his subordinates had proven themselves utterly unworthy of the solemn trust reposed in them. The men representing the British crown in Jamaica in the autumn of 1865 had disgraced the British Empire and desecrated the principles for which it ought to stand. The stain could not be wholly removed, but it could be diminished by holding those responsible legally accountable for their actions.

It may be thought odd that this investigation of Mill and the Jamaica problem has made so little of the relation between parliamentary reform and the Eyre altercation. The connective tissues figure prominently in Bernard Semmel's study, *The Governor Eyre Controversy*. It is surely no accident that many members of the Jamaica Committee—Beales, Bright, and Mill most obviously—had close ties to the movement for parliamentary reform. Nor is it strange that some of Eyre's champions, Carlyle in particular, heartily disapproved of the reform agitation and what they saw as the feeble governmental response to it. Many of Eyre's opponents drew on a common fund of political attitudes that assured a measure of correspondence over a range of issues—parliamentary reform, Ireland, and Jamaica among them. The same can be said of Eyre's supporters. Yet few of the participants bound together the reform agitation and the Eyre controversy so tightly as did Carlyle.[124] As for Mill, the issues were kept quite distinct, be it in his letters, speeches, or *Autobiography*. Had there been no agitation for parliamentary reform, his answer to the Jamaica question would not have been substantively different from what it turned out to be. Had he not been a member of parliament, the *depth* of his involvement might not have been so great. The bent of Mill's mind during the Westminster years was decidedly activist in nature.

Mill's relentless pursuit of Eyre made him the object of much hostility. In the *Autobiography* he refers to "the abusive letters, almost all of them anonymous, which [he] received while these proceedings were going on. . . . They graduated from coarse jokes, verbal and pictorial, up to threats of assassination."[125] If enough Westminster electors felt even a fraction of such enmity, whatever its causes, Mill's days as an MP would be numbered.

123 *Considerations on Representative Government*, *EPS*, *CW*, vol. XIX, p. 569.

124 See Thomas Carlyle, "Shooting Niagara," in *Critical and Miscellaneous Essays*, 7 vols. (London: Chapman and Hall, 1872), vol. VII, pp. 208–11.

125 *A*, *CW*, vol. I, p. 282.

SEVEN

The Election of 1868

The election of 1868 was quite different from that of 1865: Palmerston was buried, as was the reform issue, if not as permanently; both Derby and Russell had resigned, leaving Disraeli and Gladstone facing off across the country for the first time with the prime ministership as the prize.[1] Their confrontation signalled a new kind of party conflict as platforms became more clearly defined, especially on the Liberal side in spite of the strain caused by the Adullamite distaste for full Gladstonianism.

The effects of the 1867 Reform Act on the size and coloration of the electorate were anxiously anticipated, and speculation about them affected the election strategy and practices of the parties and candidates. The intensely hot summer saw, both before and after the House rose, great political activity in both conventional and unconventional ways. The relatively quiet but extremely important and expensive job of finding, listing, and validating claims of electors, an ever increasingly laborious task since 1832, was greatly intensified by the parties' desire to identify all the new electors, especially the lodgers, created by the recent act. Much noisier and far less conventional was the great oratorical progress—the "magnificent" campaign[2] through the country by Gladstone and Bright, who made the disestablishment of the Irish church the key issue in the election. Disraeli, the more flamboyant by reputation, wrote only the traditional letter to the electors of Buckinghamshire and made a speech after the borough elections.

In this fourth stage of Mill's parliamentary career (see p. 81 above),

1 Derby had retired because of ill-health (he died the following year) in February 1868, two months after Russell told Gladstone that he would give up the leadership of the Liberal party before the next election.

2 John Morley, *The Life of William Ewart Gladstone*, 3 vols. (London: Macmillan and Co., 1903), vol. II, p. 251.

GOING TO THE COUNTRY.

John Bull (as Guard). NOW, GENTLEMEN, TAKE YOUR SEATS! TAKE YOUR SEATS!

the campaign of 1868, he identified himself thoroughly with the Gladstonian Liberals. However, he still did not act in the traditional way: he did not canvass, and though he fully supported disestablishment of the Irish church, he did not specially argue for the measure, which in his view was a reform already "prosperous" and therefore not requiring his energetic support.[3] In fact, his campaign was, as in 1865, mainly his committee's campaign, especially through registering voters and countering Conservative appeals, though he was more visible and vocal on the platform than he had been three years earlier. He was, unfortunately for his chances of re-election, also more visible in the newspapers, where the echoes of his third parliamentary stage, his comparatively independent advocacy of measures during the Conservative ministry, continued to attract attention, and where what was seen as his "impetuous eagerness" was exposed as his initially personal reactions were made public. In any case, one must not be misled by later developments into thinking that the electors of Westminster had a full appreciation of the national campaign. Although Gladstone's tactics were to become commonplace, elections, even national ones, were still for the most part very local affairs.

Westminster in 1868 was traditional and the contest concentrated on the local candidates. The campaign, run on party lines, began while parliament was still in session, once it became clear that an election would be held in the autumn. In this election, unlike that of 1865, Grosvenor and Mill had, as sitting members, the advantage of position and first-hand knowledge in getting their plans under way—though, as in the previous election, in Mill's case it was his supporters who became active. Another major difference from 1865 was that the Westminster electors were now addressed from the beginning by a joint Grosvenor-Mill Committee, whose advertisements equally promoted both, and whose meetings featured both as speakers.[4] Yet another difference is revealed by the advertisements, which appeared as early as 22 July (the polling day was not until 17 November). Two of these advertisements on behalf of Grosvenor and Mill, signalling the Liberals' recognition of the importance of the new electorate, mentioned that forms for claims by lodgers were available at 21 George St., Hanover Square, and another gave the address of the Liberal Registration Office (47 Charing Cross).

3 *Public and Parliamentary Speeches* [*PPS*], ed. John M. Robson and Bruce L. Kinzer, *Collected Works* [*CW*], vols. XXVIII–XXIX (Toronto: University of Toronto Press, 1988), vol. XXVIII, p. 16 (3 July 1865).

4 Grosvenor, incidentally, always appeared before Mill, apparently because he had polled more votes in 1865 than Mill, and was therefore considered the "senior" member for Westminster, and not because he was an Honourable rather than an Esquire, or because his name was alphabetically prior.

The Liberals held two public meetings in July, on the 22nd and 24th, at both of which the sitting members spoke and answered questions. At the first of these (an account of which was printed by the committee for general distribution), Grosvenor spoke at length and with the kind of knowing charm that helped him materially in both campaigns, concentrating on the history of the current parliament with reference to reform and other leading topics. The main themes of Mill's speech were pauperism, the need for better men in the new parliament, and the virtues of that "great leader of progress," Gladstone. In reply to questions on that occasion, both candidates declared themselves in favour of the equalization of poor rates, and Mill said he was unequivocally opposed to giving the revenues of the Anglican church in Ireland to any other sect.[5]

For the second meeting, on the 24th, a major card was played in the presentation of a letter from Gladstone to Dr. Brewer, who occupied the chair as he had at the meeting on the 22nd. In the letter, which the committee had printed and distributed throughout the campaign, Gladstone, regretting his inability to attend the meeting, dismissed the Conservative candidate swiftly:

> I have not a word to say against Mr. Smith in any capacity except as a candidate for Westminster, and against him in that capacity I could say a good many words, for I am associated with your actual representatives in a good and great cause, the progress of which it is his purpose to impede.

And his commendation of Grosvenor was polite rather than enthusiastic:

> Captain Grosvenor, who was first recommended to us by the connection of his family with the city, and by the cordial and deserved respect in which they are held, has shown himself to be an able and faithful representative, whom his constituents might well have chosen from his personal merits and ability alone.

But of Mill the account is celebratory:

> Of Mr. Mill, who has obtained a world-wide fame, it would almost be impertinent in me to speak the language of eulogy. Yet I will venture on two assertions, both having exclusive reference to his Parliamentary career. Firm in the maintenance of his own opinions,

5 *PPS*, *CW*, vol. XXVIII, pp. 319–25.

> Mr. Mill has ever exhibited the largest indulgence for those of others, and with this liberal tolerance of differences he has shown in the most remarkable manner how to reconcile on the one hand a thorough independence, and on the other an enlightened sense of the value and power of that kind of union which is designated by the name of political party. More than this, Mr. Mill has set us all a rare example—a forgiving temper, a forgetfulness of self, an absolute devotion to public duty; and I do not hesitate to express my deliberate opinion that his presence in the House of Commons has materially helped to raise and sustain its moral tone.

In his speech Grosvenor acknowledged the reappearance on the electoral scene of W.H. Smith, Jr., referring to "the requisition signed by the Premier, and he did not know how many members of the Government, asking Mr. W.H. Smith to come forward as a candidate for Westminster. He said that when he read the paragraph in the papers announcing what had been done he looked to see if it was an extract from *Punch.*" Mill dwelt specially on current topics, undoubtedly reflecting his main preoccupations: he had spoken in the House twice that day, and had been engaged in debate continuously for the previous week. He alluded particularly to his opposition to the Metropolitan Cattle Markets Bill, and his support for anti-bribery legislation. Questioned, he explained his opposition to the secret ballot, answered (apparently rather sharply) a query about his view of the House of Lords by saying that his opinion could be obtained in a book for 18*d.* (the People's Edition of *Considerations on Representative Government*), adding that if there were a better House of Commons there would be better Bishops. Other questioners elicited miscellaneous views, such as his belief that game should belong to those who fed it, and that (as Grosvenor had averred) the average length of parliaments, three to five years, was short enough for effective responsibility. Finally, Mill was called on for comment about the Abyssinian excursion, and replied that he had favoured it as a necessary evil, carried out with every sentiment of honour and justice.[6]

On the 29th there was a meeting of Liberals, without Grosvenor and Mill, to promote their candidacy. The main theme was the danger of the methods being used by Smith's supporters. One motion agreed to was "That, seeing the unscrupulous means being employed by Mr. Smith's committee to secure that gentleman's return, we call upon every lodger to come forward and enrol himself on the electoral roll." Further, a

6 Ibid., pp. 329–32. For explanation of the question about Abyssinia, see pp. 227–9 below.

house-to-house canvass of St. Anne's district was decided upon, "ten volunteers having offered their services."[7] It would appear that, despite the threat from Smith's agents, there was reason for the Liberal committee to be quite happy about the progress of events. The questions at the meetings had not been particularly troublesome, campaign workers were coming forward, and Mill, with Grosvenor, was expressing what could only be thought of as orthodox and pragmatic as well as enthusiastic support for the party's leader, Gladstone.

Mill's recurrent problem over the ballot arose at this time when he felt compelled to correct the impression, given in a speech by John Bright, that he might be wavering on the question; he responded in detail in the press, saying he opposed its introduction anywhere in the United Kingdom, had in fact spoken against it on the very evening (24 July) when Bright had suggested his views were uncertain, and called attention to his having voted against it in the House when it was proposed for adoption in Ireland.[8] But this was not an opinion repugnant to many Liberals, and those Radicals who would be offended were unlikely to repudiate Mill because of what was by then one of his well-known crotchets.

Parliament was proroged on 31 July,[9] and Mill departed for Avignon the following day, with no expectation of returning until the eve of the general election.[10] And, summoned by the committee to attend and speak at meetings, he returned only in time for the meeting of electors on 2 November, having indicated that he would (as he did) return to Avignon right after the election, whether successful or not. During his three-month absence from August into November, Mill of course left the registration campaign solely in the hands of the committee, who worked through local unpaid volunteers with paid legal aid. But his opinions and actions, more commonly made notorious by his opponents than by his own will—and certainly not by the desire of his local supporters—kept him in the public eye. Indeed, the Westminster Conservatives were only too pleased to keep his views in the spotlight. As they cannily surmised, public reactions were many and strong. From the time the general election was anticipated until the polling day and beyond, Mill's full

7 This meeting was covered by *The Times*, 30 July, p. 10.

8 Letter to the editor, *Daily News*, 31 July 1868, p. 5; in *Newspaper Writings* [NW], ed. Ann P. and John M. Robson, CW, vols. XXII–XXV (Toronto: University of Toronto Press, 1986), vol. XXV, p. 1218.

9 It was not formally dissolved until 11 November, but the resulting election was keenly anticipated throughout the intervening months.

10 *Later Letters* [LL], ed. Francis E. Mineka and Dwight N. Lindley, CW, vols. XIV–XVII (Toronto: University of Toronto Press, 1972), vol. XVI, pp. 1429, 1433.

parliamentary career came under scrutiny, and he was constantly called on to defend his behaviour.

By any measure, the most commented on issue involving Mill during this period was the Governor Eyre case. While in retrospect the strength of the Jamaica Committee in principle as well as in the quality of its adherents attracts our attention and admiration, there can be little doubt that a majority of the public—certainly a vocal majority—was on the other side from the beginning. The satirical magazine *Fun* provides an instructive example.[11] On 25 November 1865, not long after news of the incidents reached Britain, it featured a full-page cartoon of a rampaging Jamaican black, wielding cutlass and fiery brand, white corpses in the background, with the caption, "The Black Question," and the legend, playing on the famous emancipationist slogan: "*Am* I a Man and a Brother?"[12] From then till the end of the case—and even beyond[13]—*Fun* kept up a constant barrage against the Jamaica Committee,[14] expressing fervently the views better known as those of Thomas Carlyle and other members of the Eyre Defence Committee, especially attacking Exeter Hall philanthropy with its purported bias towards distant blacks and its neglect of poor whites at home. One cartoon catches the tenor exactly: a shackled poor labourer, with hungry wife and babies in the background, is refused aid by a "Distinguished Philanthropist" carrying an anti-slavery leaflet and a paper with Exeter Hall on it, who says: "Really, my good man, I can give you no further attention, I am so engaged with those interesting blacks!"[15]

11 For a full account of the satirical papers' treatment of the Jamaica issue, see John M. Robson, "Mill in Parliament: The View from the Comic Papers," *Utilitas*, 2 (May 1990), 102–42.

12 Nearly a year later, on 22 Sept. 1866, *Fun* noted that by "general consent" the Jamaican negro would be known as "a man and a bother."

13 See "Don't Dissolve," 13 Feb. 1869, p. 236, where it is ironically suggested that the Jamaica Committee should turn its attention to New Zealand, whence came reports of the slaughter of white colonists by natives. This note is repeated in the "Preface" to *Fun*, n.s. 8, p. iv. The French action in New Caledonia, in similar fashion, is given as a cause for the Jamaica Committee on 1 September 1866, p. 250. See also 20 Feb. 1869, p. 239.

14 The list is a long one, including, in addition to those cited above and below, in 1865: 25 Nov., p. 102, 9 Dec., p. 122, 16 Dec., p. 132, 23 Dec., pp. 142, 149, 30 Dec., 152; in 1866: 13 Jan., p. 180, 20 Jan., p. 187, 3 March, p. 247, 26 May, p. 104, 29 Sept., p. 26; in 1867: 16 March, p. 7, 13 April, pp. 48, 49, 27 April, pp. 68, 75, 25 May, p. 110, 8 June, p. 195, 18 July, p. 201, 3 Aug., p. 215, 17 Aug., p. 235; in 1868, 13 June, p. 149, 20 June, p. 159 (the poetic clue to a double acrostic, beginning, "In far-off lands a manful blow / He struck for law and England's right. . .").

15 10 Feb. 1866.

With reference to Mill, it should be noted that *Fun* saw itself as a friend to the working class, with generally anti-Conservative views. And even the leading liberal satirical paper, *Punch*, was far from "liberal" in modern understandings on the Eyre case. An early comment indicates that the matter is still moot:

> Suspend Gordon—says the *Times*.
> Suspend Eyre—says the *Star*.
> Suspend Judgment—says *Punch*.[16]

But the ruling tenor is pro-Eyre and anti-Jamaica Committee, Exeter Hall, and "Quashibungo."[17] The Liberal papers generally managed to leave Mill's name out of the indictment,[18] but the Conservative ones were pleased to feature him, especially as the election approached. *Judy*, the leading Conservative satirical paper, not founded until 1867, from its inception made its allegiances clear, and in 1868 it consistently took Eyre's side against "the persistent outrage of all decency of which the Jamaica Committee have been guilty for the last two years."[19] In June, exultant at the failure of the Eyre prosecution, *Judy* says she would take great pleasure in seeing "Messrs. Mill, Buxton, and Taylor, and the rest of the self-appointed persecutors, in the dock of the Old Bailey for conspiracy. The philosophic Mill, the forgiving Buxton, and the tolerant Taylor 'doing time' at Cold Bath Fields would be a really pleasant sight, and a fitting reward for their disgraceful conduct towards the man who saved Jamaica."[20] *Judy*'s assurance that her attitude is shared by the public is evident in a cartoon showing John Bull in a rage at a Royal Academy "hanging" by Mill, Buxton, and Taylor.[21]

16 16 Dec. 1865, p. 237. Compare ibid., p. 138.

17 See, for example, in addition to others cited below, in 1865: 16 Dec., p. 235, 23 Dec., p. 252; in 1866: 10 Feb., p. 62, 16 Feb., p. 69, 24 Feb., p. 81, 10 March, p. 98, 8 Dec., p. 231 (compare 9 March 1867, p. 94); in 1867: 26 Jan., p. 37, 13 April, p. 154, 20 April, p. 166; in 1868, 30 May, p. 238, 6 June, p. 245 (a full-page cartoon in which the ghost of Palmerston, pointing to a disconsolate Eyre, says to Disraeli, "Benjamin, Benjamin! *I* wouldn't have left him in the lurch"), 20 June, p. 268, 4 July, p. 114.

18 Even *Punch* was not shy about mentioning others on the Jamaica Committee, attacking by name Charles Buxton, Jacob Bright, Peter Taylor, and (of course), "Mr. Beales, (M.A)," and (as "Shammyrumstuff") Chamerovzow (see, for example, 6 April 1867, p. 11).

19 27 May, pp. 39–40; see also 4 March, p. 246, 27 May, pp. 47 and 48, and 1 July, p. 89.

20 10 June, 1868. For other references to Mill in this context, see 17 June, pp. 75 and 77, 1 July, p. 95, and 29 July, p. 131.

21 10 June 1868.

"THE HANGING COMMITTEE."

[See Page 59.

Will-o'-the-Wisp, a less significant paper that paid close attention to the Westminster election, also gave particular prominence to the Eyre case because of the paper's very special interest in East Surrey, where Charles Buxton was running for re-election. "Will" felt "perfectly convinced" late in October that the electors would send Buxton "packing to the retirement of Mr. John Stuart Mill at Avignon, where the two amateur hangmen may dwell in safety." And the article goes on to note that Buxton and Mill had subscribed to a fund for the "penniless negro" Phillips in his suit against Eyre, and adds pointedly: "It is well these things should be known on the eve of a general election."[22] Continuing the attack in "a few parting Notes for the Electors of East Surrey and Westminster," *Will-o'-the-Wisp* says: "Mr. Mill, who has brought a great name into the gutter, may safely be left there; we doubt whether the Westminster Electors will feel disposed to help him out."[23]

The reaction to the Jamaica rebellion and its repression was not isolated from general attitudes towards "lesser breeds," and Mill's support for the blacks resulted in a flurry of small attacks in addition to the main assault. One of the most curious is reflected in the question, alluded to above, that was put to him about Abyssinia in the election meeting of 24 July. Emperor Theodore, a ruler of mercurial and wayward temper, had imprisoned and held hostage the British consular corps. After repeated objections and demands, the British government had sent a relief expedition under Sir Robert Napier, which, following a brilliantly organized and almost bloodless campaign, captured the capital and the

22 31 Oct. 1868, p. 91.

23 Buxton, *Will*'s main target, "never had a name" (14 Nov. 1868, p. 105). *Will*'s standard of performance is well captured in its use of a pun after the election, when it suggests that Gladstone, having changed "his principles, . . . should also change his name—say to Mill-stone. No offence to poor Mill—he's a 'gone coon'" (25 Dec. 1868, p. 176). As this passage suggests, *Will-o'-the-Wisp* continued a savage attack on Mill after his defeat, unlike the other comic papers, which tended to ignore him. An instance is its attempt to associate him, with Buxton and Taylor, in the New Zealand atrocities, first in "The Moral of the Eyre Case" (16 Jan. 1869, p. 216), and then in a particularly nasty supposed letter from him to the editor, headed "Gibraltar and New Zealand," in which, evidently prompted by Jonathan Swift, but not ironically, Mill proposes "to boil down our indigent classes and those working men of whom I have asserted in my world-renowned treatise on Political Economy, that when they cease to be servile they become insolent, have them potted and sent off in cases, hermetically sealed, to New Zealand for the consumption of the natives, to whom, as an act of simple justice, we owe some reparation for our long usurpation of territory and sovereignty" (13 Feb. 1869, pp. 264, 269).

ruler, who committed suicide.[24] Very quickly an analogy was drawn with Jamaica, and Eyre was compared with Napier (who was elevated to the peerage as Lord Napier of Magdala). Before the campaign, *Fun* purported to doubt, for example, the truth of the rumour that the Jamaica Committee was "taking steps to prosecute Lord Stanley if he takes any steps to persecute or threaten that amiable and Christian black, the Emperor of Abyssinia."[25] And after Napier's triumph, *Fun* speculated that he might be prosecuted by the Jamaica Committee for "killing that amiable black person, Theodore"; the concluding sentence in the account represents more than mere satire: "If anything could raise him in the opinion of his countrymen it would be that he should become an object of persecution at the hands of that body."[26] And others made the same analogy, including *Punch* and *Tomahawk.*[27] The *Owl* followed suit, with a series on the pretended prosecution of Napier by "Bright, Mill, Taylor, and Beales,"[28] and a proposal that Eyre should stand against Mill for Westminster.[29] It also offered a parliamentary notice to Buxton per the Jamaica Committee about the Australian aboriginal cricket team having been "cruelly beaten at Kennington Oval" by the Surrey Club.[30] This last parallel was not alone in its extravagance, for *Punch* in the early days of the Eyre case had said in a "Contradiction": "We do not believe the statement that the Jamaica Committee intend to follow up their proceedings against Mr. Eyre by a prosecution of M. Du Chaillu for shooting and stuffing so many of our African relations, the Gorillas."[31]

With seeming total unawareness of the danger, Mill, in support of an unrelated principle, turned the red carpet spread for Napier into a personal minefield. On 5 June 1868 he presented to the Commons a petition from the Foreign Affairs Committee of Macclesfield representing "the injustice of the Abyssinian War, and praying that the House will not

24 See Freda Harcourt, "Disraeli's Imperialism, 1866–68: A Question of Timing," *Historical Journal*, 23 (1980), 87–109; and Nini Rogers, "The Abyssinian Expedition of 1867–68: Disraeli's Imperialism or James Murray's War?" ibid., 27 (1984), 129–49.

25 17 Aug. 1867, p. 245. The link with Exeter Hall is established at the beginning of the incident: see 20 Jan. 1866, p. 184.

26 9 May 1868, p. 92.

27 For *Punch* see, for example, 16 May 1868, p. 212, 15 July 1868, p. 117, in the latter of which it is proposed that Eyre, like Napier, should be granted a peerage. For *Tomahawk*, see 16 June 1868, pp. 225–6.

28 6 and 13 May 1868, p. 6 in both issues. These are prepared for by a notice in the issue of 29 April 1868, p. 6.

29 10 June 1868, p. [3].

30 10 June 1868, p. 6.

31 17 Nov. 1866, p. 202.

confer its thanks upon General Sir Robert Napier and the army, and will appoint a Select Committee to inquire into the whole of the transactions relating to Abyssinia."[32] Mill most certainly had no close connection with the Macclesfield committee, and its petition was signed by only two persons. Knowing that some Westminster Liberals had been alienated by Mill's leadership of the Jamaica Committee and by this further indiscretion, William Sims Pratten, who had been a member of Mill's committee in 1865 and acted as chairman of one of his local committees in 1868, wrote to ask for explanations that could be used with the voters. Mill's reply of 9 June was, as Pratten had expected, mainly on the Governor Eyre matter, but also mentioned the Abyssinian affair. He explained that he did not agree with the petition, but had presented it because he believed that the power of petitioning was important to certain groups and that the opportunity of petitioning was too limited.[33] And, as noted above, this same question was asked in the second election meeting later that month—perhaps asked by a supporter just to get the response once again on the record. This minor incident is significant in that it again demonstrates Mill's adherence to a stated principle: while he usually agreed with the petitions he presented, his presenting them in no way signalled his agreement with the plea. It can hardly be doubted, however, that this distinction was too fine for some constituents, especially in the light of the general practice in the House.

Another major contribution to Mill's notoriety came to public attention in the second week of September when, under the heading "Election Intelligence. Westminster," this paragraph appeared in *The Times*:

> The supporters of Mr. John Stuart Mill are greatly concerned by the publication of a letter, signed with their representative's name, stating that it is his intention to give the sum of £10 towards any fund which may be raised to defray the election expenses of Mr. Bradlaugh. By some it is thought that the letter is a hoax, as the views of the person whom it supports on religious matters are such that he felt compelled to offer his resignation to the Reform League, but the Conservatives in Westminster hold that the letter is genuine, and they are doing their best to bring it before the general body of the constituents, believing that its contents will injure the Liberal cause all over the kingdom. The letter is addressed to Mr. G.J. Holyoake.[34]

32 *PPS*, *CW*, vol. XXIX, p. 592.

33 Mill's letter (*LL*, *CW*, vol. XVI, pp. 1410–12) was published by Pratten along with his on 15 June in *The Times*, p. 4.

34 *The Times*, 12 Sept. 1868, p. 6.

Mill had indeed written the letter (though to Austin Holyoake, the younger brother of G.J.), and was plagued with the implications of his support for Bradlaugh throughout the campaign. His defence, which he had often to present, took the form of asserting that his subscription was offered because Bradlaugh was one of the few representatives of the working classes being given a chance for election, and that Mill was supporting him, as he supported all such representatives, solely on the basis of their political opinions and their working-class affiliations; the religious opinions of Bradlaugh, he averred, were as irrelevant to him as they must have been to the workingmen (all of whom could not be atheists) who had chosen him as a candidate in Northampton, or to those (again, not all to be thought of as atheistical) who elected him to the executive of the Reform League. He also referred specifically to two of Bradlaugh's expressed tenets, support for women's suffrage and proportional representation, either of which might, it may be thought, have been sufficient to engage Mill's support, but he obviously preferred to put the more general case. What he did not refer to in public, however, was Bradlaugh's Neo-Malthusianism: it is hard to believe that the active Conservative canvassers failed to play that card in every promising deal.

The issue continued to surface throughout the campaign, with an exchange of letters between Frederick Bates and Mill appearing as late as 11 November.[35] Bates, a canvasser for Mill in St. Anne's Ward, was concerned that some voters were alienated by Mill's presumed atheism. Mill's letter refused comment, as always, on his religious beliefs, but made a strong attack on the Tories, who had raised the issue on other inadequate grounds in the previous election, and went on to say again that Bradlaugh had been supported by others who could not all be supposed to be atheists.

That Mill was here wildly impolitic is all too evident—and he was severely taken to task for pusillanimity by his principal adviser and confidante, Helen Taylor.[36] Whatever one may think of his frankness or honesty, it would appear *prima facie* that his folly lay only in supporting someone as odious in the public mind as Bradlaugh, and that there could be no strong objection simply to his having offered support to a candidate. But the fact is more complicated.

Mill had long believed that his old and dear associate Edwin Chadwick deserved a seat in parliament, and he initiated efforts on his behalf early in 1868. Through solicitations addressed to his friend Professor John

35 See *LL*, *CW*, vol. XVI, pp. 1483–4.
36 See *PPS*, *CW*, vol. XXVIII, p. lv.

Nichol of Glasgow, he had determined that an opportunity presented itself in Kilmarnock for an advanced Liberal such as Chadwick, and he wrote a strong recommendation that was used to open the campaign. However, the sitting Liberal member, E.P. Bouverie,[37] took great and perhaps not unreasonable exception to the entry of another Liberal in the race at Kilmarnock, with the effect of endangering the Liberal cause there. Also, Bouverie, like many another, had no desire for an expensive contested election; he had been elected six times for Kilmarnock, four times by acclamation.

Bouverie accordingly wrote on 25 September to Mill objecting to his endorsement of Chadwick, on the grounds that the result would be a division within a previously united Liberal constituency that had returned him for nearly a quarter of a century. Admitting to some differences of opinion between himself and Mill, he mentioned that he had given his "hearty adhesion" to Mill's candidature in Westminster, and asserted his own creed—"Toleration for minor differences, union for common public objects"—as essential to party success. Mill responded on 4 October in a typically unrepentant tone, hinting, in his praise for Chadwick's "exceptional" qualities, at Bouverie's shortcomings. Without special emphasis on the matter, he indicated that "it would be an honour to any other man to give way" to Chadwick.

Bouverie responded with another letter of 13 October, which he sent, with the previous exchange, to *The Times*, where it was published on 16 October. In his second letter, Bouverie took new ground, asserting that Mill was insisting on making the issue a personal one between Chadwick and himself, a matter that the electors should decide. Mill was attempting to act for them in advance, by assuming that it "devolve[d] upon [him] to indicate to each constituency who is 'the very best man each party possesses'" (Mill's words in his letter of 4 October). Bouverie declined the advice to "give way" to Chadwick, pointing out that Chadwick, much better known in London than in Kilmarnock, had nonetheless been unable to find a constituency in the Metropolis (including, of course, Westminster).

In a leading article accompanying the correspondence, *The Times* weighed in heavily on Bouverie's side, denigrating Chadwick as "an elderly public servant, not at all in the political line." It also attacked Mill for intervening in the contest, citing his support for George

37 He, it will be recalled, was an early and active supporter of Grosvenor in the 1865 campaign, and chaired one of the meetings at which Mill supporters challenged the Liberal credentials of Grosvenor.

Odger in Chelsea, and for Bradlaugh in Northampton—or indeed anywhere.[38]

Chadwick gave further publicity to the exchange by quoting Mill's letter in speaking to the electors of Kilmarnock, at the same time seizing the opportunity to reply to the editorial animadversions on himself in *The Times*.[39] But *The Times*, while reporting Chadwick's speech, unleashed a strong and heavily ironic editorial attack on both Chadwick and Mill. Although the criticism of Mill was generalized, the burden of the complaint was against the practice, admittedly not invented by Mill but now condemned "by men of all parties alike," of giving public character references to those who sought parliamentary seats. It was too bad, the leader said (happily passing by Mill's endorsement of Gladstone and vice versa), that Mill had wasted his support on such as Bradlaugh and Odger, when he could have sought out other paragons of virtue such as Chadwick, whose "sanitary" knowledge was such an outstanding qualification. Mill was attacked also for criticizing Bouverie as an "independent," when he himself was surely acting in this affair as an independent rather than a faithful Liberal.[40]

Mill was quite unrepentant. He had already been explicit in a letter to Chadwick about the line that should be taken against Bouverie: he had been associated with the defection from Gladstone by Whig Liberals, referring in the House to Gladstone as a leader who could not lead and the Liberals as a party who could not follow. Without having seen the leader in *The Times*, but undoubtedly knowing that Chadwick would use his letter, Mill wrote to Bouverie on 19 October, sending the letter to the press and justifying his writing publicly by pointing out that Bouverie had printed the earlier correspondence without his prior knowledge.[41] (Bouverie later objected to Mill's lack of courtesy, without exculpating his own.) Mill's letter asserted that the Reform Bill had made a great

38 Later Mill was to assert privately that only his contribution to Odger, of all his subscriptions to working-class representatives, had been unsolicited—probably he exempted unconsciously Chadwick, of whom he would think not merely, or perhaps most significantly, as a working-class representative, even though it would appear that Chadwick's unsuccessful campaign in Kilmarnock was aimed primarily at and responded to by the newly enfranchised less wealthy.

39 *The Times*, 21 Oct. 1868, p. 7.

40 Ibid., p. 9.

41 As Mill acknowledged in his *Autobiography*, during these years much of what purported to be his correspondence was actually composed by Helen Taylor—and some of hers was his, and much was mutual. Without essaying the low trick of assigning to her all that was unwise, we think it likely that she collaborated in what was written in Avignon during these months. Compare pp. 121–2 above.

difference in the electorate, and the Kilmarnock voters, like those elsewhere, might feel that, loyal as they had been, it was time for a change from an "old" to a "new" man (the terms, of course, do not refer to age—for Chadwick was not young—but to attitudes towards reform). Here Mill did not laud by name any other "new men,"[42] but his goal of introducing more Radicals to the party was clearly evident. Consonant with it was his focus on the danger in the new parliament of unfaithful quasi-Liberals standing in the way of Gladstone. Not he, but Bouverie and the Adullamites threatened the unity of the Liberal party. Here Mill was recognizing one of the major issues in the campaign—support for Gladstone—on which grounds Bouverie was dispensable.

On the same day that it published this letter of Mill's, *The Times* again referred to the matter in a lead-in to an editorial attack on Lord Westbury for publishing private correspondence, incidentally warning Mill against his injudicious revelation of his warm admiration for Chadwick by comparing him to a lover whose epistolary effusions, become public, were "read aloud by a middle-aged barrister for the benefit of a British jury."[43] Bouverie had the last epistolary word in an allusive and ironic letter to the editor two days later, on 24 October, and a supporting letter signed "C" also attacked Mill on that day.[44]

There can be no doubt that this exchange, though it received less public attention in the final weeks of the campaign, had done Mill damage in centre-right Liberal circles. Whatever their disaffection from Gladstone and some of his supporters, this group had a firm realization of electoral realities and saw all splitting of Liberal ranks at this juncture as bad, especially when the splitters were Radicals who had declared affinities with working-class political demands. That is, the negligible Chadwick aside, if it came to a test between Bouverie and Mill, the former was more to be trusted. Even the views of the still untested Smith, who had earlier declared his sympathies with Palmerston and who described himself as a "Liberal-Conservative," might when put to the test not be very far from those of the Whigs. In any case *Judy*, on behalf of the Conservatives, was delighted that the Liberals should so go at one another,[45] and the issue of Mill's support for radical candidates proved much more interesting to the public as a result of this exchange. In the event, Bouverie retained the Kilmarnock seat easily, and Chadwick,

42 *The Times*, 22 Oct. 1868, p. 3.
43 Ibid., p. 7.
44 Ibid., 24 Oct. 1868, p. 3.
45 For her response after the correspondence between Mill and Bouverie was published, see 21 Oct. 1868, p. 251.

though he received not inconsiderable support, was not a serious threat.

By this time, then, there was a general impression that Mill was scattering his opinions about candidates more widely than was compatible with decorum, sense, and party and social stability. *Judy* seized on the issue with joy, identifying Mill as "A Friend in Need" to candidates, and extending his enthusiasm into fantasy by printing his supposed letters in support of James Finlen, a notorious Reform League lecturer with Fenian connections whose neglect of his children made him newsworthy;[46] of G.W.M. Reynolds, the wildly successful pulp novelist and radical editor of *Reynolds' Newspaper*, whom Mill is made to praise as one who offers "the well of English pure and undefiled"; and of George Odger, on the ground that he "was with the mighty Beales when, at one and the same time, the usurped rights of purse-proud aristocrats and the Hyde Park railings were trampled under foot."[47]

Perhaps because of its special interest in Brighton, where Mill's support for Fawcett might be crucial, *Will-o'-the-Wisp* took keen delight in Mill's sponsorships,[48] calling him "Examiner-General and Issuer of Certificates to Liberal candidates."[49] For instance, it copied Mill's letter of 28 August, to Austin Holyoake, which announced his subscription to Bradlaugh, commenting that it expects to announce in its next issue that Gladstone has supported "his friend Mr. Finlen." "In the meantime we recommend the consideration of the above letter to those ladies and gentlemen who are touting for subscriptions to return the 'Prosecuting Philosopher' for Westminster. We believe, as doubtless they will also, that 'Charity begins at home.'"[50] Again in a double-inkpot barrage,

46 For Finlen, see *The Times*, 26 May 1868, p. 11; 24 and 25 July 1868, p. 11 in each; and 21 Aug., 1868, p. 9.

47 *Judy*, 28 Oct. 1868, p. 10. Compare *Tomahawk*, 7 and 21 Nov. 1868, pp. 198 and 221.

48 In one of its few cartoons showing Mill, with an accompanying text, headed "The Professors," "Professor Benjamin" outdraws (and puts down) "Professor Paucit" at the country fair. In the background of the cartoon is "The Ladies Roundabout" with a flying banner, "J.S. Mill." The text says: "Another Professor, named Mill, used occasionally to pay Paucit a visit, for they were remarkably attached to each other. He always brought with him his 'Ladies Roundabout,' because, having proved a miserable failure on the London boards, he knew in his own heart he must prove the same everywhere, and so he took to this 'Ladies Roundabout' in the hope of keeping up his popularity in the provinces." *Will-o'-the-Wisp*, 12 Sept. 1868, p. 4.

49 Ibid., 7 Nov. 1868, p. 96.

50 Ibid., 12 Sept. 1868, p. 2; Mill's subscription to Bradlaugh is mentioned again in passing on 26 Dec. 1868, p. 178.

Will-o'-the-Wisp presents a long "advertisement," mentioning specifically Mill's support for Bradlaugh and Chadwick (and Finlen), and saying: "Mr. Mill has recently returned from Avignon, accompanied by half-a-dozen Jamaican negroes, who distinguished themselves during the late insurrection there, and whom he intends to start for the Universities of Oxford, Cambridge, and Dublin."[51]

Meanwhile, the candidates' committees were working away in the constituency, especially attending to voter registration. Those newly enfranchised had claims presented, with apparently more success, as might be expected, on the Liberal side. (That is, however the votes of the newly qualified might eventually be cast, there was on one side an expectation, on the other a fear, that most of the less wealthy would favour the Liberals.) *The Times* reported the state of play on 29 August, saying that the Westminster Liberals had as many as 4000 lodger claims, the Conservatives scarcely one-quarter as many. It appeared that a large proportion of the artisan lodgers supported Mill, and the main question in the mind of the reporter on that occasion was whether "the cordial union now existing between the two sections of the party continues, as there is every reason to suppose it will, and stand the test of the polling-day," in which case Grosvenor would benefit from Mill's popularity with those lodgers. Also, the number of householders on the list had grown by 3500, "and a very large gain both from lodgers and householders is, therefore, confidently expected by the Liberals."[52] But when the time came for the Revising Barristers to address for the first time the problem of judging the validity of claims to the suffrage under the new act, some unexpected claims appeared. On the day when the first reports of the revision courts appeared, *The Times* felt compelled to comment in a leader on the folly and unseemliness of the attempt by Lydia Becker to get 5750 women's names on the electoral role in Manchester. There had also been similar attempts in Westminster and Lambeth and, as appeared the next

51 Ibid., 14 Nov. 1868, p. 107. Compare another "Advertisement" of 21 Nov. 1868, p. 126: "The undersigned begs philosophically to inform his numerous admirers that he is now prepared, being at present out of an engagement, to undertake the business of returning members to Parliament, at the shortest possible notice and regardless of sex, colour, age, or condition. / John Stuart Mill, / Agent. / (N.B. References kindly permitted to Mr. W.E. Gladstone, 11 Carlton House Terrace, S.W., whose return for Greenwich, in case of a slip in South Lancashire, has been confided to J.S.M.)." For similar material, see ibid., 7 November 1868, p. 103, concerning Odger, and 21 November 1868, p. 119, and 19 December 1868, p. 174, concerning Bradlaugh (the latter also side-swiping Dean Stanley for his support of Mill).

52 *The Times*, 29 Aug., 1868, p. 10.

day, in North Staffordshire, as well as in other places not then specified. *The Times* almost as a matter of course referred to Mill's defeated amendment on women's suffrage, which would of course have made these applicants eligible: the reference, while almost perfunctory, may be seen in context as certainly unkind.[53]

The revising barrister in Westminster, Nassau John Senior, was meanwhile making heavy weather of the job. On the first day, having disposed of the claim of Harriet Bainbridge on the ground of her sex, he continued through the first of the electoral districts, St. Anne's, beginning with the lodger list. The Conservative representatives mounted a consistent and time-consuming challenge on two grounds—first, that persons were not sufficiently known to be what and who they claimed to be on the basis of a declaration, and, second, that they did not pay sufficient rents to be equivalent to £10 householders. Eventually both issues were settled more or less to the Liberals' satisfaction,[54] after ruling and counter-ruling, more evidence and argument, and consultation with other revising barristers, each of whom was also having considerable difficulty in interpreting legislation that was less than clear in its wording. But the battle dragged on day after day, as the proceedings moved from ward to ward, from lodger to householder—with occasionally a woman's claim to complicate, though briefly, the deliberations.

On 17 September, for instance, Lisette Macdougall Gregory claimed the franchise as a householder; the revising barrister, Senior, said she must be struck out, being a woman; whereupon the Liberals' solicitor said Senior "had no right to assume that the claimant was a woman; but the claim," continues the account disappointingly, "was disallowed"—as was that of Lady Cicely Georgiana Fane. A slightly different ploy was attempted, equally unsuccessfully, when, upon Senior's ruling against the claim of Anne Arthur, it was asserted that he could not do so, because no one had objected to her inclusion.[55] Mill was not alluded to in the published accounts of these disputes, but since Westminster was his constituency and the cause was especially his, he was no doubt in everyone's mind each time a claim was made.

Meanwhile the Conservative lists were not going without challenge, although only two Westminster cases are reported in *The Times*. In both of these instances the problem arose over the listing of sons as lodgers in

53 Ibid., 16 Sept., p. 9, 17 Sept., p. 10.

54 Declarations in proper form were accepted, and 4*s*. per week was held to be the equivalent of £10 per year, allowing for a small deduction from the 4*s*. for the landlord's rates.

55 *The Times*, 18 Sept., p. 4, and 24 Sept., p. 5.

their father's houses, the claim being based, in the one case, on the son's paying his father £30 per year for a room; in the other, on the father's reducing the allowance he gave his son for contributing to the family business by 8*s*. per week for room rental. Both were finally ruled eligible.

September, like August, was a quiet month electorally, with no advertisements in the press, except with reference to the revising process and the beginnings of the canvass. In that cause the Westminster Liberals issued two forms to elicit information and initiate further recruitment, both headed "Westminster Election. Grosvenor and Mill Committee." One of these, over the names of the honorary secretaries of the committee, H.H. Seymour, J.W. Probyn, and W.T. Malleson, said:

> We are requested by the above Committee to ask your attention to the accompanying List of Committee, Public Addresses of the *Liberal* Candidates, and Letter from Mr. Gladstone.
>
> We beg at the same time to ask your votes and interest in favour of the Hon. R.W. Grosvenor and J.S. Mill, Esq., the sitting members.
>
> Your reply upon the annexed form will greatly oblige.

The annexed form, above the three candidates' names, read: "I intend voting for the undermentioned at the approaching election," with a postscript, "Please to run your pen through any name to which you object."

During the later days of September, only one new action by Mill was given publicity, one that, from the point of view of his Liberal supporters, presumably was impeccable: he wrote to the Liberals of Greenwich who, fearing that Gladstone might lose his contest in Lancashire, had nominated him for their constituency. His letter of support was read out at a local meeting and then published in the press.[56] This endorsement was unchallenged by the Conservatives, presumably because to object to it would itself be ludicrous.

In October the campaign began to heat up. One of the most interesting and perhaps the most curious document is a cartoon with accompanying text that appeared in *Will-o'-the Wisp* on 3 October, a forecast in the past tense of the election result. The election is portrayed as a steeplechase, in which *True Blue* is pitted against *The Philosopher* and *Cash-box*. As the race is about to begin, the "line" is given thus:

> The Westminster Cup, value £4,000, by subscription of £1,000 each. Weight for age, with penalties and allowances. The owner of the second horse to save his stake. The Election course. Gentlemen riders.

56 See *Daily News*, 17 Sept., p. 3; *The Times*, 22 Sept., p. 7.

Mr. W.H. Smith's *True Blue*, by Union Jack—
Mother's England, 3 yrs 1
Captain Grosvenor's *Cash-box*, by Ebury—
Grandmother's Money, 3 yrs 2
Mr. J.S. Mill's *The Philosopher*, by Tommy Dodd—
Mrs. Partingtom [sic], aged .... dist.

Betting: 100 to 1 on *The Philosopher*, 20 to 1 against *Cash-box*, and 50 to 1 against *True Blue*.[57] The outcome, "Will" and his sporting correspondent "Rat" being true-blue supporters, is never in question, and *The Philosopher* exhibits nothing but senile ineptitude.

Some other evidence of the accelerating campaigns is less spectacular. An elector, John Lancaster, having received the list of Smith's committee through the post before the end of September, had found his own name mistakenly on it, and had complained to John F. Isaacson, one of Smith's agents. Isaacson's reply, a not very humble apology asking for pardon on the grounds of the large number of names on the list (about 600), appeared in *The Times* on 15 October, after Lancaster's complaint had been published on the 13th. This minor skirmish probably scored no points for either side, but from this point on, with one exception, the reporting on the campaign, especially in *The Times*, was demonstrably blue for Smith rather than red for Mill, with the buff of Grosvenor fading into the background.

The Conservative strength was being gathered in quite a new way. Smith had been busy in local affairs during the parliament of 1865–8, becoming steadily better known as a concerned and effective citizen and as a generous philanthropist.[58] There could have been little doubt that he would emerge as the Conservative candidate at the next election, and little surprise when, in autumn 1867, he accepted an invitation with 3000 signatures, presented by a deputation headed by the Earl of Dalkeith on behalf of the Conservative party in the borough.[59] Knowing that Mill had offended and disturbed many people, Smith and his friends worked hard during the winter of 1867–8 and intensified their efforts in the succeeding

57 For the full text, see appendix A, which also gives the post-election celebration of the accuracy of the forecast.

58 Herbert Maxwell remarks that Smith's "reputation as a good, paternalistic employer probably stood him in good stead with the newly enfranchised artisans, in whose political sagacity Disraeli claimed to place so much confidence—not without justification, as events were ultimately to prove." *Life and Times of the Rt. Hon. W.H. Smith, M.P.*, 2 vols. (Edinburgh and London: Blackwood, 1893), vol. I, p. 56.

59 Ibid., p. 137.

THE WESTMINSTER STEEPLE-CHASE.

"*Cash-Box*," Jockey, CAPT. G———R. "*Philosopher*," Jockey, Mr. J. S. M—LL. "*True-Blue*," Jockey, MR. W. H. S—H.

[*See* SKETCH.

summer. Among those friends the most effective and strenuous was the Honourable Robert Grimston, third son of the first Earl of Verulam, described by Smith's biographer as a "remarkable character" and "a popular sportsman and barrister (in that order) with immense drive and panache." Grimston, a close friend of Smith's, was his neighbour in Hertfordshire, a co-director with him of the Electric and International Telegraph Co., and generally a close personal friend. Maxwell comments: "Grimston had supported Smith in his earlier attempt, but had not had time sufficiently to organize the effort. This time he flung himself unreservedly—and entirely voluntarily—into the fray, becoming chairman of the key Ward of St. George's Hanover Square [the "In Ward"], where he was of great value in bringing over the more aristocratic elements, who might otherwise have stood aloof from the 'newsagent.' "[60]

Grimston's personality and behaviour are worth description because they indicate, in their enormous diversity from those of Mill and his supporters, the difference between practical and successful electioneering and ideal moralistic and (in the strict sense) reckless appeals. Grimston (1816–84), who gave up his practice as a barrister when he became a director of the telegraph company, was celebrated as a sportsman, famed for feats as cricketer, huntsman, and boxer.[61] Every "man who was not opposed to him, and was in any way connected with manly sports, would work for him for the love of 'Bob Grimston.' "[62] Disliking expediency, and professing principle, Grimston averred: "I look to what a man is, not what he thinks," and sought in a man what was "straight and honest."[63] He volunteered to help Smith in 1868 because, "independently of his own political bias, some of the late Mr. John Stuart Mill's announced principles were to his mind un-English." In particular, he was offended by Mill's views on "religious and social matters," that is, his scepticism and Malthusianism.[64] Not his views, however congenial to some of the

60 Ibid., pp. 56–7.

61 The principal source of information about Grimston, a typical Harrovian and younger son who left no diary, letters, or documents of any kind, is Frederick Gale, *The Life of the Hon. Robert Grimston* (London: Longmans, Green, 1885); the material relevant to our argument is mainly in chapter 12: "As a Man of Business. The Westminster Election [of 1868]" (pp. 198–220).

62 Ibid., p. 201. Unquestionably that well-known sportsman, the Hon. Bob Grimston, thought the "Westminster Steeplechase" in *Will-o'the-Wisp* one of the best jokes of the time, and may well have been its prompter.

63 Gale, *Grimston*, p. 198. "Mine," he said, "are family politics."

64 Ibid., pp. 199–200. It seems likely that "social" here includes not just Mill's advocacy of birth control, but also his opposition to the Contagious Diseases Acts. Local opinion was undoubtedly divided in Westminster, but probably its main weight was behind the view expressed in a petition to the Commons, presented

electors, but his social standing and character made him valuable to Smith. Grimston "was known and trusted by all people of his own *status* in society who were of the same politics, and who would strain a point to serve him; and his bluff, free manner, and comical way of putting things in a few words, were sure to make an impression on those whom he met for the first time. As sure as he got a voter by persuasion or conviction he would make him work on his side, and tell him of some one or another whom he must get hold of."[65]

His biographer, Frederick Gale—who seems to have been enlisted by Grimston in Smith's campaign—testifies to his zeal, shown in his being last in the committee room at night and first in the morning going the rounds. He was especially keen "in 'fly posting,' *i.e.* seeing that his candidate's bills were posted over those of the other side on neutral premises. This is," Gale adds, "perfectly fair in electioneering." Taking an "active part in an election meant endless work night and day, attending meetings, committees, interviewing deputations, knowing all the time that the enemy had spies in every hole and corner. In a metropolitan contest, quarter is never asked or given—it is war to the knife." Paid agents—some of them not particularly savoury—were hired in the different wards for canvassing and other activities such as "fly posting," money not being, as Gale notes, "the slightest object, as it was admitted, on the inquiry into the Election Petition, that Mr. Smith had paid a large sum, and in those days, and in fact in all days, a Westminster election meant a hard, stubborn fight," particularly because in that quarter of London it was uphill work battling against the Grosvenor interest. Although Smith's troops were not actively opposing Grosvenor,[66] Mill, "as a '*Sequitur*,' acquired a great deal

---

(we infer sympathetically) by Mill's colleague Robert Grosvenor on 15 May 1866, from the Vestry of St. James's for extension to the Metropolis of the Contagious Diseases Act then before the House. The petition asserted that the 1864 act was working well, and argued that "labourers of every class are as fully and equally entitled to the like protection as is awarded to soldiers and sailors in the garrison towns," while "continued strolling of foreign and other prostitutes in the principal streets of the Metropolis is found to be an intolerable nuisance." It concluded, "it is an error to permit an open and shameless solicitation, alluring the young and unwary, and thus spreading over the land a fearful and loathsome disease, the deleterious effects of which have hurried many to a premature grave. . . ." *Reports of the Select Committee of the House of Commons on Public Petitions*, 1866, App. 640, p. 258.

65 Gale, *Grimston*, p. 201.

66 In repudiating the "current story" that Grimston had "the base of the Duke of York's column placarded," Gale goes on to mention that "some one stuck 'Smith for Westminster' on the Marquis of Westminster's Mansion." But this would have been "a bad joke" on the part of Grimston (who denied doing so), because his

of the influence of the family in fighting under the same banner."[67] Grimston attended assiduously at meetings where Smith spoke, always eager to second motions and to speak *ad hoc.* Gale notes that "loud cries of 'Go it, Bob Grimston!' were perpetually heard." Perhaps the sharpest image comes from an anecdote about an occasion when Grimston threatened "one of the regular London bullies who go to all meetings to make a disturbance, and who care nothing for either side"; when Grimston "gave his name" to the rough, "the excitable Briton used the better part of valour—discretion—and walked out."[68] In fact, for his friends the best joke of the election was his being mistaken by roughs on

---

family and Grosvenor's are "neighbours and great supporters of cricket in their county" (p. 208).

67 Ibid., pp. 202–3. In the light of the inquiry into bribery and corruption at the election, Gale's observations on Grimston's tactics deserve mention: "It being very difficult to find spaces for placarding at the West End, Mr. Grimston, to obviate this difficulty, invented a scheme of his own, and inaugurated a flying brigade who were engaged in finding shops, the owners of which would allow boards similar to the theatrical boards, with Mr. Smith's address to the constituents and other printed matter relating to the election, to be put outside at a shilling a board a day." This scheme cost £209, but to avoid the implication of bribery, Grimston "instructed those who had care of the advertising boards on no consideration to canvass those who exhibited them, or to ask what their politics were." In such circumstances, Gale observes, £200 was "a mere flea-bite" though their opponents made much of it (p. 204).

Concerning the imputations of bribery, Smith and Grimston had what Gale describes as "a narrow escape" from "a trap" laid "by the enemy." "An invitation was sent to Mr. Smith to address some of the Conservative Working Men's Association at a tavern at the West End, it matters not where (as it is no use reproducing all the details of an election petition which has long since been dead and buried). They arrived in due course, and found quite a different gathering present from the audience they had expected, and quite a different kind of place from that which a candidate would have chosen.

"When there Mr. Smith was obliged to speak, as he could not tell them that they were not worth talking to; and a lot of champagne was uncorked and handed round, and a glass was put into Mr. Smith's hands, and he put it to his lips and went on for a short time, and retired much disgusted with the place and the company" (pp. 205–6). The "plot" was "got up by a renegade spy, who tried to trick Mr. Grimston afterwards into sending ten pounds to the landlord," but Grimston was onto him, and denounced the whole operation; the landlord testified at the inquiry that "he never asked for or expected to be paid a farthing by Mr. Smith or his party. No doubt it was a public-house draw for custom, and an advertisement . . . for filling his house during the election." Had Grimston paid the £10, in Gale's opinion the election would have been lost (pp. 206–7).

68 Ibid., pp. 204–5.

the hustings, because he seemed to be a "deep-thinking man of business," for the dean of Westminster.[69] Mill's troops, worthy bourgeois and artisans all, had no such champion in their lists.

By the third week in October, advertisements concerning the now imminent election again began to appear. Mill's strong supporter, James Beal, surfaced in one of them in a different role, as honorary secretary to the Metropolitan Municipal Association, inviting the electors of the Metropolis generally to demand pledges to attempt to secure an improved government of the Metropolis.[70] In making this one of his special causes, Mill, unusually for him, became the organ—willingly enough, of course—of a well-organized extraparliamentary group. Although, in Mill's view, this was not an issue of great interest to the parties, it was not without its heat. While his behaviour strengthened his attraction to some of his supporters, it might also have alienated special interests who thought of themselves as regular Liberals, and it certainly was not sufficient to win over Conservatives who took exception to other of his views.

Among the advertisements were those of another candidate for Westminster, B.V. Hutchinson, whose campaign attracted no press attention at all; he does not quite disappear from the story, however, as we shall see.

The first meeting advertised in the fall campaign was that of Smith, in St. James's Hall, on 22 October. The advance notice of this meeting given by *The Times*, though brief, shows the same spirit as its leaders on the Bouverie-Chadwick issue during that week:

> The first meeting on behalf of the Conservative candidate for the representation of the city of Westminster will be held to-morrow, and it is evident that much interest will attach to this election. The feeling against Mr. J.S. Mill is exceedingly strong, even among those who were his former supporters, the countenance he has given to "Iconoclast" [Bradlaugh] having given great offence to the middle classes.[71]

Smith's meeting was a success, though seemingly not an overwhelming one. Presented as the "Constitutional" candidate, he made perfunctory reference to the effect of the Second Reform Act, spoke against Irish Church Disestablishment and in favour of denominational educa-

69 Ibid., pp. 208-9.

70 See, for example, *The Times*, 19, 21, 24, and 28 Oct. 1868, pp. 6, 8, 6, and 8, respectively.

71 "Election Intelligence," ibid., 21 Oct. 1868, p. 7.

tion—these were the mainstays of all his speeches throughout the campaign—and asserted that there were no real differences between the interests of capital and labour. Questioned about a local issue, the compensation of tenants required to move because of development, he made no pledge, but said he had worked for the compensation of those displaced by the construction of the Law Courts. The resolution in favour of Smith was moved by the Hon. Robert Grimston, who is reported to have said that "Mr. Mill had lost the favour of many of his former supporters by his vindictive persecution of Mr. Eyre, his attack on Lord Napier of Magdala, and his patronage of Mr. Bradlaugh."[72]

Liberal meetings had not yet begun (Mill, it will be remembered, was still in Avignon), but the Tories held two more, of markedly different character, in the following week. In the meeting on 26 October, to which admission was by ticket only, the general character of the first meeting was repeated, with more attention being given, either directly or by implication, to attacks on Mill than to the virtues of Smith's position. Smith spoke again against Irish Church Disestablishment, and then said, with respect to the "general position of public affairs, . . . he thought that we had gone far enough in the way of headlong progress; and he hoped the electors of Westminster would no longer advocate the policy of those who desired rapid and violent changes." In foreign affairs, he asserted, he was not an interventionist, but nonetheless the British position must be asserted. Then he touched on a more important issue for the local electorate, and though his remarks, at least as reported, are as anodyne as those on intervention, he does appear in the camp opposite to that of Mill: he objected to the removal of local government—that of the vestries—though he conceded that some improvement was needed. He closed with another statement in favour of denominational schools, and then, during the *pro forma* presentation of motions, Mr. Anderson Rose "adverted at some length to the attitude which Mr. Mill had occupied during the several trials of ex-Governor Eyre, and expressed his ardent desire that Mr. Smith's name should stand at the head of the poll at the ensuing election."[73] Once again there was no mention of Grosvenor, nor indeed any direct attack on the Liberals: the attempt was certainly then, and throughout the election, to pick off Mill.

The next Conservative meeting on the following day, 27 October, was described as "public," in that people without tickets obtained from the Conservative committee were able to obtain admission, though not on

72 Ibid., 23 Oct. 1868, p. 6.
73 Ibid., 27 Oct. p. 6.

equal terms with those having tickets. Not until the hall was nearly full with Smith's supporters were others admitted; two-thirds of the space, at the front, was reserved for the faithful; the remaining area, cut off from the front by "a very strong barrier" of unspecified nature, was crowded before the meeting began with persons whose adherence to Mill was soon evident. And, *The Times*'s account avers, the only agreement in the hall was that nobody should be heard. The chair was taken by George Cubitt, MP, but to no effect; he might as well, says the report in a gratuitous and sly reference to one of Mill's supposed peccadilloes, "have taken it at Magdala." The Conservatives, continues the report—and this is the only time in these last weeks of the campaign when *The Times* gave an account at all critical of the supporters of Smith—"eliminated from the meeting the most prominent of their Liberal antagonists, and this was sometimes done with an amount of violence and ill-usage which, to say the least, seemed unnecessary." Even then, however, nothing could be heard, and the meeting was more or less abandoned at 10 p.m.[74]

On 30 October the Liberals finally announced their plans for meetings: on 2 November for electors of St. John's, on the 4th for those of St. Anne's, and on the 6th for those of St. George's Out-ward and Knightsbridge. And early in the next week the regular Liberal advertisement giving the location of the daily sitting of the Grosvenor-Mill committee—Smith had been listing the fourteen locations of his local committees throughout Westminster from 21 October—was joined by others. The first advertisement was of an unusual sort: "The Grosvenor and Mill Committee earnestly request their supporters *not* to *disturb* any of the *meetings* held by Mr. W.H. Smith."[75] To the notice of the daily sittings was added a request: "Volunteer canvassers wanted, and the loan of conveyances for the polling day." Further subscriptions were again requested for Mill's election fund (payable to W.T. Malleson)—here there was no mention of Grosvenor. And, finally, the dates for the three meetings were again listed.

Mill had been recalled by his committee and, though still in Avignon on 30 October, arrived in London in time to speak at the meeting of 2 November. The tone and content of his speeches in these final days of the election indicate that he had become aware of the seriousness of his predicament. His supporters, one may infer, believing that he had put himself in a dangerously exposed position and that he must try to undo some of the damage, must have counselled moderation, restraint, and

74 Ibid., 28 Oct. p. 10.
75 Ibid., 2 Nov. 1868, p. 8.

discretion. In particular, they must have encouraged Mill in his own predilection for Gladstone, who keeps recurring in Mill's speeches as the essential totem-carrying Liberal. Such lauding of the leader was the staple of Liberal candidates' speeches, as Walter Bagehot observes:

> Mr. Gladstone's personal popularity was such as has not been seen since the time of Mr. Pitt, and such as may never be seen again. . . . A bad speaker is said to have been asked how he got on as a candidate. "Oh," he answered, "when I do not know what to say, I say 'Gladstone,' and then they are sure to cheer, and I have time to think."[76]

That remark can hardly be attributed to Mill, but it is uncomfortably close to what he is reported to have said, for instance on 2 November:

> I do not believe that any one here will contradict me when I say that the one statesman in this country who, perhaps, more than any other within living memory has the confidence of the people, is Mr. Gladstone—(*loud cheers*)—who has the confidence of the mass of the people.[77]

Some indication of the problems Mill faced is found in *The Times*'s reporting of his campaign. The meeting on 2 November was given a slight notice in *The Times*, but it passed by in silence those of 4, 6, 9, and 11 November. Mill's usual supporters, the *Daily Telegraph*, the *Daily News*, and the *Morning Star*, paid heed, though not uniformly, with the former two showing signs of partial disaffection. Writing to Chadwick on 7 November, after the third of his meetings, Mill complained somewhat petulantly: "the papers have given only the most trumpery reports of any of my speeches except the first, which was comparatively commonplace."[78]

That first meeting, on 2 November in the Regent Music Hall, was densely crowded, many women being present; undoubtedly Mill's reappearance was a good draw, and the committee must have been anxious that a strong impression be made on the electorate. In the chair was Dr. Lankester, who reminded the audience that he had chaired the

76 Introduction to the second edition of *The English Constitution*, in *Collected Works of Walter Bagehot*, ed. Norman St. John Stevas (London: The Economist, 1968), vol. V, p. 171.

77 2 Nov. 1868, in *PPS*, *CW*, vol. XXVIII, p. 336.

78 *LL*, *CW*, vol. XVI, p. 1481.

enthusiastic meeting of 5 July 1865. Grosvenor appeared first, speaking unexceptionably of the necessity of following the great leader, Gladstone, and expressing his support for the ballot. One may infer that there had been an understanding that this topic would be aired, so that there would be no confusion about the difference between the two Liberals, but that equally there would be no heated debate between them on the issue.[79] Mill's speech dwelt on the need to perceive this election as not one between Liberals, but between two Liberals on one side and a Tory on the other; Smith, he said, had no claim except as a Tory, and, since Mill went on to slang the Tories (drawing loud cheers), he can have left no doubt in his hearers' minds that such a claim was very slight. He also praised Gladstone again, and commented on the effects of the Reform Bill. His replies to questions about the Permissive Bill, the Irish church, poor rates, and legal protection for funds of trade unions were in general accord with Grosvenor's and were well received.

Mill's only reported remark that might have been injudicious was his expression of regret that George Odger had withdrawn as a Liberal candidate in Chelsea, though his main message was that Odger deserved praise for withdrawing to avoid splitting the Liberal vote.[80] This episode helps highlight the predicament Mill's adherence to principles had created. Odger's withdrawal, on the sought advice of parliamentary Liberals, again provoked delighted responses from the Conservatives.[81] *Judy*, who had taken particular note of Mill's support for working-class candidates, could not resist celebrating in cartoons their withdrawal when, the election becoming imminent and constituency-counting a preoccupation, their candidacies became a liability. "Lightening the Ship," of 30 September, shows the Liberal leaders (now significantly including Robert Lowe) getting rid of such dangerous cargo as Bradlaugh, Odger—and Mill. Mill, of course, was not cast off, and in "No Third Class," of 11 November, just before the election, he, with his ally on this matter, Thomas Hughes, stays aboard while Odger and Bradlaugh are left on the station platform.

In this connection it should be mentioned that Mill, however strongly he felt about working-class representation, was not without a sense of the

79 A question was put to Mill on the subject, and his principled response elicited only "hear, hear," and "cheers." *PPS*, *CW*, XXVIII, p. 340.

80 Ibid., p. 335.

81 Odger retired on the advice of the left-Liberals Stansfeld, Hughes, and Taylor, on the ground that his candidacy would harm the chances for a Liberal sweep of Chelsea. *Punch* applauded his decision on 14 November 1868, pp. 209 and 210. Bradlaugh, however, ran and was defeated at Northampton.

party's needs: there is no reason to doubt that he was sincere both in his praise of Odger for withdrawing and his regret that he had had to do so. He also argued that, whatever people might think of his offering a subscription to Bradlaugh, that offer had been accompanied with a caution about the danger of contributing, through splitting the Liberal vote, to the election of a Conservative; as late as 23 October, however, there was no danger of that in Northampton, where Bradlaugh was running, since the four candidates were all Liberals of one stamp or another. And as we have seen, his advocacy of Chadwick in Kilmarnock was based, genuinely if also conveniently, on his perception that Bouverie was not a reliable Liberal. However one interprets these matters, there is no doubt that Mill's most insistent public note throughout the campaign was the need for men who would support Gladstone.

On the following day, 3 November, Smith's next meeting was held, the first after the disruption on 27 October. Again advertised as open to holders of tickets, but with no reference to attendance by non-ticket-holders, the gathering was keenly anticipated by observers of the electoral scene. The report in *The Times* of the occasion is worth quoting both as an instance of a reporter looking for a story and as an example of consistent bias:

> Admission to the reserved seats near the platform was by ticket, but in or out of the body of the room persons appeared to walk at pleasure. The gathering was decidedly favourable to Mr. Smith, the recent forcible disturbance of one of his meetings having produced, as acts of violence often do, a reaction beneficial to the interest assailed. [*The Times* itself, it will be recalled, had reported that the Conservatives "eliminated" their opposition at that meeting.] The committee, moreover, of Messrs. Grosvenor and Mill have issued an appeal to their friends which, from some awkwardness in its wording, is ludicrously suggestive of the "You-are-requested-not-to-nail-the-gentleman's-ears-to-the-pump" story;[82] but is nevertheless an honest, well-meant attempt to spare the metropolis the reproach of acts of violence such as have occurred in different parts of the country. Before the proceedings commenced last evening much curiosity was manifested concerning the identity of the hon. candidate, till one of the crowd, wearing a blue guernsey, but evidently well posted in current political literature, settled the matter thus:—"That is 'im, I tell you; I seed 'im in the Tommy-ock."[83]

82 Not a story we know, alas.

83 In *Tomahawk*'s issue of 7 November, the main cartoon, "'Not for Jo'(hn Stuart

Smith's speech is equally interesting. He touched on his regular themes (admitting he was repeating himself, but saying that since he had not been heard at the previous meeting he would be forgiven), but added some new touches. He opened his remarks, for instance, by saying he had no personal feelings about what had happened, or been said about him, in the campaign. He had praise for Roundell Palmer,[84] and went on to assert that he was not really a party man, though it was necessary at this juncture for people to align themselves with one or the other of the two parties. Having spoken for nearly an hour, and having, the report says, had every sentence listened to, Smith closed with his statement of support for denominational education, saying "religion was at the root of all our greatness."

The rest of the proceedings at the meeting are also of more than normal interest for, though there were "interruptions and running commentary" through the speeches, the vote supporting Smith was unanimous and there was an intervention that, given the name of the speaker and of his organization, is likely to come to the unwary as a bit of a shock: "a Mr. Potter, representing the London and Westminster Working Man's Association, came upon the platform to explain why that body supported Mr. Smith"—the reasons were that he was against Irish Church Disestablishment and Popery—and called for plumping votes for Smith.[85]

The Liberal meeting on the next day, 4 November, held in Caldwell's Assembly Rooms, Soho, was once more well attended. Grosvenor alluded to his record and attacked that of the government, saying the Reform Bill would have to be amended in the next parliament, and again referred to his difference from Mill on the ballot, which he hoped would not alienate his supporters from Mill. Mill was, the *Morning Star* reported, "accorded a reception of quite a remarkable character. All present stood up and for some time waved their hats and handkerchiefs, and cheered with much genuine enthusiasm."[86] Mill alluded to his record, but concentrated on the way in which the vote in Westminster would affect the Liberal chances nationwide. He chanced his hand more than at the previous meeting, referring not only to Odger but also to Edmond Beales, and alluded

---

Mill), or, a Smith for Westminster," portrays a fishing contest for voters, in which Smith is the clear winner over a Mill who is consorting with grotesquely vile fellow anglers, the omnipresent Odger and Bradlaugh.

84 For his earlier appearance in this tale, see pp. 50–1 above.

85 *The Times*, 4 Nov. 1868, p. 8.

86 For the full report, see *PPS*, *CW*, vol. XXVIII, pp. 341–4; the description of Mill's reception is quoted on p. 341.

unnecessarily to Eyre, while arguing that election expenses should be borne by the public purse.[87] Once again he drew no fire from the supportive audience by these allusions, or by reaffirming, in answer to questions, his stand against the ballot and the Permissive Bill.

Following this meeting, the next Liberal move was to include in their advertisements a sentence directed against Smith's team that probably gave them much pleasure, but equally probably did little for the cause: "Admission free, without ticket, to all the Liberal meetings."[88]

The following Mill-Grosvenor meeting, for the electors of St. George's Without and Knightsbridge, was held on 6 November in the Pimlico Rooms. Grosvenor's opening remarks were interrupted by the announcement from the chair that pickpockets were about; his response suggests the general tone of his campaigning—he said (winning applause) that he did not see the connection between pickpockets and the Irish church. Again Mill attacked the Conservative record, he too demonstrating the playful temper so often missed by his critics: "When everybody was perfectly happy and comfortable," he is reported as having said, "there would be a state of things worth conserving; but the world was not just yet happy enough for anybody to be conservative in it. (*Loud laughter.*)" And again:

> Mr. Disraeli had professed to educate his party, as the Irishman did his pig when he tied a string to its hind leg, and took it into Limerick backwards. The Irishman was asked the meaning of his getting his pig to walk backwards, and replied in what is known in Ireland as a "pig's whisper:" "Hush! The pig must not suspect where I'm taking it to; walking this way it does not see where I'm taking it to; the pig thinks it's going home; I couldn't get it into Limerick otherwise." (*Laughter.*) Mr. Disraeli had also taken his party into Limerick [on the Reform Bill]. There was, however, this difference between the Irishman and his pig, and Mr. Disraeli and his party. The Irishman made his pig go

87 Mill again complained, this time to John Plummer, about the newspaper reports, commenting that he had said "a good deal" about "the expense of elections and the difficulty of getting working men's candidates into Parliament" that "was not reported"; however, the *Morning Star* account that is here summarized certainly does not avoid the issue. Indeed all the dangerous references here listed come in that connection; the allusion to Eyre being prompted only by the assumption that his solicitor had come out against the electoral corruption that made the process so expensive. His dragging in Eyre seems even more disingenuous when one notes that he was mistaken in identifying Eyre's solicitor, the remark having been made by Philip Rose rather than James Anderson Rose.

88 See *The Times*, 5 Nov., p. 6, and thereafter.

forward by making it fancy it was going backward, but Mr. Disraeli made his party believe they were going backward when they were really going forward. (*Laughter*)[89]

The Liberals now announced another meeting for local voters, this time for those of St. Margaret's, on the 9th, and soon after advertised their last two meetings, on the 11th for electors of St. Martin's-in-the-Fields and St. Mary-le-Strand, and then for all the electors of Westminster on the 13th.[90] They were buoyed by support from Dean Stanley, who again threw his strength behind Mill in a letter asserting that Mill was even more needed now than in 1865, not least because he had shown himself on at least three important occasions (not instanced by Stanley) to be willing to act "independently not merely of the general party, but of the particular section of it with which he is connected."[91]

But the Tories were now flying high and probably—though they may well not have known it—clear. Smith's next meeting on 6 November, the same day as that of Grosvenor and Mill, was crowded. Though intended for St. John's Ward electors, it clearly was more broadly attended, the private boxes overlooking the platform in the Regent Music Hall being filled with "Ladies." Smith, received with great enthusiasm, identified himself once more as "an independent member of the Liberal- Conservative party," undoubtedly sensing that, however the Grosvenor-Mill committee might feel about their happy cooperation, there were Grosvenor supporters who might be persuadable that an independent member of the Liberal-Conservative party, whatever that might be, was preferable to an independent member of the dangerously flapping Radical wing of the Liberal party. Smith's speech was otherwise much as before, though in reply to a question he expressed opposition to the Permissive Bill.

On this issue, all the candidates chose not to make whatever mileage was at least potentially available from a sympathetic response to the strident demands of that bill's proponents. It may well be, however, that they all objected in principle and saw no practical gain from support for a basically unpopular measure. Mill got in more trouble than the others, however, because he refused to meet with a deputation from the United Kingdom Alliance, the promoters of the bill, while both Grosvenor and Smith had agreed to such meetings.

89 For the full account, see *PPS*, *CW*, vol. XXVIII, pp. 344–7. Again his allusions (another to Beales) and his responses to questions seem to have raised no objections.

90 *The Times*, p. 8 on 6 and 7 Nov., and subsequently.

91 Ibid., 6 Nov., p. 8.

At Smith's meeting there was an amendment to the vote of support, by a Mr. Maynard, on the grounds that Smith's opinions on Irish affairs were not satisfactory, but it gained few adherents—one would like to think because then, as now, no one's opinions on those affairs is satisfactory. There was also a complaint, by T.W. Helps, against the attempts by Dean Stanley and Gladstone to bias the minds of the electors in favour of Grosvenor and Mill—surely an objection that no one could have taken seriously, though *The Times* chose to report it.[92]

At the next Liberal meeting, on 9 November in the Regent Music Hall, after some bland remarks by Grosvenor, Mill made an unusual move in answer to the Conservatives' rumour campaign against him, proposing that any of those "who had anything to say against him" should "get up at once like men and Englishmen, and tell what was the cause of complaint."[93] The only result was an intrusion by a man, "attired in a white smock," who called out "in a stentorian voice, that he was a working man and a Constitutional man," and that he wanted to know why the Liberals did not do as much for the working men as Smith, the "Constitutional candidate" had. The audience wanted nothing of this, and though Mill repeated his appeal, even saying he would attend a Conservative gathering just to answer attacks, the meeting returned to the usual form; however, Mill addressed somewhat different topics, arguing for universal elementary education, free to those who could not afford to pay, and asserting the need for uniform tax rates in London, with the goal of alleviating the poverty of the East End. He also alluded to the need for a metropolitan government of the kind outlined in the legislation he had been promoting in the House.

At this point in the heat of his own campaign, Mill on 10 November went down to Brighton to offer strong support to his Radical ally Henry Fawcett, who was running against William Coningham. It will be recalled that Mill's practice of offering support was condemned especially by the proprietors of the *Will-o'-the-Wisp*. Mill's speech in support of Fawcett dwelt on his beliefs and actions, with special reference to his advocacy of compulsory education, of placing the burden of election expenses on constituencies rather than candidates, and his exposure of the deplorable condition of agricultural labourers.[94] Such views on such matters would

92 Ibid., 7 Nov., p. 8.

93 It is interesting that the only other theme that led Mill to make such a seemingly untypical remark was the ballot, which he objected to on principled grounds, where he was joined by others whose criticisms that the measure was "unmanly" and "un-English" now seem less appealing.

94 *PPS*, *CW*, vol. XXVIII, pp. 350–5.

of course be welcome to those who staunchly supported the radical views of Mill and Fawcett, and would not have done any harm in the eyes of most Liberals in Brighton or Westminster.[95] Mill's speech appeared in the London papers, as did a thoroughly vindictive letter from Coningham, who had been (though not in the last parliament) a member for Brighton and who went down in this election to ignominious defeat, trailing in the poll well behind the two successful Liberals, of whom Fawcett was second. Coningham, stung at what he claimed were accusations by Mill that he advocated corruption in elections, retorted by saying that Mill's interference in the constituency was improper, and then saying publicly what again must have formed part of the canvassers' bag of tricks:

> Let me remind the electors that at the last general election you [Mill] were brought forward to liberate Westminster from the alleged dictation of the Marquis of Westminster by opposing his relative Captain Grosvenor. Finding yourself too weak to stand alone you coalesced with your opponent and intended victim, and your supporters were carried to the poll in his conveyances. While declining yourself to contribute one farthing towards the cost of your own election, you profited by his lavish expenditure, and your friends and the public were for a long time afterwards pestered with begging circulars from your committee, crying to the charitable "subscribe, subscribe."

Coningham continued by recalling to the voters' minds Mill's well-known activities, such as his opposition to the ballot, his support for minority representation, and his uncalled for interventions at Northampton for Bradlaugh and at Kilmarnock for Chadwick. Probably not all of this mud stuck, and its throwing did Coningham no good in his own constituency, but it is hard to think that it was totally ineffective in the wards of Westminster.

On the following day, 11 November, Mill and Grosvenor again addressed a meeting of electors, this time those of St. Martin's-in-the-Fields and St. Mary-le-Strand in the Polygraphic Hall, King William Street,

95 One issue, while it may not have meant much to Fawcett's campaign, may have indicated again to the shopkeepers of Westminster (who, it will be recalled, were sufficiently attached to the Liberals for some Tories to make the connection matter for satire) that Mill and his allies were not dependable: that was the matter of workers' cooperatives. This, however, is but an inference, there being no direct evidence that there was such a reaction in Westminster.

with James Beal in the chair. Mill opened with well-received abuse of the Tories and praise for Gladstone, but he also commented in some detail on Irish problems, mentioning not only the Irish church, the main Liberal plank, but also the more contentious issue of land tenure, saying that the present form was the last "relic" of the system that "treated the Irish as a conquered and alien people." These remarks brought cheers in the hall, but probably hardened the opposition outside. The question period was more boisterous, and it can hardly be doubted that the Hon. Robert Grimston was making sure that the Liberal meetings were not free of turmoil as the election approached. For instance, it was asked—almost incredibly—whether Mill had been, as rumoured, guilty of forging a ticket order for some theatre, and whether he and Grosvenor were against the separation of married couples in workhouses.[96]

Smith met his supporters on the same day, in the Conservatives' last meeting before a grand spectacular on the 13th. An apology was needed from the chairman, Richard Twining, for the exhausted condition of the candidate, who, it was asserted, was not very fresh after his canvass of the constituency. Smith, again warmly received, once more identified himself as a Liberal-Conservative, and went on to reiterate his principal notions. He added, however, opposition to the ballot, and asserted that there must be legislation to prevent the embezzlement of trades unions' funds. To questioners he replied, yet again, that he was opposed to the Permissive Bill, and then said that he was opposed to the opening of museums on Sundays because the working-man's one day of rest must be preserved.[97]

On the day that speech was reported, the Conservative finale was advertised, a combined assembly of the electors of Westminster and Chelsea, with the Conservative candidates for Chelsea, C.J. Freake and W.H. Russell, joining Smith at the Duke of Wellington's Riding School, Knightsbridge, by permission of the duke. Addresses, it was said, would be made by Lord George Hamilton, the Conservative candidate for Middlesex, "and other noblemen and gentlemen."[98]

On the next day a different kind of exhortation appeared in a Smith advertisement, one that Grimston also lithographed and sent to every outlying voter:

96 This question, from "a middle-aged man," roused loud laughter, the *Daily Telegraph* reported, because the "querist seemed so likely to have a direct interest in the matter." For the full account, see *PPS*, *CW*, vol. XXVIII, pp. 355–8.

97 *The Times*, 12 Nov., p. 6.

98 Ibid.

To the electors of the City of Westminster.

Gentlemen

At the last Westminster election, Mr. Smith was defeated by a majority of 710 votes, having failed to poll 2,000 of his promises, among whom were those of two personal friends of my own, the ten whippers-in of the Conservative party, 46 of Mr. Smith's committee, and 900 well-known Conservative gentlemen.

Upon the present occasion Mr. Smith has received such numerous promises of support that, if realized, he cannot be beaten.

The election, however, will not be won by gentlemen remaining at their county seats, and writing up at the last moment asking for a pair, but by putting themselves into the train for London on Monday next, the 16th inst., and polling early on Tuesday morning.

Colonel Taylor intends to set a good example in this respect, by coming over from Ireland, and returning there, for his own election, immediately after recording his vote for Mr. Smith.

If other gentlemen will follow so good a lead, I can promise them a crowning victory.

Gentlemen, I have the honour to remain,

Your obedient servant, Robert Grimston.

No. 24, Mount-street, Nov. 12th, 1868.[99]

Smith's private solicitor attributed his victory "in a great measure" to this document, the force of which is indeed evident.[100]

The joint Conservative meeting on the 13th was a resounding success, though Freake was unable to attend, being ill. The crowds were such that hundreds had to be turned away; the platform party, with General Wood in the chair, was most impressive, and Smith spoke first, getting a warm reception. He now returned to an earlier label, describing himself as being of the "Constitutional Party." Mentioning the benefits of Conservative legislation to the people since 1866, and repeating his themes, he concluded, "amid great cheering, by avowing himself an advocate of advancement combined with security—of reform, but not of revolution."

Russell, of Crimean fame, spoke next, in a manner more calculated to rouse the audience: "He was not, he was happy to say, the delegate of a philosopher, nor was he a thinking mill. (*Cheers and laughter.*)"[101] The

99 Ibid., 13 Nov., p. 8.

100 Maxwell, *Smith*, pp. 210–11 (who mistakenly dates the document to 12 March 1868).

101 Lest this example of paranomasia be thought unique, see the examples of puns on Mill's name in Robson, "Mill in Parliament: The View from the Comic Papers."

references here, caught by the audience, were not only to Mill, but to his "delegates," Odger, now retired from the Chelsea election, and to Dilke, though the latter was not yet recognized by Mill as a sound ally. Campaigning for Smith even more directly, Russell also commented: "All revolution was preceded by a war of philosophers against religion."[102] Whatever Russell's aims and methods, however, he went down to defeat in Chelsea, as did Freake, with Dilke and his Liberal colleague being returned.

The final Westminster Liberal meeting in St. James's Hall on the same evening, though not so splendid, was also a success, even *The Times* breaking its silence.[103] Thomas Hughes was scheduled to take the chair, but was detained by his own contest, and Serjeant Parry took his place. Grosvenor, in lambasting the Tories, won cheers and laughter by quoting a remark made by Mill during the meeting of the 11th: "the people, while accepting a household bill from Mr. Disraeli, seemed to say mechanically, 'Thank you, Mr. Gladstone.'" Mill's reception, the *Daily Telegraph* indicated, was "enthusiastic, the audience rising *en masse* . . . waving hats and handkerchiefs for several minutes," and, the *Daily News,* added, "cheering at the top of their voices."[104] Mill's speech appears aptly strong for the occasion, centring on the differences between the Liberals and Conservatives on issues of importance to the general welfare of the people, on many of which he again touched. However, in his desire to elevate Gladstone over the common run of politicians, Mill dwelt on the limitations of Palmerstonian do-nothingism; this was not a welcome message to those Whigs who were very edgy about Radical enthusiasms for change and who still had influence, especially in Westminster. The meeting concluded with "a second most flattering demonstration of respect and admiration," but those who evinced those emotions were solidly committed; the waverers who read reports probably were pushed a bit more to the right.

Mill hastened down to Greenwich the next day to speak at a meeting

102 *The Times,* 14 Nov., p. 5.

103 As noted above, *The Times* did not cover any of the Liberal meetings between 2 November and 13 November, though it reported all the Conservatives' and had reported all Mill's meetings in 1865—but its report of the Friday meeting appeared only on Monday the 16th, the Conservative meeting of the same night having made the Saturday paper. It may be—anyone who has worked for a newspaper will be alert to the hint—that no invidiousness was intended, for the report of the Liberal meeting says that it was "protracted to an unusually late hour." Indeed the report in the *Morning Star* also appeared on the 16th, though both the *Daily Telegraph* and the *Daily News* managed to get accounts in on the 14th.

104 For a full account, see *PPS, CW,* vol. XXVIII, pp. 358–63.

in support of Gladstone. His rousing eulogy is unexceptionable; perhaps the most noteworthy aspect is that Mill was seen by the Liberal electoral committee in Greenwich as one of the most valuable (as well as available) supporters to speak for the Liberal leader.[105]

The nomination meeting for Westminster on 16 November was held, for the first time, at the base of Nelson's column rather than in Covent Garden.[106] The arrangements, the *Morning Star* reported, "were an immense improvement over the old *regime* of dirt and disturbance at Covent Garden Market, where a candidate and his friends seldom escaped without making acquaintance with the flavour of decaying turnips and cabbage-stalks." Mill and his supporters, who had, in response to an advertisement, assembled in the committee rooms in Cockspur St. to walk together to the hustings, arrived on the platform just after Grosvenor (who had probably walked with them), and the Liberals took the traditional place for sitting members on the right of the High Bailiff. The nomination of Grosvenor by Sir Erskine Perry provided an opportunity for an attack on Smith's only qualification, "his large expenditures," for praise of Mill, and for the assertion that Grosvenor's representation of a great family should be seen in its proper light, for the Liberals could not be thought to be moving too quickly if the great houses of Grosvenor, Cavendish, and Russell were with them. Grosvenor's seconder, H.H. Seymour, pitched in with a reference to the illustrious Colonel Taylor's coming from Ireland to vote for Smith; he hoped that there were enough Liberals on the spot to elect their two candidates.

Malleson proposed Mill in glowing terms on the basis of his parliamentary performance, his character, and his devotion to the popular cause; Mill was "not only one of the greatest, but one of the best loved of living Englishmen. He had been assailed with insult and contumely of every kind, but his vilifiers had not dared to accept his challenge to attend one of his public meetings, and there repeat their accusations." Beal seconded, remarking that "the rancorous hatred" of Mill's opponents for him "was the best proof of the value of his services." Such attention to the opposition's attacks on the character of a candidate was of course not uncommon in nineteenth-century elections, but it deserves remark that at this point Mill's supporters clearly saw the main problem not as Smith's qualities or platform, or the Conservative platform, or Disraeli's leadership, or, on the other side, the platform of Gladstone and the Liberals, or even the particular political tenets that Mill was noted for—though

105 For a full account, see ibid., pp. 363–7. Gladstone was defeated in South Lancashire and elected in Greenwich.

106 For a full account, see ibid., pp. 367–8.

"The General Election: Nomination of Candidates for Westminster," *Illustrated London News*, 21 November 1868

these were cited—but as the personal attacks on him by Smith's supporters.

Grosvenor's and Mill's nominations were heard on the hustings, but trouble broke out when the speakers on the other side of the platform tried to present Smith's nomination. There was "a surging movement" in their direction "by the rougher element immediately beneath the hustings which of course was productive of reaction and uproar," and little else was heard. Beneath the din, Smith was proposed by George Cubitt and seconded by G. Tavener Miller. At this point, presumably, a nomination of the putative fourth candidate, B.V. Hutchinson, could have been expected, but there was no surprise when no other candidate was proposed, and the three nominees spoke and were (partially) heard. Grosvenor asserted that while he was aware that his family position contributed to his first election, now it could be seen that his Liberalism was itself reason enough; he always had voted on the popular side. When he averred that household suffrage was proper, some dissent was elicited: "(*Cheers, groan, and a Voice — 'You did not vote for it.'*)" Mill's speech was sensibly brief:

> This is not the time or the place for many words, and, if it were, you could not possibly hear them; so I will say only this, you and the people of this country generally have got to decide something more important than the particular merit or demerit of candidates that present themselves for your suffrages. You have got to decide whether this country shall have a Tory Government or a Gladstone Government. (*Cheers, cries of Gladstone, and interruption.*) If the new electors who have supported Reform care nothing about the rights that have been acquired, and desire things should go on after the Reform Act exactly as they went on before it, they will do quite right to vote for the Tory candidate; but if the old electors are as much attracted to Reform as ever—if the new electors desire that their newly-acquired rights should be exercised to the best advantage—and if both new and old electors wish the Reform Bill to bring forth abundant fruits, then they will, I have no doubt, vote for the two Liberal candidates. (*Cheers.*)

After Smith's equally short address, in which he avowed once more his Liberal-Conservatism, an unexplained confusion took over: Mill and Grosvenor would appear to have refused to move the traditional vote of thanks to the returning officer, and eventually it was offered by Smith, seconded by his agent Grimston. The show of hands was judged to be in favour of Smith and Mill, with Grosvenor then, of course, calling for a poll. Mill, with his supporters, returned to the committee room, where, "presenting himself upon the balcony," he "bowed his acknowledgements to his supporters."

It is reasonable to assume that no one would be very confident about the outcome of the poll on the next day. Grosvenor must have been fairly sure that his support would not diminish; anything that might be held against him by left Liberals because of his family connections would be overridden by his record in parliament, and, unlike the previous election, this one had seen no attempt by Mill's supporters to discredit him. The Tories had concentrated their fire on Mill, who had also been assailed by those disgruntled Liberals like Coningham who had no serious objection to Grosvenor. Mill did not run against Grosvenor in 1868, nor could he have done so. As we have seen, in 1865 the animosity between Mill's and Grosvenor's supporters had been overcome shortly before polling day, and in 1868 there had been a single Liberal committee. While Grosvenor had not distinguished himself in the House, no one had expected him to do so. Unlike his kinsman, Hugh Lupus Grosvenor, the future Duke of Westminster, he had kept his distance from the Adullamites and had done nothing to irritate either Gladstone or advanced Liberals. Any tension between him and Mill would have harmed only the latter, and might indeed have aided the former. Given the nature of the campaign, it was almost impossible to imagine anyone voting for Smith and Mill.

For Smith, the outlook may have been more doubtful. His letters at the time reveal the common reactions of political candidates, especially those who have never been successful. Indeed, apart from the idiom, these letters might pass for Mill's. On 10 November he wrote to his wife: "I don't want people . . . to suppose I sulk if I lose the battle or am too much elated if I win." The next day his note to her said: "I certainly hope to succeed, but the relief of rest will be so great that if I fail I shall be compensated by a return to home comforts." And on the 12th his daily report was even more Millian: "If I go down home on Tuesday evening beaten I shall not feel I am disgraced, and I intend to put a good and cheerful face upon it. It will all be for the best, and I shall be quite content to spend more time with my family and with you. . . . Everything is going well with me at present, but it is quite impossible to tell what the issue may be."[107] His report to his sister on the nomination day seems, in the circumstances, more hopeful even in its caution: ". . . I have never passed through such

107 Maxwell, *Smith*, pp. 139–40; Akers-Douglas, *W.H. Smith* (London: Routledge and Kegan Paul, 1965), pp. 57–8.

a fortnight of hard labour as the past has been, but am very well all things considered. . . . My *promises* of support are very satisfactory, but I shall only feel assured of success when there is a majority declared in my favour."[108]

There could be little question about Smith's and his supporters' efforts having been more powerful than in the previous election, both in the constituency organization and in the attacks on Mill; the results were to be seen in press reaction to him and to Mill and in the encouraging reports he had been getting from his canvassers, many of which must have been both reliable and strongly hopeful. What he probably had some question about was the success of his attempt to split the Liberal vote by his avowal of a Liberal-Conservative position, the concentration of his campaign on the dangerousness of Mill, and his status as a businessman among the Liberal businessmen of Westminster. It was, however, patently easier for someone to consider it reasonable to vote for Grosvenor and Smith than for Mill and Smith. And there was the support, perhaps worth little, but undoubtedly worth something, of the mysterious London and Westminster Working Men's Constitutional Association.

What of Mill's chances? He had lived up to his promises of 1865, if such they may be called, in his parliamentary behaviour, and his supporters in Westminster were—at least such of them as were not known to have become alienated over specific matters—just as vociferously in his favour as before. Indeed they were more so, having been enraged by the tactics of Smith's supporters. On the favourable side also was the now effective coalition of the Grosvenor forces with his: whatever he may have felt about expenditure directly for Grosvenor's purposes, he could not but benefit from it, since most of the efforts were clearly marked as Liberal and designed to help both. Furthermore, it could be expected, *caeteris paribus*, that the newly enfranchised, especially the lodgers, would on balance reward his championship, which was unchallenged, of the less privileged classes, both politically and economically. Still, he was not, and could not well be, blind to the strength of the reaction against some of his actions, and must have realized from the reports of his committee members, as well as from his personal mail and the press reports, that his support in parts of his Liberal constituency had been eroded. He knew that some of his behaviour had been injudicious from the point of view of one wishing to be re-elected, and he might have guessed that, while in the election of 1865 a few might have thought merely that he was not running, in this election more might have concluded he was running in the wrong

108 Akers-Douglas, *Smith*, p. 58.

direction. However, Mill's perception of his chances might well have been dulled by his conviction that he was right in what he had done, and by his (we think) genuine feeling that he might do more good out of the House than in it. And, finally, one must consider the bolstering effect of the supposition which, he had told Cairnes in 1865, it would give him great pleasure to show valid: that there is more to be accomplished "by supposing that there is reason and good feeling in the mass of mankind than by proceeding on the ordinary assumption that they are fools and rogues." Smith, he would believe, had acted on the latter assumption; he himself had taken the higher road.

And it was the road that led away from Westminster, and back to his beloved Avignon. Whatever the speculations beforehand, the poll was conclusive from opening to closing: the first report at 9 a.m. gave Smith 1020 votes (presumably Colonel Taylor having stepped up smart and early, and then departed for Ireland),[109] Grosvenor 660, and Mill 632; the last, at 4 p.m., gave Smith 7698, Grosvenor 6505, and Mill 6185.[110]

At this stage in the development of British electoral practice, the election centred on three consecutive days of public excitement, the first being nomination day, the second polling day, and the third the day of declaration of the poll. Though the result, at least approximately, was known—as it is now with usually much greater precision—the declaration, public and outdoor, attracted large partisan crowds. By noon on 18 November the crowd began to gather at the hustings, and by 2 o'clock, when the declaration was expected, it filled the whole space between Nelson's column and the statue of Charles I. Those "in the immediate neighbourhood of the hustings were of the roughest sort and refused to tolerate a decent hat in their midst," but reasonable order was kept. Mill and Grosvenor appeared together and were cheered. The reporter for *The Times* found his colour commentary in a "lad of 14" (one wonders at his ability to know the age so exactly, in the circumstances—the *Morning Star* guessed at 10 to 12), who, "hoisted on the shoulders of another, acted as fugleman, and raised a general cheer by assuring Mr. Mill that 'They'd pop him in for Greenwich.'"[111] This same lad, displaying to the surprise

109 Grimston had been resolute in preaching the virtue of polling early to influence others to join the winning side. Gale, *Grimston*, p. 211.

110 At this point an audience in the late twentieth century expects, quite reasonably, to be offered a sophisticated psephological analysis of this result and that in 1865. This we cannot supply, because there is simply not enough evidence extant to permit a reliable analysis.

111 The reference is to the likelihood that Gladstone would be elected for South Lancashire as well as for Greenwich, and would vacate the latter.

of the reporter a "considerable knowledge of the state of political parties," led cheers for Gladstone, Beales, and Bright, as well as Mill and Grosvenor, and elicited hisses for Smith and Disraeli.

The High Bailiff, it soon appeared, was much delayed, and the crowd became more active, some roughs throwing stones at anyone on the hustings conceived to be "a Smith's man." Conservatives replied by posting a Tory cartoon, but the hustings were immediately invaded and the offensive paper torn away.[112] Police were not to be found near the hustings themselves, so there was no protection from insult or even assault, according to *The Times*. "At 3 o'clock," the report continues, "Mr. Mill, who was suffering from a bad cold, asked permission to speak and retire." Comparative silence being achieved, he said:

> To be defeated in a contested election is so common an occurrence that there is no reason why any sensible man should be much moved by it—and least of all is that any reason in my case, who, as you know, did not seek the honour which you conferred on me; but, on the contrary, the acceptance was and has been throughout a sacrifice to me. (*Hear, hear.*) Whatever regret I feel, therefore, at the result of yesterday's election is solely on public grounds. (*Cheers.*) I regret the loss of a vote to Mr. Gladstone and the Liberal party. (*Great cheering.*) I regret that Westminster, which was so long at the head of the Liberal interest, should have had the unenviable distinction of being the only metropolitan constituency which has at this election sent a Tory to the House of Commons by the vote of the majority. (*Hisses.*) And I am sorry for one reason more. I think it was an encouragement to young men ambitious of parliamentary distinction—it was a good lesson to them when they found that a great constituency like this was willing to be represented by a man who always told you plainly when he differed in opinion from you—who told you that he differed on a few important points, though he agreed on more,[113] and that he should maintain his opinion by his votes, and who never, for the sake of preserving his seat, ever said or did anything which he would not have thought it his duty to do if he had not been your representative.

He concluded by thanking his supporters, including those electors who had given him "an amount of support, favour, and countenance very far above [his] deserts," to which the crowd replied with "*Cries of No, and*

112 Probably that reproduced on p. 290 below, from the Hambleden Archive.

113 *The Times* reports his saying simply "differed on so many important points."

MISS MILL JOINS THE LADIES.

cheers," and then many of them joined him in walking back to the Liberal committee rooms in Cockspur Street.[114]

Those who remained, including the successful candidates, were detained even longer, for after another invasion of the hustings, and a good deal of fighting, policemen finally came and cleared the roughs away in time for the High Bailiff's arrival at 4 p.m. He apologized for his lateness, pleading the "large addition to the number of voters," and announced the poll as Smith, 7648, Grosvenor, 6584, Mill, 6284.[115]

When Smith finally got up to speak, he was "inaudible, through the groans of the crowd, except to those immediately around him." In offering thanks to his supporters, he said they "had accomplished, not a personal triumph, but had vindicated great principles of right and justice, of moderation, law, and order. The voice of Westminster would be heard throughout the country with an effect greatly exceeding that of the single vote he might be able to give in Parliament."

Grosvenor was honoured, but not so pleased. He was gratified that, having before been accepted on trust as a "member of a Liberal and respected family," he was now established as a member through "faithful service." But he was disappointed, he said, in that the opposition "had adopted a method of appealing to the constituency which he had prophesied would not command respect, but he was sorry to find he was a false prophet"; as a result, he would have to serve face-to-face rather than side-by-side with a colleague whose political opinions were antipathetic ("however much he might respect him personally") and whose votes on all important matters would neutralize his. He also expressed keen disappointment at the loss of "a colleague with whom it was both a pleasure and a distinction to serve"; he acknowledged that Mill's departure was a great loss to Westminster.[116]

Two more events merit mention in this chronicle of the election of 1868. On 9 December a dinner was held to celebrate Smith's election, and it was given by none other than the London and Westminster Working Men's Constitutional Association in St. James's Hall. Presided over by Lord George Hamilton, it included 750 guests at the dinner itself, "of whom," we are told, "a considerable proportion were working men." The galleries were also needed, where several ladies watched over the festivities. After expressions of thanks to those who had worked in the

114 *PPS*, *CW*, vol. XXVIII, pp. 369–70.

115 These represent a reduction of fifty from Smith's total, and an increase in Grosvenor's of seventy-nine, while Mill's was up by ninety-nine—but Mill still trailed Grosvenor by 300, and Smith by 1364.

116 *The Times*, 19 Nov., p. 4.

campaign, Smith spoke of the way in which "old Constitutional principles" had prevailed. Though he made no specific reference to Mill, at least as reported, his remarks included these two sentences: "He had addressed persons in that hall who three years ago were warm supporters of the other side. There had been a distinct, positive, and powerful reaction in Westminster, Middlesex [where Hamilton had been elected], Lancashire [where, as noted, Gladstone had by now been defeated], and many other parts of the country, especially in the large constituencies." But these remarks were as prospective as retrospective.

The second event concerns the fact that, throughout the election, Mill and his supporters had complained about the vast expenditures on the Conservative side. Only one day after the declaration of the poll (when, one is happy to hear, his cold was much better), Mill, replying to a letter from John Chapman, told him that, if he wished to raise the issue of bribery and corruption by the Tories during the campaign, he should speak to Beal or Malleson. "I believe," he said, "they have information of some already. I cannot do anything myself in the matter."[117] Beal and Malleson did have some evidence, and they decided to act, with the result that a hearing into charges against Smith of "bribery and treating," the petitioners being "Beal and others," was begun on 12 February 1869 by Mr. Baron Martin under the Election Petitions Act of 1868.[118]

The particulars of the case, given in fine detail in the press, provide an insight into the actual process of electioneering that is not available elsewhere, whatever one thinks of the final judgment, the judge, the witnesses, or the counsel. Fitzjames Stephen opened for the petitioners with an account of Smith's reported expenditures, which came to £8908.17.7; on behalf of Grosvenor and Mill together £2296.2.7 had been spent. In 1865 it appeared that Smith had expended about £5000; no mention is made of the Grosvenor or Mill expenses then. After listing the expenses for Smith's central committee, for the fourteen district committees, and for "agency" and advertising, Stephen claimed that on these accounts some £2484 was either not vouched for, or vouched for in an incomplete and "colourable manner." The example he cited is certainly coloured, and looks further colourable: seventeen receipts to the Central Committee were in the name of one Edwards, a farmer of St. Albans, for "so many weeks' 'expenses' as per account rendered." The

117 *LL*, *CW*, vol. XVI, pp. 1488–9.

118 In this, the first case under that law, Fitzjames Stephen, with Murch and Littler, instructed by Cobb and Southey, acted for the petitioners; Hawkins, with Sergeant Ballantine, Hugh Shield, and D. Kingsford, instructed by Rodgerson and Ford, for Smith.

Edwards family, father and two sons, had earlier been implicated in bribery, one of them having been imprisoned as early as 1851 for "keeping witnesses out of the way at the St. Albans inquiry," where he was reported to have been the principal agent in bribing to the extent of £24,600 during eight elections. Grimston, Smith's agent, had been constantly in touch with Edwards throughout the Westminster contest, and Stephen bluntly said that Edwards "was employed for the very purpose of bribing."

Another issue was the payment of electors as canvassers, which should have disqualified them as voters. Six of them acted for Edwards, by ostensibly paying for the display of placards or "boards," as they were also called. They had been giving 7*s*. per week per placard for such display, when the going rate was more like 7*s*. per week per hundred placards.[119] Then there was treating, ranging from lavish supplies of champagne at the Merlin's Cave public house while Smith was there, to free tea tickets at a meeting, paid for by a clergyman called Waldo. There were also offers of employment or money.

And what of the London and Westminster Working Men's Constitutional Association? They had in fact invited Smith to come forward as a candidate; he had earlier been elected and then resigned as their president; and they had transferred their committee rooms just before the election to public houses, had been supplied with canvassing books, and been recognized by Smith's Central Committee.

Finally, two examples of illegitimate attempts to split the Liberal interest were documented. First, a man using the name Howard had called on Lieutenant-Colonel Dickson of the Reform League, then a Liberal candidate for Hackney, offering £500 on the spot and £5000 more if he would stand as a Liberal for Westminster. Dickson said he would not stand against Mill, upon which Howard suggested that he stand against Grosvenor. Dickson replied that if a deputation of electors asked him to, he would consider, just so long as everything was above board. Nothing came of this, but after the election Mr. Jenkins, one of Smith's agents, told Dickson he had been a fool, since he could have had £5000 and been returned as Smith's colleague. "Howard" was Jenkins's own father, sent by him, he confessed to Dickson. Second, and here another apparent puzzle has light shed on it, an attorney, Barry V. Hutchinson, who had tried to become an agent and then to induce a Radical candidate to come forward, decided to run himself. Thereupon he was offered £200 by

119 A witness later commented that there "was not much advertising on the Liberal side. They had large posters, but no boards." This witness was of opinion that boards were unnecessary.

Jenkins's clerk, Purcell, on condition that he retire; if he agreed, Howard was again to carry the cash.

These were the charges advanced by the petitioners through Stephen. The proceedings were lengthy, rancorous, and detailed, with examination and cross-examination that produced some surprising evidence, and some that caused considerable amusement in the court, largely because of its manner of presentation and/or its callousness. The judge was, he said before his summation, greatly impressed by the presentation of evidence on both sides, but during the proceedings he would appear to have been less pleased, perhaps only in the manner of his kind. After removal of the hearing to more salubrious quarters, threats of adjournment, offers of condensation and withdrawal of evidence, and some procedural problems, on the seventh day after hearing the defence's summation Baron Martin made his judgment immediately. The cases of treating he thought trivial, the bribery not strictly proved, and so he found Smith properly elected. He conceded, however, that others might interpret the matter differently, especially in view of the truly extravagant sums of money expended by Smith, who had been surprised when, having paid £4000 before the actual election, he had been called upon for a further £4500 after it. As *The Times* commented in a leader: "A good character has, to Mr. Smith at any rate, certainly proved better than riches. It may be a question whether the latter won his seat for him, but there can be no question that the former has saved it."[120]

And his it was. Why was it not Mr. Mill's?

120 For the full proceedings, see *The Times*, 10 Feb., p. 6, 11 Feb., p. 8, 13 Feb., p. 7, 15 Feb., p. 5, 16 Feb., p. 7, 17 Feb., p. 7, 18 Feb., p. 8, 19 Feb., p. 5, and 20 Feb., p. 8.

EIGHT

Judgments

Having seen the record, can one answer our initial question: Why was Mill defeated in the 1868 election, having been returned in 1865? Since we have been using *The Times* as a "newspaper of record," which, despite its bias, by and large it was, it seems only fair to let it have a first word. In fact, more than one word. On 19 November, a leader assessed the general election results as showing a "moderate, though decidedly Liberal" feeling in the country, and continued:

> when the candidate has promised to stick to his party and support Mr. Gladstone the general moderation of opinion he may profess has been in his favour. There is hardly an instance of a sound Liberal losing his seat for not going far enough, and the waverers of the last Parliament have, as a general rule, been leniently dealt with. On the other hand, the candidates of the Reform League, and the extreme men generally, have met with almost universal rejection. The Liberal electors of Westminster, who are in an immense majority, have simply stayed away from the poll rather than support Mr. Mill; while the chief of the Radical celebrities, Mr. Beales, has been rejected by the most Democratic constituency in the kingdom, and stands in the poll below even the Tory candidate.

With some satisfaction, *The Times*'s leader also records the defeat of all working-men's candidates and university Liberals, concluding that on this evidence the Second Reform Act has proved a success.

So here Mill's failure is attributed simply and generally to his having been an "extreme" man; his loyalty to Gladstone and the party, which he himself had stressed strongly in the campaign, was not mentioned, presumably on the ground that even so he was not "sound" as well as not "moderate."

A broader view of public attitudes, as reflected in *The Times*, was given in early December 1868 when, though Mill is not mentioned directly, he certainly is implicated. It will be recalled that Charles Buxton, the Liberal member of parliament who had been instrumental in establishing the Jamaica Committee, had later resigned from its chairmanship because he wished to have no part in the attempt to establish the criminal guilt of Eyre. During the election campaign Buxton's part in the affair was used against him, and there had been a complex and vindictive exchange in the press.[1] After the election, Buxton himself wrote to the editor of *The Times*, including a long extract from his self-exculpatory account to his constituents that he had distributed during the campaign. In a leader, *The Times* praised and exonerated Buxton, and criticized Eyre, while continuing its attack on those whose vengeful feelings had led them to prosecute him for murder. This topic, the editorial writer says, "was naturally turned to account in the late Elections, and with remarkable effect. To describe a candidate as a member of the Jamaica Committee was like putting him on the black list, and giving him a terrible stigma to fight against."[2]

And *The Times*'s fullest treatment of Mill's defeat returns to this theme, but by a curious route. On 23 December it picked up the public exchange of letters between Priscilla McLaren and Mill[3] in which McLaren, writing on behalf of the Edinburgh Branch of the National Women's Suffrage Association, offered condolences on his defeat and expressed the hope that he would continue to pursue his worthy goals, instancing the Eyre affair; and Mill, replying, said that he was pleased to believe that his most important public service was in the cause of women and that he regretted greatly that some women supported Eyre. This was too great an opportunity for *The Times* to miss, and the letters appeared on the leader page with a lengthy comment. Many even of Mill's admirers will not regret his absence from parliament, *The Times* asserts, for his conduct as a politician has diminished his influence as a writer; indeed, they may regret that he had been elected at all. Though there is no real connection between his parliamentary conduct and the value of his writings, many people would now just as soon choose Bradlaugh as Mill for a "philosopher and guide." The trouble is that, having been admired by men of all parties, he has "estranged many even of his best friends . . . by his vehement, narrow partisanship, and apparent inability to see a redeeming point in a political adversary." Now that Mill has retired, it may

1 See above, p. 227, and *The Times*, 4 Nov. 1868, p. 8, and 9 Nov. 1868, p. 7.

2 *The Times*, 7 Dec. 1868, pp. 4 and 8.

3 Letters of 1 and 12 December, respectively.

be that the grudge against him politically will be forgotten in a restored popularity as a writer, but this hope is based on the assumption that he will resume "his old attitude of dignified reserve" and, if he must comment on current affairs, "select occasions worthy of his interference, and not be perpetually rushing into the fray with an impetuous eagerness." He has, however, become "the apostle of a small and not very select band of zealots," and is drawn into "the part of a petty Providence" by his friends—and here the point of the argument emerges—such as in the exchange of letters with Priscilla McLaren, where more credit is done to his heart than his head. After asking almost parenthetically why the Edinburgh branch arrogates to itself the task of condolence, the article draws attention to the references to Eyre. Here Mill's acrimony, it is asserted, of a kind foreign to his earlier behaviour, becomes almost comical, as he is led to attack those thought "to be under his special protection and his most favoured clients"—women. While the leader also attacks the weakness of Mill's logic in the letter, as well as denigrating "the 'coming woman' " and Priscilla McLaren, its central purpose is obvious: after a passing reference to Bradlaugh, Mill's feminism and his pursuit of Eyre are linked together as examples of his utter failure to practise the tenets that his writings had made his supporters expect; his extremism has simply caused him to fail as a politician, and, from that point of view, good riddance is the wisest judgment.

A view from the opposition camp, taken long after the smoke had cleared, is also worth scanning. Commenting on Smith's success his first biographer, Herbert Maxwell, points out that in 1868

> Westminster was not . . . the same constituency he had courted in 1865. The effect of household suffrage on the political complexion of such a borough could only be darkly surmised. It was true that people had begun to get tired of Mr Mill: in those days the advocacy of woman suffrage was regarded as an eccentric novelty, and if there is one thing of which the English middle class is more suspicious than of novelty, it is eccentricity. Mill had also disgusted some of his supporters by relentless prosecution of the charges against Governor Eyre; and by espousing the cause of Charles Bradlaugh, the infidel and revolutionary lecturer, he had roused the alarm of members of all the Churches. Still, the new electors were an untried contingent, and nobody could predict what their action might be.[4]

4 Herbert Maxwell, *Life and Times of the Rt. Hon. W.H. Smith, M.P.*, 2 vols (Edinburgh and London: Blackwood, 1893), vol. I, p. 137.

But Mill's behaviour, Maxwell argues, made Smith's road to victory a much easier one. To demonstrate, he quotes newspaper accounts from papers sympathetic to Mill, accounts that delighted the Conservatives when they appeared. The *Pall Mall Gazette* wrote:

> It is extraordinary that a man of his [Mill's] acuteness and discernment should fail even now to perceive how much he himself did, not only to bring about this result, but to jeopardise the seats of other Liberals by his patronage of Bradlaugh. . . . At Westminster the Conservatives, if they had only known their strength, could have put in two Conservatives instead of one; and if both the Liberals had been ousted, Mr. Mill would have been mainly to blame.

And, Maxwell points out, the *Daily News* was "even more vindictive":

> From the date of his letter commendatory of Mr Bradlaugh to his journey, a few days since, to Brighton, where he delivered himself of a diatribe against the Palmerstonian Liberals,[5] Mr Mill has neglected nothing which could prejudice against him men whom, for the sake of his party and his cause, he might at least have abstained from offending. The late member for Westminster has himself principally to thank for his defeat. The great follies of small men may be dismissed with contempt or with indulgence; but the serious errors of a man of Mr Mill's character, intellect, and reputation are too mischievous to be passed over in silence.[6]

The voice of a strong supporter of Mill, Thomas Beggs, may also be heard. Writing on 20 November 1868 to the editor of *The Times*, after outlining the campaign of 1865, Beggs goes on to say rather surprisingly that in 1868, despite the good faith of Grosvenor and his immediate friends, the Westminster Liberals had

> to work with separate committees, with a strong and powerful opponent in front, and lukewarm supporters and hollow friends among the Liberal ranks, and many old Liberals working and voting against us. . . . The main cause of our loss was the want of cordial union in our own ranks.

5 For an account of Mill's speech in support of Fawcett—another instance of his campaign to radicalize the party—see chapter 7, pp. 252–3 above.

6 Quoted by Maxwell, *Smith*, p. 141.

> There were, no doubt, subordinate causes, such as the feeling caused by the part Mr. Mill had taken in relation to Governor Eyre; his views on the ballot; and there is sufficient validity in the old No-Popery feeling to influence the elections everywhere. Latterly, in the support he had rendered to several aspirants for parliamentary honours, he had lost friends, and cooled the ardour of others. I know and respect Mr. Mill's feelings, but I think a little consideration was due to the men in Westminster who were fighting a battle of principle with him, and making sacrifices to attain a great end. Giving to Mr. Mill the utmost liberty of action, and conceding all that he would claim for the men he so much wished to help, we felt that Mr. Mill's return was of far greater consequence than that of any of the others, and it might have been well had he taken that in view, or rather considered how his actions would affect his own position in Westminster, and his party in Parliament.
>
> All this was known and calculated upon by the Conservative party. Mr. Smith is an honourable man; and if I could vote for a Conservative, I should prefer him to anyone I know. But his supporters adopted the well-known tactics of the Tory party. They began by traducing Mr. Mill, and misrepresenting his views on many social questions. Extracts were taken from his books, which, without the context, were made to read very differently to the author's intention. Nothing but blank pages could save an author under such treatment. The walls were covered with them, and it was the stock article of the canvassers. Some of them carried about with them printed matter, which it was alleged Mr. Mill had written, but took care not to let this pass out of their hands. We were thus undermined by a number of agencies that we could not confront. When such liberties are taken with a writer there is no protection against misrepresentation and no vindication possible.

Turning to the actual election, Beggs comments:

> I was about all the day, and can bear witness to the admirable organisation of the Conservative canvassers and assistants. There was no lack of numbers, no stint of zeal, the blue canvasser was everywhere. So far as Mill's own supporters were concerned we were a mere handful, deficient in numbers and the superintendent of every booth was complaining of want of sufficient assistance. We did nothing out of Mr. Mill's pocket—we paid the expenses by our subscriptions, and none of us had a sandwich or a biscuit that was not

> purchased at our own expense. Thus, with a machinery and a discipline against us that I never saw surpassed, and a number of men that would do good service in a campaign, if their bravery in the field equalled the alacrity they displayed on the polling day, they have secured 1,600 more votes than we have done with a machinery ludicrously small and inefficient.

The lesson must be for next time: "The city has been represented by many great men—by none greater than John Stuart Mill, and even his loss will be compensated if it lead to the thorough reorganisation of the Liberal party."[7]

What of Mill's own immediate response? In letters he wrote during the campaign the analysis is not subtle. He shows himself usually as not willing to see any serious danger to his election in what others saw as rashness or extremism. The Bradlaugh subscription he thought did not at all diminish his "weight," for anyone offended by it either had already given him up because of his other "crotchets," such as "Women's Suffrage, Jamaica Committee, representation of minorities," etc.—or more likely had never supported him in the first place.[8] For, as he reminds Chadwick before the election, "my Malthusianism and religious heresies, and my accusing the working people of not speaking the truth, were all brought up against me at the [previous] Westminster election, and all increased my popularity." He here also expresses belief that his anti-ballot views will not cost him any votes in Westminster, and finally returns to the Bradlaugh affair to say, even more confidently, that it might indeed gain as many votes as it might lose.[9] Writing to Cairnes almost three weeks later, near the end of October, just before returning from France for the final days of the campaign, Mill, obviously having been badgered by his committee, felt less confident, and was for once willing to admit that Bradlaugh might do him some harm; his helping Chadwick against Bouverie, he notes, is causing considerable stir in the press, but voters in Westminster are more likely to be alienated by the Bradlaugh subscrip-

7 Printed in *The Times*, 21 Nov. 1868, p. 5.

8 He wrote to Bradlaugh immediately after their defeat, on 19 November, to say: "I may have lost some votes by my subscription for you, but neither that nor any one thing is the cause of my losing the election. Many things have contributed to it, & I sh[d] very likely have been defeated if my name had never been coupled with yours. In any case it was the right thing to do & I do not regret it." *Later Letters* [*LL*], ed. Francis E. Mineka and Dwight N. Lindley, *Collected Works* [*CW*], vols. XIV–XVII (Toronto: University of Toronto Press, 1972), vol. XVI, p. 1487 (to Chadwick, 19 Nov. 1868).

9 Ibid., pp. 1458–9 (to Chadwick, 9 Oct. 1868).

tion. (He here, incidentally, expressed indignation at Coningham's attempt to unseat Fawcett at Brighton.)[10]

Two more bits of information before turning to Mill's post-defeat judgments. The question of the Liberals' mode of organization had clearly been a matter of contention during the campaign itself, though Mill's mention of it to Chadwick is not marked by judgment either way. William Sims Pratten, he remarks, "one of my local chairmen, says it is all nonsense employing paid agents for election purposes, and that the whole thing is much better managed by the local committees. Even at the registration, he says, the thing would have been boshed if it had been left to the agents; it was only by the exertions of the Committees that they got on a greater number of lodgers than have been got on in almost any other place."[11]

The second additional point comes after the election from another Mill supporter. William Malleson, the honorary secretary to the Grosvenor-Mill Committee in 1868, expressed interest in Mill's account to Esquiros (see below) when it was published, and commented that Mill had omitted one of the chief causes of his defeat, "namely, the apparent incapacity on the part of a large portion of the constituency to admire or even understand the rigid independence which led him, on the eve of an important election, to act and write precisely as he would have done had he not been a candidate." The contrary practice, Malleson continued, was so common that it was not wonderful, though lamentable, "that Liberals of Westminster," instead of "doubling their devotion, through appreciation of Mr. Mill's perfect honesty and matchless fidelity to his opinions, felt themselves affronted rather than otherwise at not having been taken more into consideration." He concludes:

> No doubt, reckless expenditure of money on the other side, and the perfect organization which unlimited means make possible, told against us, but all this we were prepared for and meant to beat, as we had beaten it before, by the strength of popular enthusiasm.
>
> Unfortunately, the full wind upon which we had counted to fill our sails fell away under the influence of the Bouverie correspondence and the Bradlaugh subscription.[12]

With these varied accounts in mind, one can turn to Mill's own assessment after his defeat. This comes from two sources, letters written

10 Ibid., pp. 1464–7 (29 Oct. 1868).
11 Ibid., p. 1481 (7 Nov. 1868).
12 *The Times*, 21 Dec. 1868, p. 5.

immediately after the campaign and the relevant portion of the *Autobiography*, written about a year later.

The fullest epistolary account is in a reply to a request from a French journalist, Alphonse Esquiros, for an assessment. In this letter,[13] Mill isolates and comments on three principal reasons for his defeat: first, the great superiority in organization and competency of the Tories; affairs of this kind, Mill concedes, are ordinarily better run by a man of affairs than by a committee of amateurs; second, the vast amounts of money spent by the Tories; and third, the hostility of nearly all the vestrymen and other local men of prominence who usually are at the head of political action in the constituency, and who had been greatly displeased by his attempt to reform municipal government. Other causes contributed to his defeat, Mill says without giving particulars, but the three cited were alone sufficient to have brought him down. Later in the letter Mill generalizes at greater length about the role of money in the election nationally, mentioning that £1 million had been withdrawn from the Bank of England during the week preceding the election. Money has a threefold power in the existing circumstances: through actual corruption; by conferring political status, because men of money are seen as being the right kind for parliament; and by making it possible to canvass, advertise, set up local committees, see through the expensive business of registration, and hold public meetings.[14]

In a letter to George Grote written at about the same date, Mill gives the same three reasons as having been responsible. But here he is more open about other, to him less significant possible contributing causes, under the head of his "own rashness"—he is not repentant, it should be emphasized, for independence of action was, after all, a large part of his declared purpose in running. He mentions "Bradlaugh, Bouverie, &c.," though "greatly doubting" that his actions in relation to them were "at all accountable" for his defeat.[15] In other letters he mentions the first two of the reasons given to Esquiros—superior organization on the other side (or, in one case, "want of organization" on the side of Radicals generally), and "lavish expenditure" by the Tories.[16] He quite simply, in this period, passes by the Eyre case as irrelevant to the outcome of the election.

How did Mill explain his defeat in the *Autobiography*? It is fair to say,

13 It appeared in the *Morning Star*, as well as in Esquiros's article on the election of 1868 in the *Revue des deux mondes*.

14 *LL*, *CW*, vol. XVI, pp. 1495–7 [Dec. 1868].

15 Ibid., pp. 1501–2, 1 Dec. 1868.

16 Ibid., pp. 1493, 1512–13 (to Norton, 28 Nov. 1868, and Henry G. Mackson, 7 Dec. 1868).

first of all, that his account of his parliamentary years dwells less on his personal fortunes than on what he thought were his important contributions to the progress of his ideas, the radicalization of the Liberal party, and the parallel progress of advanced movements. And because of this bias, as well as normal human urges to self-justification, especially so soon after the event, the account must be read with some caution as lacking the high level of objectivity Mill usually strives for. However, his magisterial prose is not completely self-serving; it projects at least some disinterestedness—more, it seems just to say, than most people would be able to muster in the circumstances. After saying that it was not to his surprise or, he believes, to that of his principal supporters, that he was defeated, he enters into four reasons for that defeat, the first of which is only hinted at, and all four of which occupy only about two pages of the text.[17]

The first point, made obliquely, is that the failure to pass a strong anti-bribery bill in 1868 meant that "the practices which we sought to render more difficult prevailed more widely than ever in the first General Election held under the new electoral law." More explicitly: "an unscrupulous use of the usual pecuniary and other influences" was made "on the side of my Tory competitor while none were used on my side."

Mill's second point is that greater efforts were made by the Tories to defeat him in 1868, because the Tory government was struggling for existence and needed every seat, and because all Tories were far more embittered against him; whereas earlier some were indifferent and some had even been favourable to him (on the mistaken view that he was anti-democratic because he had wished to control the damaging effects of democracy), now all of them were vehemently opposed.

Third, the Liberals were less enthusiastic about him because he had concentrated on issues on which they differed from him or in which they had little interest. He had not been, as some obviously had expected him to be, a great organ for the party's opinion. He had, he recognized, "differed from most of the Liberal party" on the very issues for which he received most publicity—just those issues involving advanced radicals.

The fourth reason (which in Mill's account is rather entwined, one may say improperly, with the third) has to do with his having given offence by particular actions, two of which he mentions: "the persecution of Mr. Eyre," as his opponents called his behaviour in and through the Jamaica Committee, and, what he says gave "still greater offence," his subscription for Bradlaugh. He spends more space defending himself on the latter

17 *Autobiography* [A], in *Autobiography and Literary Essays*, ed. John M. Robson and Jack Stillinger, CW, I (Toronto: University of Toronto Press, 1981), pp. 288–90.

issue (though in his account of his parliamentary career he gives more space to the Eyre prosecution than to any other issue of any kind), and says that it was used both fairly and unfairly by his opponents in Westminster.

A conflation of Mill's accounts produces the following:

A) the opposition was stronger because
  1) without reference to Mill, they had
    a) more money
    b) better organization (not unconnected with their expenditures) and
    c) a strong inducement to win every available seat, and because
  2) with reference to Mill, they had
    a) discovered that while he was opposed to certain tendencies in democracy, he was a strong advocate of democracy, and
    b) gained vehement adherents as a result of some specific actions of his, particularly his behaviour with reference to Eyre and Bradlaugh.

B) his support was weaker, because he had
  1) not proved valuable to the Liberal party by taking on the issues they thought most important, and
  2) offended not only enemies but former adherents by his behaviour on particular occasions, such as his advocacy of municipal reform and his support for Chadwick against Bouverie.[18]

The question must be asked: Is this a reliable and satisfactory account?[19] It will be recalled that we used a sentence from his *Autobiography* as a way into the question: "That I should not have been elected at all would not have required any explanation; what excites curiosity is that I should have been elected the first time, or, having been elected then, should have been defeated afterwards." That sentence introduces his explanation in the *Autobiography*, which he concludes by saying, "To these various causes . . . it is to be ascribed that I failed at my second election after having succeeded at the first." One's "curiosity" having been excited by the question, is it satisfied with the explanation?

18 Perhaps one should be hesitant about that last matter, because it would appear that, on Mill's account, this offence might better be placed with his "crotchets," such as women's suffrage and proportional representation, as having in his view no significant effect on the outcome of the election of 1868.

19 A brief but sensible analysis of the reasons, with special reference to the Hyde Park riots, is found in Janice Carlisle, *John Stuart Mill and the Writing of Character* (Athens, Georgia: University of Georgia Press, 1991), pp. 273–8.

It is clear that, here at least, Mill underestimates the difference between the two elections. Not to be ignored are the differences nationally: the election of 1868, the first after the passing of the Second Reform Act, produced a Liberal majority, as was expected by most observers, but the "advanced" Liberals, especially those characterized as working-class representatives and university Liberals, took a heavy beating, and it might be thought that Mill's defeat was, as *The Times* implied, a special case of a more widespread phenomenon. However, some people both then and afterwards associated with Mill and his ideas were re-elected, and there seems good reason to think that had Mill succumbed to the entreaties of those who wished him to stand for another seat, he might well have been successful.

Putting these considerations to one side as at least apparently inconclusive, one may look at what differences there were locally, in the constituency itself, in the relative positions of the candidates and in the perception of Mill as a politician. First of all, there was a large increase in the number of voters, both potentially and actually. In the absence of poll-books, one cannot determine just how votes were cast, beyond the raw numbers. Certainly it was expected by the Liberals that the lodger vote would be favourable to them, and the battle over registration would appear to have swayed in their direction. Furthermore, *The Times* would seem to have been simply offering conventional wisdom in saying, after the fact, that the Liberals had an enormous plurality of support in Westminster, and that Mill was defeated because Liberals stayed away from the polls. This explanation is *prima facie* plausible. However, there is one difficult fact that needs accounting for. It will be recalled that Westminster had been well known long before 1865 as a Liberal stronghold, normally returning two Liberals without difficulty. After his defeat, Mill wrote to Amberley, expressing regret at the latter's defeat (in the Southern Division of Devonshire), and going on to say: ". . . I confess that though not mortified at present by my defeat in Westminster, I should be mortified if a Tory continues to represent Westminster, unless it should turn out that the Tories have a fair and genuine majority there, which I do not expect."[20] In the event, though he did not live to see it, his expectation was mistaken. At the next election in 1874, Grosvenor having retired, the contest was between two Liberals, Sir Fowell Buxton and W.J. Codrington, and two Tories, Smith and Sir Charles Russell. The Tories not only won both seats, but Russell's total vote, 8681, was 487 more than the combined vote of the two Liberals—a gap that surprised observers—and

20 *LL*, *CW*, vol. XVI, pp. 1494–5 (30 Nov. 1868).

Smith was very comfortably home at the top of the poll with 9371 votes. And subsequent elections confirmed that the political colour of the constituency had reversed. In 1885 Professor Edward Beesly, admittedly more Radical than Mill, ran in the Liberal interest and was badly defeated; his judgment was that "there is not a more hopeless seat in England."[21]

It would appear, then, that Westminster was no longer a safe Liberal seat in 1868.[22] Such an inference is also supported, albeit crudely, by looking at Grosvenor's votes as compared to Mill's and Smith's. In 1865, it will be recalled, Grosvenor and Mill had almost exactly the same total, with Grosvenor just edging Mill out for the top of the poll, while Smith trailed them by some 700 votes. In a constituency where the voters had two votes to elect two members, and where there is so little evidence of other kinds about how the electors actually voted,[23] percentages are opaque evidence, to say the most; however, since those conditions did not change between the two elections, and the same three candidates, and they alone, ran in both, there is some point in the arithmetic. In 1865, then, Grosvenor and Mill each received about 35 per cent of the votes cast, while Smith received just under 30 per cent. In 1868, with more than 7000 additional votes cast, Grosvenor, who now led Mill by about 300, trailed Smith by over 1000; Smith received over 37 per cent, Grosvenor about 32 per cent, and Mill just over 30 per cent. It is of course ridiculous to assume that all the voters of 1865 voted again in 1868, and voted again exactly as they had in 1865, or (to put the matter in another way) that the difference between the candidates' individual totals in 1865 and 1868 is a reflection of "new" votes; nonetheless the figures indicate that a majority of new voters can hardly have voted for Mill in 1868, unless his support in 1865 had been almost totally eroded, when one observes that Smith's total in 1868 was some 3800 higher than in 1865, while Grosvenor's went up about 2000 and Mill's only about 1750. What may be detected here, as already indicated, is illustrated by the two totals for Grosvenor in relation to the totals for the others: while his association with Mill may have cost him

21 And his explanation has a familiar ring: "We might have made head against [Westminster's] Toryism alone, or the clergy, or the Baroness's legitimate influence from her alms-giving of old date there (it being her special preserve), or the special tap of philanthropy turned on for the occasion. But all united were much too strong for us. . . . I return to my work in much contentment." Quoted in Michael Millgate, ed., *The Life and Work of Thomas Hardy* (London: Macmillan, 1989 [1984]), p. 175.

22 It may not have been safe even in 1865, as Grimston implied, though likely the change in the constituency had not become evident, if it had begun, before 1868, with the new registrations.

23 For what evidence there is about the election of 1865, see appendix A.

some support in 1868, that association, so far as Mill's extremism and crotchets were concerned, was minimal, and Grosvenor's percentage loss, and his failure (in a constituency where his family name and connections were still strong in 1868, and he was far better known than he had been) to make anything like Smith's gain, suggests that indeed the constituency was moving—indeed had moved—a long way from being the stronghold of Radicalism or even Liberalism. It may also be inferred that both Tories' and Liberals' expectations of the lodgers' views were mistaken to some extent: Mill's support for the "working classes" probably did not have an overwhelming appeal for the army of clerks who were trying to make their way in a new world.

Still with reference to the constituency, one must heed the matter to which Mill calls attention—the opposition of the vestrymen and others to his proposals for reform of the government of the Metropolis. It is difficult to come up with hard evidence one way or the other, but there is little reason to doubt Mill's assessment; certainly Smith was anxious to indicate during the campaign that he was opposed to the reform, and such opposition was unlikely to be fortuitous. There is, moreover, the matter of Mill's persistent refusal to see himself as responsible for local concerns, except such as were consonant with other issues for which he was struggling. (It is true that, as he recognized, metropolitan reform was a local issue, but evidently was not a strong vote-catcher in Westminster.) His active presentation of petitions was not specially related to Westminster issues. Smith, however, in his speeches made consistent reference to local issues, and presented himself (as Grosvenor did as well, especially in 1865) as wishing to represent all those in the constituency—Mill was, in his own eyes, a general representative of minority opinions of various kinds and of the unenfranchised, and not of the electors of Westminster; indeed he may properly be seen as the kind of representative who would be electable under proportional representation, but not under the actual voting system.

Finally one comes to Mill's own opinions and actions, and the way in which the electors may have perceived those opinions and actions. It is in the area of opinion that one can see why Mill would be likely to perceive less difference between the two elections than others would, and on other grounds. For he was, certainly within normal human limits, consistent during this period. He in fact published little new—as he said, his devotion to the business of parliament was such that he could write only during the recesses, and what he published, with the exception of *England and Ireland*, was far less controversial or indeed political than most of his later writings: the most significant productions (very important in his corpus on other grounds) were his very long review of Grote's *Plato* and his resonant *Inaugural Address at St. Andrews.* He had, to his satisfaction, given the electorate a very comprehensive account of his views long before 1865, and he constantly referred those who wished to know his opinions to his great works. But, without going into a silly counting of numbers of copies published as against the number of electors, it should be evident enough that most residents of Westminster, Liberals or not, voters or not, supporters of Mill or not, had not and did not in those years read his books at all, let alone with care and attention. Those politically active, and the electorate generally (not the same bodies, of course), would know Mill's opinions largely through what they read in the press and heard from their fellows. And what they read and heard there and then were the opinions he was reported as uttering in the Commons and at public meetings. While his books sold more widely during and after 1865 than before, their circulation could not match that of the daily papers, and their extended and qualified arguments could not compete for easy accessibility with simplified journalistic representations.

We have seen what were presented to the public as Mill's opinions. First of all, some were directly related to his view of the duties, functions, and behaviour of a member of parliament. These were given wide notice during the campaign of 1865 and, in the circumstances then, would appear to have had a favourable effect. What he stood for was purity in elections: a notion attractive enough at any time, at least in the abstract, and more attractive, because of greater corruption, then than now. There can be little doubt that his absence from the field of battle was annoying to many; hardly anyone can have actually been pleased by his behaviour in this respect, however much they may have been impressed by the principle when expressed without reference to their own desire to see and question a candidate. However, there was a major offset in the first election against whatever weakness this olympianism may have caused in the campaign: both his opponents were untried and little known. Mill was shown—and seen—as a man of international stature, to be compared with lightweights, who had to scurry around looking for support. The appeal of the unknown is often strong, but the appeal of the unknown great man is stronger still. Grosvenor, yes, but which Grosvenor? one can imagine the elector saying in 1865. And Smith? he would ask, and not bother asking which one, or, if he knew, dismiss him as a mere bookseller. But Mill—yes, it would be a personal disgrace not to know, or rather to be known not to know, who he was. And when he did appear in the constituents' midst, there was all the excitement of his formerly denied presence to overwhelm any annoyance.

In the second election, however, there were differences: Grosvenor had to some extent established himself on his own merits, and Smith, though there were Liberal attempts still to denigrate him, had more experience and more of what is now called exposure. He was showing a concern for local interests, he was a local businessman, and he was on the spot. To point out this fact is not to suggest that Mill's absence during the months before the second election directly caused him much harm, but rather that it did not do him any good, as his first abstention may have, and that his Tory opponent was, this time, making ground the while.

It may also be inferred that Mill's principled refusal to spend any of his money, or to canvass, did not win him any new votes in 1868, though again he may not on this ground have lost many old ones. Once more the value of his views' novelty (which was not unexampled, in fact) had disappeared, and they were no longer newsworthy. One wonders whether some of the electors might not even have known that he had such principles, and may have wondered where he and his money might be. The satirical magazines in fact picked up this thread: *Fun* supplied a squib, "Mill's Political Economy:—Expecting the electors to pay the expenses,"[24] while *Tomahawk* chimed in with

From Avignon to Westminster
Journeyed omniscient Mill,
Whose lucky fate 'tis to be great—
His friends', to pay the bill.[25]

In thinking of his opinions, then, one should not attempt to assess the appeal of his *Principles of Political Economy*, his *System of Logic*, his *On Liberty*, or even his *Considerations on Representative Government*, except

24 *Fun*, 28 Nov. 1868, p. 116. Compare *Judy*, 16 Sept. 1868, p. 202, where it is implied that Mill's refusal to pay his own campaign expenses ignobly shifted the cost onto others.

25 "The Ballad of the Beaten," 5 Dec. 1868, p. 247, in which the defeats of Odger, Bradlaugh, Beales, Dickson, and Chadwick, "Mill's joy and pride," are also celebrated. Not only opponents but close allies evidently worried about Mill's insistence on not spending any of his own money. Harriet Grote wrote to Kate Amberley on 20 December 1868: "Mill's cardinal mistake was, the sturdy refusal to contribute towards the exps. of the election in any form. The next, his pecuniary support of Bradlaugh. These two, coupled together were, in my view, fatal to his election." She goes on to confirm what is obvious from other evidence: "Miss Taylor is even more elate [*sic*] than Mill himself, at their recovered liberty! She writes in positively gleeful tone about it." *Amberley Papers*, ed. Bertrand and Patricia Russell, 2 vols. (London: Hogarth, 1937), vol. II, p. 251.

insofar—and it is not very far—as particular notions were aired publicly, or may be inferred to have been aired in the canvassing. The public airing includes, of course, his speeches and actions while in the House of Commons, and without doubt the three items that caught most public attention, and—at least in the case of two of them—Mill intended to catch maximum attention, were his support for women's suffrage and for proportional representation, and his opposition to the secret ballot, though he made little reference to it in the House. These, as we have seen, were called his "crotchets," and he thought they had little effect on his defeat. He does not say, it should be noted, that they did anything to win him votes.

It is hard to summarize in brief compass the effect of the first of these items on nineteenth-century sensibilities without being silly or smug. Mill's views, if not yet quite triumphant, certainly are far closer to received opinion now than they were a century ago, so much so that it often causes surprise when one mentions that Mill moved in his amendment of 1867 that the word "person" replace the word "man" in the Reform Act, just as, in virtually all cases of dubious import, it had already replaced "man" in his major writings. Our judgment, unhedged with proper explanations and qualifications, is that Mill was right in thinking that his advocacy, much as it amused and annoyed the press, had little effect on his electoral chances, because almost no one (and those few mostly his supporters) thought votes for women at all likely to result from the campaign. The general attitude is probably caught, once again, when, in describing the testimonial presentation to Smith after the dismissal of the bribery and treating case, *The Times* mentions the presence of many ladies "from whom Mr. Smith appears to have secured their prospective rights of the franchise."[26] In short, a dismissive joke was adequate to the case, and Mill's crotchet was no more than a crotchet in the public eye.

Much the same holds for proportional representation, though the jokes were not thought to be so good. The main criticisms were based on the supposed or real complications in the machinery of Hare's proposal, some of the later views of its general inapplicability to modern politics (such as the apparent incompatibility of its goals with party electoral practices) not then being raised. Whatever the justice of these criticisms, they indicate well enough that the proposal was one of those that find a very difficult road into public understanding because of their apparent complexity and real novelty. Once again, then, one may judge that Mill's championship of the scheme would continue to endear him to those who

26 *The Times*, 9 April 1869, p. 7.

were already enamoured, and have little actual effect on the number of votes he received.

The third of his crotchets was somewhat differently perceived. In opposing the ballot, Mill was of course arguing against the firm convictions not only of most of his closest allies and of his running mate, but also of his own teachers and early associates, and even against his strongly expressed opinion in his first maturity. It is amusing, but probably not very instructive, to quote the opinion of John Bowring, one of the last of the old Westminster Radicals, who had supported, it will be recalled, Mill's candidacy in 1865. Writing to Chadwick in December 1868 to offer condolences on his defeat at Kilmarnock, and commenting that Mill's "kindly interference has been mischievous to himself and his friends," Bowring adds:

> If in his own case his supporters were to *ballot*, he would find himself in a fearful minority in Westminster itself. I remember Francis Place saying that if James Mill could have anticipated that his son John Stuart should broach so abominable a heresy as the advocacy of open suffrage, he "would have cracked his skull." In the passage you quote I see a gleam of hope for the future: when he speaks of "the ballot as the possible smaller evil." I do not believe (which I regret to own) that he will ever be returned to Parliament, while the ballot question remains unsettled.[27]

Whatever Bowring thought, Mill was on this issue falling into line with the equally strongly held views of much of the electorate and certainly of a majority of MPs.[28] On this topic, too, it will be recalled, Smith was on the same side as Mill—but he was trying to gain Tory votes, not to retain Radical ones. It seems likely that only someone like Berkeley (who was on Grosvenor's committee in 1865), whose major political interest was in the ballot, might not have voted for Mill just because of this issue, and even then one must recall that George Grote, who had been its principal advocate for years in parliament, was able to support Mill in spite of this heresy. Important as the issue was, therefore, it does not seem that here too there were, for Mill, many votes in it one way or the other.

Finally, about all these crotchets one must say that they were there in 1865 as well as in 1868, and they were thoroughly aired on the former

27 Letter of 23 Dec. 1868. University College London [UCL], Chadwick MSS, 355, ff. 1–3.

28 See Bruce L. Kinzer, *The Ballot Question in Nineteenth-Century English Politics* (New York: Garland, 1982).

occasion. It is true, however, that through Mill's efforts—and he is self-congratulatory about how successful his efforts were—the first two had become much better known throughout the country between 1865 and 1868, and there were many new electors in 1868 to express their views for or against through their votes. And so it is possible—though we do not have the evidence—that specific electors, especially new electors, saw some or all of these crotchets as sufficient reason to oppose Mill. More likely, however, the effect was more subtle: because Mill had particularly taken upon himself the advocacy in parliament of the first two of these, women's suffrage and proportional representation, and had not strongly identified himself with the main body of Liberal politicians and platforms—his trimming his sails during the Liberal stormy passages could not be observed outside his own head—he was likely known to many of the electorate in 1868 just as a man of enthusiasms, given to lost causes, and not very comfortable as an associate. While by themselves these stands by Mill would not have led to his defeat in 1868, and probably, again by themselves, had little to do with his election in 1865, they were differently perceived in the two elections and had their effect by their consonance with other perceptions. In 1865 they would be seen as interesting, if perhaps not totally sound, examples of the thought of the leading political theorist of the time, and examples that one wanted to know something more about. There was no chance that either of his untried and largely unknown opponents would confront the electors with different views of comparable authority and greater persuasiveness. In 1868, however, these opinions might well appear as the consuming passions of a man who would be better employed in considering the central problems facing the country. And, worse, they were associated in the public mind with specific actions during his tenure of office that made him appear even more a man of unwise enthusiasms.

These actions encompass six other matters that then received attention and merit it still: Mill's apparent advocacy of critics of General Napier, his support for the Irish, his intervention in the Kilmarnock election, his subscription for Bradlaugh, his connection with the radicalism of the working classes, and his part in the Eyre prosecution. These were all broadly publicized at the time, all but the second played a part directly in the election campaign of 1868, and all but the first and third are dealt with in the *Autobiography* (though two of them are not treated by Mill as instrumental in his defeat).

The first of these items is the most trivial, but is interesting in that it could be used as a text for a sermon on Mill's parliamentary career. He asserted that he presented the petition from Macclesfield against Napier simply as a matter of principle, believing that the practice of petitioning was very important, while dissenting himself from the point of view of the petitioners. But of course most petitions are presented by persons who are sympathetic to their aims, and indeed Mill's own presentation of petitions in favour of women's suffrage was accompanied by an amendment strongly supportive of them. So it is hardly surprising that the Conservatives would attempt to associate him with the unpopular minority who were running against the growing support for heroes and for imperialism. Mill, of course, defended himself in public, asserting his support for Napier's action in Abyssinia, and explaining his attitude towards petitioning, and it seems likely that once again there was little electoral mileage in the issue. But what little there was the Tories would benefit from, because it appeared that Mill had adopted an unpatriotic stance.

Mill's attitude towards Ireland need not be summarized in detail. What should now be recalled is that here one can see a most unusual example of Mill's taking thought and even advice about the dangers of what appeared to be extreme advocacy. During his first days in the House of Commons he voted and spoke on Irish affairs as though he did not know what everyone knows—that to do so is to move into a bog whence no politician can hope to emerge clean, let alone bright-shining as a star. He was advised by Roebuck, through Chadwick, to keep quiet until a favourable opportunity arose during which he might redeem himself from the opprobrium into which he had so quickly fallen, and he took the advice.[29] Mill recovered and indeed developed his stature in the House, but he continued publicly to show an interest in Irish affairs, particularly in land reform and the Fenians, that can hardly have done him much good in his own constituency. Did it do him much harm? Again there is little evidence. Among fanatical Protestants, and Westminster was not free from them, anyone expressing concern for the Irish masses was likely to be thought a Papist. Or it may more sensibly be said, almost anyone, for Mill surely was not thought to be a covert Catholic. However, hatred for the Irish was at least a strong undercurrent in all classes, and Mill's support for radical Irish views, and what could be construed as support even for radical Irish actions, would mark him as unsound among many who based their political creeds on prejudice rather than on reason—and we all know how highly the shrewd Walter Bagehot would rate that proportion of the electorate. These were the years of the Fenian bombings

29 Roebuck, it may be recalled, was vainly trying to repair the rent torn in their friendship thirty years earlier by his advice that Mill should show caution in his relations with Harriet Taylor. Roebuck was usually a man for caution—and ever for advice.

and the Murphy riots. And so, once again, his attitudes on the Irish question would not win him votes in Westminster,[30] and would undoubtedly have lost him some.

What finally can be said of his intervention in Kilmarnock in support of Chadwick? In Liberal eyes, the intervention was less in support of Chadwick than in opposition to Bouverie. Mill would not have bothered himself to oppose Bouverie, much as he disliked him, had it not been for the chance he perceived, or wished to perceive, for Chadwick, whose faults as a potential parliamentarian Mill knew as well as anyone, but whose virtues he ranked more highly than anyone (certainly more highly than did Chadwick's wife, who bitterly assailed Mill for his part in encouraging Chadwick to seek a seat). To the public, we suspect, the stain on Mill was twofold: he was a meddler and he was vindictive. This was at least the line taken by the press. It is likely that in general it was not Mill's meddling that was specially offensive, but the objects of his meddling. Had he confined himself to Gladstone, he would not have been seen as a meddler—did not many a Tory, from Disraeli to William Russell, support the candidacy of Smith, without the slightest hint of opprobrium? And there are countless other examples on both sides. But Mill had the bad habit of recommending Liberal candidates in constituencies where, in most eyes, there were already suitable and sufficient Liberal candidates. In this way, his support for Chadwick could be seen as just a particularly egregious example of his dangerous—to established Liberal interests—habit of offering support to working-class candidates such as Odger, even though Chadwick was not of that class. Mill's support for Fawcett against Coningham probably did his own campaign no good, and may have caused some slight harm as a result of the publicity given Coningham's vicious response;[31] his support for Gladstone in Greenwich probably helped slightly to establish him as a staunch Liberal supporter, and was, of course, of a piece with his explanation that Bouverie was dispensable because he had attacked Gladstone. There can be little doubt, we believe, that, specifically, his intervention in Kilmarnock did him some harm in right-Liberal circles, at least to the extent of lessening their enthusiasm for him (their number might include some of the Liberals who just did not bother to vote in 1868), and that, generally, this intervention was seen as an instance of his unwanted meddling, caused by a lack of common sense.

30 Except to the limited extent that there was support for Irish Disestablishment, which Mill certainly concurred in, though he was not willing to devote time or energy to a cause ably presented by others.

31 See chapter 7, p. 253 above.

His subscription for Bradlaugh was, it seems, even more damaging. First, and least importantly, it was yet a further instance of meddling. Second, it was an example of his favouring persons with dangerous political ideas; that is, even accepting Mill's defence that he was concerned only with Bradlaugh's political views, he was advocating near-revolutionary proposals of the far left. Third, and far and away most importantly, Mill was supporting, whatever his attempts to disguise the matter, an advocate of immorality and atheism. Once again there is no direct evidence proving that Bradlaugh's and Mill's Neo-Malthusianism were used against Mill in the election of 1868. But it is hard to believe that, given the conjunction in both men of advanced feminist views with advocacy of birth control, there was no mention by the canvassers of what would most assuredly be electoral dynamite among the male working classes, a large proportion of whom were capable of extreme derision and crudity in response. The only impulse to think that it might not have been used arises from the thought that the other issue was itself strong enough: atheism was also a sufficient charge to blow a candidate off the polls. And it was used. Mill, of course, was quick to point out that it had been used in 1865 and, in fact, because of the support he was able in 1865 to gather, it is possible that then, rather than losing him votes, the crude accusation—for such it was in the *Record* and the *Morning Advertiser*—faced as it was with the brave nobility of the passage from Mill's *Examination of Sir William Hamilton's Philosophy* and the exalted language of praise from clerics, actually gained him support. The situation in 1868 was different. Mill continued to practise reserve, refusing to comment on his own religious opinions, but this time he was not expressing admirable, if controversial, sentiments on a moral-theological matter, he was offering financial support to the campaign of an avowed and outspoken atheist—and he was not surrounded by a crowd of defensive and holy witnesses. If it was difficult to believe that someone would present petitions, like the Magdala one, which he did not support, how much more difficult was it to believe that someone would support the election of a person whose most blatant opinions one found abhorrent? Furthermore, in supporting Bradlaugh, Mill appeared not simply to be expressing opinions but engaging in a campaign against religion, for that was what "Iconoclast" himself was doing and seen to be doing. And the propagandizing was, it must be remembered, directed most definitely to the working classes, in conjunction with revolutionary political ideas and destructive moral ideas.

The Bradlaugh affair is connected not only with the Chadwick-Bouverie episode, but also with the fifth of the actions here under

PUBLISHED BY BEMROSE & SONS, 21. PATERNOSTER ROW. COPYRIGHT.

THE WESTMINSTER GUY.

consideration—Mill's advocacy for the working classes. While he was active in several ways, the one that had most occupied the public mind was the role he played during the crisis over the Hyde Park riots. Then, it will be recalled, he claimed apparently with justice that he had intervened with the Reform League to prevent a confrontation between the authorities and the working classes that might have led to bloodshed and revolt. But once more the public interpretation was undoubtedly somewhat different from Mill's and probably less in concurrence with the facts of the matter. To simplify greatly, it may be suggested baldly that he was seen as an ally of the Reform League extremists and not as a moderating force who did not even belong to the League. His name, after all, was linked with Beales's in *The Times* editorial on the results of the 1868 election, as illustrating the fate of extreme men. No particular measures needed to be mentioned: the tar and brush were ready for those who were seen to push policies beyond the mean, beyond measure, beyond what was needed for reform. And Mill was so seen.

And not only that: he was also vindictive and shrill. Here one comes to the final action of the six—the Eyre trials. There were those such as Carlyle, not insignificant in number or stature, who supported Eyre's behaviour in all respects and who would have no sympathy and only contempt and hatred for Mill. These he knew of, for they delivered private and public attacks of the most savage kind. But there were also those—probably many, some of whom supported Mill on other issues—who found fault with some aspects of Eyre's behaviour, who even wished him to some extent to be punished, but who thought that public disgrace was quite enough in the way of retributive justice, and could not countenance the attempts of the Jamaica Committee to bring Eyre before the dock on a charge of murder. Even Charles Buxton, instrumental in the first formation of the committee, backed off when the policy began to be formulated and, though he certainly never relinquished his detestation of Eyre, would not associate himself with what was seen as vindictiveness and unreasonable rage. Among the electorate generally one may reasonably believe there was a revulsion from Mill's position, a revulsion of a kind often seen in similar circumstances. So far as we have seen, the only actually recorded reason given by an inconspicuous and newly enfranchised voter for not giving his vote to Mill was his attitude to Eyre, and there is no hint whatsoever of Mill's gaining votes by his stand.[32] He was, of course, totally convinced of his rectitude in the matter—and judgment about the principle behind his actions is irrelevant to the

32 See *The Times*'s report of the Smith bribery inquiry.

questions here asked—but given the amount of space he gives to explanation in the *Autobiography*, he knew that some defence was necessary. His near silence about the issue during the campaign itself suggests not that it had no importance, but that even he realized that no defence was likely to be effective in the circumstances, beyond that already given by the committee's publications and by his own speeches in the House.

In summation, then, Mill was not totally candid with himself about, and perhaps was unable clearly to see, the effects of his actions on his election chances. One reason for his inability to see fully has only been hinted at: while it does not seem right to suggest that he wished to be defeated in the election of 1868, it may be less wrong to suggest that he did not wish wholeheartedly to be elected. When still in Avignon before returning for the election in 1865, he had written to Hare about his reading in preparation for his review of Grote's *Plato*, saying: "I do not find that this by any means quickens my zeal in my own cause, as a candidate. It is an infinitely pleasanter mode of spending May to read the Gorgias and Theaetetus under the avenue of mulberries which you know of, surrounded by roses and nightingales, than it would be to listen to tiresome speaking for half the night in the House of Commons."[33]

While Mill's letters to Helen Taylor immediately after his defeat are not known, two of hers from Avignon to him surely embody what they both genuinely felt, as well as revealing much about their relations. The first, written on Thursday evening of the election week, begins:

> Dear Mr. Mill— How I wish you were not obliged to stay all these tedious days at Blackheath! I want you to be here that we may enjoy together the strange feeling of liberty and respose; instead of which you are surrounded by circumstances which bring forward all the disagreeable side of the Westminster failure—all the excitements and interests of party politics. I have just got the "Temps" from which I learn the result in the City and West[r], although of this last I have of course felt certain since I got your letter this morning. If I thought you would feel the result as a disappointment on the whole, I should so wish to be with you—indeed I think I should start off to meet you; only then I think you would laugh at me, not for sympathising with you but for supposing you could dislike the result!. . . How I wish you were here! I shall be so impatient till you arrive! and now today it is

33 *LL*, *CW*, vol. XVI, pp. 1060–1 (29 May 1865).

divinest Avignon weather; the Ventoux streaked with sparkling snow; the air warm and balmy the sky intensely blue, the after-glow its most glorious. And then the two pussies seem to mew for you to come and admire them.[34]

The second, a day later, is equally revealing:

Dear Mr. Mill— your letter this morning is a great comfort to me, for it seems to imply a feeling of relief, such as I myself feel this morning. Yesterday I felt chiefly the public aspect of the event; and did not get to sleep till four o'clock this morning for turning it all over in my mind. I slept soundly and waking this morning asked myself what had happened that made me feel so well and happy; it took me sometime to remember; and yet I had gone to sleep feeling it a disappointment! It is a bright morning and I cannot say how I long for you to be here to enjoy it. . . .

I am clear that you are not in any way to blame for the defeat. It is owing to the strength of the tories wielded now by D'Israeli a man who knows how to use his weapons, and your letter has removed the only anxiety I felt this morning—respecting Gladstone. There will be a deal for us to talk over as to all these things. . . . We have leisure for everything now![35]

To this account must be added Mill's genuine doubt whether he was not of more use to the causes he so ardently believed in as a writer than as a politician;[36] since the newspapers had made this judgment also, and unequivocally, after his defeat, his account in the *Autobiography* should be read in the light of that consideration—nothing has changed in my

34 Mill-Taylor Collection, British Library of Political and Economic Science, London School of Economics, vol. LIII, no. 56.

35 Ibid., no. 57.

36 In the letter last quoted, Helen Taylor refers to one she had received from Caroline Lindley reporting on Mill's reaction to the declaration of the poll. In it Lindley says that Mill said to her and her brother that "never for the sake of preserving his seat would he abstain from doing that which he felt his duty just the same as if he had not been in parliament at all." She went on to say: ". . . I will picture you in your sacred home and see you welcome your Father there. . . . Be sure our Helen that it is quite impossible for us to dream you are wanting in public spirit—no, you feel for us deeply in our loss [Mill's defeat]—most knowing *all* we lose—but, you also feel Mr. Mill may, and we anxiously hope will, be able to do much out of the House of Commons, when he quietly and healthfully enjoys your oneness with him in your home." Ibid., vol. XXII, no. 438; 19 Nov. 1868.

attitudes and those are foolish who think there has been a change; so, while it is possible to understand why I was defeated, there is no reason for regret, and so no reason for serious self-examination. And, finally, his reluctance must be associated with his relation with Helen Taylor. She suffered his tenure "nobly," he once said, and "heroically," he said again, for she sacrificed ease and health for his career, as she let him know. Since she, like her mother, was virtually always right in his eyes, her willingness to see him defeated, and her insistence on his upholding his principles, contributed materially if not measurably to his own attitude, and hence to his defeat.

What, then, is the conclusion? In the first place, Mill underestimated greatly the differences between the two elections. It was in fact not surprising that he was elected in 1865. Such a shrewd observer as Lord John Russell said in June 1865: "I expect Mill to come in for Westminster, and tho' I am far from agreeing with him, I think he is too distinguished a man to be rejected."[37] If a public perception can be summarized, it lies there in Russell's statement. But in November 1868 things were very different: far more people were further from agreeing with Mill, and he was not seen as too distinguished a man to be rejected; the mystery had evaporated in the parliamentary limelight. National considerations had some effect on the Westminster election, but more important were local ones and the comparative perception of the candidates. Mill could not see, as no one saw clearly at the time, that the constituency itself was moving to the right. What had been seen as admirable if odd distancing from the heat of the battle in 1865 was now seen as odd and perhaps insulting. But both on this ground, and on that of consistency of principle, Mill was unaware of much change. His adversary was better prepared, and better known, in the second election, and his money and organization were put to better effect; as an offset, Mill was from the outset in 1868 running with, not against, his Liberal colleague, Grosvenor: however, the alliance in 1865 had been forged in time, and both committees then were insisting that plumping was wrong, just as they did in 1868. Grosvenor too was better known in 1868 than he had been in 1865, but it would be difficult to argue that his family's position was more advantageous than, or perhaps even as advantageous as, it had been on his first attempt. There apparently was a swing towards the Conservative side in Westminster but, even given that swing, there would appear not to have been any non-individual reason for Grosvenor to do better than Mill in 1868—yet he did. The reason would appear not to lie in Mill's crotchets,

37 *Amberley Papers*, vol. I, p. 394.

nor even in any one of his individual acts, repugnant as many of them were to certain sections of the electorate, but in the cumulative effect, in the way his behaviour as a whole was perceived.

There was in Britain then—and not only then, and not only in Britain—a prejudice against men of theory, a prejudice that Mill himself had identified and repeatedly written against. In 1865 some of his supporters had been eager to point out that someone with his experience in the India House could not be thought of as without practical experience, and he himself advanced this argument tellingly in the *Autobiography*. However, he did have some doubts about his capacity: one of the most revealing analyses he ever engaged in was his discussion of the Art and Science of life, in which, when personal instances were involved, he saw himself as the Scientist, the abstract reasoner, rather than, like his wife and his step-daughter, the Artist, the doer. And his whole interpretation of his usefulness in or out of the House of Commons bears on his self-doubts. In any case, the press and the public were only too willing to assert that he had made a mistake in thinking that he was wise in practice, whatever he might be in theory. The proof, in their eyes, was seen in what they perceived as his extremism, his flight from calm consideration to hasty impulse, his unwillingness to compromise, his single vision. All this made him a danger to the polity, at a time when there were threats enough. A step towards democracy had been made with the Reform Act of 1867, a mad step, in the eyes of such as Carlyle for whom it was "Shooting Niagara," but at all events a large enough one for the moment. Let us see our way, before making another, was the broad mood. And into it Mill did not fit easily.

Taking all into account, then, it seems likely that, given the money and organization of the Tories, and the tendency towards the right in Westminster, Smith would probably have won a seat in 1868, no matter what Mill had done in the intervening years and during the campaign.[38]

38 It is unlikely that Mill thought of applying to his own case what he had written in 1859, but anyone with a taste for quiet irony will appreciate its relevance: "A member who had already served in Parliament with any distinction, would under [Hare's] system be almost sure of his re-election. At present the first man in the house may be thrown out of Parliament when most wanted, and may be kept out for several years, from no fault of his own, but because a change has taken place in the local balance of parties, or because he has voted against the prejudices or local interest of some influential portion of his constituents. Under Mr. Hare's system, if he has not deserved to be thrown out, he will be nearly certain to obtain votes from other places, sufficient, with his local strength, to make up the quota of

However, it seems also plausible that, had Mill taken a middle Liberal line during those years, pursuing his crotchets but also taking his place in the central ranks—where he could have been accommodated—and had he not chanced his arm on Eyre and Bradlaugh, he would have himself been the other member for Westminster, heading Grosvenor—and perhaps even Smith. But, of course, he would not then have been a moralist in or out of parliament; he would not have been John Stuart Mill.

2000 (or whatever the number may be) necessary for his return to Parliament." *Essays on Politics and Society*, ed. John M. Robson, CW, vols. XVIII–XIX (Toronto: University of Toronto Press, 1977), vol. XIX, p. 363.

Appendix A

Polling by District in Westminster, 1865 from *Mr. J.S. Mill and Westminster: The Story of the Westminster Election, 1865*, pp. 19–21

[Though there are no known pollbooks for either election, Mill's committee kept a detailed record of the voting in the districts of the constituency in 1865, reporting it in these terms:]

TABLE 1

District or Parish	Mill	Grosvenor	Smith	Majority Mill	Majority Smith
St. Anne's	226	209	147	79	–
St. Clement's	170	159	378	–	208
St. Mary-le-Strand	26	23	35	–	9
Savoy	8	9	16	–	8
St. Paul's	92	78	104	–	12
St. George's Inwards	514	556	554	–	40
St. George's Outwards	1202	1217	921	281	–
St. James's	727	698	647	80	–
St. Margaret's Ward No. 1	133	140	99	34	–
St. Margaret's Wards 2 & 3	306	335	280	26	–
St. Peter's	3	3	5	–	2
St. John's	762	762	279	483	–
St. Martin's	356	345	359	–	3
Total	4525	4534	3824	983	282
				282	
		Gross majority		701	

These returns are very instructive, as showing the geographical political areas of Westminster. Mr. Mill, in a majority in St. Anne's, a densely packed but small area, with numerous disfranchisements for non-payment of rates, was in a minority in St. Clement's Danes, Savoy,

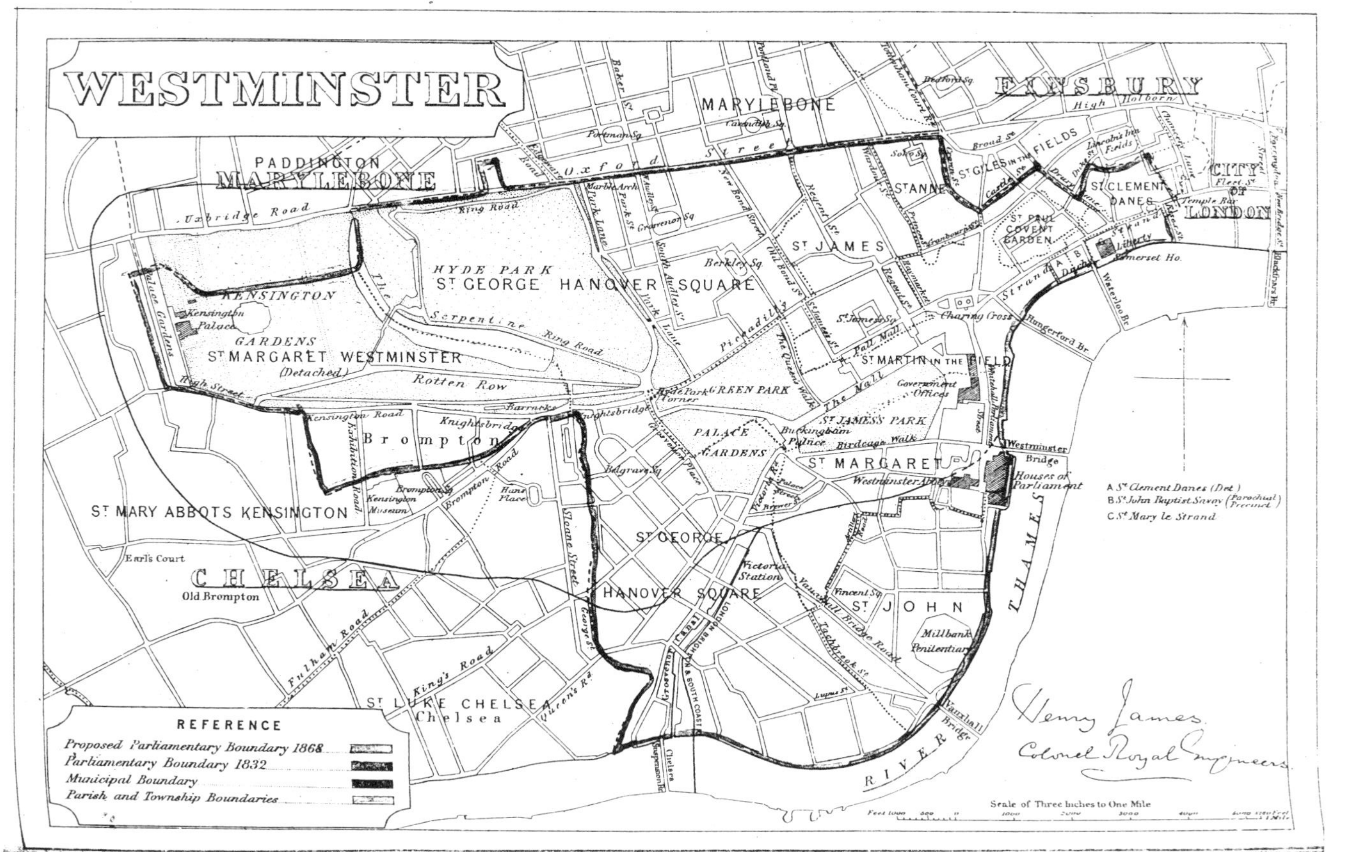

Parliamentary Papers, 1867–8, Vol. xx, p. 748

St. Paul's Covent-garden, and St. Mary; there Mr. Smith was thoroughly known and appreciated as a tradesman and neighbour. Old Liberals were found voting for the Conservative. Mr. Lewis, of the Strand district board, an old Liberal and leader of the district, was an ally of the Conservatives. It was here that the personal influence of Mr. Beggs, Mr. Storr, Mr. Ellis, Mr. Horton, contributed to the polling, even to the extent apparent. St. Martin's was a keen contest, giving to the Conservatives a majority of three only, whilst St. George's Outward and St. John's, in which are hives of industry, factories and breweries, despite the efforts of Mr. Carter Wood and Mr. Elliot, respected Conservatives and large employers of labour, gave the most decided and emphatic majority, giving the victory its real significance, defeat being barely held at bay in other districts of the borough.

The returns show that a considerable number of Liberals split with Smith, but few of the Tory supporters of the latter returned the compliment with either Grosvenor or Mill; though more so with the latter than the former. The attention of the Tories to the manufacturing of votes is shown by the polling of Lord Ranelagh, the Hon. R. Bourke, C.J. Chetwynd, Talbot, Newnham, and Winstanley for Smith, all on the qualification of 33, Norfolk-street (offices of the Conservative Land Society). Lawrence Palk, though qualified on the same rating, did not vote. The following distinguished and well-known names appear on the polling-books in favour of Smith: Mr. Disraeli, Lord Chichester, Lord William Godolphin Osborne, General Peel, Sir W. William Wynn, Dean Wordsworth, the Hon. and Rev. Lord Thynne, Sir E. Antrobus, and the four well-known members of the Trollope family. The name of Carbonnel, the great West-end wine merchant, appears in the same category.

For Mill and Grosvenor we find the following distinguished names recorded: Sir A. Cockburn, Chief Justice of England; Barons Anthony and Meyer Rothschild, Viscount Enfield, the Right Hon. W.E. Gladstone, and Albany Fonblanque. It is also worthy of notice that Mr. Higgins, the "Jacob Omnium" of the *Times*, plumped for Mr. Mill. Another Mr. Higgins, the son-in-law of Lord Chelmsford, plumped for Mr. Smith.

Taking St. James's vestry as a specimen of the parochial mind and voting on this election, we find that out of 50 voters, 15 voted for Mill and Grosvenor, 7 for Grosvenor and Smith, 1 for Mill and Smith, and 4 plumped for Grosvenor. The rest of the 50 did not vote. Lords Cosmo Russell and Huntingtower plumped for Grosvenor, as also did Mr. Agar Robertes. The Drummonds, as a rule, split their votes between Grosvenor and Smith. It is further a singular fact that the well-known city Liberal, Mr. George Moore, voted for Grosvenor and Smith.

We have to report some neutrals that, from their character and position, might have been expected to vote, but did not. Charles Dickens, the popular novelist, is a qualified elector, but he did not put in an appearance on the day of the poll. This was also the case with the Biddulphs, the Berkeleys, Sir J.V. Shelley, Sir S.M. Peto, and the Broadwoods. There are other interesting items illustrative of the action of parties in this electoral *mêlée*. These, however, will sufficiently indicate the sub-currents that flowed out of the steady and general stream of one of the most notable, if not the most notable, electoral conflict of modern times.

The following is a complete analysis of the votes given in the various districts of the city of Westminster on the day of the election:

TABLE 2

	Mill/ Grosvenor	Mill/ Smith	Grosvenor/ Smith	Grosvenor	Mill	Smith
St. Anne's	182	20	19	7	22	107
St. Clement's	124	24	26	9	24	328
St. George's	1453	72	128	178	194	1258
St. James's	600	35	56	33	95	561
St. John's	682	25	50	41	51	218
St. Margaret's	390	16	49	30	33	319
St. Martin's	289	21	29	33	42	301
St. Mary's & St. Paul's	94	21	9	6	16	124
Total	3814	234	366	337	477	3216

This shows that 7844 electors voted.

Appendix B

The Westminster Steeplechase,
from *Will-o'-the-Wisp*, 3 October 1868, pp. 36–41

Sporting Intelligence.
[*Slightly Anticipated.*]
The Westminster Steeplechase.
[*See Cartoon.*][1]

The great event has come and gone! It is over, and a rare "pot" has been upset! All doubt as to the tactics of the "confederacy" has been put an end to by the starting of both the representatives of that stable, who, as will be presently seen, cut anything but a pleasant figure, and must have thoroughly disgusted their backers. One of these gentlemen informed me that it was the last time he would ever support either of them with a penny of his money, and he knew a great many others who entertained a like opinion. I am not in the least surprised, as all along I have advised readers of this journal to bide their time, and only stake money at the post. *The Philosopher* I have always endeavoured to expose as a rank impostor; on every occasion of his performing in public he has betrayed a want of stamina and physical incapacity that should have warned his friends in time, while, as I fully anticipated, he has turned out a regular "roarer," and will require a great deal of rest and care before he can show again. The position he has for some time past occupied in the betting, was chiefly due to the pressure put upon his trainer to keep him quiet for this race. All sorts of tricks and dodges have been resorted to by those in the secrets of the stable to keep the horse in favour with the public, among others making him give 25 lbs. to Odger's *Working Man* for the Chelsea Meeting, when, upon public form, he is scarcely his equal at even weights,

1 That on p. 239 above.

and, over the Westminster course, is obliged to have pounds allowed him. *Cash-box*, the other representative of the "confederacy" stable, has always run a more honest race than his companion, as although he is well-bred, no one ever gave him credit for being a first-class animal, and he has never risen above the level of an ordinary "plater." There was a talk, some little time since, of getting up a match between him and *The Philosopher*, both to run on their individual merits, but the supporters of the latter, when they were informed that they would have to find the money for it by themselves, jibbed, and so it came to nothing. During the last few weeks *Cash-box* has suffered in the betting from the metallic fever, consequent, so I was told, on a rumour that he had been beaten in his trial. The result of yesterday's race satisfies me that this could not be the case, and that *The Philosopher's* friends were at the bottom of the report being put into circulation. *True Blue*, who ran so well in the same race once before, has gone on improving and came to the post in splendid condition, exciting the admiration of all beholders. He has been kept in steady exercise for some weeks past, and his preparation as been carried out in a way that left nothing to be desired. In fact, both his trainer and owner have every reason to be proud of him. With this much of preliminary, I now proceed to describe the race itself.

The Westminster Cup, value £4000, by subscription of £1000 each.

Weight for age, with penalties and allowances. The owner of the second horse to save his stake. The Election course. Gentlemen riders.

Mr. W.H. Smith's *True Blue*, by Union Jack—
Mother's England, 3 yrs 1
Captain Grosvenor's *Cash-box*, by Ebury—
Grandmother's Money, 3 yrs 2
Mr. J.S. Mill's *The Philosopher*, by Tommy Dodd—
Mrs. Partingtom [*sic*], aged . . . . dist.

Betting: 100 to 1 on *The Philosopher*, 20 to 1 against *Cash-box*, and 50 to 1 against *True Blue*.

There was considerable difficulty at the first, owing to the refractory conduct of *The Philosopher*, who let out right and left and displayed the eccentricities of his temper, putting his head obstinately down between his fore-legs, and refusing to stir. Getting tired of this, his next performance was to take the bit between his teeth and bolt, giving his rider an ugly hurl over the first fence and quieting his own transports by a crashing fall, that brought him back to his horses [*sic*] quivering all over in a fashion that anything but inspired his supporters with confidence. A worse display of temper I seldom if ever saw in the course of a lengthened experience; the nearest approach, in my recollection, was that of Mr. Gladstone's *Policy*, in the Great Reform Stakes last year, when he made such a dead set at Mr. Disraeli's *Little Bill.* While *The Philosopher* was thus delaying the start, *Cash-box*, who seemed very fresh and skittish, stood first on his hind legs and then on his head, to the delight of the spectators and the undisguised dismay of the jockey, who turned exceedingly pale and looked as if he anything but enjoyed his painful position. "I'll back *Cash-box* for a monkey," exclaimed a well known Northern speculator, who happened to be down at the post, and he was immediately accommodated by a well known book-maker, whose residence is not a hundred miles from Charing cross [*sic*], and who remarked with a sneer of contempt as he entered the bet, "Why I'd back myself to perform better than he ever will over this course."

It was nearly an hour before the starter was able to get the three away, and the public in the Grand Stand were getting quite tired out when the welcome sound of "They're off" secured their attention, and all eyes were strained in the direction of the post. Sure enough they were off, *The Philosopher* leading by some twenty yards, almost pulling his rider out of the saddle, with *Cash-box* next behind him and *True Blue* bringing up the rear well in hand and running grandly. The first obstacle that presented itself was some very rusty posts and rails with a deep drop on the landing side, which, owing to the elections going on in the neighbourhood, had been utilised by the bill stickers and was plastered all over with printed slips bearing the word *Disestablishment.* Both *The Philosopher* and *Cash-box* refused at this; the former doing his best to put his jockey over his head, while the latter slipped up and sat down on his hind quarters. *True Blue* went over it in fine flying form, and from this point led to the finish. *Cash-box* having been restored to his legs again, was rammed at the fence and managed to bungle over to the other side, carrying away the top bar; *The Philosopher* followed immediately upon his stable companion, with the difference that he went blindly through the whole thing making a terrific smash, and, as it ultimately turned out, doing himself no end of injury. *True Blue* was a field's length ahead by this time, going well within himself, his jockey knowing how necessary it was to keep him in wind for the finish; consequently *Cash-box* was enabled to make up some of his lost ground. The *Gordon** difficulty got *The Philosopher* into terrible trouble, as both horse and rider went head first into it, the latter running a slight risk of being drowned. A sympathising bystander of the name of Taylor, how-

* [Note in original:] By a printer's error, this word has been spelt with G, instead of J [that is, the executed Jamaican rather than the famous water jump].

ever, pulled the latter out and very properly remonstrated with the bystanders who crowded round him, entreating them to give the unfortunate man "Eyre."† In a few minutes he was enabled to remount *The Philosopher* again, who stood shivering and shaking, presenting anything but an interesting spectacle, and they once more were going. It is unnecessary to add more than that *The Philosopher* endeavouring to make up for past misconduct, and no doubt wishing to promote active circulation after his wetting, went a great deal better than he did before, and managed to get near to *True Blue* and *Cash-box*, who had been going well together, at the last fence. Over this *True Blue* flew like a bird, but *Cash-box*, who seemed to have had enough of it and was nearly pumped out, swerved round to the indignation of his rider, who proceeded to punish him severely, finally managing to force him over, only, however, to see *True Blue's* plates as he cantered in first, and just with time enough to save being distanced. As for *The Philosopher* he got in a most dreadful mess at the last fence, and was so crippled that his rider had to dismount and lead him in amidst—I am sorry to say—the derisive cheers of the spectators, who now know how to appreciate this much valued but useless "crack," who has figured so long in the quotations as first favourite, who started with long odds on him, and who seems best fitted to be kept at home in the stable for inquisitive people to look at if so inclined.

The Rat.

A Retrospect of the Westminster Steeple-Chase, from *Will-o'-the-Wisp*, 21 November 1868, pp. 127-8

Sporting Intelligence.
A Retrospect of the Westminster Steeple-Chase.
[A letter from The Rat to Will, congratulating himself.]

[The] winner literally walked in, having led from start to finish. . . . *Cashbox* [*sic*], who carried with him the money of the Westminster confederacy, as I anticipated, beat his stable companion hollow, and proved himself incontestably the better of the pair. But it was clear from the first that neither of them ever was in it; indeed at the end of the first mile the arms of both jockeys were seen moving; and though *Cashbox* struggled bravely on, it was Lombard street to a Chinese orange against him. As for *Philosopher*, he was all over the place, rushing blindly at his

† [Note in original:] Another printer's error, this, [*sic*] really is too bad.

fences, and getting some ugly spills. He came to terrible grief over what a spectator gravely termed the Bradlaugh "bullfinch," pitching his jockey and cutting his knees dreadfully. It was with the greatest difficulty that he was steadied after this *contretemps*; and though he was persevered with, the catastrophe I apprehended in my prophecy attended him at the water jump, out of which he was extricated with the greatest difficulty. The cold bath appeared to have freshened him up somewhat, and for a few yards he seemed to make up for lost ground, but the last fence was too much for him, and, as I predicted, his jockey had to dismount from his high horse, and lead him in amid the derisive shouts of the crowd, most of whom had set themselves all right by backing the winner at the last moment. *Cashbox*, who refused badly at the last fence, cut a very different figure to his cracked-up stable companion, whose merits have now been satisfactorily ascertained. I understand it is the intention of the owner of *Philosopher* to lay him up for the winter, as he hopes by dint of patching and doctoring to turn him out again for this race on a future occasion. If I were to offer my advice, I should say, put him in for some small country handicap on the "*flat*;" he is scarcely, either by breed or stamina, fitted for steeple-chasing, and he may possibly manage to come in front. I understand that *Philosopher's* owner, when the race was over, expressed himself as perfectly satisfied with the result, as it was a matter of principle with him, in every phase of life and under all circumstances, to see the best man or the best horse win. If this be true, the Christian spirit shewn is beautiful to contemplate, and I trust that the gentleman who could thus express himself will, in his retirement, find that solace he so eminently deserves. . . .

Index